HV
6542
.C47
1982

74800

Charny, Israel W.
    How can we commit the unthinkable? :
genocide, the human cancer / Israel W.
Charny in collaboration with Chanan
Rapaport ; foreword by Elie Wiesel. --
Boulder, Colo. : Westview Press, 1982.
    xvi, 430 p. ; 24 cm.
    Bibliography: p. 419-420.
    Includes index.
    ISBN 0-86531-358-X : $25.50

    1. Genocide. 2. Genocide--
Psychological aspects. 3. Genocide--
Prevention. 4. Holocaust, Jewish
(1939-1945) I. Rapaport, Chanan.
II. Title

31 MAR 83   7998273   OMMMxc   81-19784

HOW CAN WE COMMIT
THE UNTHINKABLE?

HOW CAN WE COMMIT THE
UNTHINKABLE?
GENOCIDE: THE HUMAN CANCER

ISRAEL W. CHARNY

EXECUTIVE DIRECTOR, INTERNATIONAL CONFERENCE
ON THE HOLOCAUST AND GENOCIDE

IN COLLABORATION WITH CHANAN RAPAPORT

FOREWORD BY ELIE WIESEL

WESTVIEW PRESS • BOULDER, COLORADO

Copyright © 1982 by Israel W. Charny

Published in 1982 in the United States of America by
  Westview Press, Inc.
  5500 Central Avenue
  Boulder, Colorado 80301
  Frederick A. Praeger, President and Publisher

Library of Congress Cataloging in Publication Data
Charny, Israel W.
  How can we commit the unthinkable?: Genocide, the human cancer.
  Bibliography: p.
  Includes index.
  1. Genocide. 2. Genocide–Psychological aspects. 3. Genocide–Prevention. 4. Holocaust, Jewish (1939–1945). I. Rapaport, Chanan. II. Title.
  HV6542.C47   364.1'51   81-19784
  ISBN 0-86531-358-X   AACR2

Printed and bound in the United States of America

To Adam, Rena, and Chana

Daddy, do you think if a Nazi were living, and even if he was just a little crazy already, that he would stop? He wouldn't! He would just throw the book out and burn it!

—Chana (age 9)

It makes me hope that it will be a good book that will prevent more holocausts and hurting of people that would like to live in this world.

—Rena (age 9)

You want to show how easily the Holocaust can happen, but it's also important to help that it doesn't happen. Did you write how to prevent it from happening? Did you also write how to deal with it when it does happen?

—Adam (age 11)

If we are all innocent, then the mystery of evil, drawing its strength from our very innocence, will crush us in the end. For in order to realize himself, man must fuse all levels of being into one; every man is all men. Every man can and must carry creation on his shoulders; every unit is responsible for the whole. . . . Created in the image of the One without image, man is so constituted that as he comes close to one extreme, he advances towards the other. It is frightening because in the name of the absolute, he is called upon to do good and evil at the same time, relying on identical gestures and inventing identical forms.

—Elie Wiesel, *The Oath*

CONTENTS

FOREWORD

The subject of this book is fear; the subject of this book causes fear. Condemned—if not damned—by a past fraught with terror and shame, is man still capable of recovering his innocence? After Auschwitz, is hope still possible? Since history suffers from cancer, what is left for us to do?

Psychologist by education, moralist by vocation, Israel Charny confronts these questions with a courage no one can dispute. Having diagnosed the evil, he tracks it down and unmasks it. To fight it. Perhaps even to defeat it. Certainly, all is lost; yet all remains to be saved. Evoking the millions of dead becomes part of a humanitarian design for safekeeping: it is *because* the genocide has taken place that it will never happen again. Provided, of course, that we remember it. The memory of suffering becomes a safeguard against suffering.

And here is the importance of this work: it serves as warning as well as reminder. The past is invoked not to make us weep, but rather to make us reflect. The future, born of the past, must break away in order not to repeat it. But, paradoxically, that very act contains its own share of risk. Bringing about such a break with time and conscience may only lead to ruin and night. How do we go about resolving this contradiction? We cannot, yet we must at least try to confront it.

This is where, at times, Israel Charny and I might find ourselves in disagreement. Not being a scientist or an expert or a clinician, I confine myself to exploring the questions; the answers escape me. Treblinka, for me, is a perplexity. Belsen and Birkenau compel me to put everything back into questions. I still do not comprehend why some men become killers, and others victims.

That said, I understand the victims better and more than their executioners. I could never say "I" in the name or in the place of a killer. Is it because, by killing, he dehumanizes himself? Perhaps. Victims, by giv-

Translated from the French by Anne Ketchum, associate professor of French at the University of Colorado in Boulder.

ing their life, become more human, while killers, by giving death, become less human. It is a question, then, of two separate categories nothing can reconcile. To say that the victims might have become executioners is unjust. Malraux is right: death transforms certain lives into destiny. Let us accept the dead in their irrevocable "situation." By what right can we suspect them of actions that, under other circumstances and in face of other pressures, they might have committed? No, we cannot look for the murderer among *them*. Let us look for him where he has perpetrated his crimes—in the eyes and the heart of the killer. In his being; that is, in his difference, in what sets him apart from his victims, apart from humanity in which he is the cancer.

This term seems just to me. The SS system was exactly that—a cancer. It spread to an entire social body, the entire human species. Its noxious, destructive effects can be observed almost anywhere in the world where minorities endure poverty, hunger, fear, humiliation, and death. All those paroxysmal violences that are taking place in Paraguay or in Cambodia, all those mass slaughterings, all those oppressive measures reported almost daily by the press—we must link them to the Holocaust. To be more specific: I am not saying that we should compare them to the Holocaust, but that we must decipher the signs connecting them to it. It is Auschwitz that opened the way to Hiroshima. Does this mean that Hiroshima should be compared to Auschwitz? Not at all. This kind of comparison can only diminish the event. Auschwitz defies every analogy and transcends all forms of description. Auschwitz is the point zero of history, it is the beginning and the end of all that exists. It is the ultimate reference—everything is judged in relation to it. In other words, the massacre of the Cambodians is not Sobibor, but it is because of Sobibor that we must do everything possible to assist the victims in Cambodia. Because we have seen the triumph of night, we must tell of the suffering and the resistance of its victims. Because we have seen evil at work, we must denounce it. Because we have seen the near annihilation of the European Jewish communities by the nazi "cancer," we must fight without ceasing to save the world from its contagion.

Is it possible that we may have a chance to succeed? It is our *only* chance.

Elie Wiesel

ACKNOWLEDGMENTS

There are many people I want to thank very deeply for their assistance with this book that is so dear to me. First and foremost, my thanks go to Ian Baldwin, Jr., former editor of the World Order Series of the Institute for World Order. Ian and I first met when we were both invited to participate in the organizing conference of the Consortium on Peace Research, Education, and Development (COPRED) sponsored by the Institute of Behavioral Science at the University of Colorado in 1970. Even then, Ian grasped quickly my deep interest in applying psychodynamic concepts of personality along with social-psychological and sociological concepts to studies of evil, destruction, and especially genocide. We agreed that to date man's collective destructiveness has been treated largely from sociopolitical, historical, and legal points of view without sufficient study of the humanness of the people who commit the terrible acts of mass destruction.

I shall always be grateful also for the timing of Ian's invitation to me to develop this book under contract with the Institute for World Order at a time when I was already packing for my move to Israel. This choice was based in no small part on my sense that Israel would be an especially appropriate context for work on the book. Needless to say, the formalization of my contract with the institute provided a great deal of encouragement to me at a time when, naturally, I also had my share of doubts about the major move I had elected to make. As it was to turn out, we barely had arrived in Israel when the Yom Kippur War broke out, and the meaningfulness of this writing loomed larger than ever.

I also gladly express my appreciation to the former president of the Institute for World Order, Dr. Saul Mendlovitz, now director of the World Order Models Project, and to Saul's successor as president of the institute, Dr. Robert Johansen, for their continuing and various support of this work. It was because of my deep regard for the Institute for World Order and its efforts to develop new ways toward peace that I did not hesitate to undertake the book as an institute project, despite the fact that more lucrative offers had been received directly from commercial publishers.

In Israel, I have enjoyed the heartwarming support of the Henrietta Szold National Institute for Research in the Behavioral Sciences in Jerusalem under the direction of Dr. Chanan Rapaport. Dr. Rapaport, a specialist in social indicators research, has also been my active collaborator and is coauthor of the culminating chapter, "Toward a Genocide Early Warning System." Although Chanan is not responsible for any other material in the book, there is considerable continuity between the earlier chapters of the book and the concepts developed for the warning system, and I acknowledge with deep appreciation the contributions Chanan has made to my thinking on many levels. I shall always treasure the long afternoons and nights of work in his charming Jerusalem apartment, including the warm hospitality of Dr. Judith Rapaport and their children. Most of all, Chanan and I found in one another a common language not only as behavioral scientists, but also as human beings who share deep feelings about the terrible Holocaust that befell our people.

In this connection, it might be noted that wherever we have chosen in the book to speak of the historical process of our people, the intent, ultimately, is to underscore the universal need of *all* peoples everywhere to be strongly on the side of life. For the Holocaust is not only an unspeakable tragedy in its own right, it is also an example of the universal plight of peoples everywhere on earth since the dawn of man, and, tragically, such events will occur again and again in the years ahead. Whatever the bias of our positive identification with our people, in no way is this book specifically about the Holocaust of the Jewish people, any more than it is about any other specific instances of genocide. The intention is to conduct an inquiry into the nature of all holocausts that befall human beings everywhere.

Technical preparation of the manuscript has been the province of Sonia Neu of Herzliya, Israel, and Barbara V. Meyer of Bamberger-Rosenheim Ltd. Word Processing Service Bureau, Tel Aviv, and I thank both for their patience and helpfulness. I also note appreciatively the earlier work of Doris Sherman of Herzliya and the still earlier work and comradeship of my publications assistant in Paoli, Pennsylvania, Frances Johnston, who helped develop research notes and various projects that led toward the development of the book.

There are several colleagues I want to thank for their critical reading of part or all of the manuscript. Dr. Alberto Podorgny of the

Weizmann Institute of Science agreed to review the several chapters that refer metaphorically to biophysical concepts, especially the book's theme-metaphor of destructiveness as a cancerlike process that, like physical cancer, is latent in all of us and the treatment of aggression as a basic energy process. Dr. Podorgny was also kind enough to consult a number of his colleagues who are involved in these areas of science. The entire manuscript was read by Dr. Leon Shaskolsky-Sheleff, my colleague at Tel Aviv University's Institute of Criminology and Criminal Law, and his creative contributions to our understanding of violence are referred to in the book. The manuscript was also read by Dr. A. Paul Hare, head of the Department of Sociology at the University of Cape Town, South Africa, and he also gave freely of his time earlier as a consultant on issues of group dynamics. Dr. Hare's own highly creative contributions, both to group dynamics research and to research on non-violence, are also acknowledged in the book. Finally, the book was delivered into the capable hands of Rinah Lipis Sheleff, whom I thank both for her professional editing and for her considerable encouragement. The usual demurrers as to the lack of responsibility of the readers and my editor for any remaining errors and shortcomings are, of course, understood; what should not be taken for granted is my sincere appreciation for their thoughtfulness and assistance.

In the course of our work, Chanan and I received a request from Richard Arens, professor of the School of Law at Temple University and also counsel to the International League for the Rights of Man, to see our work toward a Genocide Early Warning System in connection with the work of his research group on the little-known, ongoing genocide of Indians in Paraguay. The result for us was an invaluable opportunity for a critical reading of our developing work on the early warning system, which proved to be highly encouraging. We were invited to include our work in *Genocide in Paraguay* (since published by Temple University Press and hailed by reviewers around the world), but because of our own upcoming publication, we had to reluctantly decline the invitation.

Finally, at Westview Press, I have enjoyed not only solid professional expertise, but also the enthusiasm and warmth of a remarkable publishing team including Fred Praeger, publisher; Lynn Arts, senior editor and head of the Editorial Department; Megan Schoeck, copy editor; and Jude Biggs, marketing manager. I especially want to express my appreciation to Lynne Rienner, executive editor and associate publisher, who heads the spirited team at Westview, for really understanding my goals and dreams for this book and for believing they could be achieved.

As is true for the book itself, I know of no way to conclude these acknowledgments. The concern of this book is for me a lifelong commitment. I thank all those who have helped me in my study thus far.

Israel W. Charny

The author wishes to thank the following for permission to reprint material appearing in this book:

Macmillan Co., *A Sign for Cain* by Frederic Wertham (Copyright ©1966 by Frederic Wertham)

Marjorie Housepian Dobkin, "The Unremembered Genocide," *Commentary*, September 1966

Overseas News Service, "Amin: Ruthless Killer Plays the Buffoon" by David Martin, June 14, 1974

United Press International, "Tens of Thousands Dead Under Khmer Rouge Rule," June 17, 1975. Reprinted by permission of United Press International

Jerusalem Post, "A Million Cambodians Slain by Khmer Rouge," June 3, 1976

Fellowship Magazine, "Army Film Says Soldiers Must Refuse Illegal Orders," June 1, 1975, and "The Massacres in Indonesia," September 1966

Donald C. Drake, "Margaret Mead on Indonesia," *Philadelphia Inquirer*, November 2, 1965

United Press International, "Mass Grave Found in Cypriot Garbage Dump," September 3, 1974. Reprinted by permission of United Press International

Philadelphia Bulletin, "Peasant Woman Stomped to Death By GI's at My Lai, Sergeant Writes" by Seymour M. Hersh, December 2, 1969

United Press International, "South Africa Accused of Massacre," July 26, 1974. Reprinted by permission of United Press International

Associated Press, "Soviet Charges China Killed 12,000 Tibetans in 1972," November 11, 1973

Hadassah Magazine, "Shame of Switzerland" by Harold Flender, November 1969

Jerusalem Post, "A Fascist Regime Which Stood by the Jews" by Geoffrey Wigoder, November 6, 1975

Random House, *The Oath* by Elie Wiesel

Lionel Rubinoff, "Auschwitz and the Theology of the Holocaust," Address at Lutheran Theological Seminary, Columbus, Ohio, May 1973

Penguin Books, *The Politics of Experience* by R. D. Laing

Hadassah Magazine, Review of Elie Wiesel, *One Generation After*, by Jack Riemer, November 1970

Heinemann Educational Books, *Licensed Mass Murder* by Henry V. Dicks

Jerome D. Frank, *Sanity and Survival*, Random House, 1967

Elsevier Scientific Publishing Co., *Theory and Society*, "Three Faces of Cruelty" by Randall Collins

Temple University Press, "The Beginning Not the End of the Age of Genocide" by Chaim S. Shatan, in *Genocide in Paraguay*, ed. Richard S. Arens

The American Academy of Political and Social Science, *The Annals of the American Academy of Political and Social Science*, "Violence and Human Development" by Elton B. McNeil

Center for the Study of Democratic Institutions, Santa Barbara, Calif., Paul Tillich, *To Live As Men: An Anatomy of Peace*

Kenneth Vaux and Harper and Row, *Biomedical Ethics* by Kenneth Vaux

Robert Jay Lifton, "On Death and the Continuity of Life"

Arthur Kovacs, from *Psychotherapy* (Bulletin of the Division of Psychotherapy), American Psychological Association

Journal of Humanistic Psychology, "Some Fundamental Questions That Face the Normative Social Psychologist" by Abraham H. Maslow

Leon J. Saul, *The Hostile Mind*

Harper and Row, *Invisible Loyalties* by Ivan Boszormenyi-Nagy and Geraldine M. Spark

Society for the Psychological Study of Social Issues, *Collective Violence and Civil Conflict*

Scarecrow Press, *Systems Theory, Science, and Social Work* by Irma Stein

Associated Press, story of U.S. Public Health Service study of untreated syphilis, September 12, 1972

Penguin Books, *Conflict in Man-made Environment*, © Anatol Rapoport, 1974. Reprinted by permission of Penguin Books Ltd.

Philadelphia Bulletin, letter by Anatol Wolf Holt, June 5, 1959

United Press International, March 11, 1976, dateline Heidelberg, West Germany. Reprinted by permission of United Press International

Williams & Wilkins, *The Roots of the Ego* by Carl Frankenstein

American Medical Association, *Dynamics of Violence*, ed. Jan Fawcett. Reprinted with the permission of the American Medical Association

C. G. Jung Foundation, *Depth Psychology and a New Ethic* by Erich Neumann, copyright 1969 by the C. G. Jung Foundation for Analytical Psychology

Grune & Stratton, *Evil in Man*, 1968, by Gustav Bychowski. By permission

Association of Humanistic Psychology, "The Achievement Ethic and the Human Potential Movement" by Larry LeShan

W. W. Norton, *Power and Innocence* by Rollo May

International Humanist and Ethical Union, Utrecht, Holland, from the *International Humanist*

Psychosynthesis Institute of the Synthesis Graduate School for the Study of Man, 3352 Sacramento St., San Francisco, CA 94118, from *The Balancing and Synthesis of the Opposites* by Roberto Assagioli. Reprinted with permission

Grune & Stratton, *Strategies of Psychotherapy*, 1963, by Jay Haley. By permission

R. D. Laing, *The Politics of the Family*

The Clinical Psychologist, Newsletter of the Division of Clinical Psychology of the American Psychological Association

American Academy of Psychotherapists, from *Voices: The Art and Science of Psychotherapy*

Fellowship Magazine, from "An Interview with Alfred Hassler"

University of Toronto Press, *Charisma* by Irvine Schiffer (published in the United States by Free Press)

Robert Jay Lifton, *Boundaries*

Society for the Psychological Study of Social Issues, *The Justice Motive in Social Behavior*

Reconstructionist by Alan Miller, 1967

Alfred Knopf, *The Madman* by Kahlil Gibran

Curtis Brown, "Chants to Be Used in Processions Around a Site with Furnaces" by Thomas P. Merton. Reprinted by permission of Curtis Brown Ltd. Copyright © 1961, 1962 by Abbey of Gethsemene, Inc.

Opera Mundi, *The Murderers Among Us* by Simon Wiesenthal, © Opera Mundi, 1968

Jerusalem Academic Press, *Psychological Bases of War*, ed. Heinrich Z. Winnik, Rafael Moses, and Mortimer Ostow

Addison-Wesley, "Mass Phenomena" by Roger W. Brown, in *Handbook of Social Psychology*, ed. Gardner Lindzey, © 1954, Addison-Wesley, Reading, Mass. Reprinted with permission

Society for the Psychological Study of Social Issues, "Man and World Politics" by J. David Singer

The New Yorker, "Notes and Comments" in the *New Yorker*, October 2, 1971. Reprinted by permission, © 1971 The New Yorker Magazine, Inc.

Council on Religion and International Affairs, *Modern War and the Pursuit of Peace* by Theodore Weber

William H. Blanchard, "Messianic Feeling Can Lead Us Into Trouble"

Y. Harkabi, "The Position of the Palestinians in the Israel-Arab Conflict in Their National Covenant"

Random House, *The Last 100 Days* by John Toland, © Random House, Inc. Reprinted by permission

Harcourt Brace Jovanovich, *The Origins of Totalitarianism* by Hannah Arendt

Simon & Schuster, *Treblinka* by Jean-Francois Steiner

Vahakn N. Dadrian, "A Typology of Genocide"

Robert Jay Lifton, *Death in Life*

Sifriat Hapoalim, *Childhood Under Fire*

Hadassah Magazine, "Israel Was Alone" by Elie Wiesel

Delacorte Press, *Slaughterhouse-Five* by Kurt Vonnegut, Jr.

Academic Press, London, "Possible Substitutes for War" by Anthony Storr, in J. D. Carthy and F. J. Ebling, eds., *The Natural History of Aggression*, copyright by Academic Press Inc. (London) Ltd. Reprinted by permission

Charles Scribner's Sons, *Human Aggression* by Anthony Storr

Fellowship Magazine, "Nhat Hanh on Meditation" by Jim Forest

Westview Press, *Strategies Against Violence*, ed. Israel W. Charny
Paul Wehr, "Conflict Education Through Experiential Learning"
Johan Galtung, "Theories of Peace"
Dryden Press, Mohandas Ghandi, in Thomas E. Hackey and Ralph E. Weber, eds., *Voices of Revolution*
Philadelphia Bulletin, "Only a Sick Society Would Applaud The Godfather"
Adam Curle, "The Scope and Dilemmas of Peace Studies"
Institute for World Order, *Macroscope* and *Alternatives*, "Contending with a Planet in Peril and Change"
    by Burns H. Weston
Izre'el Publishing House, Tel Aviv, *Psychohistory of the Holocaust and Rebirth* by Fishel Schneorson

HOW CAN WE COMMIT
THE UNTHINKABLE?

Many Extensive Massacres and Exterminations

We should not regard the Nazi mass killings of civilians in isolation. Many extensive massacres and exterminations have occurred in the past: The Crusades (a million victims); the Inquisition (a quarter of a million); the burning of witches (at least 20,000); the subjection of colonies in South America (more than 15,000,000); the island of Haiti (24,000 survivors out of 1,000,000 inhabitants after thirty-five years of colonization); the extermination of the Indians in Argentina and Uruguay, the island of Mauritino (the work slaves died so fast that 1,000 had to be imported annually); Java (the Dutch East India Company extorted in twelve years $830,000,000 from the slave labor of 5,000,000 natives, untold numbers of whom perished); the Congo (of 30,000,000 inhabitants at the time of its colonial takeover, 8,600 were still alive in 1911); . . . Nanking (the massacre by the Japanese); the Hereros in Southwest Africa (40,000 men, women, and children were surrounded, driven to the desert, and left to die of hunger and thirst. Neither the German Parliament nor the traders or missionaries protested. Report of the German General Staff: The Hereros had ceased "to exist as an independent tribe"); Armenians (1,500,000 were driven from the place they had cultivated for more than 2,000 years; many men, women, and children were massacred or left to perish in the desert); and so on and on.

—Frederic Wertham, *A Sign for Cain* (New York: Macmillan, 1966), pp. 140–141

1

INTRODUCTION TO A BOOK ABOUT LIFE AND DEATH

The central problem . . . of psychology and other behavioral sciences is the handling of violence. . . . It may seem utterly absurd to suggest seriously that this can be done, even if we allow a generation or two for its achievement. It must have seemed equally absurd to ancient Romans who were told that their flesh-rending gladiatorial combats should be abolished.

—Irwin A. Berg

Picture men somewhere lining up the human beings they are about to kill.

The somewhere is here, there, or anywhere on this earth.

The time is today or tomorrow.

It hardly matters whether it's a frozen wintry day or a sun-streaming summer afternoon.

A human being on his way to death is sobbing. One of the captors moves toward him almost calmly and clubs him senseless. Then, suddenly, he kicks the silent body and, with a final gesture of disdain, empties his revolver into the once-person.

A mother clutches her baby to her breast. The baby, who will not be comforted, is heaving spastic, agonizing cries. A soldier runs up and snatches the baby from the mother. Laughing loudly, he mounts the baby on top of his bayonet.

Can we picture ourselves among the victims?
Can we picture ourselves among the killers?

1

THE HOPES AND LIMITS OF THIS BOOK

This is a book written in pain and in hope. For reasons that have since become clear to me, I realized a good number of years ago that it was this book I was listening for in my everyday work as a practicing clinical psychologist engaged largely in the private practice of psychotherapy. What I was listening for were the inner sounds (in myself as well as in my fellow human beings) that might explain to me something of the horrible facts of man's bizarre destructiveness everywhere on this planet. It seemed to me that through the veil of the everyday agonies of human beings, in our hurts and disillusionments and in our hurting of others, we should be able to learn something about man's larger madness of destruction and genocide.

Much of my deepest feeling had been formed in the course of my childhood experience of watching my mother struggle against and then succumb to the mass killer within her, cancer. She was a sweet woman, too sweet it was to become clear to me, and my being cried out against the injustice of her death and my loss.[1]

Much of my caring and outrage was forged by my encounter from afar with the deaths of my people in Europe. It was, of course, altogether natural for me to picture myself as the Jewish child in Germany, Poland, Holland, or Hungary who was taken to his death. Over and over again, I tried to encompass the pictures of my fellow people—six million men, women, and children—taken in cattle cars, led to their death on forced marches, lined up on grim concentration camp parade grounds, clubbed, shot, hanged, subjected to sadistic surgeries, marched naked into gas chambers, and on, and on.

My mind and heart cried out, How could this be? How could human beings do this to one another? Who were the people who did this? Whenever I would meet a clean-shaven German businessman who had obviously been in Germany during the Holocaust, I would look him up and down and scrutinize him from every angle to try to fathom whether he was one of *them*—and if so, how could he have done what he did?

Slowly but surely, the picture broadened for me. Everywhere I looked in history, it was the same. The Germans were, essentially, the same as all peoples—and ultimately, so were the Jewish people. None of us are immune from the danger of possibly becoming mass killers, and none of us are entirely lacking in humanity and decency. Whatever it is that makes people monstrous destroyers is somehow potentially in all of us. The seeds of the cure, it seemed to me, were also potentially in all of us.

My mind and spirit began to realize that all around me there are new acts of genocide being executed all the time and that potential genocides are even now developing in different places. I myself was privileged to live in the United States of America where for the longest time, I had enjoyed a sense of safety and decency that was not the lot of my contemporaries in so many other lands. Yet, all around me too, I sensed the same forces of destructiveness at play, alternately seeking to spend themselves and biding their time until it was safe to do so.

Sometimes sitting in a staff meeting of a modern psychiatric hospital, I could see how it could happen. The ingredients were all there: the bitter, hating factions among the staff disguising themselves in the pomp and circumstance of a mental health staff conference; the barely disguised superiority and disdain for the hapless patient; the patronizing professional sympathy and righteousness that barely concealed the brutality of the so-called modern therapies of electric shock and brain surgery; the dehumanizing everyday herding of anonymous patients into anonymous routines.[2] Everywhere. In lovely families that persecuted one or more of their members. In the universities I loved, where faculty intrigues and hatred knew no bounds. In the ruthless coups de grace of business killings. In the pompous coldness of exalted physicians turning away from the death fears of their patients.

The world news never ceased to report new episodes. In far off Iraq, the Kurds were being driven relentlessly to death by the Iraqis. In Africa, the tall northern Sudanese massacred the stocky black southern Sudanese. In Bangladesh, the Bengalis were murdered en masse by the Pakistanis. In Tibet, the Communist Chinese were said to be putting thousands of Tibetans to death. On and on it goes.

I would read of these events and, like so many other caring people, momentarily shake my head in disbelief and sadness, then quickly turn away. Partly, it was because the picture was too horrible to bear. Largely, it was because there was nothing to be done about it all. It occurred to me that this is the way it was with the world that didn't care about the massacre of the Jewish people. Maybe a great many people wanted to care but did not know how.

As a psychotherapist, I was fortunate to be working with many most thoughtful and searching fellow human beings, people who had allowed themselves to feel the stress of their inner world and who had the courage to examine their way of life. It came to me that, more than anything else, what I wanted to learn from these privileged encounters with the inner minds of my fellow human beings was, What is it about our otherwise beautiful, creative species that makes it possible for us to be drawn into playing vicious roles as mass killers or as their henchmen and assistants? Ironically, my laboratory for the study of man's*

*Throughout this book, the words "man," "mankind," etc., are used to refer to all people.

availability to genocide contained no genociders. Yet, I was convinced that that laboratory contained as many would-be genociders as appear so readily on the human scene in countries and cultures where the flow of historical, political, and other circumstances builds a climate in which genocidal destruction erupts.

This book is not about the holocaust of the Jewish people, nor is it about any one or another specific instance of genocide. Rather, it is a search for the underlying rhythms, patterns, and meanings within the human mind, individually and collectively, that make it possible for us human beings to be drawn to the worst possible side of ourselves.

It has been a difficult, even an agonizing, book to write for many reasons. Not the least of the difficulty is the awareness that when all is said and done, this book will not be so wise, nor will people be so open to its possible wisdom, that very much good will issue from it, at least not quickly and certainly nowhere close to what my heart would wish. In psychotherapy, at least, the situation is somewhat otherwise. Although the really effective therapist learns not to have that much of a stake in the outcome of the treatment of a patient (and therefore is freer to care and help but not to invade, control, and repeat all manners of oppressive maneuvers that the patient suffered in earlier relationships), there is at least a reasonable hope of helping a good many people come to their own strength. For the subject of this book, it is obviously too early in human history for such a hope. The processes we are searching to understand are deeply complex and rooted in aspects of human nature that cannot be observed concretely or analyzed separately from an incredible complex of forces. We are faced with a total configuration of events that is determined on many levels of political, economic, and sociological forces acting through the barely understood power of the group process on an individual human nature we know too little about. The best we can hope for—and for this I hope very much—is to advance somewhat in our understanding of the essence of man's destructiveness and of what we can try to do about it. It is hard to write a book that can't really solve a terrible problem, especially when one cares so very much, yet it must be done.

HOW MUCH THIS BOOK NEEDS TO BE TRUE
TO BE MEANINGFUL

As a final note of introduction, there is no question but that much of this book will be incomplete. There will be errors, and there will be partial truths. I also know that time will bring far more effective ways of approaching what this book is attempting to do.

The biggest fault of this book has to be its overambitious effort to track the process of how destructiveness can be generated on any of several levels of human experience and behavior—from the "nuclear" level of generating energy, to the individual's experience of life's meaning, humans in their family lives, and to humans in their larger group experiences. It is utterly impossible that scholarship can do justice to so many levels of experiencing. Inevitably, there will be many instances in which observations that are accurate or meaningful on one level fall far short or are downright inappropriate on another level. Parallels and similarities between different levels of human behavior do not make them really equivalent to one another, and inevitably this book will sometimes be superficial or somehow off the mark in submitting that behavior on one level of human experience is analogous to behavior on another level of human experience.[3]

Still, it is my hope that this work will demonstrate that man's genocidal destructiveness can be seen as a process to be studied, charted, and managed correctively. This book proposes a frame of reference for attempts to understand human mad violence alongside the genius of human creativity, as both issue from the very givens of life and death in human existence. Even if virtually all of the details of these observations eventually need to be discarded or revised, I hope that this book will engender a sense that the cancer of man's destructiveness can be studied with new hope.

It also seems very much in order to emphasize that my efforts to understand man's killing ways in no way should be taken to excuse, absolve, or forgive such deeds. God forbid that this book should be taken in any way as an apology for the horrors of mass human destruction. Still, it is my conviction that we must plumb the cancer of human destructiveness at any cost, even if we must discover that human nature itself opens our hearts and minds to the destructive option. If ever we are to curtail holocausts of human life, we must understand the cancers we are fighting.

The Unremembered Genocide

During the night of April 24, 1915, the intellectual and religious leaders of the Armenian community in Constantinople were seized from their beds, imprisoned, tortured, and ultimately put to death on charges of sedition. Simultaneously, all Armenians serving in the Turkish army—these had already been gathered into separate "labor battalions"—were taken aside and killed. Then, when the leaders and fighting men were disposed of, the final phase began. Lord Bryce[1] describes the opening procedure as follows:

At one Armenian center after another, throughout the Ottoman Empire, on a certain date (and the dates show a sequence), the public crier went through the streets announcing that every male Armenian over age 15 must present himself forthwith at the Government building. . . . The men presented themselves in their working clothes, leaving their shops and work-rooms open, their ploughs on the field, their cattle on the mountainside. When they arrived, they were thrown without explanation into prison, kept there a day or two, then marched out of the town in batches, roped man to man along some southerly or southeasterly road. . . . They had not long to ponder over their plight for they were halted and massacred at the first lonely place on the road.

After a few days' interval, the Armenian women and children, as well as any remaining men, were ordered to prepare themselves for deportation. Many were turned out on the road immediately, but in some towns they were given a week of grace which they spent in a frenzied attempt to sell their personal possessions for whatever was offered. Government orders forbade them from selling real property or stocks, as their banishment was supposed to be temporary. Scarcely were they out of sight, however, when Moslem refugees from Europe, who had been gathered nearby, were moved into their homes. Since the Turks of the interior were almost totally unskilled, a representative Armenian craftsman in each area—a shoemaker, a tailor, a pharmacist—was permitted to remain. All the rest were set upon the roads leading to the deserts. According to Morgenthau,[2] hundreds and thousands "could be seen winding in and out of every valley and climbing up the sides of nearly every mountain." In the first six months alone, over 1,200,000 people joined this unearthly procession.

By now the story bears a chillingly familiar quality, the more intensified when one remembers that the victims of this last, most hideous phase were almost exclusively women and children. They were marched south from the plains of Anatolia, through a region that is a no-man's land of treacherous ravines and craggy mountains forbidding to the most hardened traveler, and finally into the bleak Syrian desert, fiercely hot by day and frigid by night. On the way, they were beset by all the Moslem populations they encountered. First there were the Turkish villagers and peasants who robbed them of their few provisions, their clothes, and took such of their women as they pleased; then the Kurds, who committed blood-chilling atrocities, first butchering any males in the convoy, then attacking the women. According to the Bryce Report: "It depended on the whim of the moment whether a Kurd cut a woman down or carried her away into the hills. When they were carried away their babies were left on the ground or dashed against the stones." Then came the "chettis," savage brigands who had been loosed by the thousands from prisons and set in the victims' path, and dervishes who roared down from their convents in the hills and carried off children "shrieking with terror." And always there were the gendarmes, prodding the exhausted and terror-stricken figures with whips and clubs, refusing them water when they passed wells and streams, bayoneting those who lagged behind, and committing increasingly perverted atrocities.

Apologists have claimed that these atrocities were simply the work of barbaric and fanatic tribesmen, but Morgenthau has shown that they were a matter of deliberate policy. Thus, an educated state official told him with some pride that "all these details were matters of nightly discussion at headquarters. . . . Each new method of inflicting pain was hailed as a splendid discovery, and the regular attendants were constantly ransacking their brains in an effort to devise some new torment.

He told me that they even delved into the records of the Spanish Inquisition and other historic institutions of torture and adopted all the suggestions found there."

Nor can there be any doubt that the policy of extermination as a whole was planned by the central government. The official record includes the following orders, sent on cipher telegrams and in all but one case addressed to the provincial government of Aleppo (the lightning advance of Allenby's forces prevented the Turks in Aleppo from destroying these compromising documents):[3]

September 3, 1915
We recommend that the operations which we have ordered you to make shall first be carried out on the men of the said people, and that you shall subject the women and children to them also. Appoint reliable officials for this.

[Signed] Minister of the Interior
Taalat

As a result of Turkey's policy, over one million Armenians died.

1. James Bryce, English statesman, historian and author, *The Treatment of the Armenians in the Ottoman Empire* (edited by Arnold Toynbee).

2. Henry Morgenthau, Sr., American ambassador to Turkey who proclaimed the Turkish crimes to be unparalleled in the history of the human race.

3. First published in the *London Daily Telegraph*, May 29, 1922.

—Marjorie Housepian, *Commentary*, September 1966

2

NORMAL MAN
AS GENOCIDER

We are all of us, Christian and Jew alike of a generation and a tradition that has been brought up to believe that culture was the basis of salvation. As George Steiner has often reminded us, we believed that if people read good books, went to museums, subscribed to the opera and loved symphonies, certain decencies would follow. . . . Auschwitz, Hiroshima, and Mai Lai have taught us that murder and culture do not exclude each other. If these events prove anything, it is that it is possible for a person to both love poems and kill children.

— Lionel Rubinoff

This is an age that is impressed with the significance of one or another disease or social problem by way of its statistics. In the United States, for example, we are alert to facts such as these: one out of twelve people will spend some time in a mental hospital; one out of eight people can be expected to turn to some form of psychological help; one of every two to three marriages ends in divorce; the number one killer is cancer. However, we have never allowed ourselves to be fully aware of the greatest killer of all, which from 1820 to 1945 is reputed to have claimed some 54 million human lives: man himself, in his forever murdering of his fellow man.[1]

With tongue in cheek and, yes, with barely suppressed tears and rage, I propose that humans' killing humans should be defined as the Number One Public Health Problem! In the metaphor of this book, the number one killer of all time is the cancer of human destructiveness. Psychiatrist Ronald Laing has written:

We are all murderers and prostitutes—no matter to what culture, society, class, nation, we belong, no matter how normal, moral, or mature

9

we take ourselves to be. . . . In the last fifty years, we human beings have slaughtered by our own hands coming on for one hundred million of our species. We all live under constant threat of our total annihilation. We seem to need death and destruction as much as life and happiness. We are as driven to kill and be killed as we are to let live and live.[2]

In this book, we are addressing ourselves to genocides more than to other killings, such as formal wars between armies, because the insane genocides point out to us more clearly than the other killings the agonizing truths of our species.[3] Here we see the full, utter madness and evil of man as he commits to death helpless masses of men, women, and children without mercy.

The toll of this all-time destroyer is staggering, and its threat is ever present, yet, in so many ways, we pretend to disregard its presence all about us. It is bad enough that eventually each of us must die a natural death and that all our lives we know that is our fate—though we tend to deny this truth too. It is harder yet that all our lives none of us ever knows whether he or she will be cut down shortly by a cruel illness or cruel accident. But to die at the hands of another human being who willingly authors our premature death is an even more cruel blow. Realistically, the fact is that at any given moment, the odds are unbearably high that such a death will be the fate of many of us and many of our children.

NEARLY ALL "NORMAL" PEOPLE ARE CAPABLE OF BEING GENOCIDERS, ACCOMPLICES, OR BYSTANDERS

All evidence points to the fact that according to the mental health standards of our age, genociders are not generally distinguishable as "sicker" than most other people. In fact, psychiatrist Frederic Wertham has documented how the actual beginnings of mass killing in the Nazi period were under the direction of psychiatrists and pediatricians, who intended to solve the problem of mental retardation and mental illness by exterminating "inferior peoples":

> The mass killings of mental patients during the Nazi regime . . . was sponsored, planned and organized by leading psychiatrists and pediatricians of the universities (Berlin, Heidelberg and others) in psychiatric hospitals. At least 275,000 patients, men, women and children, were declared "worthless" and were put to death in hospitals. To this day there are no accurate figures on how many children were destroyed in this program. It is known that even bedwetting was enough for a death warrant issued by psychiatrists.[4]

A grotesque note is that at one point, Jewish patients were denied such a solution of their problem, because they were not as deserving as the Aryan patients!

Availability to Genocide in a Basically Democratic Society

Some people have sought refuge in the notion that the readiness to commit genocide was particularly characteristic of the Germans and that it would not occur so easily in another people, such as Americans, with their far deeper tradition of democracy and their ideal of the inherent equality of men. The evidence does not support this thesis. For example, psychiatrist Douglas M. Kelley studied the Nuremberg prisoners who had been the leaders of the Nazi regime and concluded:

> No. The Nazi leaders were not spectacular types, not personalities such as appear only once in a century. They simply had three quite unremarkable characteristics in common—and the opportunity to seize power. These three characteristics were: overweening ambition, low ethical standards, a strongly developed nationalism which justified anything done in the name of Germandom.
>
> Let us look about us. Have we no ultranationalists among us who would approve any policy, however evil, so long as it can be said to be of advantage to America? Have we no men so ruthlessly eager to achieve power that they would not quite willingly climb over the corpses of minorities, if by so doing they could gain totalitarian control over the rest of us? . . .
>
> What of the followers? Shocking as it may seem to some of us, we as a people greatly resemble the Germans. . . . we have a very similar background of ideological concepts, and we are similarly inclined to base our thinking on emotional rather than on intellectual evaluations.[5]

Americans have committed mass murder on a variety of occasions. Consider the bloody history of the whites' treatment of the Indians in the United States. For example, in 1830 Congress passed a removal act that gave the president the right to remove Indians east of the Mississippi River. One of the resulting events was the Trail of Tears: Thousands of Cherokee Indians were forced to march a thousand miles through the winter from Appalachia to Oklahoma, and conservative estimates are that 4,000 died along the way.[6]

Few Americans are aware that at the turn of the century, U.S. troops fighting an insurrection in the Philippines committed a series of genocidal atrocities that led to a whole sequence of court martials. Writing in 1970 under the apt title, "Our My Lai of 1900," Stuart Miller recorded:

By 1900 letters from soldiers to relatives back home, describing the use of dum dum bullets, torture, retaliatory shooting of prisoners and the creation of concentration camps for civilians, began to reach the desks of local editors. One soldier bragged in a letter that Americans were shooting Filipino men, women and children "like rabbits." Lieutenant Hall reported that General Funston had all prisoners shot as a matter of course, and described how one was dispatched on his knees still begging for his life. This disclosure dampened the Administration's plans to give Funston a hero's welcome back to the United States.[7]

In recent years, many people believed that U.S. actions in Vietnam actually constituted a near-genocidal campaign against a whole people, and in some specific instances, such as at My Lai, clear-cut scenarios of genocide were played out. Of course, the U.S. involvement in Vietnam was defended by many as a legitimate "war," but it has always been that way. Genociders rationalize and extenuate their actions so that, quite sincerely, they believe they are acting in self-defense of one sort or another. There comes a point when people no longer recognize their bloodthirsty destruction for what it is. Before long, it is as if man's marvelous machinery for experiencing has itself been killed.

It has to be admitted that the U.S. tradition in some ways has succeeded in preventing the worst types of mass political violence, and in the chapter on the Genocide Early Warning System, we cite U.S. democratic institutions as examples of a society's safeguards against mass destructiveness. The historical evidence of the great U.S. experiment, however, shows clearly that a serious potential for genocidal destructiveness is present even in a great democratic society.

Civilized Peoples as Accomplices
and Bystanders to Genocide

It is also true that the U.S. historical process has evolved a tradition of humanitarian concern for victims. Yet, history finds the U.S. people playing not only the role of killer, but also the role of accomplice to other more vicious genociders. Arthur Morse has documented how the United States was an accomplice to the Nazi destruction of 6 million Jewish men, women, and children. In his book, *While Six Million Died*, Morse documents the indifference and inaction of U.S. diplomatic and political leaders in the face of increasingly clear knowledge of the German "final solution."[8] So too with other "civilized" peoples around the world. Judah Pilch writes in *The Story of the Jewish Catastrophe in Europe:*

The world knew and was silent. . . . The masses of the German population were *aware* of the anti-Jewish measures. Many were also aware of the ghettos and concentration camps. . . . The Germans as a people heard the brown-shirted fellow Germans singing "When Jews' blood drips from the knife, then things are fine and dandy," but they did not condemn this bloody slogan. . . . The Poles . . . too were indifferent to Jewish sufferings in the ghettos and they were unmoved in the hour of the Jewish deportations to the extermination centers. . . . The Ukrainians regarded the liquidation of the Jews calmly and with some satisfaction. It is on record that the Ukrainian participation prompted the famous poet, Yevgny Yevtushenko, to write a poem, "Babi Yar" in which he deplores the participation of the civilian population in the mass killings of forty thousand Jews in the ravine Babi Yar of Kiev. . . .

America was not prepared to change its national quota system. The French insisted that they could not receive any more Jews. The Swiss complained of the mass crossing of the borders by Jewish refugees. Admission of Jewish refugees to Palestine, the only country whose Jewish population was willing and ready to find room in their own community for unlimited numbers, was prohibited by Britain. . . . And the most painful of all questions was the silence of the Christian church. . . . Righteous acts were the exception to the rule. That fact is that no official representation was ever made by the Church to the German leaders which would have expressed in the strongest possible terms the protests of all true believers. . . .

It is told that the famous Jewish historian, Simon Dubnow, when he was driven to death in the gas chambers, cried out to the people as he passed: "Record everything! Remember!"[9]

It is perhaps tempting to imagine that such acts of national policy are different from a sheer, direct refusal by an individual to help a fellow human being when his or her life is threatened. Sadly enough, we also have evidence that many individuals will stand idly by while fellow human beings are being hurt and killed. In fact, people often exhibit only thinly veiled interest, let alone enthusiasm, for the "exciting" spectacle they are witnessing. In many of these situations, the observers could help to some extent, without endangering themselves, yet they do not. The story of Kitty Genovese has been told and retold. The young woman was murdered on Long Island, New York, in full view of thirty-eight people who were in their apartments. The attacker stabbed her several times within a period of forty minutes. Not only did none of the observers go out to help her, not one even went to the phone to call the police![10]

OBEDIENCE TO AN AUTHORITY WHO ORDERS TORTURE AND DESTRUCTION

A fascinating seminal research series by psychologist Stanley Milgram points out the extent to which people are ready to obey leaders who call for violence against innocent people.[11] Milgram's basic research design has come to be known, appropriately enough, as the Eichmann Experiment.

Milgram's experimental situation is one in which an apparently traditional learning study is under way. A subject is required to demonstrate his mastery of certain material, and when he fails, he is given an electric shock. In actual fact, the subject is a paid actor hired by the experimenter, and he receives no shock at all. The real subject is the person who is engaged by the experimenter to administer the shock. In some variations of the experiment, the true subject is alone; in other experimental variations, a member of a team of three who together must determine what dosage to deliver – except that the other team members are actually assistants of the experimenter, and they call for the administration of increasingly severe shocks. The real subject and the two other team members are seated at a console that offers an apparently wide range of shock severity. The buttons indicate low voltage; moderate voltage; painful and possibly dangerous voltage ("extreme shock"); and finally, very dangerous, possibly even lethal shock ("danger: severe shock"). To add to the vividness of the situation as the shock dosages apparently increase, the actor-subject protests more and more, even to the point of begging and shouting to be let out. The basic experimental situation has been varied in a number of ways, but the results have been tragically consistent and clear cut:

Given the instructions of an authority, a majority of people from all socioeconomic levels are capable of doing serious, perhaps even lethal, harm to fellow human beings.

As indicated, Milgram himself attempted a series of variations. When the experiment was conducted at Yale University, the overall rate of subjects who administered all shocks as instructed was 65 percent. When the experiment was removed to a run-down commercial building, so there would be less of the authority of the university science setting, the percentage of people who administered the maximum shock was 48 percent – still an unbelievably high figure when we remember that we are talking about administering a shock that was identified in the experiment as "danger: severe shock." A more reassuring result was found when the experiment was run without an authoritative command to increase the shocks. In the absence of an authority commanding the subjects to go on, the percentage of those who administered the maximum shock dropped to 23 percent. This important finding obviously says a good deal about the crucial role of leadership in bringing people to execute evil acts. However, in another sense, the figure is hardly reassuring if one realizes the full meaning of even a single person being available to administer the full deadly sequence of shocks the Milgram "passion play" prescribed, let alone 23 percent of a population.

Another U.S. experimenter, David Rosenhan at Stanford University, reported that when he removed the "models" from the situation (the experimenter's assistants), so that the subject was deciding on his own how much shock to give, he still found an 85 percent level of compliance with administering the maximum shock.[12] In another variation of the experiment, Milgram went so far as to bring the subject close to the victim by requiring the subject actually to hold the victim's hand forcibly on the shock plate. Under these conditions, a smaller but still terribly large 30 percent of the subjects administered the maximum shock.

It is pertinent, and also of some special symbolic significance, to report that another replication of the Milgram study done in Germany by David Mantell yielded the same overall results. In other words, there was no significant difference between the percentage of people in Germany who would comply with the experimenter's instructions to hurt fellow human beings and the percentage of people in the United States who administered the maximum shock.[13]

An important extension of the basic experiment was built into the study in Germany, as well as into the work conducted by Rosenhan in the United States. The central dynamic in the Milgram experimental structure had been that the subjects were instructed by an authority to administer the shocks. In fact, Milgram himself had defined his research as a study of conformity rather than as a study of the extent of human destructiveness. What both Mantell in Germany and Rosenhan in the United States now independently sought to test further was, What happens if the authority is discredited to the subject? Would the subject cease to follow instructions?

In Rosenhan's study, after reaching a point when the subject was apparently administering shock of some 210 volts, one of the experimenter's assistants, posing as another subject, would spontaneously ask the experimenter about his credentials and learn that the experimenter was not a member of the university faculty, as had been supposed all along, nor even a graduate student. In fact, under futher questioning, the experimenter would be unable to defend his position in any credible manner. At that point, the subject who was pressing the experimenter would refuse to go on with the experiment and stomp out. Now the question was whether the real subject would continue with the full series of shocks. Rosenhan's results were that a dismaying 53 percent of the subjects continued with the entire shock series. Similarly, in the Mantell study in Germany, there was a procedure for attacking the authority of the experimenter by having the true subject observe a fake subject's refusal to administer the shocks: again some 52 percent of the true subjects went on to complete the full series.

The study in Germany also introduced another variation. The subjects were not instructed to administer a progressive series of shocks but were put on their own to decide if and how much to punish the apparent subject of the experiment for his or her errors. Under these conditions, only 7 percent of the true subjects adminstered an entire series of shocks.

Psychologist Philip Zimbardo has written about the Milgram research:

> The question to ask of Milgram's research is not why did the majority of normal, average subjects behave in evil (felonious) ways, but what did the disobeying minority do after they refused to continue to shock the poor soul, who was so obviously in pain? Did they intervene, go to his aid, did they renounce the researcher, protest to higher authorities, etc.? No, even their disobedience was within the framework of "acceptability," they stayed in their seats, "in their assigned place," politely, psychologically demurred, and they waited to be dismissed by the authority. Using other measures of obedience in addition to "going all the way" on the shock generator, obedience to authority in Milgram's research was total![14]

It is revealing that in the wake of these studies, many psychologists protested the psychological brutalization of the true subjects in the experiment, because they were forced to encounter their true potential for destructiveness. There are, of course, very real limits to the amount of damage scientists can be allowed to inflict on subjects of experiments—thus we dare not forget how the Nazis conducted brutal medical experiments—but the Milgram experiment is not brutal so much as it forces all of us to realize that someday we must gain control over our violence. In this sense, the assaulting quality of the Milgram experiment is really a valuable attack on the denial and indifference of all of us. Whatever upset follows facing the truth, we must eventually face up to the fact that so many of us are, in fact, available to be genociders or their assistants.

THE NONPSYCHIATRIC STATUS OF GENOCIDERS

Diagnostic concepts in mental health leave a good deal to be desired, insofar as they derive from attempts to distinguish between normality as a capacity to function without symptoms and abnormality as a state of impaired functioning. So often, the really disturbed person who brings great pain and suffering to other human beings is free of "symptoms" of impaired functioning. To my mind, the most important psychological issue is whether a person has respect for human life and human experience, beginning with a deep feeling for the miracle of his or her own being, and then, by extension, has respect for the integrity of the lives of others. Such inner integrity is far more important than the number of tangible symptoms a person shows. Thus, even a deeply disturbed, truly mentally sick person who has given up functioning for himself in everyday life may show great potential for such integrity, and it is my belief that this fact changes the patient's overall diagnostic picture radically. Many times the long-range emotional prognosis of such a patient is better than that of people who show no symptoms in their current functioning but lack an inner respect for life.

Still, given the general acceptance of the traditional distinctions between normal and abnormal, it is important that we see that by and large, genociders have not been found to be abnormal in terms of current clinical concepts. Only if we redefine the goal of psychological diagnosis to focus not on how sane or realistic or competent a person is, but on how *human*, do matters make more sense. There is depersonalization in the genocider, that is, an inability to feel the grandeur of the life process in himself or in another human being. The genocider sees people as flat-surfaced objects to be ordered and put in place. Conformity to the dictates of the group, a fuehrer, or an "electric-shock god" is the genocider's ultimate value.

Such was the case with the master killer-organizer of the Nazis, Adolf Eichmann. Psychological and psychiatric studies of Eichmann by the Israeli husband-wife team of Drs. Shlomo and Shoshanna Kulcsar yielded a picture of a man utterly lacking in a sense of being.[15] He paled at and was embarrassed by sexuality. He was upset by emotional themes of aggression. What mainly mattered for Eichmann was to reduce all of life to order, nonmovement, and nonpassion so that all of life could be controlled.[16] The late Father Thomas Merton wrote:

> One of the most disturbing facts that came out in the Eichmann trial was that a psychiatrist examined him and pronounced him *perfectly sane*. I do not doubt it at all, and that is precisely why I find it disturbing.
>
> If all the Nazis had been psychotics, as some of their leaders probably were, their appalling cruelty would have been in some sense easier to understand. It is much worse to consider this calm, "well-balanced," unperturbed official conscientiously going about his desk work, his administrative job which happened to be the supervision of mass murder. He was thoughtful, orderly, unimaginative. He had a profound respect for system, for law and order. He was obedient, loyal, a faithful officer of a great state. . . .
>
> It is the sane ones, the well-adapted ones, who can without qualms aim the missiles and press the buttons that will initiate the great festival of

destruction that they, *the sane ones*, have prepared. What makes us so sure, after all, that the danger comes from a psychotic getting into a position to fire the first shot in a nuclear war? Psychotics will be suspect. No one suspects the sane, and the sane ones will have *perfectly good reasons*, logical, well-adjusted reasons for firing the shot. They will be obeying sane orders that have come sanely down the chain of command. And because of their sanity, they will have no qualms at all, when the missiles take off, then *it will be no mistake.*

We can no longer assume that because a man is "sane" he is therefore in his "right mind." The whole concept of sanity in a society where spiritual values have lost their meaning is itself meaningless. . . . Perhaps we must say that in a society like ours the worse insanity is to be totally without anxiety, totally "sane."[17]

Of course, there are some genociders who are passionately driven people. In the genesis of various revolutionary and dictatorial movements that are the breeding grounds of much later genocides, there are obviously ambition-ridden, power-mad personalities. Some of them even warrant one of the various severe psychiatric diagnostic labels such as "paranoid" or "psychopath." However, even in the case of these more obviously "sick" people, it may be that a great deal more can be understood by thinking about how their destructiveness is a desperate effort at aliveness instead of pinning sterile labels on them. Other mental health observations of the Nazi leaders of the Holocaust are in agreement that one cannot see the principal Nazi personalities as abnormal.[18] Psychologist G. M. Gilbert, who studied the Nazi war criminals at the Nuremberg trials, wrote:

Psychopathic personalities undoubtedly play an important part in major manifestations of social pathology, particularly when they achieve positions of leadership in social groups and movements. It is all too clear that they played a decisive role in the revolutionary nucleus of the Nazi movement, and thus determined the complexion of the government of Nazi Germany. But that does not mean that the crux of our problem is the detection and elimination of such personalities from political life. Even if that were possible, it would be an endless palliative process at best. We have seen that without the support of "normal and respectable" leaders in that society, without a considerable following among the masses of the people, and without the facilitative action of certain cultural trends, it would hardly have been possible for the Nazi leaders to precipitate as great a social catastrophe as they did.[19]

The Holocaust convincingly brings home the truth that genocide is a complex of forces that can be set off in virtually any society of normal human beings.[20]

MAN'S CAPACITY TO BLOT OUT THE PROSPECTS
OF BEING BLOTTED OUT

It has long been understood in mental health work that to the extent that a person avoids experiencing the truths of his situation, he sets himself up for those truths to return to plague him the more. This is true whenever a person denies either the actual facts of his life situation or the feelings and emotions that must naturally accompany the circumstances in which he finds himself. For example, failure to grieve over the death of a loved one is often followed by illness or emotional breakdown.

The extent to which a person denies critical aspects of reality is crucial for emotional health. *"There is nothing wrong with me, I am God" is the classic statement of extreme denial by the paranoid psychotic. "No, I don't have anything worrying me, it's just that I have so much work to do" is the classic cry of the psychosomatically ulcerated executive who denies his or her dependency needs through overwork.*

Not that it is hard to understand why humans engage in denials; it is bitterly painful to feel loss, hurt, or weakness. Following surgical removal of a part of the body, there are a certain number of patients who imagine, even insist, that nothing has been taken from them. Following the breakup of a marriage, many people insist that it was they who rejected their spouse; heaven forbid the possibility that they might have been on the receiving end of rejection. The mechanism of denial serves the very legitimate function of blunting pain that could be too difficult to bear. However, in the long run, the price of undue denial, or denial sustained for too long, is that it prevents a person from working through the loss he or she has suffered. (This working through is essential if one is to take preventive action to guard against renewed losses – to the extent that we can reasonably protect ourselves against certain events or their consequences.)

When it comes to human violence, there is no end to our denial – both of the violence that can befall us ("It can't happen to me") and of the violence that we may inflict on others. If ever there were an area of human experience that denied reality, this is it. Day after day, year after year, people die by the thousands and millions, and although there are deep (and I believe increasing) swells of caring and protest, the overall quality that prevails is the unreal one of going about everyday life as if there were no terrible dangers about us and upon us. Violence is always happening to someone else who is not really related to me; it can't ever happen to me – neither my being a victim, nor, even more remotely, my becoming one who does violence to others. The denials continue unendingly, until it happens, as it does, relentlessly, over and over again.

Even our behavioral and social sciences, which are delegated to advance our knowledge of how to live with our emotions and how to improve human society, often have joined in denying the extent of violence in human affairs. For many years and until quite recently, one could look in *Psychological Abstracts,* where thousands upon thousands of contributions to psychology and the other behavioral sciences are regularly abstracted and indexed, and find only a mere handful of entries dealing with violence—both the facts thereof and certainly the whys thereof.

In this respect, there has been a significant change in the past fifteen years. More and more behavioral scientists are concerned with aggression and violence. However, the quality and depth of the scientific work in this area are in their beginning stages, and how much the work will deepen remains to be seen. There is some sense that U.S. psychologists, in particular, have been drawn to studies of violence by the increasing violence in everyday life in the United States and by the trauma of U.S. destructiveness in Vietnam. It is hard to tell yet whether there is a truly deep concern over the bedrock destructiveness of the "normal" human being, for even now, psychology books rarely contain an honest description of how the normal personality includes an explicit penchant for destructiveness.

Why is there such denial of violence? I suggest that there are two essential reasons:

1. People deny the reality of never-ending violence because they feel powerless to cope with the problem. So long as people feel essentially powerless in limiting or preventing violence, it serves their emotional stability not to be too aware of the likely possibility of new acts of violence about which they will be able to do virtually nothing.

2. People also deny the realities of violence because they cannot bear their own unknown destructiveness. Individuals shrink from their own deep potential for doing violence and destructive deeds. We are accustomed in our civilization to relegate all impulses and energies that in any way are committed to violence to the realm of the "ugly," "sick," "disturbed," "immoral," "inhuman," and the like. If, in fact, we do admit that there are violent roots deep in human nature, we see them as the "base," "primitive," or "pathological" qualities of human nature, not at all as necessary and desirable aspects of being. People try as much as possible to put their potential for destructiveness far away from their awareness. Even when people are faced somehow with the necessity of acknowledging the serious destructiveness going on about them, say, in a society that engages in genocide, they still seek to isolate the facts of those events from any awareness of the violent impulses that exist within their own personalities.

THE NORMALITY OF EMOTIONAL WEAKNESS
AND PROBLEMS AS AN EVOLUTIONARY CHALLENGE

To understand better the roots of man's violence, we might profitably ask just how natural are any number of other distortions, "illnesses," and weaknesses in the psychological lives of people. Once one gets past traditional and romanticized medical concepts of mental health and illness, one discovers that just about everybody is "sick" in some significant way fairly often in life. Most human beings struggle deeply with themselves at one point or another, and often for long periods of time, with considerable problems and symptoms.[21] Most people suffer serious underachievement in one or another important aspect of their personal or family lives, and all too many people permanently destroy a great deal of their potential.

The whole human race is so "sick" that a growing number of mental health clinicians believe there is a far better way to think of human problems than in the sense of mental health, which distinguishes between sick and healthy. I would say that, overall, man is at a primitive point in his evolution. In other words, it is not because people are sick that they suffer problems, it is because they are human. Of course, there still is some useful meaning to the concept of sickness. Among other things, it is used for identifying a degree of breakdown and inability to function that correspond to the breakdowns and inability to function that mark physical illnesses. But in the broad sweep of human behavior, it is more useful to see each person as a case study in evolution. The question then is, How can each person tap more of his or her enormously rich potential and limit the rampages of weakness and limitation that are evidently quite natural in the drama of evolution?

In matters of physical health, we have achieved a staggering lengthening of our longevity as a result of step-by-step triumphs over various illnesses that were once naturally epidemic. There is no reason we cannot seek a similar evolution from our overwhelming emotional weaknesses to greater emotional sturdiness. The real psychological health-illness issue is not whether people feel or show symptoms of weakness, vulnerability, or distress at any point, but whether the meanings of the distress are experienced and followed through—even honored—as challenges to further development. Each experience of our vulnerability is a rich opportunity to learn more about how to live better and how to become stronger and less vulnerable.

The critical and exciting implication of such a point of view is that more than focusing on restoring sick people to health, and even more than studying how to prevent emotional illness, the real goal is to learn how to help people increase their potential for experiencing their humanness. How can people turn problems into opportunities for growth? How can the inevitable conflicts of life be directed to peaceful solutions? How can we be both strong and peace seeking when we are under attack? It is not that no useful questions at all issue from the traditional model of human beings as either mentally healthy or sick, but many more useful questions issue from a model built around the concept of how humans cope with the serious problems that are natural in life.[22] By not pushing our deepest weaknesses off into a realm of pathology or sickness, we invite ourselves to acknowledge these terribly difficult parts of ourselves and master them. For example, it is natural to be depressed after losing out in a love relationship, it is appropriate for a young person to be frightened and anxious on entering a new career, and it is human to become upset when one realizes he or she has hurt another person. These and many other symptoms of upset are not really problematic; essentially, they are indications of an organism healthily at work. Even when we are talking about people who are really psychologically sick—that is, their terror and disturbed functioning have reached some degree of breakdown of their ability to function in everyday life—the disturbance may be remarkably productive. If the "inner sounds" indicate that a person is using a period of inner craziness to regroup, rebuild missing strengths, and get rid of forces that have been in the way of reaching more of his or her potential, that patient is not as "sick" as he or she appears. Such people may require professional help to shorten the period of their reorganization and to guide them in strengthening themselves, but basically they may be trusted as people who are working to be more alive.

The people to worry about are often those who are not really living. Not infrequently, these people are free of symptoms for a long time. They appear not to suffer, but often that is because they don't take emotional risks. They do not try to grow, so they don't get "sick" as readily as people who do try to live and grow. It might also be said that the nonriskers are not participating in the evolutionary process. They are trying to sit out nature's grand plan. They simply "exist." They are often smug. And they are often dangerous. Their dangerousness issues from their brutal reduction of life to routineness, banality, and an ordering of things; a life in which human values do not exist and the creative is not sought. Life is reduced to a kind of pretending not to be different in any way from the common picture of society. When these people become sick—and they do because eventually their disguises can break down in the face of nature's constant mysteries and challenges—their condition is likely to be particularly sad. Often, their mildest symptoms may resist change no matter what the treatment effort, and their severest symptoms may well go as far as one or another irretrievable "death." For example, studies in both the United States and England have shown that the all-too-perfect marital couple is especially prone to severe breakdown by way of sudden divorce, psychosomatic breakdown, or even murder.[23] There can be no emotional wholeness without contending with the terrible, fascinating truths of the two sides of man's being, the creative and the destructive.

THE CRITICAL ROLES OF SOCIAL INSTITUTIONS IN TEACHING AND EVOKING RESPECT FOR LIFE

If there has been any attempt at a sensible explanation of genocide over the years, it has been along the lines of understanding how historical, political, and economic forces build to legitimate destructiveness in the name of this or that national, religious, racial, or whatever group purpose. Nothing of what I have been saying is intended in any way to dismiss or minimize the critical significance of these large-scale sociohistorical processes. The problem is that these large-scale events in themselves do not really explain the ultimate human phenomenon of man's ability to destroy his fellow man.

So often when we talk about major sociohistorical forces that cause genocide, we know in our hearts that we are avoiding encountering what really goes on in the hearts and minds of people that makes it possible for them to kill others wantonly. When we hear analyses of human destructiveness that relate only to sociohistorical forces and not to the inner nature of humans, it is as if we hear a depressing refrain: "Human destructiveness has erupted many times before and will many times again; there's nothing we can do about it, because we don't really understand our need to be destructive." What we need is to be able to see simultaneously how group forces stimulate people in the direction of destructiveness, how the personalities of people allow them to accept the group's influence, and how it is people who contribute to the group's destructiveness.

Ultimately, we need to have a machinery for understanding acts of genocide by a single individual who is not himself clinically disturbed and whose life is marked by a fair quality of affection for family and other human beings. We need to understand how such a person is capable of being influenced by group processes that excite, trigger, and legitimate genocidal violence. We also need to understand the role that such an individual plays, both as leader and as follower, in the group processes of conformity to authority and idolatry of charismatic leaders who call for genocide. The social sciences need to have a language that makes it possible to think about how a human being who is not clinically mad or morally perverse can become a killer of many people.

What is "normal" to the human condition is the combined readiness of human beings to be destructive and the readiness of social institutions to evoke and sponsor violence. This discussion of the normality of man's availability to genocide cannot be complete unless we see the inner weakness of human beings in relation to the social forces that trick people (all too successfully) into believing that they must kill others on behalf of their own desire to live. On the one hand, the normal human being's struggle to encompass life and death seems to leave him virtually mad and available to primitive destructiveness. On the other hand, a society will label one or another group of people as outsiders who are a dangerous threat to the lives of the members of the society. If it were not for our terror about life and death, we would reject these scapegoating mythologies; if it were not for society's authorization of scapegoating, we would not translate our terror into collective destruction. It is only the combination of personal and collective forces that can explain the huge evils of genocide.[24]

Does it matter which comes first, our availability to destroy or the authorization of acts of violence by society? There is, of course, an historical sequence. From the dawn of time, man has moved across the stage of history suffering terrifying anxieties about being alive. Primitive man's basic model of life is that of a perpetual contest between his survival and the survival of another. He thus builds varied and numerous social institutions, such as governments and armies, to protect him from his enemies. These institutions then frequently set men against one another and over and over again sponsor untenable violence under the guise of self-defense.

Once we develop a language that makes it possible to see that it is human beings, individually and collectively, who are responsible for the eruption of violence, then we will want to return to the political, economic, social, and historical forces to link our understanding of people as destroyers with our understanding of social-institutional forces. Throughout this book, we want to see psychological man and social-institutional man as being on separate levels but at the same time appreciate their continuous interrelationship. An effective treatment of the cancer of human destructiveness clearly requires major changes in the fabric of our social institutions, but such changes must be based on an understanding of which qualities of human nature generate and support injustice and cruelty. If we are to change the fact that a normal person is available to genocidal destructiveness, we need a concerted campaign on behalf of life both by the individual and by society.

The Limits of Religious Ideals in Reducing Mass Killings

A special word seems in order here about the role of religious institutions in the societal process. After all, religious institutions historically have done the most to bring human beings forward to a measure of "civilized" regard for life. At this point in history, however, it appears that religious institutions have reached the limit of their potential, at least for the foreseeable future. In truth, if we look carefully at the role played by the traditional religions with regard to war and peace, we find a striking paradox. There is, on the one hand, a god who calls on humans not to kill. This is the god who enjoined our savage forefathers from their head-hunting, and this is the god whom we credit with inspiring so many of our noblest aspirations for peace. On the other hand, not only have there been countless incidents in which ostensibly religious human beings have stood prominently among the genociders and their henchmen, but there have also been many instances in which the church itself fomented and even assisted in executing genocide. Throughout history, men have gone off to war in the name of their god, and the mass killers, too, have done their ugly work in the name of some god. Man's gods freely call for death to man's enemies even as the gods preach the injunction, "Thou shalt not kill."[25]

The religious ethic also seems to be lacking in power, not only because of its duplicity, but also because something very basic is missing in the way religions conceive of man. By and large, traditional religions see people as either good or bad, yet scientific study of human behavior concludes that all people must deal with destructive impulses and that those who cut themselves off from their natural aggression are more prone to be violent. As long as religious thought is not prepared to help people relate more to their natural destructiveness, the religious establishment sets itself too far away from man's true nature to be a genuine influence. Perhaps when the social scientists understand better how to teach us to respect life, theologians will be able to draw new tools from the social sciences that will help religions regain the momentum of their former promise as inspirers of men and women toward their better selves.[26]

THE PARADOX OF HUMAN NATURE

I have already said that genociders, like all of us, are trying to transcend the terror of death and that at its root, man's violence is the result of natural or normal processes. There are analogies in human physiology. For example, many bacteria serve very important functions in normal life. Without these friendly bacteria, we are in serious trouble, but if the bacterial processes run rampant, they cause disease. It is the task of our organism to select, filter, and control the bacterial processes. We understand that deadly cancer cells may be present in all of us all the time, although their natural function, if any, is not known, and we know that under certain circumstances, not yet entirely understood, those cells develop runaway growth processes and become life-destroying cancers. Researchers have established that in healthy people there are forces that counteract and check the cancer cells so they do not become runaway and that some as yet unknown process breaks down this checking or policing action in those people who become sick.

Similarly, destructiveness is a characteristically normal process of our species on the simplest or inner levels of our construction, but that does not mean that cancerous, bloody, ugly, and brutal violent behavior is normal or must forever exist. Destructive violences are runaway, pathological, cancerous exaggerations of an originally normal process.

Once one begins to think in this way, one is free to acknowledge the hitherto intolerable contradiction, namely, that human beings are at one and the same time beautiful, generous, creative creatures and deadly killing genociders. Human history is both a glorious epic of achievements and love and a dreadful blood-soaked nightmare of destuction. For many people it is inconceivable that under certain powerful conditions, otherwise good people become mass killers or partners to killing. Few people have the strength to conceive of the possibility that human beings can be naturally both good and bad. Seeing good people as capable of being killers shatters one's basic hope and faith in humanity, and in oneself. So we press on in the face of all the repeated historical facts of destructiveness to keep alive a series of illusions that genocides don't really happen; certainly they do not happen to me and mine; and if and when genocides do occur in history, they are the work of madmen or mad cultures. Rarely do we encounter the suggestion that genocides are, in fact, the result of a process in human beings like ourselves – who wanted to be good people but who became, in the metaphor of this book, "cancer-ridden" when their once-natural aggression grew wild and became life-destroying violence.

WE NEED A PSYCHOLOGY OF NORMAL MAN BECOMING DESTRUCTIVE WITHOUT INTENDING TO DO SO

How does it come about? How do "normal" men become genociders? We know a good deal about how a society invites, justifies, commands, and legitimates violence. We also know a good deal about how human beings are blinded and intoxicated by the collective process. But we know far less about how deep inside of human beings they can be drawn to and bear serving destruction and death.

More than anything, we need a psychology of how it is possible for normal, everyday people to end up destructive when they did not intend to become so.[27] Perhaps the worst of it is that they often do not really realize what they are doing even in the midst of the destructiveness—not only because they cannot bear to acknowledge the truth, but because they connect the experience of what they are doing to some sense of trying to be alive and to the good they intended to do when they started life's journey. Psychologist Elton McNeil once wrote:

> The comprehension of individual or group violence will continue to be a mystery if the form of development of human personality and the form to which human psychic structure can be modeled are treated as nothing more than an annoying gadfly pestering the concept of large-scale violence. Man's psychic nature cannot remain an unknown in the equation of violence or we will find ourselves presiding over the dissolution of the human race.[28]

What are the "simple" universal processes that underlie the buildup toward violence? The point of view I develop in this book is that at its root, man's violence is the result of natural or normal processes, but those processes in themselves are not at all identical to the actual *acts* of violence. I believe one of the great aims of the social sciences should be to help man tap the enormous power and mysterious genius of his nature without being drawn to violence.[29]

There have been many opinions rendered over the years that violence is natural or instinctive in humans, but the simplistic conclusion most people have drawn from that thought is that if it is normal for humans to be violent, it is all hopeless. The mistaken assumption that sets off that reaction is the belief that if something is natural to humans, it must always be expressed in its totality and cannot be modulated. Few people see the alternative possibility that there can be natural processes that serve quite healthy purposes and that they turn into pathological or destructive processes only if they are not paced and phased correctly. It is these natural processes, and how they can lead to cancers of destructiveness, we want to study.

* * *

Dare we really listen inside ourselves—even those of us who are now reading this book out of a deep caring about life? Notice how hard it is to keep up really *caring* as we go with the discussion. After a while, even an emotionally powerful illustration of cruelty leaves us fairly unfeeling, and the subject becomes more a matter of intellectual exercise, even though we did not want it so.

If one can really bear listening inside, after a while, beyond the zone of unfeeling, I believe all of us can also hear echoes and refrains of a muted excitement that resonates and vibrates to the very horrors being committed by others all around us. Within us too there beats a pulse of pleasure as we read about mass murders. Here is a note I made for myself one day as I read Simon Wiesenthal's *The Murderers Among Us* and listened for the echo of my own inner man as genocider:

> All of us must know how depraved men can be so that we can fight the madness around us . . . and in us. . . . The reading becomes exciting. . . . One murderous incident follows another. . . . My excitement mounts. . . . It is almost a sexual feeling . . . I flow into the next account of a killing and become one with the murderer. . . . Part of me still says this could never be me. . . . But I am increasingly excited, and it is almost as if I am experiencing myself as one of the killers whom I swore I could never be.[30]

Is it possible that the bedrock capacity and urge to kill are present latently in all human beings?[31] In all of us there are terrifying fears of being annihilated, not only because history dictates the reality of such fears, but because we ourselves are afraid that we too can be destroyers, and we project our fears of ourselves onto others. It does not take an awareness of history, but simply contact with the inner nature of man through ourselves, to know that there is a danger within us and therefore around us all the time.[32]

On the other hand, there is also a deep human desire to be alive and on the side of life, not to be a destroyer. Nature builds into us both natural feelings of wanting to destroy others and deep wishes to support life and not act out our potential for destructiveness. The fear of being a destroyer can be so powerful that often people literally choose to go mad rather than run the risk of succumbing to the destructive forces they sense within themselves.[33] Altogether, our world is full of millions of people who do go too far; then, too, our world is full of other millions of people who, at any given point, are struggling not to go too far.

Part One

WHAT ARE THE ORIGINS OF HUMAN DESTRUCTIVENESS?

Amin: Ruthless Killer Plays the Buffoon

Since General Idi Amin seized power in Uganda on January 25, 1971, between 25,000 and 250,000 people, almost all Africans, have been killed in Uganda, according to a report released recently by the International Commission of Jurists. The 63-page report has been sent to the U.N. Secretary General, Dr. Kurt Waldheim, with a request that it should be submitted to the Commission on Human Rights.

For General Amin the report could not have come at a worse time. He is in the throes of trying to improve his image where variously he has been cast as a buffoon and a ruthless murderer. Some months ago he approached "Markpress" (who handled Biafra's publicity) to undertake public relations work on his behalf.

In addition, a 90-minute documentary is showing in France this month—and on Ugandan television every week—in which the general dances, plays the accordion and wins a swimming race. But even this ploy fails to improve the image, and an advertisement in the International Herald Tribune for the film had as a caption one of his typical remarks: "You can never run as fast as a bullet."

The Jurists' report shows just how many people in the past three years did not run faster than the bullet—or avoid the hammers, knives, machetes and other implements of death that have become part of Uganda's nightmare.

The report is broken up into three sections: the first dealing with the much publicised Asian expulsion in 1972, the second with the political and legal structure under General Amin, and the third is a chronological account of the "reign of terror." This latter section takes up over half the total report, and is a horrifying record of the slaughter in Uganda. Anyone—and there are still many—who believes that General Amin is a funny figure should read this.

"It is not possible to give any reliable estimate of the number of people who have been arbitrarily executed since January 1971," the report states. "Estimates received range from 25,000 to 250,000. All that can be said is that they are to be numbered certainly in thousands and very possibly in tens of thousands. With the exception of a handful, all were Africans. The Asians are perhaps fortunate to have been expelled."

Immediately after Amin came to power, when many in the West were still welcoming the overthrow of Dr. Milton Obote as Uganda's President, the murders and massacres in Uganda began. The report says: "In the first few months of the new Government a pattern of random and continued violence began to emerge. . . ." Throughout 1971 doctors, eye surgeons, civil servants, businessmen and politicians joined the mounting list of missing.

The Ugandan Government consistently blamed the disappearances on Dr. Obote and his supporters, on the Chinese, on Southern African freedom fighters, on an array of neighbouring countries and finally, after the break with Israel, on Zionists.

There is little anyone can do to stop the killing, which is still going on. The likely outcome is an assassin's bullet, but every time an attempt to unseat Amin fails — and there have been a number — that is the signal for a new purge.

—David Martin, Overseas News Service, June 14, 1974

3

THE CANCER OF EXPERIENCING: THE INTIMACY OF LIFE AND DEATH

As an existentialist philospher, I see human nature determined by the conflict between the goodness of man's essential being and the ambiguity of his actual being, his life, under the conditions of existence. The goodness of his essential nature gives him his greatness, his dignity, the demand embodied in him to be acknowledged as a person. On the other hand, the predicament in Nhich he finds himself, the estrangement from his true being, drives him into the opposite direction, preventing him from fulfilling in actual life what he essentially is. It makes all his doings, and all that which is done by him ambiguous, bad as well as good.

— Paul Tillich

The two immutable facts of life are life and death. It is in the human being's experience of these basic facts of life that I believe we can understand much of how people turn to sacrificing others' lives. My suggestion is that human destructiveness is a cancer of human experience, much like the dread cancers that haunt the physical existence of humans. We have learned that the cancer cells that may bring about disease and death are, in fact, always present in the normal human organism. In states of disease, the process of life is somehow overwhelmed by these ever-present cancer cells, which previously were held in balance by the larger life system.

I propose that man's terrifying ability to bring death to others grows from a similar "cancer," as it were, of the very process for experiencing aliveness. For here, too, the normal state of life is always accompanied

33

by seeds or silent experiences of our death-future and the necessity of our relating to that future. My suggestion is that when a human being becomes a monstrous killer, the death-future breaks forth from a system of checks and balances to overwhelm the larger process of life and the destruction of life is an effort to resolve the dilemma of being alive while heading toward one's own death.

Before proceeding further, it has to be clear that whatever conclusions are reached, we are not *really* going to understand how human beings can put others to death. For one thing, there is no way we can presume to put into words the ineffable meaning of even a single human life or the brilliance and beauty of the human essence, so it is virtually impossible to understand the process of its destruction. In attempting to describe the destruction of human life, we run a great risk of dishonoring that life, for no words or symbols can possibly express the real meaning of that vital process of human aliveness that has been destroyed before its time.

Moreover, we are concerned not only with the meaning of the lives of the victims we mourn, but also with the essence of the lives of those hapless members of our species who kill their fellow human beings. Evil as they are, their acts are the acts of alive human beings, in some way playing out aspects of the human condition whose miracle we barely begin to comprehend.[1]

Do our efforts at understanding the killers as human beings in any way imply forgiveness or extenuation? If we argue that the potential for being drawn to the role of killer is in all of us and that there are natural processes through which not-bad people are easily seduced or called to a murderous destructiveness that was not chosen by them purposely, it might appear that there is a case for understanding – hence accepting – the heinous crimes of murder and mass murder, let alone the lesser crimes of being an accomplice or a bystander to murder.

What I see as the deeper human truth needs to be stated very clearly, and more than once: Whether or not we are driven by deterministic forces, each of us must bear full responsibility for the choices we make whether or not to be destroyers. There can be no forgiveness; there can be no dampening of our outrage and protest against the killing of men. My desire is to understand how these terrible events come to be and what we might do to stop them, not to forgive.[2]

THE TWO UNCHANGING FACTS OF LIFE ARE LIFE ITSELF AND INEVITABLE DEATH

We begin with two fundamental universal truths:

1. We are alive!

2. We are dying!

It follows that these unchanging givens of life in themselves necessarily define the boundaries of the life experience.

3. We wish to feel alive. There is no greater drive than to be alive — and stay alive — and in a larger sense, too, to feel alive. The "life instinct" is a prime mover in all human experience.

4. We wish to die well. Given the fact that we must inevitably die, we understandably want to die well. We wish ourselves a death that will come after a long life. We hope our death will be quiet, simple, and sleeplike. We pray that our death will mark an ending to a life that has been richly lived and not be a cruelly wrenching end that will throw bitter salt on the already painful reality that die we must.[3]

Each fact is immutable, hence a powerful immutable dynamic. We wish to feel alive. We wish to die well. Link those two profound truths of life together, and a still further reality is generated. We wish both to feel alive and to die well.

5. We wish to feel alive, and we wish to die well. People who feel alive in the course of their lives are readier to die well when their time comes. People who are prepared to die well are more likely to experience the richness of aliveness during their life.

Mental health evidence confirms the profound interrelationships of the life experience and the death experience.[4] Over and over again, it has been seen that people who ask for mental health help because of a fear of dying are speaking largely of their dread that they are missing out on creating a meaningful aliveness during the time that they have.[5]

Over and over again, it has been seen that those who dread not being able to feel alive are too afraid of dying — of either the ultimate fact of dying or the short-range "dying" that means not succeeding at being alive even after trying hard. Because they cannot stand the possibility of dying, they elect unconsciously to quit on trying to live fully, and the result, of course, is that they do not feel alive enough.[6]

There are still other sides to the profoundly paradoxical interrelationship of life and death. It is not true that we only want to feel alive until the far-off day of the death that must be. Even under the best circumstances along the way of life, it is intrinsic to the human condition that one suffers a never-ending series of little "deaths" — injustices, disappointments, unfairnesses, betrayals, and worse. Many of these bitter hurts will be at the hands of people one loves and whose love one seeks the most. Little wonder, then, that one will also be drawn toward moments of wishing to be relieved of the pain of life itself. It is natural that one should wish that the risks of life and its agonies could be eliminated. When pain, unsureness, humiliation, and dread of the future mount up beyond one's "fail-safe" or bearable limit, there will follow naturally enough wishes not to be alive, even wishes to be dead.

6. *We often wish not to be alive when the hurts of life mount.* We wish we could be free of the risks and hurts of life; when these become too great, we partly wish to be not-alive (which points in the direction of being dead, though the wish to rest from life is not necessarily a full-blown wish to die).

We see these moments at the bedsides of patients who, we sense, want more not to be alive than they want and are able to fight to be alive. Often their unhappy disposition is confirmed by the outcome of their illness. We see many other moments of giving up in life. Many people abandon their dreams for a real love – then deny to themselves that they ever cared, because that would only add to the pain they are trying to escape from. Others give up the precious dream of their potential creativity. We see the wish not to be alive in countless "accidents" on the highways and elsewhere, as well as in chronic styles of "accident proneness." The wish not to be alive also seems to play an unknown, but oft-sensed, role in initiating many germ- or virus-derived illnesses. Apparently there are secret barriers and defenses in us that let down when we wish not to be alive, and then the diseases that are always present about us move in to seize the advantage.[7]

There is yet another side to man's need to prepare for death and wish to die well, for we well know that we also dread and resist dying.

7. *We dread and resist dying.* It is good that humans dread and are angered by the fact that they must die. We are thus faced with the maddening truth that unless we live well now, we never shall. Many a person has reported experiencing the call of death, resolving to fight back spiritedly and angrily, and consequently, taking a brilliant turn in life toward new health and fulfillment.

In many areas of life, the human spirit carries the day by fighting back against "sure" predictions of imminent death or loss. Even in the prosaic, pleasurable area of sport, it is not difficult to see nature's wise purpose at work. Success often follows a player's and team's resolve to "fight to win," to overcome "a sure loss," or to "steal" an upset victory.

What we have done in deepening our understanding of the two sides of the human experience (the wish to feel alive and the wish to die well) is to add to the contradiction of life and death the idea that each side of the human condition is linked from the outset to its own inner complement or contradiction. Not only do we want to live well and die well; we are also given to further contradictions on each side of the experience. The same person who wishes to feel alive is also naturally given to a continuous stream of wishes not to be alive; the same person who wishes to prepare to die well is also fighting against death.

A new picture of the human condition emerges when we put together the contradictory processes in our orientation to life and death, in addition to the larger contradiction of life and death as the two basic facts of the human experience. Now we see that it is natural for humans to live out a never-ending cycle of the contradictory processes of seeking life and yearning for the restfulness of nonaliveness, preparing for death and fighting bitterly against dying. For us to appreciate fully either side of the reality of our lives, we must simultaneously experience the contradiction within each side of experience.

To the extent that man falters, panics, or tries to grab a false sense of security by emphasizing only one side of the experience—either too total a push for life or too ready a surrender to death—the natural process is seriously distorted. It is not true that we only wish to feel alive. When living becomes difficult, it is natural to suffer times of wanting not to be alive. When we overcome that side of ourselves, we are strengthened against the danger of being drawn prematurely to giving up life, and we renew our experiencing of life with even greater vigor and creativity. Similarly, it is not true that we only wish to prepare well for death. When death threatens or beckons, it is natural that we resent death and fight against it. We then become more alive—and thus prepare ourselves better for the ultimate death, whose finest meaning comes from marking the end of a vigorous life.[8]

Let us look at how each side of the human experiences of life and death is extended through the linkages of these inner complementaries or contradictions.

8. *We wish to feel alive (3), and we wish not to be alive when the hurts of life mount (6).* People who want to feel deeply alive must also know how to yield under severe stress to experience their equally natural wishes not to be alive, so that they may gain strength from that side of the cycle of human experience to return more resolutely to battle and fulfill their aliveness. To avoid being overwhelmed by wishes not to be alive, which mount with life's inevitable hurts and agonies, one must seek as much as possible to feel alive. A faith and joy in one's ability to

experience aliveness can sustain hope and the ability to renew oneself during difficult times.

It is not always enough simply to be a courageous warrior for life. Even the basic thrust of wanting to be alive can be overdone, and it then works against its own interests. Thus, the person who is "never sick a day in his life" seems to be more vulnerable to sudden and total death-dealing illnesses, because he has not practiced or rehearsed wanting to retreat from life's pains and hurts and then coming back—much like a plant that is pruned—to a renewed, strengthened living experience. The never-sick ones, the always-sure ones, the never-troubled ones are paradoxically drawn toward disaster because they do not allow themselves to acknowledge their weaknesses and learn how to recover from them. Then comes an accumulation of stress too great for them to avoid, and the too-perfect people may break down and suffer severe illness or madness, or their spouse or one of their children may develop a serious problem that cries of an inability to live with a paragon of pseudoperfection. To try only to win at life without learning also how to lose along the way is to lose much more in the long run. Losing well is a part of the larger process of winning. People who have the courage to live out times of loss and even to flirt with the wish not to be alive may turn back aggressively and resolutely to live even more effectively. Ernest Becker has written in his powerful book, *The Denial of Death:* "If there is tragic limitation in life there is also possibility. What we call maturity is the ability to see the two in some kind of balance into which we can fit creatively. . . . No organismic life can be straightforwardly self-expansive in all directions."[9]

There are many ways of living out loss. There is a kind of letting go to a "Who cares" or "Who gives a damn" attitude, which is good to enjoy at times when the pressure is too much to handle but not as a permanent way of life. There are times to get sick and have a good rest. There are times to become emotionally upset and even disorganized, and then bounce back more purposefully and wisely. Studies of the creative process show that artists (which really means all of us, as we are all in part potential artists in our many different ways and walks of life) know how to use "creative disorganization" to become more productive and original.[10]

People who risk little gain little. People who avoid trying hard for success and vibrant aliveness protect themselves from feeling the depression and despair that come from disappointed hopes. Yet, when the great, overwhelming hurts in life occur, they will know very little about bouncing back from such agonizing periods of demoralization and wanting not to be alive.

On the other side of the life-death experience, we find a parallel complementary process.

9. *We wish to die well (4), and we dread and resist dying (7).* People who prepare for death are more likely to have the strength to fight off actual death when it threatens before its time. Those who fight hard against death and all the smaller "deaths" of sickness, loss, and ineffectiveness seem to be better prepared for death when their time does come.

Strength and courage to come back from hurt and demoralization seem to be nourished that much more by an ability to come to terms with one's inevitable death and to prepare for it. It is an exciting experience in psychoanalytic psychotherapy when a patient reaches the point of dreaming of his death, yet somehow surviving that death with relatively little dread and even with a sense of the mystery and joy of aliveness! This is a definitive moment in the psychotherapeutic drama that bespeaks the patient's ability to accept much of his weakness as a person, because the patient now trusts his strength to bounce back from the depth of his problems. At the same time, it appears that dying is easier for those who have fought to live more fully. People who learn to fight back against the call of death seem much readier to die when their time comes.

So we see that living and dying are linked inseparably in the ongoing process of life experiencing. We began with the knowledge that all through our lives we are faced with the truth of future death, and now we see that all through life we fight against our future death, counterpointing our wish to prepare for inevitable death.[11]

These paradoxical or complementary sides of experience are critical to the fullness of human living. People need to learn to accept the coexisting streams of life experience – yielding to feelings of wanting to give up and retreat, in order to be able to bounce back better, and knowing to turn against the "angel of death" in resolute anger and determination and to fight for life as long as they can, in order that they can die better (see Figure 3.1).

Now we can go even further in our effort to appreciate life's brilliant paradoxes by opposing the complementaries on each side of the life-death experience. In other words, we take the inner contradictory experience we saw on the life side (we also want to get away from the pain of life) and the built-in contradictory experience on the death side (we also fight against dying), and we set these two sentences alongside one another.

FIGURE 3.1   Some Variations of the Interrelationships Between Life
                and Death

---

(3) We want to feel alive,
(6) But are drawn toward wishing
     not to be alive when the hurts
     of life mount;
(4) We wish to die well,
(7) But dread and resist death.

(6) We are drawn toward wishing
    not to be alive when the hurts
    of life are too great,
(3) But we want to feel alive;
(7) We dread and resist death,
(4) But we wish to die well.

(3) We want to feel alive,
(4) But we wish to die well;
(6) We are drawn to wish not to be
     alive when the hurts of life are
     too great,
(7) But we dread and resist dying.

(4) We wish to die well,
(3) But we wish to feel alive;
(7) We dread and resist dying,
(6) But we wish not to be alive
    when the hurts of life are too
    great.

---

10. *We often wish not to be alive when the hurts of life mount
(6) and we dread and resist dying (7).* We wish to be free of the risks and
hurts of life, at times even to the point of wishing for nonlife, but we
should seek to fight back to resist dying with all our strength. We should
fight against dying with all our strength, but we should also be able to let
go to rest and repair—and even wish not to be alive at times of great
stress.

All of the many interrelationships can be spun in a brilliant
kaleidoscope, and each time we rotate the matrix of man's life and death
experiencing, we can see still another facet of the dynamics of the
human condition.

Both the simplicity and the complexity of the human living experience are staggering. We are graced with the opportunity to feel more

alive during the course of our limited mortal lifetimes to the extent that we prepare well for our deaths. To the extent that we know how to be hurt and take respite, even in occasional wishes to be free of life, we seem to bounce back with renewed courage and ability to fight. To the extent that we live well, we seem to die better. To the extent that we fight against death, we seem to live better.

Being is the integration of living and dying: on the one hand, being alive and feeling alive; on the other hand, accepting one's everyday limitations and "deaths" as well as the inevitability of one's ultimate death.

THE EVER-PRESENT THREAT OF THE CANCER OF DESTRUCTIVENESS

We have been seeing that the seeds of death are an integral part of human life, and it is striking that the same is true of physical cancers as well: The cancer cell is ever present in the healthy organism. Under conditions that we do not fully understand, the cancer cell can break out of its accompanist role to take over and swamp the healthy cell structure.[12]

A possible key in helping us look at human destructiveness may be found in the notion that when people fail to balance and integrate their natural cycle of life seeking and death seeking, they are likely to become destructive of life – of the life of others as well as their own. I suggest that it may be a useful metaphor to think of breakdowns in the integration of the experiencing of life and death as "cancers of human experiencing": When we fail to integrate our experiencing of the realities of life and death, the death-related side takes over the thrust of the whole life experiencing system (see Figure 3.2).

Just as the agony of death can tragically overwhelm us physically from within ourselves, it seems no wild stretch of the imagination to consider that the same may be true psychologically or spiritually. Certainly there is always present in our human experiencing a potential for being destroyed from within ourselves.

Cancers Grown of Not Fighting Hard Enough for Life

In everyday life, many of us observe how certain people who do not fight for their aliveness may make themselves susceptible to dying.[13] Oftentimes when such people fade prematurely from the stage of life, we have the troubling (but still unsure and sometimes also guilt-provoking) feeling that perhaps they opted for death by not fighting enough for the precious opportunity of life. Frequently, such people are very dear, sweet, and charming, and for a long time we may be reluctant to realize

---

FIGURE 3.2   Cancers of Experiencing: The Breakdown of the
Integration of Life-and-Death Experiencing

WE ARE ALIVE!

We may demand and pretend to feel so omnipotently alive as to not suffer hurt, incompleteness, or fear, but one day we can no longer maintain our denials of weakness and are shattered.

We may retreat from the hurts and disillusionments of life to the point of wishing we were not alive; by then it may be too late to fight back to the feeling of wanting to live.

WE ARE DYING!

We may be drawn toward seeking peace, wholeness, and reunion with nature itself to the point of welcoming and seeking death.

We may so dread our death that we deny its existence and try to remove everything that brings home the truth of our mortality, but one day we can no longer keep up the show; then we have to give up life itself, because it is now a reminder of the truth of death.

---

how much they may be hurting themselves. What hurts so much is that these people seem to have so many of the good qualities that mankind so desperately lacks on this planet. Yet these too-sweet people are often losers, quitters, and "fadeouters." Too often, they fall short in their life experiencing: Whether in their marriages they do not make themselves equal to their spouses or in their working lives they fall short of their potential for leadership, a weakness of spirit prevents them from being the fuller people they might have been. When their life force is required to battle against natural wishes to retire from the stresses of life, such people may not be able to invoke enough energy to fight against nonlife and death. Often they actually seek death.[14] Unconsciously, they allow themselves to be called to a fantasy of wholeness and reunion with mother nature in the peace of death. They are sadly dear flowers that fade after a short, too-tender bloom.

There are also people who are so extremely careful about any and all risks in life that once they realize that they must someday die, it is as if they begin to make their preparations right away, thus taking the spirit out of life itself. They are retiring and unrisking, sometimes to the point of virtual paralysis. They reduce the joy and richness of being to a droning humdrum of being in which there is only bare survival and the security of unconsciousness. If and when a burst of vivid life experiencing nonetheless flames in these people, they are not ready because they have not learned to live enough, and they may run from the experience to the reassurance of nonbeing. When troubles and disasters threaten, they are not seasoned enough to know how to fight back with powerful enough wishes to live. They do not know how to push death back when it comes to their door.[15]

Cancers Grown of Trying to Live Too Much

There are also people who try to live too much and do not yield to the side of life that quite naturally calls on them to know how to give up, at least to rest and repair themselves and thereby find the strength to come back to fight another day. In effect, these people do everything they can to dismiss the reality of an inevitable death. In such cases, the cancer of experiencing takes its vengeance of their efforts to live too much. These people try never to be weak, incomplete, or vulnerable. Always they insist on being on top, thriving, and triumphing. When other mortal men cry, they are grimly resolute, masking their trepidation with what may pass as great courage. Because such people do not enrich their experiential flow with an awareness of incompleteness and loss, they do not develop a seasoned, proved capacity to recover from stress. They may seem to be stronger than most other human beings, but the truth is that inside they become progressively less capable and competent until the time may come—as it generally does—when they are hurt by life in some way that is greater than they are capable of handling. Once they cannot keep up their illusions of immortality and omnipotence in their emotional lives and interpersonal experiences, they often succumb to one or another "cancer" of an actual death-dealing illness—such as a sudden, massive heart attack, stroke, or cancer—or they succumb to a cancer of experiencing and unwittingly become devotees of death rather than of life.

The remarkable similarity that exists between those who withdraw from trying to live fully and those who attempt too hard to conquer the prospect of death has been pointed out by Jane Pearce and Saul Newton, who describe

> the similarity of the . . . person whose main operation has been the avoidance of danger through the limited investment of life, with . . . the person whose preoccupation has been the act of defiance of danger. When the chronic repudiation of aliveness in either of these attitudes has been seriously challenged, the person suddenly becomes acutely and intensely

aware of his subjective expectation of being destroyed. He experiences his creativeness, his enthusiasm, his intense wish for succor not only as painful, but in the literal and immediate sense as imminently fatal. He is overcome by a paralysis which would be appropriate to the feelings of someone stepping in front of a firing squad.[16]

Destructiveness as a Cancer of Experiencing

How do we relate the metaphor of cancers of experiencing to the specific issue with which we are concerned: man's devastating destructiveness? It seems reasonable to assume that if a person is overwhelmed in the first place by a lack of comprehension of life and death, much of that person's consequent madness will be expressed in the very terms of the life and death issues that are tearing away at him and driving him mad. A good deal of what culminates in destructiveness may have its origin in man's natural efforts to free himself of his utter misery and agony in the process of struggling with life and death.

To the extent that a person is desperately unsure that he will succeed in being alive, he may seek to reduce and destroy his own life, the lives of others, or both. Certainly it seems credible that many people who are afraid of dying will be capable of thrusting the fate they fear onto others in unconscious maneuvers that are like primitive magical sacrifices of another to spare oneself: "You before me" or "If I have to go, then you go too" or "You instead of me." Ernest Becker wrote: "Modern man's defiance of accident, evil, and death . . . carried to its demonic extreme gave us Hitler and Vietnam: a rage against our impotence, a defiance of our animal condition, our pathetic creature limitations. If we don't have the omnipotence of gods we can at least destroy like gods."[17]

In summary, when humans fail to integrate the life and death sides of experience, they are prone to cancers of experiencing, which destroy them and/or are translated into a desperate killing of others to save oneself. Such killing can be experienced as essentially innocent. When someone is terrified, he may attempt to gain mastery over life and death by committing others to death, not because of any desire to kill the other, but "coincidental" to the need to prove his own omnipotence. "I'll prove that I am not terrified of death. I'll prove that I can control life and death. If I am powerful enough to bring about your death, then I can keep death from my own door."

The intimacy between life and death suggests that there are several innocent ways of being drawn to destructiveness because one does not succeed in mastering the interplay between life and death. Eruptions of cancers of destructiveness can represent a largely innocent outcome of the fact that we simply do not know how to build, pace, and channel our basic energy, which is always intense and volatile and therefore explosions of destructiveness are likely when the energy process gets out of hand.

Intense overflows are also likely to take place when one fears not being alive enough. Panic over the possibility of one's own death may cause one to reach out too desperately and intensely to experience the life force. The resulting unbalanced effort may trigger unmanageable destructiveness. There are times when all of us are so driven and "mad" with desires to feel more alive that we lose track of how to pace and gauge the extent of the power that we set off, and that power can turn toward destruction. Indeed, there are many situations that cause us to panic over our impotence and vulnerability and over the threat of our death and many occasions when we want so much to explode with power and potency that we explode with an energy we know not how to master.

Moreover, there are also the gratifications that come from the very gaining of power ("power tends to corrupt"), and there are many other simple laws of energy and structure, such as the tendency of a momentum or process to seek its maximum or completion, which slowly but surely can draw us to excesses we did not really want. Later chapters consider much more systematically different situations that draw us to destructiveness in our very quest for life, but to summarize the overall frightening and even repulsive conclusion: Much of our utterly depraved destructiveness may well have its roots in natural processes where we originally seek nothing more than to feel alive. Yet, because there is so much we do not know about how to manage the natural processes of life and its ever-present counterpart, death, many of us move ineluctably toward illness, insanity, and all manner of evil deeds, including the destruction of others.

Nature poses for us a series of interlocking dilemmas, paradoxes, and contradictions that are mind boggling. Although many men and cultures have effected brilliant penetrations into one or another aspect of the life and death processes, no Western culture to date has really solved the problem of how to teach people to deal with death as part of life: how to prepare for death and yet fight against the inroads of premature death; how to live deeply and fully and yet yield to loss and the need for rest. There is a whole curriculum for living waiting to be developed to teach us all how to mix our basic wish to be alive with the qualities of nonaliveness and preparing for death that are integral to life.[18] For is it not possible that the terrible problem of genocidal destructiveness is born of the ultimate paradox that life and death are intimately intertwined all through our living experience?

Tens of Thousands Dead Under Khmer Rouge Rule

London—Tens of thousands of Cambodians have died, some of starvation, and others by execution, under the new regime there, the "Daily Telegraph" said here yesterday.

"Reliable reports indicate that Cambodia is now in the midst of what may prove to be one of the most profound human tragedies in recent times," the newspaper said.

The dispatch, datelined Bangkok, quoted Western diplomats as saying "tens of thousands have already died, and are continuing to die as the doctrinaire Khmer Rouge victors ruthlessly pursue their goal of establishing the only true peasants' revolution in Southeast Asia.

"The old and the infirm have died after having been forced at gunpoint from the towns into the countryside by the Khmer Rouge," the "Telegraph" said.

Many more have perished as a result of starvation, for the millions who have been pushed out of the towns are competing one against the other for anything they can lay their hands on to eat.

"There are also deaths by execution to be taken into account. Reporters from the few Cambodian refugees who have been able to flee into Thailand since the Communist victory say these are widespread and numerous."

"Cholera, widespread since the Communist take-over, has now reached epidemic proportions as medical supplies have collapsed," the report concluded.

—United Press International, June 17, 1975

4

THE SOURCES OF HUMAN AGGRESSION

Aggression, hostility, strife, conflict, cruelty, sadism certainly all exist commonly and perhaps universally on the psychoanalytic couch, i.e., in fantasy, in dream, etc. I assume that aggressive behavior can be found in everyone as an actuality or a possibility. Where I see no aggressiveness at all, I suspect repression or suppression or self-control. I assume that the quality of aggression changes very markedly as one moves from psychological immaturity or neurosis up towards self-actualization or maturity, in that sadistic or cruel or mean behavior is a quality of aggression found in undeveloped or neurotic or immature people, but that as one moves towards personal maturity and freedom, the quality of this aggression changes into reactive or righteous indignation and into self-affirmation, resistance to exploitation and domination, passion for injustice, etc.

— Abraham H. Maslow

What is the secret of human energy? Clearly, the mystery of human energy in many ways is the unfathomable mystery of life itself. Yet perhaps we can attempt to understand some aspects of humanity's system for generating and channeling energy even if we cannot plumb all of the mystery. In this study of human destructiveness, we need very badly to understand what qualities of human energy are volatile, explosive, and readily turned to destructiveness, and we need to understand how humans can knowingly regulate and channel their energies and commit them to peaceful purposes. I will call basic life energy or built-in natural force "aggression."

I think of aggression as the ever-present, purposeful, pulsating energy or strength for *being* that charges the very spirit of living organisms. Aggression springs universally not only as a reaction to stress, but also from the outset as a song of life, an affirmation of oneself, a bedrock of energy to express life, and the strength to protect oneself against threats to one's life or life force.[1]

For those to whom the issue matters, looking at it in this way means aggression is "instinctual," but it does *not* mean that I am defining destructiveness as built-in or instinctive.[2] I am defining aggression as a nonspecific, powerful energy that may be turned to all manner of life activities, not necessarily destructive ones. Such a life force naturally seeks to express itself and is spent in a variety of powerful, climactic ways. We commit our tremendous energy to fulfilling a whole variety of drives, beginning, of course, with the elemental drives to satisfy our needs for food, shelter, and other protection, and then there is the need to satisfy the pressure of powerful talent drives, such as exploratory and self-expressive desires, and to fulfill our intellectual potential. Aggression or the life force stimulates, subserves, propels, and in effect energizes our various drive systems, individually and then all together in the marvelous orchestration that is called being alive. In this symphony, fulfillment of one's drives is hardly synonymous with destructiveness, and the propelling life force or aggression that is the "psychoatomic energy source" of humans does not in itself connote a bad force at all. Aggression or the life force is a natural force; if it is anything, it is what we would always want to think of as "good."

Yet, we need to understand how man's life force so frequently turns and is turned to destructiveness. We need to understand whether human destructiveness in any way derives from built-in qualities of our underlying life energy or aggression, let alone from unthinking as well as calculated choices to be destructive. If our basic life force in itself includes a natural thrust or pressure toward destructiveness, it is easier to understand why human beings are so readily drawn to be destructive. Understanding this natural process is also essential to developing better controls of destructiveness.

The model that will be developed here is one that I call "psychoatomic energy," aggression that is formed at the outset from a basic interplay or polarization of positive and negative forces. Energy is then generated from the impact of creating and building elements poised in counterpoint against forces for tearing down and breaking down.

If we use a simple notation system corresponding to elementary concepts of electrical energy, we may designate the building elements as "positive" and the tearing-down elements as "negative." The interplay of positive and negative constitutes an energy-generating system that neither set of forces alone could produce or hope to sustain. Insofar as the powering and firing of our tumultuous basic life energy necessarily calls on explosive forces, one may be carried along unwittingly to a whole sequence of destructiveness out of one's lack of knowledge about monitoring, controlling, and channeling these "psychoatomic forces."[3]

AGGRESSION INVOLVES A DESTRUCTIVE COMPONENT ALONG WITH THE CREATIVE: HENCE, IT IS ALWAYS HAZARDOUS

The scheme I am proposing as a working theory would mean that thrusts of aggression or life forces will always involve destructive, attacking, and tearing-down qualities along with building and creating qualities. In other words, man's most basic life process of harnessing energy in itself will always involve the hazard of working with volatile forces that, by their very nature, can easily flare into destructiveness even when one is searching sincerely to channel one's energy to creative life-serving efforts. That, after all, is the story of so much of human history: on the level of small events, such as in family life, and on the level of larger international events, where, indeed, men often are truly seeking to be good but nonetheless are drawn to destructiveness.

Lest this effort at theory too quickly become abstract or wordy, let us look at one powerful area of human expression whose draw on basic energy we already know a great deal about. I am referring to the world of human sexuality. What we know is that this marvelously natural, irrepressible system suffers any number and variety of power and transmission failures or irregularities of functioning. By now, we are pretty well able to trace such faults and breakdowns in the utilization of sexual energy to their root causes, because we have learned a good deal about how sexual energy is best generated as well as about the optimal channeling or expression of this energy.

Specifically, we have learned that the best sexual energy is generated by an interplay or intermixture of powerful loving (building or creative or good) impulses and attacking (tearing-down or hating or bad) forces, which modify one another in an integral interpenetration to yield an optimal flow. When the intermixture becomes too heavily weighted, either by too much positive or loving feeling (for example, persons of either sex who would seek to be too nice in their relationship to their partner) or by too much negative feeling (such as when sexuality becomes overloaded with rage and a desire to hurt), the result is a significant disturbance in the draw on basic energy.[4]

We now have a substantial and well-grounded body of psycho-therapeutic literature on disturbances that result in impotence, premature ejaculation, frigidity, all kinds of failure to experience pleasure, and unnatural reductions of sexual activity – all deriving from serious imbalances or inequalities in the apposition of loving and hating feelings or building and attacking forces. It is also extremely interesting to note that the disturbances may express themselves for some time in excesses of sexual energy. Such excesses are often spurts of power born of intense feelings of hate, which the person seeks to discharge or spend through ever more frequent sexual releases. But however frequent or boastful, these sexual discharges never yield the wholeness of pleasure and relaxation that characterize sexual climaxes built of a more balanced interplay of positive and negative feelings.

The empirical information we have about human sexual energy is so tangible and measurable that it offers a fairly convincing sense of the realistic possibility of a similar, broader theory of basic life energy for the larger spectrum of human experiencing.

A METAPHORIC PICTURE OF NUCLEAR HUMAN ENERGY

Let us try to build a metaphoric picture of human psychoatomic forces at work on their simplest nuclear level. Of course, it is very hard to put such a picture into words. No one has ever really succeeded in translating into words the positive and negative forces that are polarized in the construction of that marvelous energy we know of as electricity. Yet, we learn in the physics classroom that it is possible to sense and understand the metaphoric picture of electrical energy as a system of plus and minus forces: neither type of force can energize the system by itself, but together they produce a marvelous flow of power. Also, their combination can become seriously imbalanced, thereby creating a kind of short-lived power that is out of control, capable of burning up or short-circuiting part or all of an energy system.

We can also note another analogue in existing scientific knowledge and theory, one that has proved useful for understanding basic life phenomena: the biologist's conception of anabolic or life-building processes and catabolic or breaking-down forces forever swirling and working within our organism. If a serious imbalance develops – for instance, the building forces grow, multiply, and extend themselves without a balancing, limiting, catabolic force – the result is a grotesque mimicry of life, which can result in death to the whole energy system.

Let us at least attempt to picture metaphorically the two sides of human aggression. Consider that on some indefinable level of the mystery of our living, there are positive psychoatomic forces whose spin or propulsion or intention is to push at the reality of space and objects around us to build and make more of the same—to create, to "love," and to construct. These energy forces carry with them that irrepressible genius of a human being's wishes to add to life and to generate newer and newer aspects of the life experience.

There are also complementary negative forces. Their direction or intention is to attack and tear down, break down, pull away, and dismantle—in effect, to seek to destroy the reality of objects or experiencing in which the human organism is engaging. As an example, picture these destructive forces as they contribute to the everyday process of learning. These tearing-down forces represent a momentum for tearing apart an issue, for dissecting a problem and breaking it down into components. Or think of the process of sexual penetration: The attacking forces represent a momentum for *penetrating* the other and capturing the object of one's sexual desire. If we again think of analogies in nature, attacking forces are crucial to the human's biological defense system, as in the case of white blood cells, which stand guard and fight infections. That analogy can also be extended to demonstrate the terrifying destructiveness that those same attacking forces can unleash when they are uncontrolled by a balancing opposite force: If the white blood cells that first stand gloriously in our defense run rampant because they are not sufficiently checked by a counterbalancing force, there emerges the dread state of cancer that we know as leukemia.

We seem now to have a metaphoric picture of positive and negative energy forces that makes a simple kind of sense. We now want to press further to see how successfully we can develop a metaphoric picture of these complementary forces operating together, both antagonistic to one another yet simultaneously meshing, interpenetrating, cooperating, and balancing one another.[5]

Everywhere one looks in nature, it seems that there is considerable value in the counterpointing of opposite forces.[6] We operate the limbs of our body through a counterpointing of agonistic and antagonistic forces that alternately contract and release our muscles. We evacuate our bodies through an interplay of pulling in and releasing. We derive a sense of well-being from an interplay of activity and resting. Cancer scientists tell us that our healthy, life-giving cells are forever accompanied by cancerous cells that threaten to destroy us. Even if we do not understand the natural role of these cancer cells when we are healthy, we nonetheless can conclude that normally the cancer cells are being held off by the strength of our healthy forces and what the disease of cancer represents is a breakdown of the natural tension of that apposition.

What I am proposing (in metaphoric terms) is that to the extent that the human basic energy forces of creating and tearing down are brought together in apposition and smooth interplay with one another, the process activates and sustains the energy potential inherent in each and both together. Balanced one against the other, building and attacking energy forces or components yield a summative energy that is a controlled, manageable power that can be marshaled, channeled, gauged, and corrected.[7]

Working with such a metaphor of basic energy firing, we can think of human beings as possessing a potentially safe power, which they learn to pace, monitor, and correct by gauging and adjusting the flow of the component forces of their energy. Of course, there are serious choices as to how to use the energy.[8] It still remains to be determined to what ends (goals) each person and each society will commit its energies, and it still remains to be seen how people choose to go about achieving their commitments (what means they choose to reach their goals). But we have achieved a theoretical freedom as to the basic stuff of aggression or power of humans: at once potentially healthy and life creating even though it is built of volatile, destructive forces; at once potentially explosive and life destroying when it gets out of balance.

We now have a metaphor or theory that we can apply to a rich variety of observations and experiments as to how one might seek to monitor and correct one's basic energy building—whether in prosaic everyday activities or in serious conflicts that threaten to erupt into mayhem. We have achieved a metaphoric definition of energy that in its best state, is a marvel of checks and balances that might eventually be monitored, regulated, and channeled for peaceful purposes. Of course, we do not yet know enough about how to become aware of and correct the inner flow of our building and tearing-down energy forces. But we have come a long way from where we have been—stuck with the pessimism of a theory of man that considers destructiveness as an all-or-nothing underworld, forever threatening and finally succeeding in erupting and overpowering the higher-level "civilized" goodness of man. For now we have located our potential for "badness" within the continuous stream of our natural energy. Hence, it is available to regulation long before it assumes the fuller dimensions of satanic killing and murdering. Human "badness" is no longer a superior alien force waiting its inevitable vulturous turn to overpower us, but a natural side or component of the basic energy-building process, which, like so many other natural functions, is a mixture of positive and negative forces.

THE CONSEQUENCE OF EITHER EXCESSIVE BUILDING OR EXCESSIVE TEARING-DOWN FORCES IS DANGEROUSLY UNSTABLE POWER

The optimal mode of the human energy system is one that achieves an interplay of positive and negative energy elements standing in equal or complementary balance to one another. Consciously, we do not yet know how to achieve and maintain such balance, but I argue that it is possible for us to build an information feedback system that will continuously adjust the flows of positive creating and negative, tearing-down energy forces. At any given point, there is a flux of natural imbalances and irregularities, but under healthy circumstances, one checks and regulates these imbalances and achieves a relatively smooth-flowing energy system, which one commits to aliveness for oneself and for others.[9]

The history of human events, of course, clearly tells us that so far in our current stage of human evolution, individually and collectively, we frequently do not succeed in marshaling a balanced controlled flow of energy. All too often, humankind explodes in madness. In the metaphor, I propose to think of such madness as failures to balance out the positive, building and the negative, tearing-down components. If there is an excess of either positive or negative forces, the instability of the energy system will be greater, and the energy for transmission to the target behavior systems will be more unmanageable.

If we are brave in creating the metaphoric picture of man's energy system, we can go further and theorize that when a significant excess of either the positive or the negative force develops, there is compensatory activity on the part of the opposite or complementary force. We can then speculate that to the extent that the rush of that compensatory opposite force is too rapid or too intense to be met, checked, and integrated by its opposite number, the result will be a serious increase of instability, storminess, and explosiveness. In other words, opposite forces will rush into the breach, seeking to settle the energy flow into a renewed stability in which the creative and tearing-down forces are again linked as equal-energy partners, but the result of that effort at correction and restabilization can be an unbridled, unchecked storm that must be spent in some manner of energy discharge.

In this case, there are biological analogues. For example, there are some bodily reactions in which an initial hurt is met by a rush of compensatory forces—e.g., an extension of a muscle around a wounded area—but if the organism is not strong enough to balance or check the compensation, the well-intended state of compensation itself can add insult to the original injury—e.g., the extended muscle group goes into a spasm that is more harmful than the pain and limitation of the original injury. Note especially that the resulting destructiveness is unwitting; the original intent of the compensatory mechanism was to aid and balance, not to destroy, but the result for the patient is more pain.

Let us now try to translate this further extension of our metaphor into everyday, familiar pictures of human behavior. We want to see whether there is a possible usefulness of the metaphoric model we are experimenting with on the recognizable level of everyday human experience. Specifically, we want to see whether our metaphoric picture can encompass some of the complications of the human capacity to be both good and bad. Such demonstrations in no way "prove" the theory because description of human behavior on any one level does not tell us about behavior on another level. However, such is the way of theory building that it is at least helpful to look at the possible correspondence of a theory constructed for one level of behavior and observable facts on another level of behavior, if only because of our faith in the considerable correspondence of nature on different levels of organization.

THE EVERYDAY BALANCE OF LOVE AND HATE

There are many everyday-life demonstrations of the inseparability of love and hate. The very intensity of much of our anger is the result of our wish to love—otherwise there would not be such great anger on our part. Our very loving necessarily opens the door to future hating—if only because terrible hurt must inevitably occur in any relationship with a person one wants to be close to. On the other side of the coin, we find hating often opens the door to new loving. A good example is the reunion of lovers. Although many people do not know how to make their way through hurt to reunion and renewal, happy lovers who are able to make the transition tell us of marvelously sweet reunions after the hating.

In all areas of life, we see that loving and hating are interrelated. Many times when we seek to help a person, we must first attack and tear apart in order to be constructive and helping. The surgeon first cuts a patient in order to heal. We prune plants in order to stimulate further growth. We often attack the self-confidence of a person in order to shake up some system of behavior that is stopping the unfolding of that person's greater potential. On many levels of human experience, "negative" phenomena pave the way for the emergence of positive experiences and a deeper pleasure in those experiences. In psychotherapy, we have learned that a balance of powerful, even attacking, confrontations and loving support is the most effective treatment.[10] The same is true for the process of stimulating growth in family groups. With children, a balance of loving, caring, and even hateful discipline makes all the difference; we know only too well that an excess of either love or hate or an absence of either will have decidedly negative consequences.

WHEN LOVE AND HATE DO NOT BALANCE EACH OTHER

Let us look specifically at life situations in which either the positive and loving or the negative and hating force outweighs the other. Four general conditions of imbalances are possible in our metaphoric model:

1. An excess of the constructive and loving
2. An excess of the destructive and tearing down
3. The constructive, loving energy force is lacking in strength
4. The destroying, tearing-down energy component is lacking in strength

When There Is an Excess of the Constructive and Loving

People who overemphasize the building and loving side of their personalities often turn out to be essentially weak people who are unable to fulfill their wishes to be constructive. For example, loving that is "too much" often turns into bitter demanding and possessiveness. In terms of our metaphor, we might say that the effort to be too loving brings on negative or nonloving feelings, which then take over. The unseen negative feelings come in to correct the imbalance created by the too-positive ones, and then the negative feelings become too strong to be balanced out by the positive feelings.

Negative or destructive feelings are also often triggered in the people who are the objects of too much loving. These negative feelings, too, are the result of an excess of positive feelings in the first person, and, of course, the negative responses on the part of the second person also lead ultimately to the emotional ineffectiveness of the too-loving one. Many times we see negative feelings rush in with the intention of protecting a person from being swamped by too much loving. A mother who loves her child too much may push him toward great hate; the child may need to hate the mother in order to throw off the excess closeness that threatens to suppress his ability to live for himself. As any well-trained psychotherapist knows, expressing caring or loving feelings to a depressed person may stimulate a terrible onslaught of self-hatred in the depressed person. Appeasing approaches to a bully may stimulate further sadism in that bully.

People who seek to dignify their excess loving are wont to rationalize their invasion of the rights of others. The privacy of many a child has been invaded by a parent under the guise of love and good intentions. On the larger stage of life, medical scientists have been known to delude themselves that their quest for knowledge justified experiments on hapless human beings. Fascist medical experiments are well known, but even in the United States medical subjects have been maimed and killed. For example, a public health study of syphilis "justified" inducing the disease in prisoners and allowing the disease to take its deadly course.[11] Psychiatrist Robert Lifton has studied the roles of physicians in the Holocaust, and he concludes that there is a basic dialectic pull between healing and destroying.[12]

When There Is an Excess of the Destructive and Tearing Down

An excess of destructiveness brings us in touch with even stranger phenomena. Some of what we see in such cases is bound to arouse considerable discomfort and distaste because we are so deeply accustomed to defining excessive attacking and tearing down strictly as destructive. However, there are all sorts of disturbing psychological data that tell us that this is not entirely the case. Happily, we will find that when we apply the framework of the metaphor we are building, it turns out that we are in a position to anticipate and understand some of the paradoxes.

The key paradox is that if we look penetratingly and honestly at evil behaviors, we find that often the original intent of the destructive thrust was to stimulate loving or building![13] How often does the hurt lover strike out in anguished hate? The inner intention is not so much to destroy the object of the hate, but to connect with that object and stimulate the loving that is lacking. In truth, on really modest levels of intensity, attack, and even "hate" and tearing down, can be used as effective stimulants or invitations to responses of love from another. Girls and boys of all ages have been known to give their handsome princes and lovely ladies a hard time precisely when 'tis yon person they seek, and it works very well for them. In numerous cases, attacking and hurting are the preconditions of loving of any sort. This is also the cause of various sadomasochistic scenes, as well as the "little" sadomasochisms in the emotional lives of so many of us.

Many times people do not want to stop to consider that a destructive person really wanted "to be loved."[14] Yet, whether we like it or not, we must come to terms with the tragic fact that the severely destructive person frequently is somebody who is so frightened by his own failure to generate enough loving connection with objects in his environment that he drives himself desperately to hurt and kill those objects. Much as we may not like admitting the fact to ourselves, many times the killers we hate and despise the most are on some deep level of their unconscious actually striving for a greater sense of life and vitality. (Once we admit this we lose much of the pleasure of hating the evil in another, and also the safety of such hatred, and we are brought closer to our own terrible potential for being among the destroyers.) In terms of our metaphor, we might say that such destructiveness is an intuitive application of the mechanism of exaggerating one side of the complementarity (hatred and attacking) in order to release the compensatory flow of the other (love and contact building).

When the Constructive, Loving Energy Force Is Lacking in Strength

Of no less interest are some of the paradoxes that follow from a state of insufficiency of either side of the energy-creating process. Sometimes the loving and building energies are insufficient. We certainly know a good deal about how people who are lacking in loving may be deeply destructive, but it is too easy a matter to dismiss such people as simply overly angry and hence destructive. Often there is a terrible unknowing ache of emptiness, and a wish for contact and love that feels so unreachable, that these lonely souls are driven to power- and destruction-seeking fantasies and acts as ways to express themselves, feel alive, and gain contact—any kind of contact—with others. *These lonely souls have been known to put on the gray shirts and brown shirts and black boots of their respective eras and bash people's brains in.* It also happens that people who are lacking in loving will reach out desperately and intensely to try to love far more than they are able—then can follow the same tragic sequence that occurs when there is an excess of loving, building energy. Such people can become host to a surge of unexpected destructiveness they do not know how to handle. *He wanted so to love her that he hurt her. He wants so to be a leader of the group that he tries to bully and push everyone out of his way. The child wants friends so much that he goes around knocking other children down.* In the case of a depressed person, the terrifying paradox is that the possibility of suicide is greater following an experiencing of hope and a moving out to attempt to be more loving of life than at times of deep depression and demoralization. The experienced psychologist knows that the happier moments of improvement in a depressed person are a signal of danger as well as of possible progress. Similarly, oppressed peoples generally do not revolt as long as they are given to hopelessness. A revolt usually builds after there is some significant improvement in a people's situation that gives rise to new hopes. There then follows the drama of how a revolution's thrust of destructiveness is to be managed, whether truly in the service of the revolution's intent to free and enrich life or as a new scourge of blind destructiveness on the part of people who were oppressed so long that they are unable to embrace life. *The people bring down the oppressive regime and lift the hated restrictions on their lives. However, before long, the revolution turns into a new bloodbath led by the new priests and nobles of the revolution.*

When the Destroying, Tearing-Down Energy Component Is Lacking in Strength

There are some people who are too lacking in power to attack and in natural destructiveness. It is all too true that the best intentions in the world are not enough to put a real winning team across in countless real life situations. The cad often gets the girl. Lovers who are too nice are not exciting; they do not stimulate enough loving because they are not "attacking" enough. In political life, many a "good guy" cannot put together a powerful enough political force to win an election. However wise and beautiful a person a political leader may be, it may be difficult for him to command popular devotion to his cause if he is not "attacking" or "hurting" enough. In the terms of our metaphor, the absence of attacking, tearing-down forces fails to catalyze the complementary devotion or loving forces. Too little destructiveness, in effect, yields too little energy or momentum.

Some people who are not destructive enough may have moments of deep panic at not having enough energy available to implement their wishes to love and be alive. There then may follow a terrible outburst of destructiveness designed to provide the missing power. *A rather disturbed, brooding young man in psychotherapy described how he would fantasy shaking his head and waving his hand to make the whole world disappear. Was he so angry that he wanted to destroy the world? "No, it just happens, and I don't even feel like I'm doing it. And besides, I just feel I have to in self-defense. When I feel angry, I feel powerless, and then I have to think of feeling violent. You'd think then I'd feel powerful, but in the midst of it I truly feel powerless, futile."*

The not-bad-enough person is vulnerable to the possibility of breaking down and becoming a ghastly killer when he is thwarted in his wishes to relate to another and to express his love. The classic picture is of the quiet, well-mannered, retiring person who is not forward and attacking, does not have any real emotional connections with others (at best, only a semblance or caricature of connections with others), and one day explodes in terrible murderousness.[15]

According to baseball's Leo Durocher, "Nice guys finish last." Nice guys of all sorts would do much better if they would get mad, not only because they are losing something in their lives but because they want to win. Were the nice guys to fight more aggressively to win and build whatever it is they care about, the fruits of their "attacking," "hurting," and tearing down often would be new flows of loving connection with others. This, of course, is what so many psychotherapists teach. "Why do you put up with such putting down? You ought to fight back. You need to assert yourself more and let the other know how you feel." "If your father is bearing down on you so hard, you ought to tell him so and that he'll have to back off." "Surprising as it sounds, I think you ought to tell your child you're angry at him." What is especially fascinating is that although the therapist's immediate intent is to separate people who are locked into each other, the long-range purpose and outcome of the tearing down and attacking often is to build a new basis for greater loving.

HOW ENERGY IS USED INFLUENCES THE ENERGY-GENERATING SYSTEM

The Energy-Building Process and One's Choices of Means and Goals Influence One Another

It is important to emphasize that the story of human behavior does not end simply with the availability of a strong and manageable energy force. There are also all the manifold choices as to the application of this energy, what goals one adopts for oneself, the means one chooses to reach those goals, and the fascinating interrelatedness of the choices. Even optimally healthy energy resources can be channeled or directed to unwise purposes, and the outcome of unwise applications of the energy resource can, at some point, affect and change the energy-producing system itself. For example, having a fine talent does not in itself mean that one will do well; one must work hard at applying that talent. What then follows continues the drama—for example, when a person uses too little of his potential talent, he sets himself up for a deep dread, even panic, that he will not be able to fulfill his real capacity, and a good deal of destructiveness often flows from this panic.

Like so many other natural processes, we can think of man's energy-generating system as a feedback system. The information that comes back from the "field" as to what has happened in the application of one's energies in turn stimulates or inhibits different aspects of the energy-building process. An example of such a feedback system is what happens to the beating of the human heart as a result of a person's experience in channeling his or her "heartfelt" emotions. It requires no impressive documentation of scientific literature to observe that a once-healthy heart can be "hurt" or "broken" by disappointments and anguish. I believe this is true of man's basic aggression-generating system too. Serious disappointments and disillusionments of the spirit can break a once-healthy power system or spirit.

Consider what happens when one leaves oneself open to excessive demands on one's power capacity. The effort to draw too much power from one's actual energy system may temporarily force through the transmission line too much energy or more than the system can reasonably handle so that the system blows out. We see this occurrence when efforts to love, win, succeed, or reform blow up in the faces of people who have sought to do too much too intensely or too quickly. For example, studies of affective psychological disorders (such as the "manic-depressive" condition) have shown that often there is an early history of deep disappointment or abandonment that leaves a child full of despair and inclines him to extremes of both depression and efforts at compensation in euphoria. Years later, such a person is inclined to overexuberance and enthusiasm in the way he goes about pursuing his goals, but the choice of that behavior really has its origin in his earlier pattern. What the person actually does in life in turn affects the energy-building process. The same overexcitable or "manic" person may be defeated in his business pursuits because he tries to grow too big too fast, and that disappointment then feeds back into the underlying sadness and uncertainty that first drove him to try to be too big.[16]

One of the great discoveries of psychoanalysis has been the extent to which all of us unknowingly seek to recapitulate the circumstances of our earlier experiences, and this concept seems applicable to our metaphor of an energy system as well. The means and goals we choose in life in many ways reflect or replay the basic style or balance that characterizes our approach to building energy. The faults that then arise as a result of what we actually do in turn feed back new critical influences on our ways of going about harnessing new power. People who are on the side of life generally go on to enjoy increased aggressive power in their further experiencing. People who are destructive of others generally end up destroyed, although, sadly, that can take a long time, and they are usually able to take down with them many other people before their cancer spends its course within them.

The fact is that any complex energy system – and we humans are certainly that – involves a whole sequence not only of mechanisms of energy generation, but also of mechanisms of transmission and application. Until we learn to describe and control these processes at least as well as we can control a home appliance, we are understandably in the muddle that history tells us we have always been in.

Two basic principles of modern psychology will be useful to us in thinking about the energy system as a feedback system. The first is that people must love themselves; if they do not love themselves, they do not feel sufficiently alive, or, in the words of our present thinking, they stop generating healthy new energy. The second principle is that if human beings care only or too much for themselves, they also do not succeed in feeling genuinely alive. As Rabbi Hillel put it in the first century, "If I am not for myself, who will be for me? But if I am only for myself, what am I?" Both of these principles can help us extend our metaphor of an energy-building system.

If I Am Not for Myself, Who Will Be for Me?

People need to know how to love themselves genuinely and deeply – especially when life's going gets rough. In recent years, a good number of psychoanalytic thinkers have revised the Freud-mandated concept that all narcissism or self-love is to be overcome in favor of connection and commitment to other relationships. It has become clear that reasonable self-love (in contrast to excessive or compensatory self-love) is a prime requirement of the healthy personality and is the only possible basis of a real caring for others.[17] Most people recognize this principle intuitively in their own experience. The idea of loving oneself has an immediate logical appeal, and it is also probably one of the most popularized principles of psychology. However, many people do not know how to love themselves. In psychotherapy, we often teach grownups how to take over being their own "mothers" and "fathers." Even if in childhood one was hurt by the neglect or callousness of a parent, it is the way we now treat ourselves that determines our spirit and optimism for living.

Being for oneself is the essence of not being destructive of oneself. In terms of our model, people who feel good in applying their energy to caring for themselves are reinforced or encouraged to generate new healthy energies for themselves. But people who are not able to love themselves sufficiently, or people who hate themselves, are unable to maintain effective energy production. In other words, self-hating people may be driven into one or another imbalance of the positive and negative sides of their energy. Thus, some people who don't love themselves may try too hard to be too nice or too loving. "She tries so hard to get people to like her because she really doesn't like herself." Others may give vent to bursts of destructiveness in an effort to get rid of their feelings of being unlovable. "He's full of hate because deep inside he can't stand himself."

The important point for our model of man's energy building is that when people do not find satisfaction in the application or utilization of their energy, their dissatisfaction affects their future energy building. People who don't know how to love themselves often stop trying to love life, and people who don't know how to love themselves often explode in a destructive rage.

But If I Am Only for Myself, What Am I?

The other side of what people do with their energies involves relationships with others. Here, too, when people find confirmation of the value of their energies, their pleasure stimulates a greater and healthier production of new energies. Theology, medicine, psychology, and other schools of thought tell us that people who love others feel good and that constructive commitments to improving matters for other people and society bring great inner rewards.

Having first committed one's energies healthily to oneself, the next challenge is to commit one's energies and caring to advancing the welfare of others. We know that many people who are actively committed to improving their family lives are likely to survive and solve the storms of family life that fell so many others. Similarly, professionals and executives who enjoy a sense of purpose and commitment to values generally seem to thrive on their hard work, while other hardworking people may break under the pressure. Similarly, citizens who commit themselves to bettering life in their community and nation are likely to enjoy far greater satisfaction in their everyday life.

As for the destructive impulses that affect our relationships, there is considerable evidence that people actually fear being destructive – a somewhat surprising finding, considering the record of the human race. People feel guilty when they don't care for others, and they fear "going too far" in their indifference and cruelty to others. In the language of our metaphor, because they want to maintain a healthy balance between their building and tearing-down energies, people become upset when their inner signals advise them that they are "losing their balance."

We have many indications in dreams, for example, that people are "scared to death" when their rage or impulsiveness threatens to erupt into actual destructive acts against others.[18] It is common that people's enthusiasm and confidence for their own energy building are upset when they see that they are bringing unhappiness and upset to people about them, and the situation is worse when they see that they are destructive, especially to people whom they want to love. Sometimes, in fact, a man or woman decides to get a divorce not so much because they do not love their spouse or family any longer, but because they have lost confidence in their ability to love and provide for their mate and children and cannot bear to continue hurting them. Conversely, some people who have hurt others so much that they can no longer bear their shame may turn even more destructive, as if to show that it doesn't bother them at all, but the truth is that at one point they wanted very much not to be destructive.

One interesting and useful way to see how many human beings are afraid of their destructiveness is to look at people who enter psychiatric hospitals. It is remarkable how much of mental illness can be understood from the point of view that people render themselves impotent (that is, mentally ill) in order to flee destructiveness toward others. Mental illness, in large part, is an effort to avoid wreaking mayhem on others. Of course, mental illness is generally a statement of being deeply hurt by others, but at the same time it often expresses a terrible fear of mishandling one's rage in response to those hurts. Surprising as it may seem, clinical observations suggest that in many cases the latter concern is the more powerful of the two. In other words, the fear of annihilating other people is often more decisive in the "decision" to become mentally ill than are fears of being hurt or annihilated. A great deal of psychological treatment of the mentally ill can thus be seen as education for constructive aggression, that is, how to stand up to those who hurt us and how to fight back against them without being destructive.

These issues also dominate the emotional experience of many human beings outside of the mental hospitals. In the "everyday psychotherapy" of quite competent people, it emerges that this issue haunts just about all of us once we dare to turn on our machinery for energy or power. For example, a good number of people opt out of trying for power and then need therapy because they have made themselves too weak (and are often secretly destructive in their weakness). Their job is to discover that they must brave the dangers of affirmatively engaging their natural power.[19]

People also fear unintentional destructiveness, and with good reason. The very power we develop for our lives is potentially explosive and destructive. Moreover, there is much that we do not know about how to store, transmit, and channel our power. The basic problem is that it is in the nature of power—when expressed or directed toward others—to press, penetrate, and ultimately attack, hurt, and fell. It is in the nature of power to be what it is by virtue of nothing more than the momentum of the thrust of energy. In other words, even though one may not want to kill, a powerful charge of strength aimed at another *can* kill. Small everyday examples of men "killing" each other without wanting to are to be found in business and career struggles. One may intend to succeed in one's own career without pushing others aside, but the sheer flow of the competitive effort may very well find one bringing others' careers to a halt.

It is also in the nature of power to be destructive of another when the other person is unable to stand up against the energy directed at him and deflect, absorb, or transform the energy for his own use. There are any number of tragic situations in which a blow that is intended to be far less damaging than it proves to be destroys another person, not because the destruction is willed on any level of conscious or unconscious desire, but because the power unleashed is too great for the recipient to manage. Some moments of unplanned violence take place in great rushes of impulsiveness. "My God, I killed him; I didn't mean to." Other incidents of unplanned violence occur because of remarkably poor, but fundamentally innocent, judgment. "We were playing with the gun. I was sure it was unloaded, but when I aimed it at him and fired, he let out a gasp and fell." Other moments of unplanned violence are simply accidental. "We received the wrong blood for the laboratory, but we didn't know it. When we gave the patient the transfusion, he went into shock before our very eyes. We weren't able to bring him out of it. Later we found out that the blood had been mislabeled and that we had given the patient a deadly dose."

In family life, many of the destructive sequences that take root and build to the tragic destruction of one or another member of the family have as their root source not a diabolic choice to hurt a particular family member, but a natural exploratory expression of aggression or power. For reasons that we may or may not succeed in reconstructing, one member of the family fails to stand up to the pressure, limit it, and turn it from its excess, and before long the family is unintentionally victimizing and making a scapegoat of that member of the family.

What happens to people once they do in fact hurt others very much? Do they or don't they pay a price for their inhumanity to others? We do know that normal human beings experience guilt because of the destruction they do to others. One of the processes served by certain religious ceremonies is to help people express this guilt along with a resolve to be better in the future. A good many psychotherapists have come to the conclusion that the same process is essential in psychotherapy. If psychotherapy was once seen largely as a guilt-relieving and impulse-freeing experience, it has become more and more clear to many therapists that human beings must also come to recognize when they have hurt others and the danger of their hurting others further.[20]

However, there is also another type of response by people who succumb to destructiveness. There can be a great deal of pleasure in the discovery that one has achieved power over others, there can be delight at the apparent confirmation of oneself as strong , and there can be gratification in finding long-standing fantasies and wishes to control others coming true. Power seems also to answer people's worst fears of not feeling alive. It takes a great deal of personal maturity to distinguish between the feeling of strength that seems to come from being more powerful than another and the genuine feelings of strength that flow from fountains of inner aliveness and confidence in ourselves that are not dependent on or fed by another's weakness. Many clinical studies tell of people who feed on false power for a long time but finally break down, bankrupt in the face of the real emptiness of their inner experiences and intimate relationships.[21] Unfortunately, a false sense of security can last a long time, and a great many people can be hurt before it falls apart.

Another side to the gratifications yielded by power over others derives from our always-lurking need to project our most feared weaknesses onto others, a tendency that is universal.[22] It is a fact of life that the machinery of our human mind tries to put on others those qualities we are most unhappy about in ourselves, and most fear for ourselves. It takes considerable emotional growth to learn to forgo the natural temptation to attribute to others those parts of ourselves that we can't stand. It seems almost beyond human nature to expect people not to take advantage of opportunities for control over others. "Here is an opportunity to prove that I'm not as vulnerable as I fear. Here is somebody on whom I can put what I can't stand in myself. I would be mad to pass this opportunity by." To renounce such power over others requires rare courage and belief in one's own real value.

It is against this background of people's desires for power that we can see more clearly what happens to people who actually become mass destroyers. Psychiatrist Robert Lifton, who previously studied the survivors of the Hiroshima atomic bombing and how that experience continued to haunt people years later, has published a study of what happened to servicemen who came home from Vietnam.[23] Lifton describes the demoralization of the Vietnam veteran who found himself to be part of a system that killed people wantonly and cruelly. He observes that something human dies in the spirit of people who become machines for killing, something vital in the core of their own aliveness or energy for life. Some critics of Lifton's work believe that he has read his own presuppositions into what he believes he hears from interviewees, but I disagree.

Other studies of mass killers have also shown that the killers are unable to feel what they have done.[24] An important question is whether that is so because it is now too late and it would literally be unbearable for the killers to experience the horror of what they have done, or whether the killers were from the outset a special breed who did not care or could not care. An interesting analogy can be found in the case of many people who are faced with their imminent death, say, to cancer. We know from countless clinical observations that many such patients cannot allow themselves to experience the truth of what is happening to them and lies ahead of them. Does this mean that they do not want to live? Hardly. Even if we find instances of people dying of a dread disease who really did not want to live, and that played a role in their illness, this does not mean that earlier those same people did not want to live as much as the rest of us. Similarly, it isn't necessary to assume that the killers who no longer seem to feel or care about what they have done never cared about life. It may well be that there comes a point where they no longer can care. Certainly, we know that once people have done great harm to others, they may invoke a more and more powerful machinery of denial to block out experiencing the reality of what they have done and are doing.[25]

HOW THIS APPROACH RELATES TO EARLIER CONCEPTS

These concepts are not new, of course. It is not new to divide major aspects of man's being into living, building, and constructing forces on the one hand and attacking, tearing down, destroying, or death-dealing forces or processes on the other hand. We find many different variations on the theme that good and bad counterpoint one another in the history of ideas: the forces of "light and darkness," the passions of the creative and the "demonic," gods of love and gods of hate and death – all these ideas and many others exist in different philosophies and cultures. After all, the ultimate fact is that creation and destruction are involved in the very beginning and end of the living process. All of life's flow is a continuity of ever-renewing creation moving toward inexorable death. These givens necessarily place these forces at the center of human experience and thinking.

Kenneth Vaux, professor of ethics in the Institute of Religion and Human Development at the Baylor College of Medicine, has written in this vein:

> Two energies activate human life. We oversimplistically call one creative and one destructive. Understood *sub specie aeternitatis* both must be creative. There is a life energy that pulses through human reality. It is found at all levels of life. It struggles to move, it gasps for breath, it yearns for communion, it defies the intrusions of disease and death. . . . The other energy is the death impulse. Darwin and Freud both noted the death mechanisms in nature. Whether it be the species' instinct for survivial or the organism's inherent drive toward death, all life is informed with the principle of destruction. Neo-Freudian disease theorists like David Bakan, for example, show the way that death is the central teleology of life. Brain neurons die, blood cells destruct, organs have a life-time. The mechanisms of aging have the essential evolutionary purpose of insuring the future. Even disease, thus understood, functions as a creative condition of life.[26]

The metaphoric model I am describing is one of many pictures of the fundamental importance of the good and the bad, the positive and the negative in human experience – whether projected onto one's gods or returned to one or another aspect of a human being's inner experience of himself. I propose seeing the process as residing within the miracle of our basic energy system. In the metaphor, I emphasize the two sides of man's human experiencing and aim at locating these two sides of man's naturalness on a basic level of energy building, which will then be useful to us in seeing the complexities of creating and destroying on larger behavior levels, but the basic elements of the metaphor in themselves are not at all unique.

In the epic work of Freud, we find most clearly an assumption of two basic instincts: Eros, whose aim is "to establish even greater unities and to preserve them . . . to bind together," and Thanatos, the destructive instinct, whose aim "on the contrary, is to undo connections and to destroy things." The latter then is to be called the death instinct, because its final aim is to render living things inorganic.[27] So it is hardly an innovation that our basic conceptual construction turns on a never-ending presence in all of nature and the human experience of life and death; or living and dying; or bringing life and bringing death; or moving with life and moving toward death. In a sense, the fact that such a concept occurs and recurs in man's efforts at understanding the universe might be taken as suggestive confirmation of such a model (although I should caution that many entirely primitive themes also occur unendingly in various cultures—for example, the search for belief in immortality).[28]

Note that theories or metaphors differ as to how much the positive and the negative components are posited as fighting one another and how much they are seen as complementing and interpenetrating one another. In Freud, generally, Eros and Thanatos are joined in a death struggle of the gods, and only one can win. Freud emphasizes not so much the value of uniting both good and evil aspects of life, but the energy that comes from choosing building over tearing down, or the affirmation of life over the taking away of life. The opposing forces of creating and destroying are posed essentially as antagonistic to one another more than as two sides of our humanness working together. My own metaphor emphasizes the interpenetration of the contradictory forces. Granted there is also a quality of "fighting" between the positive and the negative, but it is more a pressing at one another as equals rather than as antagonists who seek to destroy one another.[29]

There are also many psychologists who differentiate between a healthy and an unhealthy commitment of aggression to different life purposes. Erich Fromm emphasizes the distinction between benign aggression and pathological aggression. The former includes accidental, playful, self-assertive, and defensive aggression; the latter includes energies directed at power seeking, vengefulness, and sadism. Both have their origins in the same vitality of life. Man needs to feel the power of his being, as if to say, "I am because I effect."[30]

I suggest that the creating and tearing-down sides of man are complementary and that they give meaning to one another by triggering or catalyzing the fuller flow of energy that takes place. Man's energy fates him to deal with a built-in volatile explosiveness and to become destructive to the extent that he does not learn how to balance and integrate the contradictory sides of his still-mysterious nature.

A Million Cambodians Slain by Khmer Rouge

Paris—A million Cambodians slain by the Khmer Rouge since the fall of Phnom Penh in April 1975 "is plausible if not certain," journalist Yves-Guy Berges said in an article in a French newspaper yesterday.

After interviewing hundreds of Cambodian refugees in a camp in Thailand, Berges summed up:

"Collective assassinations, reprisals, manhunts after the middle class, massive deportations, forced labour, disappearances, death, always death, familiar, omnipress, to the point of nausea.

"In these conditions, the figure of a million victims since April 17, 1975, the date of the 'liberation' of Phnom Penh, is plausible, if not certain."

Berges quotes one 50-year-old refugee, trying to convince him of the truth of the massacre accounts, as saying: "I am like a frog. I see only water when it is right before my eyes. But when it rains, thousands of frogs see the same things as me."

The refugee said on his long journey to Thailand he had spent time searching for his missing brother, but instead of finding him had found legions of corpses "like a field of locusts."

A 23-year-old refugee who held out against the Khmer Rouge in Sieme Reap five days after the fall of Phnom Penh, said practically his whole garrison was massacred after surrendering, and "eight truckloads of corpses were dumped into wells."

The refugee and six comrades managed to escape the slaughter and head for Thailand, a journey that took 12 days, but two of them died of exhaustion en route, he said.

—*Jerusalem Post,* June 3, 1976

5

THE INTEGRATION OF "GOOD" AND "BAD" IN HEALTHY AGGRESSION

See, I have set before thee this day life and good, death and evil.
— Deuteronomy

We move beyond good and evil when we move toward an openness to the sources of creative energy. . . . Evil is best seen as the inability or unwillingness to overcome separation. It is the refusal to see the world as process.

— Charles Drekmeier

My own shadow side is a part and a representative of the shadow side of the whole human race; and if my shadow is antisocial and greedy, cruel and malicious, poor and miserable—if he approaches me in the form of a beggar, a negro or a wild beast—then my reconciliation with him will involve at the same time my reconciliation with the dark brother of the whole human race. . . . It is only when man learns to experience himself as the creature of a creator who made light and darkness, good and evil, that he becomes aware of his own Self as a paradoxical totality in which the opposites are linked together as they are in the Godhead.

— Erich Neumann

The exercise of developing a metaphor of man's basic energy force or aggression seems quite removed from the actual choices that human beings make on the battlefields of life: whether or not to kill hapless Jews/blacks/gypsies/Bengali/Communists/South Vietnamese/whichever human beings. We need to translate the life building and destruction making sides of man into the time-honored concepts of goodness and badness.[1]

The previous chapter sets the stage for thinking about "good" as largely interchangeable with, or an aspect of, what we have been referring to as creative building and "bad" as largely interchangeable with, or an aspect of, what we have been referring to as tearing down or destructive. When good and bad continuously influence one another, each offering the other the essence of its spirit in a back-and-forth stream of human behavior that is neither excessively good or bad, the inherent dangers of excess of either type of activity are contained, checked, and balanced.

When the bad, or attacking and breaking-down, forces are checked by and integrated with their opposite number, the good or building and loving forces of experiencing, the bad or attacking forces do not result in destructiveness gone amok. By the same token, the dangerous gluttony and self-righteous destructiveness that attach to a too-extreme "goodness" are checked and held in constructive balance by the bad, tearing-down, and attacking forces. The absence of such balance is, perhaps, what happens to many well-intended revolutions or to other once-positive social forces, such as trade unions, that gain too much power.

It has not often been understood that the good forces, too, can run amok, seeking to eliminate everything that stands in their way. Father Thomas Merton has written: "Humanistic love will not serve. As long as we believe that we hate no one, that we are merciful, that we are kind by our very nature, we deceive ourselves, our hatred is merely smoldering under the grey ashes of complacent optimism. We are apparently at peace with everyone because we think we are worthy. That is to say we have lost the capacity to face the question of unworthiness at all."[2] Once building forces gather a monstrous momentum that sweeps everything along in their path, they become unmanageable gluttons, even though originally they were intended to produce new growth.

On what level do we intend to think of good and bad forces? We are discussing the metaphoric meanings of good and bad as a continuation of the earlier metaphor of the creative and destructive energy components in the underlying human power plant, and, as I emphasized before, this is an area of experience we cannot actually see. Although we cannot see human goodness and badness, we have many reasons for believing there are values being experienced deep in humans that set the stage for overt behavior choices.[3] What we are trying to do is to join in the philosophic and scientific tasks of stretching toward new ways of picturing the root, building-block forces that are at work in the mystery of our nature, which are then expressed on many progressively complex levels. Right or wrong, if this effort makes possible new work toward understanding man's destructiveness, it will have fulfilled its purpose.

GOOD AND BAD IN THEORIES OF HUMAN NATURE

Man Is Naturally Evil

In virtually all cultures, as well as in virtually all psychologies, the basic construction of theory is dualistic, that is, good is seen as opposed to evil. In most cases, though not all, man is conceived of as essentially bad, dangerous, or impulse ridden (for Freudian readers, id-undisciplined) from the beginning of his existence, and the task of the good, such as when parents rear their young, is to civilize, discipline, and teach control of the hugely powerful and dangerous inner forces of instinct, desire, or primeval lust in the supposedly bad core of man. This notion is elaborated quite clearly in the basic framework of traditional psychoanalytic thinking:

> Disintegration of personality in an individual, as a result of mental illness or some special complications in development, brings about the regression of sublimation of instincts. The latter then recover their original primitive form, which they have retained in the unconscious as the heritage of an archaic past. . . . The higher emotions of sympathy and compassion, of altruism and concern for the fellow human being yield to the pressure of ruthless egoism and cruelty. Such essential elements of the civilized personality as shame, modesty and concern for basic cleanliness may disappear, leaving place for a direct discharge of infantile impulses. . . . Basic concepts of humanity lose their dynamic validity. . . . The understanding of the true image of man as never ready, always becoming and precariously maintained against the impact of ever-threatening primitive brutality can prepare us to face the evil which lies in ambush, always ready to scorn the human attainments of man.[4]

Of course, such a conception that underneath it all, man is largely evil does seem to fit the dread facts of our bloody history. Evil destructiveness certainly lurks in just about all cultures, and it is historically true of individuals and cultures that it doesn't take much for the veneer of civilization to be stripped away. However, this conception also seems to doom man to his intrinsic badness, and many of us would prefer a different conception that would explain both the dread hell of man's behavior and the indications of an evolutionary potential for something better. After all, there is also in human history a persuasive grouping of data that speaks of the capacities of some individuals and some cultures to withstand the seductions of evil, even when the flames and joys of the devil are virtually consuming everything in their paths. In general, we know that there also springs in the human heart a potential to choose in favor of life preserving and building and that this choice also mobilizes a far from insignificant power on its behalf.

What is most persuasive for many of us is that deep within our human experiencing, there is, along with our potential destructiveness, a reverence for life that seems deeper than what can be supplied by the notion of a thin veneer of civilization restraining the destructiveness that is the "real" or ultimate nature of man. On the contrary, there seems to be such depth, wholeness, and unlimited energy to the call to respect life that one senses that the potential power of these life-supporting forces must at least be equal to the power that we know exists in the tearing apart, pushing down, sadistic joys of terminating and destroying life.

Man Is Naturally Good

The other side of the same coin of good warring against bad has been the seemingly alternative conception that man is intrinsically good. Most religions have developed concepts of a depth of godliness in every soul from the beginning of its creation. Interestingly, although these religious traditions seek to affirm man's holiness as deriving from his god or gods, in most cases their concepts also have to counter a considerable burden of tradition that man is intrinsically evil. In many religions, the simultaneous presence of good and evil is handled by posing for the righteous a lifelong challenge to resist evil. Satan and the evil impulse are described as always lurking nearby to invite and seduce good people away from their alliance with God. The task of the good people is to guard against giving up their godly potential to the evil forces.

There are similar treatments of man as naturally good outside the religious framework. In modern psychology, especially in humanistic psychology circles, many hold that people are basically loving of life but that given a failure to tap or connect to their natural potentials for being, self-expression, and loving, there will follow dark sequences of hate, rage, and destructiveness to protest the absence of love.[5]

The advantage of conceiving of man as intrinsically good, but needing to fight against the specter of equally potent evil forces, is that this approach does seem to account for the many beautiful events in our individual and collective lives, yet it still provides for the ravages of human destructiveness. However, the problem with the conception of man as intrinsically good is that the overwhelming and repetitive history of evil triumphant in smaller and larger events seems to call for a much more powerful concept of man's basic natural availability to turn ugly. Human evils are much too formidable to be satisfactorily explained by an after-the-fact explanation that such-and-such conditions of goodness or love were not sufficiently satisfied and therefore man was not able to be his better self, or that the seductions of evil were too great and man's natural goodness was overwhelmed. Worse yet is the problem that many people who do seem to enjoy a feeling of satisfaction about their loving selves nonetheless may emerge as the dramatis personae in terrible, evil acts. I would propose that this is one way of interpreting the results of Milgram's classic Eichmann Experiment discussed in Chapter 2. Given certain conditions or a structure of command by authority, a majority of the people are available to engage in a terrible destruction of others, and we can only conclude that this vast majority includes many people who are, to a significant extent, reasonably self-fulfilling and loving.[6]

Other laboratory studies of man's availability to evil show that the structure of an actual situation determines to a great extent whether people will be cruel or not. This, of course, is also the evidence from psychotherapeutic studies: Life loving is not a constant, but a flow that bends and yields to life-destroying impulses when people are tired, threatened, seduced by power, or drawn by the promise of apparent immortality. There are many reasons, therefore, to conclude that *all* people have within them a fundamental potential for evil and that most people, including those who are otherwise "good" in everyday life, are capable of making dastardly choices. It is this truth of the naturalness of evil that is not accounted for in the optimistic conception of man as instrinsically good.

Man Is Neutral to Begin With

A third conception of good and evil, which in some ways attempts a radically new point of view in order to get away from the limitations of having either good or evil be the ultimate given of man, posits that man is entirely neutral and open to what will unfold in his experiencing. This point of view regards aliveness as a state of existence that has no implications for or further connections to man's choices of life-building or death-directed behavior. Aliveness is seen simply as the immediate experience of the mystery of the gift of life. Erich Fromm writes:

> Aside from the extreme cases, each individual and each group of individuals can at any given point regress to the most irrational and destructive orientations and also progress toward the enlightened and progressive orientation. Man is neither good nor evil. If one believes in the goodness of man as the only potentiality, one will be forced into rosy falsifications of the facts, or end up in bitter disillusionment. If one believes in the other extreme, one will end up as a cynic and be blind to the many possibilities for

good in others and in oneself. A realistic view sees both possibilities as real potentialities, and studies the conditions for the development of either of them.[7]

There are telling advantages to this conception. It overcomes many of the objections to positions that claim the necessity of man's basically being either more good or more evil, and it allows for the enormous contributions of ideas and cultures in determining one's choice whether to be a supporter or a destroyer of life. There is no belying the greater openness of this approach to a more optimistic view of the future, and therefore this point of view is also more likely to stimulate new creative efforts to develop ways of teaching people life-serving behaviors.

Yet, is it really enough to say that man is originally neutral? To say so is to beg some essential questions. With what qualities, after all, do we start our life? Are there not certain intrinsic connections between our disposition to both good and evil and the intrinsic nature of our life force? Is not our potential for both good and evil represented in our original nature? One might say that the concept of man as naturally neutral renounces something of life itself. Somehow, there is reason to feel that the forces that speak and act for life grow not only in environments of love that teach us to seek good, but ultimately have something to do with the life force itself. By the same token we sense that our attitudes toward fomenting deaths, little and big, are not only formed from experiences from without, but are somehow related to the ultimate truth that death is inevitable for all of us and is built into our very first experience of life. On the one hand, one senses from the very miracle of creation a deep, resonating spirit of life seeking flowing within us that is more than a neutrality; on the other hand, one senses that the call of ultimate death is heralded by little deaths, decays, and breakdowns all along the course of our experiencing and by thrusts of powerful attacking energies that tear at life to bring it to an end. The notion that life is intrinsically neutral somehow seems to bypass the fundamental issue of life itself. It seems much too unreal to think of man's life seeking or death seeking as springing entirely from experiences outside of himself without any foundation in his natural, built-in orientation toward the two most fundamental facts of life, life and death.

Once we do not see man as naturally bad, naturally good, or simply neutral, we can consider that human beings are the product both of powerful intrinsic inclinations toward life and death and of environmental influences. We are then in a position to see how man's nature and his environment act on one another and through one another to create the fantastic powers of good and evil whose interplay, in each individual and every collective group, is the fabric of human history.

Man Is Both Life Building and Life Destroying

We are led now by the sheer logic and structure of what we have been considering to a fourth alternative: In the natural essence of his aliveness, man is inherently, powerfully drawn to both life building and life destroying. This conception, too, is not a new one. In many ways, the tension and struggle within traditional thought to encompass the evidence of both good and bad inclinations in man have led not infrequently to the conclusion that man is given to both good and bad. In religious thinking, this conclusion begins to emerge in the course of movements back and forth between observations of how man is intrinsically good and observations of how man is intrinsically evil; the very movement between poles in itself implies an emergent sense that man is both good and evil. Various religious doctrines then posit a struggle between the good side of man and the bad, but both sides are generally accorded the status of natural inclinations.

This conception has also appealed to many modern psychological thinkers. It is a position that appears to solve the self-evident problem that man is both good and evil and that any theory must represent both of these powerful factors. In psychological thinking, religiously based notions of struggles between good and evil are translated into a natural competition between an intrinsic potential for good and an intrinsic potential for bad, a competition that is determined to a large extent by the influences of environment. Thus the extent to which individuals are satisfied or frustrated in their needs for love and encouragement from their family and culture will have a good deal to do with whether or not they turn toward the good or bad side of themselves.

This point of view also accounts for the influence a collective group has on its members to do evil, and yet it leaves room for exceptions—people who have the inner resources to stand alone and separate from a group that is bent on destructiveness. *To resist being numbered among the genociders and their accomplices in a Nazi Germany is a hugely heroic act of individual choice. It is extremely difficult to resist slaughtering civilians when serving in an army troop at My Lai. In contrast, the small number of Israeli soldiers who have killed civilians are morally more responsible for their choices since, for most of the years of Israel's history, the military has insisted on a very high standard of moral conduct.*[8]

This conception of man seems to do away with many of the problems previously encountered. Unlike the concept of man as a neutral person whose naturalness is channeled by experiences toward paths of goodness or badness, this theory attributes to man both an intrinsic life-supporting force and a powerful pulsation toward life destruction, and those natural processes then are shaped by experience and environment. We seem now to be in a much better position to understand the struggles of people in choosing whether to live or die on behalf of protecting life and on behalf of destroying an enemy.

We have now arrived at a position that is reminiscent of Freud's concept of the war between Eros and Thanatos. Without belaboring the variations that emerge in the course of Freud's struggle to conceptualize the role of death in human behavior, the major motif that emerges from his Herculean efforts (which has found support even among colleagues who will not adopt his more frontal focus on the death instinct as such) is that throughout life, man experiences a battle between the side of him that affirms life and the side of him that is drawn to death and waste.[9]

But there is still a problem even with this last conception of man as both good and bad. The key problem with this otherwise admirable conception of the naturalness of both good and evil in man is that the evil side of man is generally seen as just that: evil or fundamentally bad and rotten. This side of human nature is defined virtually always as taking away from the worthiness of man. Although evil is now treated as natural, and although badness or death dealing is now a fully equal component of or contributor to behavior, the destructive, attacking, tearing-down side of man is seen almost entirely as a dark, malignant force that cannot subserve the positive life-building side of man. For all that man is seen as naturally inclined to both life and death, there still remains a fundamental dualism. The determination of what choices one ultimately makes still remains essentially a function of competition between the two sides of man—one desirable, the other not, both pressing hard against the other.

But most modern psychological evidence speaks to the life-supporting roles of what we have characteristically thought of as the bad side of man. This is one of the fundamental contributions of the psychoanalytic interpretation of man. Psychoanalysis has given us a picture of the health-giving roles of our impulse life—especially pulsating, exciting sexuality—but also of the welter of aggressive, pushing, and attacking qualities. Included in the psychoanalytic picture of our natural impulses are elements that are referred to as devouring, defecatory, expulsive, demanding, competing, and attacking—even impulses to outright murder. In fact, "everything goes," that is, all impulses, no matter how bizarre or immoral from the point of view of traditional concepts, are considered natural on some level of the human experience. Of course, the critical question then becomes what part any of these impulses is allowed to play in the total symphony of a human's behavior. But on some fundamental level, all impulses are seen as life supporting and deserving of some expression.

The Goodness of Even "Bad" Impulses

In a fascinating, though not terribly productive, exchange of letters between Sigmund Freud and Albert Einstein, who agreed to discuss with one another their mutual ideas about why men so often go to war, Freud writes:

> We must not be too hasty in introducing ethical judgments of good and evil. Neither of these instincts is any less essential than the other; the phenomena of life arise from the operation of both together, whether acting in concert or in opposition. It seems as though an instinct of the one sort can scarcely ever operate in isolation; it is always accompanied – or as we say – alloyed with an element from the other side, which modifies its aim or is, in some cases, what enables it to achieve that aim.[10]

Admittedly, psychoanalytic theory strays from this germinal commitment to the inherent goodness and naturalness of bad impulses. There are times when the psychoanalytic picture of the "integrated" or "mature" person sounds like a person who has so refined his impulses that he is beyond really experiencing the bad in himself any more. The "well-psychoanalyzed" person's impulse life seems to be channeled virtually entirely through sublime expressions of dignity, lovemaking, art, philosophy, science, good works, leadership, and so on. Of course, psychoanalytic thinking does place a good deal of emphasis on the legitimacy of assertiveness, which could easily be another word for what we call life energy or aggressiveness, but this assertiveness, which was taught to patients for a long time more as an expression of healthy sexuality than as a more general life force, is not always clearly linked with a sense of man's healthy "badness." Psychoanalysis also emphasizes the naturalness of some anger and of all manner of primitive destructive wishes and fantasies, but by the time the "finished product" of psychoanalysis emerges, much of this has been forgotten and relegated to a bad that is bad that is bad. Even in psychoanalysis, there remains a need for a clearer statement of how the good/life-seeking and the bad/death-seeking qualities are both aspects of the truly human person; hence, both are good in their naturalness, and both are dangerous in the extreme. Even more important, there is a need for a fuller model that will show how the good and bad in man interrelate. We need to know not only how good and bad are both natural, but also how they are elaborated into more complex intermixtures of good and bad in the same person.

I believe that the fusion and integration of loving and attacking create moral human behavior. In the realm of sexuality, for example, excessive attacking and certainly hate destroy the capacity to function sexually; undue hate shows up in the clinician's office as disturbances of distaste, prematurity, impotence, frigidity, and the like. But so do excesses of love. When positive impulses are not balanced by an equal and a simultaneously present counterpoint of wishing to enter, attack, consume, and so on, the imbalance leads to breakdowns of sexual functioning that result in essentially the same symptoms that are caused by excessive hate. Studies of family life in recent years have shown incontrovertibly that only interplays of caring and rejecting, liking and disliking, supporting and frustrating, loving and hating are likely to yield effective family bonding.[11]

Observations of the ethical quality of people's behavior also yield evidence that good and bad support and complement one another rather than being antagonists and competitors. It has often been observed that the person who comes to terms with his or her "bad" impulses and wishes is a person whose good can be trusted the more when it really counts. Woe unto us when we are saddled with overly righteous, self-declared exponents of perfect "good" — such as Somerset Maugham's minister in "Rain" — as there comes a point of no return at which their denied other side of inner experience breaks through. Woe unto those who claim the right to throw stones against evil as if there were no evil in them.[12]

Several wise Jewish legends tell how the rabbis sought to free man entirely of the burden of his evil impulses, only to discover that the total absence of any evil meant the whole creative symphony of life was stilled.

> The Rabbis of the Great Assembly petitioned God to turn over to them the Evil Impulse. Said the Evil Impulse: See here, if you kill me, the entire world will be destroyed. They decided to lock up the Evil Impulse for three days. After three days had passed, they went to find a newly hatched egg, but could find none at all. So they released the Evil Impulse. [*Yoma* Legends]

> Were it not for the existence of the Evil Impulse, men would not build homes, they would not marry women, they would not sire children, and they would not engage in trade. [*Breishit Raba* Legends]

Elsewhere in religious thought there are other hints about the possible end of a dualistic conception of good and evil – in other words, a more integrated picture of man as good and bad is beginning to develop. There is at least the beginning of a real sense of the interpenetration of good and evil. Thus, here and there in religious literature there is the theme that no man can be good except as he taps his evil impulses. However, not surprisingly, before this theme of the goodness of evil is fully developed, traditional religious thought beats a hasty retreat to one or another of the prevailing dualistic conceptions of man either as largely good – and needing to fight off evil – or as basically evil – and needing to fight to attain redemptive good.

Similarly, in twentieth-century psychology, there are beginnings toward conceptions of man that put his opposite sides together rather than considering them as alien or competitive. Rollo May writes:

> It is a considerable boon for a person to realize that he has his negative side like everyone else, that the daimonic works in potentiality for both good and evil and that he can neither disown it or live without it. It is similarly beneficial when he also comes to see that much of his achievement is bound up with the very conflicts this daimonic impulse engenders. This is the seat of the experience that life is a mixture of good and evil; that there is no such thing as *pure* good; and that if the evil weren't there as a potentiality, the good would not be either.[13]

Physicist–peace researcher S. M. Silverman sums up concisely and effectively the overriding history of opposite forces contending against one another and the transition toward an integrated concept in which good and evil are part and parcel of the same fabric.

> The concept of antagonistic forces contending against each other repeats itself again and again in the history of man. Satan, the adversary, and God are both in the Book of Job. In the philosophies of Zorastrianism and Manicheanism, both good and evil are considered as active principles. In more recent times, the ideologies which have been quoted as justifying the world as struggle are those of evolution (the survival of the fittest) and Marxism (the class struggle whose final nirvana will be the classless society). There is, however, another repetitive theme in human history: that of harmony and oneness. In this the problem of good and evil and the concept of antagonistic forces are either meaningless or alien. While suffering exists, it becomes a part of life itself, to be experienced as one experiences joy or any other emotion. Good and evil are part of the same fabric: "I form the light and create darkness. I make peace and create evil. I am the Lord that doeth all these things" – Isaiah.[14]

Good and Bad as Two Sides of
the Same Coin of Naturalness

So we arrive at the threshold of a final and, I believe, wiser theory of good and bad. The new language we seek would convey to us that certain elements or degrees of attacking and even hurting are as natural and spiritually positive as equally desirable degrees of loving, caring, and building. What we say in present concepts of good and bad is redefined to refer to the extent to which a person is effectively balancing and fusing the two sides of himself. Good will refer to the balancing of what are currently known as both good and bad, and Bad will be defined as the extent to which man is failing to balance and integrate his two sides. Integrating the positive, creative and the negative, tearing down will become the essential act of generating the ethical good; failure to fuse the creative and the destructive – whether by being overly good or overly bad – will define the unwholesome or bad side of human behavior. Remarkably, we now are working with a concept of good and bad that is another side of the concepts of creative and destructive energy forces developed in the metaphor of man's basic energy building; both in turn derive from the basic givens of a desire for life and preparation for death.

Needless to say, there is a good deal that we do not know about how to put together the good and bad sides of man. But there is a good deal we do know, especially about how to try to look at two sides of a behavior and put them together. For example, consider the tender and the powerful sides of the human personality. Traditionally, tenderness has been valued as good, and the exercise of power has been considered at least suspect if not actually bad. Yet, to be too tender is actually to be weak, to be too assertive is to be boorish, and both are bad. But to alternate appropriately and flexibly between the two, and especially with a sense of strength in one's tenderness and a quality of tenderness when one uses one's strength, is to approach the desirable human condition, hence, the truly good.

A METAPHOR OF GOOD AND BAD COMPLEMENTING
ONE ANOTHER OPENS NEW DOORS

The metaphor of good and bad as intertwined is consistent with studies of the cultural process that speak to the vitality, hence goodness, of those social systems that include unsettled, changing, vital processes of conflicts, differences, and competition. It is remarkable how the notion of a conflict system that allows for good and bad together proves equally suited to the data of family life, to differences between people within communities, and to large intercultural and international relations. In family life, the family system that is open to the intrinsic emotional quality of all of its participants, child and adult, each of whom may speak reasonably freely of their anguish and hurt, tenderness and yearning, and criticism and hate, is less likely to trap and scapegoat one of its members as a carrier of undue badness for the pent-up "madness" and rage of the whole family group. A government system that gives free rein to differences between people, parties, and philosophies but restrains power plays and takeovers that would destroy the very system of openness is a system that makes room for constructive, nonviolent change and creative evolution.

Johan Galtung of the University of Oslo, Norway, has demonstrated brilliantly that on all levels of human experience, a flux of differences provides a better basis for stability than any imposition of a rigid pattern of sameness.[15] We have also seen how psychological studies of destructive personalities in our world such as Adolf Eichmann, show that the real focus in a destroyer's life may not be destruction as such, but an imposition of order and sameness on everything.[16] The inner compulsion is to tie down, batten down, and remove the dangers of spontaneity and naturalness, that is, to remove from existence anything that threatens risk. One may observe that the demand to order everything ends up spawning terrible evil precisely because there is too much fear of experiencing and exercising badness to begin with.

Family therapist–researcher Jay Haley describes how psychopathology generally originates from the tendency of people to overclassify. "Psychopathology occurs because man is a classifying animal. . . . To create a class of things means automatically creating another class which are not those things, and men can spend their lives pursuing a not-something, as busy philosophers demonstrate. The man who tries to avoid distress has divided the world into the distressful and the non-distressful. He cannot have one without the other because one class depends for its existence upon the other. Similarly to postulate goodness is to create badness."[17]

What is so attractive and exciting about much of the work of the psychiatrist R. D. Laing is that he repeatedly demonstrates the tragedies that follow from dualistic thinking, both on the level of family life and in the larger societal system.

> As long as we cannot up-level our "thinking" beyond Us and Them, the goodies and the baddies, it will go on and on. The only possible end will be when all the goodies have killed all the baddies, and all the baddies all the goodies, which does not seem so difficult or unlikely since, to Us, we

are the goodies and they are the baddies, while to Them, we are the baddies and they are the goodies.

Millions of people have died this century and millions more are going to, including, we have every reason to expect, many of Us and our children, throttled by this knot we seem unable to untie.

It seems a comparatively simple knot, but it is tied *very*, *very*, tight—round the throat, as it were, of the whole human species.

But don't believe me because I say so, look in the mirror and see for yourself.[18]

It is very appealing that the concept of an integrated good and bad allows us to move up and down the continuum of human experience from individual to family to societal behavior. If only from the point of view of a kind of elegance of theorizing—a kind of wholeness, or what is defined in the philosophy of science as the essential unity of all natural phenomena—we prefer and enjoy having the same theoretical model available for the whole continuum of human experience. Such a theory appeals to our knowledge that nature is often built of pyramiding structures that elaborate more and more complexly the same basic elements and processes on successively higher levels of evolution. Hard as it is to put into words, we sense that the data for all levels of human experiencing lead us more and more to a picture of man as never able to be genuinely good unless he is at home with his bad impulses and that hate and destructiveness do not run amok if they are tempered by love and a desire to build life for oneself and others. Rather than considering destructiveness and badness as the lurking, underworld side of a man, to be countered by a higher-level but essentially weaker goodness and nondestructiveness, we must call on the two natural sides of man to work together: strength and weakness, toughness and tenderness, loving and hating, resistance and forgiveness, meanness and compassion.

SOME CHALLENGES AND IMPLICATIONS

Evolving New Gauges of Our Energy and Goodness and Badness

The proposed metaphoric model leads obviously enough to the conclusion that to avoid excesses of destructiveness, we want to learn to equalize, balance, and integrate our inner creativity and destructiveness. By doing so, we can become more potent political forces, more potent lovers, or more potent effectors of any of our best intentions. To accomplish such balance, we need to develop better gauges and monitors for recognizing what the flow of our component energy forces is at any given point—just how they are mixing in the "carburetor" or heart of our individuality or in the collective groups of which we are a part.

The trouble is that we do not yet know how to teach people to gauge their building and tearing-down energy flows—at least, we don't know how to teach the use of such gauges to groups of people and in a reasonably short time—but we do have some knowledge. There is no question but that in successful psychotherapies, as well as in many other processes, we stumble and find our way toward understanding some of the mysteries of human self-regulation. People can learn awareness of deep, powerful emotions. People can learn to control the delivery of their emotional energies to complex psychophysiological processes such as the delivery of one's energy to sexual activities, the pacing of one's hunger-digestive process in order to reduce damaging acidity, or the management of complex endocrinal processes such as secretions of adrenaline and other stress hormones.[19] There are many recent laboratory studies of new methodologies for biofeedback, that is, the development of control over one's physiological functions, such as heartbeat or blood pressure, in response to continuing flows of feedback information about the physiological activity.[20] There are also constructive contributions from people in the fields of religion and ethics that tell us of man's capacity to acknowledge many of his excesses and unfairnesses and of his ability to resolve to change and to concentrate his willpower to effect those changes. There is also a growing understanding of our inner human language via dreams, fantasies, drama, and authentic encounter experiences with other people in the here and now.[21] There are exciting human relations innovations and technologies for self-disclosure, trust, conflict resolution, and the like.[22] All in all, it is clear that man has a vast, untapped potential for self-regulation. However, it is also clear that we are far from knowing how to teach processes of self-awareness. The evolutionary task of building teachable gauges of our inner energy and experience is still largely before us, but the possibility of such tools is clear enough.

Learning Not to Dupe Ourselves into Believing Destructiveness Is Intended to Bring Good

One of the most terrible sides of human destructiveness is how often and easily man is led to believe that his destruction of others serves a good purpose. Often people are led into their destructiveness quite innocently when they really did mean to exercise no more than their naturalness—but the energy unleashed proved too much. The worst of it is that we are able to call the worst evils of our killing "good" acts in the service of this or that ideal. Philip Hallie writes: "There is a paradox of cruelty writ large across the history of mankind and written intimately into the minds of men: We find substantial maiming of other men totally unjustifiable, an object of disgust and horror, and yet we find it easy to justify in a hundred expediential and even religious ways. . . . Smashing this paradox, this ambivalence in human relations, is the first step toward moral wisdom, which is a sad wisdom, and a dangerous wisdom, but one not without hope."[23]

Our metaphor helps us understand more of the paradox that so much of human destructiveness is intended, on some real level of sincerity, to generate love and to improve the human situation. Some of the most terrible events in history have been launched on behalf of social betterment. Even monumentally destructive causes, such as genocide, are characteristically announced as sincerely aimed at goodness, improvement, or virtue. Values of loving and life building are taken as justification for the most obscene killing and destructiveness.[24] Thus there have been "improving the purity of the species" by killing undesirables and physicians granting "mercy killings" to mentally incompetent patients. The implication is that we need to learn how to teach people from childhood on the dangers of attaining false feelings of aliveness through destructiveness, how to see destructiveness for what it really is, and how to fight against being seduced by justifications of destructiveness in the name of human betterment.[25]

Too often, man employs his symbolic machinery to delude himself – like feeding false instructions to a computer that doesn't know any better. Our personal and collective history is distinguished by endless self-delusions. People allow themselves to be destructive in order to be good. A basis is provided for the illusion that the destruction is somehow connected with loving and helping. People tell themselves their destructiveness doesn't "really" count because it is intended to be the forerunner of a greater good. That justification has been heard from the advocates of all kinds of destruction in human history. *"Ours is a crusade for God's glory" (Kill the infidel!), "Ours is a revolution for equality and liberty" (Kill the aristocrat!), "Ours is a noble effort to improve the race" (Kill the non-Aryans!).*

We need to teach people to test their destructiveness by looking at the actual outcome of their acts as well as at their own beliefs about their intentions. If there is a huge price in human suffering, the belief that one really means to do good should be rejected as an illusion designed to conceal one's destructiveness.[26]

Our metaphor also suggests that the more tearing-down power is unbalanced by energies for building and constructing, the more it is likely to be short-lived and burn itself out. There is some consoling evidence that that is the case. On the human level, the burningly angry person often seems to blow himself up in one of a number of ways – whether by suffering a stroke, a blowout of an intestinal wall, or an explosion of the heart muscle, or by stimulating powerful, counterattacking hostility from others around him. In international affairs, dictatorial governments generally are finally turned out by the people. Unfortunately, it also follows from our theoretical structure that he who would be a successful dictator, hater, or destroyer should seek in every possible and clever way to link his destructiveness with a "good" ideal and justify his actions in the name of loving and building. Tragically, the crushing forces that kill people in the name of liberty, God, scientific truth, or whatever pose of improving the lot of people stand to inflict their horrors for longer periods than those forces that set out blindly to destroy. Society seems to dispose of most purposeless killers relatively quickly. But those who annouce that they are trying to build a better life for man, no matter what miserable destructive demons they are on the stage of history, often hold onto their roles and places in history for some time.

Knowing When to Be Destructive

Another serious aspect of our metaphor is that there are times when peace-loving peoples must destroy those who threaten their lives. In discussing the metaphor of the energy process, we saw that the marvel of life is not gained by relying only on the loving and building side of the energy system. Some considerable destructiveness is an integral, I suggest even an equal, part of the healthy energy process, but destructive energy forces need to be modulated and balanced by the counterpoint of creative, building energies. However, there can be no effective energy unless the destructive elements are utilized. Undoubtedly, there are times when man's efforts at balance call for a good deal of destructiveness, even more than he wants to employ.

It is also a strange reality of history that often it is the meteoric flare of the destructive that triggers the creative, building forces that are necessary to address a major social problem.[27] Tragically, history teaches us there is sometimes a good deal to be gained from rioting and burning cities in revolt against years of discrimination and other abuses regularly allowed by imperfect societies. Pressed by the alarm of destructiveness,

once-indifferent and hostile authorities may turn surprisingly constructive. It is intriguing to see how there often is a split in revolutionary
movements between those who want to pursue the revolt with no holds
barred on violence and those who press for a more disciplined revolution.[28] Sometimes the challenge of a terrorist faction within a revolutionary movement catalyzes or mobilizes the majority of the people into
a more disciplined and restrained revolution, which goes to great pains
to minimize the loss of life, and later to establish a responsible, life-
respecting government. In these instances, the terrorist movement actually contributes to the saving of lives by stimulating counterforces
against the extremes of violence that so often snowball in revolutions. In
a sense, the stimulus of potentially intense destructiveness can bring
forth positive, building forces—though, of course, many times the terrorists do win out, and their violence takes over the revolution.

A Metaphor That Helps Us See the Intrinsic Normality of Evil but Calls Us to Our Better Selves

Our metaphor also appears compatible with a good many other
observations of the intrinsic universality of various bizarre psychic processes, which psychological theory has not effectively encompassed in
its overall picture of normal man.[29] Many mental health specialists now
believe that schizophrenia is not a disease but an exaggeration of those
mechanisms or processes that ward off unbearable conflict in all of us.[30]
To most contemporary students of humanness, anxiety is not so much a
fear of falling apart as a statement of the challenge to grow and fulfill
one's potential.[31] Destructiveness, too, is not so much the legacy of the
evil and corrupt, or of the abnormal—much as we would wish it to be
so—as an often unwitting outcome of an interplay of the forces of good
and evil that are inherent in all of us.

We are now armed with new concepts with which to return to the
data that tell us that "nearly all of us" are available to be the killers and
their accomplices or bystanders in any given generation.

Choosing Not to Be Destructive

Can we escape being killers and accomplices or bystanders,
especially when our cultures call upon us to play these roles? Perhaps
some of us achieve a finer pacing and balancing of the positive and
negative sides of our beings and so can play balanced roles in the larger
collective groups in which we participate.

Certainly, at any given point in history, some of us are lucky enough to be part of a group that reaches a higher level of development and directs its members toward the better side of humanness. There do seem to be certain groups that identify more successfully with man's historic wishes for peace. For example, the effort Israeli soldiers have often exerted to protect civilian life in the middle of a difficult military operation is a landmark in the history of collective self-defense, and there are certain Scandinavian countries that have an enviable history of commitment to peace, including the courage to stand up for peace values even during the country's occupation by a conqueror.

In the psychological literature, there are some hints as to what qualities make for human beings who can be trusted not to align themselves with destructiveness. Elise Boulding, for example, describes how people committed to nonviolence are very active and alive in spirit and trust their competence as problem solvers.[32] But we need to learn how to identify in objective ways the interplay of building and destructive elements in whole cultures. Perhaps peace-loving societies learn how to encourage far more open aggression or other related impulse expressions within their communities, while also emphasizing love and responsibility to one's fellow man, so that on a communal level, people are exposed to a model that calls for balancing both the constructive and the attacking sides of their beings.[33] In contrast, we might find that destruction-prone nations and cultures underemphasize constructive aggression in their dealings with one another; or emphasize unbridled, undisciplined impulsiveness; or fail to encourage loving and affection within the society; or overemphasize correct, pleasant relationships with people at the expense of natural aggression.[34]

We don't really know yet how individuals and societies can balance the two sides of their nature, but we now have a way of thinking and searching further. Everything we have been considering in our metaphor of aggression is no more than a series of fictional constructs; yet we have not been buoying up ourselves with a fantasy but working at building a theory whose real purpose is to enable the development of new tools for reducing man's terrible destructiveness. The truth is that whether or not any of these hypotheses ever prove to be valid is of surprisingly little importance. The whole point of the theory is that it is intended to help us find new ways of approaching the problem of man's acts of violence by seeing them as grotesque exaggerations of essentially normal processes that are at work in all of us but under certain circumstances, are turned toward cancerous death making.

Army Film Says Soldiers Must Refuse Illegal Orders

A new U.S. Army Training Film (21-4228), produced to explain in graphic terms "a soldier's responsibilities in warfare," says American military men must refuse to obey an order if it violates international law.

"After World War II many members of the German and Japanese military were brought to trial on charges of having committed war crimes," the film explains. "The accused often claimed that he was 'just following orders.' But this was ruled no defense. Those who had committed acts they knew or should have known were wrong, were held responsible for their acts. Convicted, they were jailed and, in some cases, executed."

—*Fellowship,* June 1, 1975

6

DESTRUCTION IN THE QUEST FOR LIFE

The psychiatrists' ideal world would have healthy outlets for general masculinity and untrammeled expression for the feminine aims of conservation and love. Destruction would be planned in order to make room for needed change. Aggression would then be directed toward construction: daring schemes for feeding billions, bold plans for lessening suffering and bringing plenty; adventurous exploration and development of creative arts. Masculine intellect and feminine nurturing would be harmonically balanced in the pursuit of common goals. . . . Myths of creation supplant myths of destruction and death.

—Robert A. Clark

Do people basically wish one another life? I think so. In fact, man feels confirmed and reassured in his own aliveness by the flourishing of life around him. The innovative encounter and sensitivity groups show us that people are basically glad to see and make contact with the aliveness of their fellow human beings.[1]

However, when life becomes too cruel, hazardous, or uncertain and when one is deeply frightened and angry about threats to one's own aliveness, one is no longer inclined to wish others well. This is true of normally decent, moral people. Psychologist Albert Bandura observes, "Much human maltreatment and suffering are, in fact, inflicted by otherwise decent moral people."[2]

Unfortunately, people often turn toward desperation in their attempts to stay alive, feel alive, and cope with the possibilities of loss and death. Scared, terrified, unknowing humans can easily go "crazy" because of a fear of nonlife and death. In desperation, they reach out for power, even at the expense of other people. When we are terrified of nonlife, we are inclined to wish no less than the same nonlife or death for our fellow human beings. The more desperate we become, the more we turn to primitive rites of magic, through which we hope to sacrifice others to the fate we fear for ourselves.

It is also true that many of our most glorious life-serving moments occur during times of great stress. It is precisely in the face of real death threats – in war, for example – that many people feel better and act better. Not only do some people mobilize their best resources to meet a war emergency, but for people who are extremely troubled by the underlying death process in their life the objective threat issuing from war can be a relief.[3] There are stories of frankly disturbed mental patients who get "out of bed" to serve in the armed forces during a time of war and then return to being crazy when the shooting is over.[4]

How people can so readily turn away from their original, fundamental wish for aliveness is what we now want to track down. We know a good deal, relatively speaking, about hate, intentional efforts to gain power over others, prejudice, persecution, and other relatively direct choices of evil. I now want to emphasize that much of human destructiveness is not a function of directly willful hate, conscious or even unconscious, but rather the result of a complex system of forces that grow out of fearfulness and uncertainty about the basic dilemma of one's being.[5]

WE KNOW RELATIVELY LITTLE ABOUT HOW TO USE THE MACHINERY OF ALIVENESS

The Human Condition Is One of Deep Anxiety Over Nonaliveness and Death

At its best, the universal state of man is one of enormous anxiety about being incomplete or "dead" in one's experiencing during the course of one's lifetime – let alone fear of a premature, cruel death before one's time. Until one achieves an ongoing sense of aliveness and a sense that one is succeeding in fulfilling life's opportunity, one is bound to dread and hate even more the fact of ultimate death. Yet, at the same time, we must strive to come to terms with death if we are to be effectively alive. Given the staggering contradictions of life and death, being genuinely alive is an altogether difficult process, and its burden is anxiety. Ernest Becker wrote:

> Man is literally split in two: he has an awareness of his own splendid uniqueness in that he sticks out of nature with a towering majesty, and yet he goes back into the ground a few feet in order blindly and dumbly to rot

and disappear forever. It is a terrifying dilemma to be in and to have to live with. The lower animals are, of course, spared this painful contradiction, as they lack a symbolic identity and the self-consciousness that goes with it. They merely act and move reflexively as they are driven by their instincts. . . . To live a whole lifetime with the fate of death haunting one's dreams and even the most sun-filled days. . . . I believe that those who speculate that a full apprehension of man's condition would drive him insane are right, quite literally right.[6]

Rollo May has taught us that anxiety is basically our fear of not fulfilling our potential for life,[7] and anxiety is the most central experience of the human condition. In nature's grand scheme, anxiety is the fuel of greater aliveness and evolution for each man and for mankind as a whole. Anxiety is the energy of the evolutionary scheme. Anxiety is the gift of nature to power the whole range of brilliant creativity of which we are capable.

At the same time, anxiety imposes an enormous and often unbearable burden on many human beings, especially insofar as they do not learn to tap the energy of their anxiety. There is no way of avoiding anxiety (as opposed to working with, resolving, or channeling anxiety) that does not turn man away from the life potential that is within him and toward nonlife and death serving. When one takes on this or that style of certainty rather than remaining open to the mystery of life and nature as a whole, one becomes less genuinely alive. Instead of openness to experiencing, one becomes committed to maintaining certainties and the pretense that this is what it means to be alive. Because they are efforts to cheat life, positions of overcertainty naturally turn into springboards for increasingly self-deluding and cruel attacks on whatever may stand in their way.

The Empty Center

Modern psychotherapy has confirmed more and more that in every person there is an "empty center."[8] In depth psychotherapy, patients painfully encounter this empty center – a terribly vulnerable, death-approaching nothingness that is at the very center of our otherwise brilliant, intricate construction. People who successfully encounter their empty centers in psychotherapy learn not to be so afraid. They are less inclined to utilize omnipotent defenses to deny their vulnerability. What results in effective psychotherapy is not a magical filling of a center that nature apparently decrees must always be empty, but a new freedom to move through that center. Anxiety over incompleteness becomes a more and more welcome, even delicious, stimulus to tapping one's potential for aliveness, although in no case do the gifts of our aliveness remove the truth of the death that is in us and ahead of us.

However, in many cases, terrified men turn to defenses against their fear of the empty center. There are a variety of mechanisms that nature makes available for self-protection under stress, but the problem with these mechanisms for defending life is that taken to the extreme, the process of fighting to defend oneself overwhelms all else and sets off psychological chain reactions that may destroy the very aliveness one is seeking to protect. In addition, whether under comfortable or stressful conditions of life, we still know very little about our natural energy system, and there are a variety of situations in which the energy process "gets away" from our control. Together, our vulnerability to extremes of defenses against anxiety and our ignorance as to how to generate, pace, or channel our energy set the stage for unwittingly powerful momentums toward destructiveness that people do not necessarily invite, desire, or approve of.

We Do Not Know How to Gauge the Extent of Our Power

Many people go through life as if life is a process one takes for granted, where one goes about "doing whatever is to be done." In a certain sense, of course, people are, in fact, the subjects of a powerful evolutionary process that commands, without question or choice, that the powerful shall survive and the weak shall pass away. However, as has been understood by many of the finest thinkers, it is in the very nature of the same evolutionary process that man represents the emergence of a fuller consciousness that allows him to choose and direct much of the subsequent thrust of his own evolution. But we still know relatively little about how to gauge our energy output, how to know when we are approaching the safety limits of our power systems, or how to evaluate the appropriateness or effectiveness of our various applications of power.

We Have a Natural Inclination to Let Our Power Out "All the Way"

There is apparently a natural tendency in nature to take a process to its whole or maximum point. There are terms in psychology such as "closure" or "gestalt" that speak of the inclination to complete a process once begun. In philosophy, too, there are concepts of wholeness and the integrity of objects. In everyday human experience, we sense the quickening need we all have to finish something that we are close to ending. We also have many indications that people like to find out "how far they can go."

We Have a Tendency to Get Drunk with Power

It is apparent that just as men are drawn frequently enough toward states of abandon, drunkenness, and orgy, abandonment of oneself to the maximum or near-maximum of one's power is also in the category of intoxication. In some of the more obvious situations of a human being's indulging himself in hurting and oppressing others, we say he is "drunk with power." We know that in "high" or manic states, people cultivate "power trips" in order to spare themselves anxiety, dread, or inner emptiness.

We Know Little About How to Gauge the Intermixture of the Constructive and Destructive Sides of Our Emotions

Not only is the human energy system inherently an unstable, volatile system, but it becomes more unstable to the extent that people don't know how to manage, channel, and balance their emotions. The intermixture of loving and hating in intimate relationships is, of course, a crucial issue. We now know that people also hate quite a lot those whom they love the most: Parents hate their children, spouses hate one another, children hate their parents, friends hate one another, colleagues who otherwise respect one another are drawn into complex hate relationships.[9] If one studies carefully the gods man has created to epitomize his sense of himself, they are no exception either. There are many moments when the gods roar their hatred of man; there are fearful, agonized moments when man curses his gods. Although our overriding wish in all of life is to love and be loved, nature has ordained that the pursuit and conquest of love is tied inseparably to accompanying experiences of protest, pushing off, and hatred.[10]

Hatred must play a partial role in a larger symphony of loving, but in many instances, people do not know how to regulate the role of hatred. On the other hand, too many human beings try to deny the role of hate altogether, and they build up a backlog of dangerous and malevolent anger. Other humans express their hate irresponsibly and without control, and they do not discover their underlying wish to love until it is too late. Donald Winnicott, a great British psychoanalyst, has emphasized that a critical developmental task for each human being is to be able *as if* to destroy the person he loves the most without actually destroying him.[11] In other words, the essence of a truly secure love relationship is to be able to hate one's love without feeling that one is obliterating the other or wiping out one's future connection to that person.

We Suffer Power Excesses and Insufficiencies in Our Natural Energy Cycles

There are various cyclic qualities to our power systems, just as all manner of problems beset any known energy system. We are poorly trained to live through our cycles. In large part, we are afraid of the natural ups and downs of the cycle and often do rash things out of our hysteria to regain our balance. We frequently do not know when to trust our moments of excess and those of insufficiency as natural parts of a cycle that can be relied on to move back to a new balance. Nor do we always know when our excesses and insufficiencies are in fact alarms that our system is running out of control.

WE KNOW RELATIVELY LITTLE ABOUT MAKING CHOICES OF MEANS AND GOALS

We Are Not Trained to Choose the Means Toward Our Goals

People are not taught how to go about making choices of the means they will use to pursue their various goals in life. Even modern science seems to imply that the best means are those that lead most directly and effectively to the goal one is after. We have not learned to consider systematically the spin-offs, fallouts, and implications of any particular set of means. For example, it is only in recent years that we are beginning to realize the long-term ecological implications of many of the environmental decisions that have been made.

We Are Not Trained to Choose Our Life's Goals

When it comes to choosing goals, most people are inclined to select the goals that are set for them by their immediate environment. This slavish acceptance of one's environment is a security-seeking way of avoiding risk and vulnerability. Because these goals are not truly related to the inner being of their followers, any threat to the fulfillment of such goals often triggers disproportionately powerful counterattacks and a kind of destructiveness that is typical of efforts to protect insincerely held values.

Of course, great visions of goals that affirm and honor human life have been clearly defined in many of the great religious, philosophical, and literary works of all ages, but few peoples and cultures have discovered how to translate those visions into operative goals. We do have some notion that there are ways of helping man move toward "oceanic feelings" of oneness with nature. Such experiences are reported in various psychotherapies, and such experiences do emerge from various powerful moments of reorientation to one's self and to nature at times of crisis and near death. But we are far from knowing how to teach large groups of people how to go about choosing genuinely life-affirming goals.

We Know Little About Interrelating Means and Ends

We learn in the philosophy of science that means and goals are inseparable. The paths we choose to reach our most vaunted ideals of life, such as liberty and happiness, themselves determine whether we are serving life and liberty or more truly serving the guillotine or another ideology that commands human sacrifices. No matter what we say we are doing or what great goal we announce for ourselves, *how* we go about reaching our goals defines those goals as much as, or more than, any statements made about them. Similarly, the goals we choose as individuals and communities in turn influence and define the means we choose to implement those goals. If we commit ourselves to wealth or another power that is intended to overcome and overwhelm people, we will naturally be more inclined to seek and authorize power-seeking means to reach that goal. If we select goals that aim at denying volatile and aggressive aspects of our nature–as various ascetic, sensation-denying persons or groups do–then we will be drawn to a severe flagellation of ourselves as well as of others when we or they threaten to indulge in forbidden impulses and joys.[12]

To the extent that we do not see our choices of means and goals as statements of our own wishes to be alive, irrespective of prevailing authorities or the pressures of tradition, we are more likely to be drawn to idolatry of an ideology and overidentification with this or that group, and to yield to the group our individual right to choose what we shall be and how we shall arrive at what we shall be. We are then prone to extremism in defense of the cult and ideology we have chosen.

We Know Little About Differentiating Inner Experience from Overt Acting Out of Feeling

One of the crucial emotional challenges that we now understand should be a focus of emotional education in the early years of life is knowing how to differentiate between feelings and actions.[13] We want first of all to teach children to trust their various natural feelings. It is natural to hate mother at various times. It is natural to want to be up until late at night. It is all right to imagine all manner of things in our dreams and waking fantasies. Children and people should be encouraged to accept their feelings, even the outlandish and the "bad" ones. People should enjoy the creative expression and even humor of their wishes in song, dance, storytelling, inventions, or whatever. However, children and adults who treat feelings as if they are in no way different from actions either turn into bullies, tyrants, or worse, or they have no alternative but to attempt to suppress many of their feelings to stop themselves from doing undesirable and terrible things. The result is a vast reservoir of resentment and intensity of emotion, from which ill-chosen actions are likely to erupt in time. We know that people who do deny their anger are more likely to "act out" destruction. On the other hand, people who accept the naturalness of their feelings are more able to establish a healthy working distinction between feelings and actions; conversely, people who know how to distinguish between the two are more able to accept their feelings.

It is quite natural for all people to experience *wishes* to hurt other people, even to bring an end to their lives. After all, we all experience dread and hurt and fears of death, and in the process, we all at least test out imagining the various solutions to anxiety that spring naturally to the human imagination, which include deflecting those death blows onto others. However, it is clearly wrong to actually destroy another human being.

This principle of differentiating between feelings and actions has immediate and useful applications in psychotherapy. Take a married man who is beating his wife. Experience shows that it is possible to be very effective by saying, "You're obviously furious at your wife, and you deserve to be able to express that anger. You deserve to be heard. But it is wrong for you to do actual harm, and that you must stop immediately." Experience shows it is possible to speak in this way even to some people who suffer known brain damage (and thus have a built-in weakness in their emotional self-regulation).[14] It is truly exciting and reassuring to see in such experiences just how such human beings do want to be recalled to their basic wishes to respect the lives of others as well as their own. In this connection, Lawrence Kohlberg has documented a universal sequence of development of moral values that can be tracked in widely different cultures, including seemingly undeveloped, primitive ones.[15] Kohlberg's work supports the conviction that the wish to affirm life is an integral part of human nature. However, we need help in knowing how to act on this basic wish so that we are not trapped by weakness and ignorance.

WE FACE SERIOUS THREATS OF ANNIHILATION

Now add to all the above areas of ignorance of our powerful machinery of aliveness the simple truth that we are faced with serious, recurring threats of actual annihilation all through life. Besides the anxiety and instability in our natural state (where aliveness is always accompanied by the awareness of death), we actually are beset throughout life with literal threats of annihilation from without. We must be forever on guard and ready to seize defensive postures and actions. Life visits on all of us never-ending hurt, injustice, misery, and tragedy in all of our human relationships and in the interactions between groups with which we are affiliated, which are continuously under attack by other groups of human beings. It is no wonder that we are utterly terrified!

These threats to life seem to derive from a variety of sources, not from one source alone. For example, nature seems to legitimate one animal species' taking another's food. There is also a natural animal legacy of groups' seeking territory at the expense of one another. Nature is often unstable and dangerous; our natural environment is staggeringly beautiful, but it is also treacherous. In human life, there are special complexities because of our extended period of dependence at the beginning of life. A protracted state of dependency necessarily generates anger, and the process of separating emotionally from the sources of one's original dependency calls for thrusts of aggression (or else people remain emotionally unseparated). In the affairs of men, there are unending wars and murders. Everywhere we turn, life is unquestionably hazardous.

The Hazards of Annihilation in the Ecology and Environment

Although a large number of human beings live out their natural life cycle, many do not because of one or another "fault" or disaster of nature. We are part of an environment in which there are cataclysms on small and large scales. There are earthquakes, flash floods, tornadoes, hurricanes, and killer tidal waves. There are freezes and scorches and cycles of famine. There are natural poisons, and there are beasts of prey. As if these threats from without were not enough, there is also a whole world of disease and illness that springs at us and from within us, often entirely unannounced. Often enough, even when medical sciences do succeed in limiting a disease, the human being is left shaken and marred for the rest of his life by the damage wrought by his illness before it was stopped. There is also the mystery of the biological clock, as we are fated to a short or a long life potential by a heredity we cannot control.

The Hazards of Destructive Experience in Dependent Relationships

In addition to the random and unpredictable threats of annihilation that are rooted in the unknowns of nature, there are hazards in human relationships themselves. These seem less random and unpredictable, and therefore more unfair and undeserved, but in many ways these hazards, too, issue from the unknowns of life. Often they are rooted in the limitations and ignorance of the particular parents whom chance assigns to us for the period of our critical dependency.

We have learned that in all parents there is a natural and necessary anger and destructiveness toward their children—if only as part of the separating process that enables children to go on to be themselves.[16] But we know there is also an unnecessary and extreme parental destructiveness, both in spirit and in body.[17] There are parental demands to perform for the parents' needs rather than for the child's wish to feel alive. There are parental retaliations by way of deprivation of the spirit of and affection for a child. There are near-total obliterations of many children by parents who are in a frenzy to salvage their own sinking feelings of aliveness.

There is little question that those people who suffer bitter deprivation of needed human warmth and care in their personal development and are treated instead to brutality or neglect, become, in turn, prime candidates for what Erich Fromm has called the expression of an "archaic bloodthirst."[18] Psychologist Harry Harlow's brilliant researches into the mothering and other early social experiences of monkeys has demonstrated that monkeys that are deprived of necessary affection in their infancies become aggressive, short-tempered parents to their own young.[19] In human society, there is evidence that there is an unbelievable amount of actual child beating and assault among ostensibly civilized people, including the well educated.[20] In general, Western society in recent years has been characterized by increasingly massive breakdowns of family units via divorce, which deprives children of the whole of their natural parental love and support systems.[21]

The Hazards of Annihilation by Our Fellow Men

What can be said about the dread that haunts us throughout life that we and our loved ones may be among the next to fall at the hands of human beings who are bent on genocidal destruction? We are all seemingly players in a great worldwide "lottery" in which it is decided whether or not we and our loved ones will be among those who fall victim to human destructiveness. Who would not become upset and downright crazy under such circumstances? The Holocaust of the Jewish people in Europe spelled out irretrievably how fully man can dissociate himself from the humanity of his fellow human beings as he callously masses people for destruction as if they were no more than toys to serve his diabolical humor. The same situation exists in the holocausts that are taking place this very day here or there on the face of this blood-soaked earth. Could we be anything but terrified?

WE DO NOT KNOW HOW TO MONITOR AND PACE
THE THREAT PROCESS

We see that there is every reason in the world for us to be terrified. It is therefore prudent and natural that we erect huge warning systems for spotting emerging threats to our survival. However, in the process of trying to be aware of threats of annihilation, we may be drawn toward a paranoid, exaggerated state of vigilance, and we may become unable to distinguish among real threat, potential threat, and nonthreat; among actual foe, still would-be friend, and innocent other. We can become so sensitive that we are easily triggered into labeling the innocent other as an enemy and a would-be destroyer. Oftentimes, people correctly perceive wishes to annihilate them but fail to appreciate the fact that those wishes are nowhere near being translated into actions. Understandably enough, people respond to what they experience as threatening with their own counterthrusts and counterattacks, but often those responses in turn confirm the no-less paranoid fears of the people that posed the threat, and they then escalate their own threats and attacks. Before long, there is a system of mutual escalation and counterescalation that builds to a zenith of maximum destruction.

Isn't that often much of the story in many marriages? Many couples who once genuinely loved and wished to love one another, become unable to stem the tide of escalating attack and counterattack, hate and counterhate. Is it not also the case in many small group situations, such as in business and professional matters? People who really wanted to work with one another polarize themselves into fixed positions as enemies. They are then unable to find a way back to cooperate with one another or to utilize their very conflict to contribute to an even more spirited and a better-quality effort toward their common goals.

What we also know of the human condition is that once a situation has been defined as a major threat, that is, once another person or a group has been categorized as our would-be annihilator, we allow ourselves to consciously enter into actions that we otherwise would never countenance. The justification for these actions is, of course, the very legitimate and natural feeling of defending one's life. The tragedy is that often the situation is nowhere near as extreme as it is believed to be, but neither party can stop itself from confirming for the other that what is under way is a war unto death.[22]

We Often Don't Know the Difference Between Self-defense and Its Illusion

Faced with terrible threats of annihilation from our fellow man, we gird ourselves for the battle of self-defense. For this battle, we are powered by the energy of feeling that it is our natural right to defend ourselves against death-dealing attack. Certainly, there is no more convincing justification for aggression than the need to slay one's would-be killer. Even as a legal defense, self-defense has been recognized by virtually all religious and legal systems as a justification for killing. In man's inner mind, the feeling that one is fighting in self-defense sets off energies of heroic proportions. The trouble with fighting and killing in self-defense is that serious mistakes are made. *A relatively innocent night prowler is shot to death. Worse yet, following reports of many prowling incidents in the neighborhood, a terrified citizen arms himself and ends up shooting an innocent person who happens to stumble into that citizen's terror-filled world.*

If and when we really appreciate the extent of our terror and how we turn in desperation to our instinctive feeling of the right to defend ourselves, we may be able to approach the saddening, maddening truth that many of our most aggressive acts are intended as self-defense and not as attacks to beat down, take over, or annihilate others. This situation is seen over and over again in many "small wars," such as on the "marital battleground." In psychotherapeutic practice with marital couples who are seeking help in disengaging themselves from their unhappy wars, one never sees a spouse who does not feel himself or herself the victim of the machinations and destructions of the other. Each spouse claims sincerely that his or her own aggressions are in response to the other's destructiveness, that is, entirely on the basis of self-defense. If we honestly search our minds and hearts, we will find that in just about all situations in which we have been involved in conflict with another person—when we were children, in our married lives, in our business and professional connections—our predominant, and certainly first, reaction to conflict has been to feel that we are under unfair attack by the other. It is a real hallmark of maturity to be able to question oneself as to one's own role in a conflict and to search for our own unwitting contributions to the spiraling of hate and destructiveness.

Some people seek to handle the difficult distinction between legitimate needs for self-defense and the illusory feeling of self-defense by proposing that under no circumstances whatsoever can the taking of a human life be condoned.[23] The ideal proposed by the true pacifists is deeply appealing in many ways. There is no question but that in many situations, terrible destruction can be averted because the spiral of threat and counterthreat is cut by the courage to "love one's enemies." However, when human destructiveness is wanton and megalomanic, the result of a total commitment not to fight back even in self-defense often leads to the death of more human beings.[24] There is also a whole body of evidence that shows that when sadistic power is left unchallenged, the sadist grows more vengeful toward the victim as the latter remains passive and that once the sadist damages his victim and renders him helpless, the sadist turns even more cruel.[25]

It would seem that the really desirable ideal would be to learn how to deal with our feeling of being under attack and wanting to fight back in self-defense. Perhaps someday the social scientists will provide us with methods for differentiating between claims of self-defense that are essentially appropriate to the facts of an attack or an imminent attack and claims of self-defense that, though sincere, are objectively untrue. As things stand now, the painful facts of history are that even in cases of the most ugly and depraved genocidal destructiveness, many a genocider sincerely holds the conviction that the victim group is a source of real danger to his own survival. Survival may be defined in "psycho-ideological" terms—for example, the nonbeliever will destroy our chances of immortality by defiling and offending the true god in whom we believe—or survival may be defined in terms of a perception of the victim group as threatening racial impurity and therefore poisoning the eugenic life stream of our people. There is no end to the variations, and all self-defense is phrased in the available terms of a culture's sociohistorical circumstances and images. Shocking and uncomfortable as the conclusion is, the genocidal killers, whom we despise and detest, are usually quite sincere in their intention to defend their own people against destruction.

Psychiatrist Ronald Laing has brilliantly described the dynamics of convincing oneself that one is fighting in self-defense.

> We must defend *reality* against the emptiness, deceit, and the evil, of *Unreality*. This is what we are fighting for. To defend the real against the

unreal. The true against the falsehood. The full life against an empty life, the good against evil. What is against what is not.

But then what are we defending ourselves against? Nothing? Oh no! The danger, the menace, the enemy, Them, are very real. So we have to start again. . . .

They are Real. They are dangerous, because they are. So long as they *are*, we are in danger. So we must destroy them. If we must destroy them, they must destroy us to prevent us destroying them, and we must destroy them before they destroy us before we destroy them before they destroy us . . . which is where we are at the moment. . . .

We need not worry that the kill ratio between Them and Us will get too high. There are always more where *they* came from. From *inside Us.*[26]

Once begun, acts of attack on and destruction of another that were originally intended as self-defense take on their own momentum, and power begets more and more power. We human beings seem to create a tradition out of just about anything—even though it may have stumbled into being inadvertently—and thereafter we treat the pattern as if it is always to be repeated.

The Unknowing Corruption of Increased Power

There are good reasons for terrified people to fight back, not only to defend themselves but to capture more of life, and there follow huge new flows of energy drive or aggression. What that means, of course, is that all the hazards of the energy system are doubled and tripled because the system is at its greatest intensity, and there must be efforts to regulate the flow of the surging energy power. In addition to all the "simple" unknowns of monitoring, gauging, and pacing the power, and in addition to our problematic natural inclinations "to go all the way," we know little about how to guard against the corruptions that seem to set in when greater power is attained. To the extent that man is somehow apparently successful in gaining new mastery over life, he becomes the more dangerous. To the extent that man seems to achieve the greater aliveness he is fighting for, he is faced with the beguiling recklessness of his new power. In his intriguing analysis of the Milgram experiment, described in Chapter 2, social psychologist Philip Zimbardo has written that the key to people's availability to destroy lies in the fact that human beings seek to maintain an illusion of personal invulnerability and personal control. It is the quest to maintain invulnerability that makes people insensitive to the power forces they are dealing with, forces that are directing them toward destructiveness.[27]

Many people who attain a measure of power allow themselves to be drawn into the illusion of having found a permanent way to be spared further feelings of vulnerability and anxiety. Some power-crazed men seemingly declare that they will dethrone and overpower the life-gods themselves. However, no matter how much people may strut and boast about their new majesty, they cannot help but be aware that they still have not become masters of their destiny and that they will never be free of the ultimate terrors of life and death. They may then become increasingly desperate and increasingly angry at how life still cruelly mocks them. Now their newly gained power is no longer cause for celebration but demands more and more bolstering. Power now begets more power seeking, and there develops a need to seek out objects for one's venom and vengefulness.

Few people escape the seductions of corruption by power. Power begets further power and unending efforts to attain even more. A terrifying spiral is now spinning and thrusting toward its ultimate consequences. The grotesque passions of power often build toward destruction of the very sources from which power first springs.

WE RESORT TO PRIMITIVE MAGICAL MECHANISMS IN OUR ATTEMPTS TO SALVAGE LIFE

The drama gathers pace. We respond altogether naturally by counterattacking against the many threats of our annihilation. If life is so unsure, then we must assert our right to feel alive. We feel there is an inherently self-justifying purpose in seeking to be alive and to protect ourselves against attack. This sense of justness and purpose provides us with a base of excitement, drive, and mission that can hardly bear to leave anything in its way as it gathers force. Thus, all the hazards of not knowing how to pace our energy machinery are that much more intensified as the increasingly dangerous momentum gathers.

Enter now, for better and for worse, the fact that nature has granted us a variety of extremely powerful mechanisms for defending ourselves against severe stress and unbearable anxiety. Many observers of the human condition agree that in the present stage of our evolution, we are still at the dawn of consciousness of our mind and its unique powers for shaping reality. The processes on which we call when we are in serious trouble are rooted in the primitiveness of the relatively recently evolved mind and its origins in earlier forms of life. It is to such powerful mechanisms of projecting responsibility for our fate onto others, and determining to get rid of them, that we turn when we are caught up in powerful sequences of stress, and the primitiveness and lack of reality testing that are inherent in these magical mechanisms play a further role in determining the outcome of the forces that are gathering momentum.

We are faced with the utterly mad spectacle of a brilliantly evolving organism that is making breathtaking penetrations into the secrets of nature, extending life, and building fascinating and beautiful civilizations on the one hand and on the other, given to simple-minded, primitive, magic-ridden devices to create and maintain illusion, self-deception, and actual psychotic delusions to protect itself from terror.

We Experience a Primitive Terror over Contact With Other Life

Earlier I suggested that people are basically glad to see life in other people and nature but that under stress, they turn toward another side of their experiencing and wish others the nonaliveness and death they fear for themselves. There appears to be built into the human experience a basic ambivalence about actual close contact with other human beings. On the one hand, contact is eagerly sought after because it is caring, reassuring, and stimulating. On the other hand, contact is seen as dangerous and potentially annihilating.

Recently, there has been something of a rediscovery of contact in the Western world in the wave of encounter groups. In these encounter groups, people affirm the pleasure and simple joy that lie in wordless touch experiences with other people, including those whom one does not and never will know and often including people who otherwise fall short of one's general standards of attractiveness and interest. Life enjoys life; warmth is nourished by the warmth of another; something tense and hurried and angry lets go in us when we are touched by human warmth.

At the same time, those whom we love the most and whose love we seek the most can drive us mad with their touch. There are times when our bodies recoil in fear and repulsion from those very people we basically wish to be closest to. The same arm around our shoulder that was (and again will be) a source of camaraderie and protection turns into a clawing, preying, gouging, monstrously taloned limb that makes us creep into ourselves with fright.[28] Perhaps fundamentally this repulsion is a continuation of the human terror that strikes deep into the hearts of all of us when we learn that even our beloved mother (like all people) has an angry, hurting side to her personality—even if she doesn't know it and pretends always to be loving.[29] Perhaps it is the projection of our own agonized anger that makes us believe that another is monstrously angry at us.[30] Whatever the reason, the fact is that one frequently attributes to others repulsive, dangerous, noxious ugliness. It then becomes entirely legitimate for one to want to push off touch or contact with the disgusting and frightening creatures; ultimately, it begins to appear legitimate even to remove the possibility of their ever again seeking contact with us. It may be that the genocider, too, may find something of his definition of legitimacy in his overwhelming conviction that he has to get the other's dirty hands off him.

Projecting That We Can Bear Least in Ourselves onto a Scapegoat

Whether in brief words or in longer essays, every elementary psychology textbook describes the mechanism of projection clearly enough, but rarely do their definitional explanations capture the dramatic power of that process. The mechanism of projection grips people. It is a powerful force that serves much of the destructiveness in this world. No human being seems to be exempt from projection, and formal education seems to offer very little protection against people's succumbing to this mechanism when they are under stress.[31]

Projection seems to derive from a deep, primitive conviction that because aliveness is obviously granted to some when it is not to others, the best defense against serious threats to one's aliveness is to take away the aliveness allotted to another. That aliveness is doled out to some and not to others hardly seems to need arguing. Life itself seems to "prove" that fact at every turn. At the best of times, there are people all around us who die unfairly before their time, and each such event necessarily strikes terror into the hearts of every one of us as to whether we will be the next to be struck down. At the worst of times, some people seem to hold on to the life raft while others are swept to a bitter death. To the terrified hearts and minds of all of the survivors, it can only seem that behind these unpredictable events there must be a mysterious guiding force and the trick must be to learn how to connect oneself to the sources of strength. It seems almost instinctive that if one wants to gain something that is in short supply, the thing to do is to push others out of the way.

The mechanism of projection enables a person to attribute to others whatever one fears in oneself. Since the central fear in man's experience is nonaliveness and death, that is the essence of what men are projecting onto others in one or another form: "I will cast my fears of death onto you; I will claim for myself the life force you appear to possess."

One of the truly remarkable contributions of the approximately twenty-year-old field of family therapy (in which whole groups are seen as the "patients" rather than the one or more obviously symptomatic members of the family) has been the identification of how projection is centered on a particular member of a family. We have seen how a family that is beset with problems of aliveness will stigmatize one of its members with this or that failing, impotence, or craziness and thus spare the rest of the family the truth of everyone else's nonrealness or nonaliveness. In so-called pseudomutual families, in which differences of opinion or feeling are not expressed openly, the members feel that if they were to allow themselves to be their real selves, sheer pandemonium (divorce, desertion, murder) would break out. So it is tacitly agreed instead to drive only one person crazy.[32] Family therapists have demonstrated that often the historic role of the so-called schizophrenic patient is to be the scapegoat for his or her family. What is exciting is how family therapists can then apply an understanding of these mechanisms of pseudomutuality and scapegoating in treatment innovations that may succeed in relieving the patient and in reopening the entire system of disorder within the family as a whole.

From the point of view of our concern with the hideousness of man's choosing fellow human beings to be victims who are sent to premature death, the mechanism of projection can be seen as the main dynamic through which people who are overwhelmed with fears of their own possible death seize on other people and consign them to the fate they fear for themselves. Irvine Schiffer describes the sequences of terror and projection vividly.

> The spectre of death — one of mankind's most elemental dreads, something over which one has no ultimate control despite man's endless struggle to deny the fact — hovers constantly over the barrier of the will; . . . the surreptitious *threat of dissolution to our illusory sense of self-control* . . . anything that hauntingly reminds us that, though we may have indeed *acknowledged* the reality of death, we have by no means accepted *living* with this reality. . . . We experience ourselves at the mercy of fate or destiny. This recognition we find repugnant, and we set about ridding ourselves of this trauma to our narcissism, this loop-hole in the armour of our self-determination. . . . An outside agent is chosen to portray the "enemy" that threatens all our hard-won illusions of equilibrium, of self-control, of complacent "surmounting" of the theme of death. By projection onto suitably symbolic and enigmatic objects that are sufficiently estranged and beyond the pale of conscious familiarity, we manage to "discover" alien monstrosities.[33]

The projection mechanism operates on many levels, of course. There is first of all a general devaluing of the worthwhileness, and even the validity, of the existence of another that we call dehumanization. The feeling that is developed and nurtured is that the other people are not really as human or as alive or as deserving of life as we are. We assign such a feeling to whatever may be the lower class in a given culture and/or to a less valued racial or national group, so that they become representative of all that is vulnerable, unattractive, and undeserving.

Obviously, this dehumanizing process in itself yields a bad enough state of affairs, as it divides human beings from one another. Dehumanization spawns and perpetuates classes of lower and undesirable peoples, with all the grief and pain that such distinctions bring to the less fortunate people as well as the denuding of dignity and aliveness in those people who fall unknowingly into the trap of pretending to be better than others.

However, the process generally does not stop there. What has been accomplished by dehumanizing a particular target isn't really enough to justify doing further damage to those hapless undesirables, and if we are to prepare a justification for hurting those people, we need also to "prove" that they are out to hurt us. Granted that we have already projected onto them that they are less than us and not the same as us, not even as deserving of life as we are, but there is nothing yet in this bill of particulars to justify the extreme of killing them. By any test of the simple logic of man's still natural wish to be decent, what needs to be added to justify taking away people's lives is proof that the others are also a terrible threat to our lives and that it is their intent to take our lives away from us unless we stop them first.

In that process, too, the mechanism of projection plays a part. For not only do we project onto others our fears of being destroyed by making the others the objects of the fate we wish to escape, but we also project onto others the hateful wishes to destroy that we cannot bear in ourselves. We justify our own hatred and destructiveness on the grounds that that is what the others harbor toward us. First we project our feared weakness onto the others, then we project our destructive murderous impulses onto them, and most of all, what we project onto the hapless target group is that they are to be the objects of the death we so fear for ourselves.

Now, of course, all that is inherently self-justifying about fighting back in self-defense is invoked. There can be no further doubt about it. Not only are those hapless others less deserving of life to begin with, for they are not quite as human as we are, they are also threatening to take away our aliveness, and it is entirely justified that we destroy them.

We have now defined a deadly basis for retaliation. There is nothing to stop us. We are one with the ancient sacrificing rite of man. We come alive with the battle cry of our self-defense. We shall destroy the other and thereby remove the threat to our own aliveness. Moreover, we will claim the other's aliveness as our booty. Already the sheer energy and excitement of our attack make us feel more alive. And if despite all, we still die — which we desperately fear will happen even after we sacrifice the other — at least we will go down alive with the passion of our violence.

Unfair? Logically, of course. Morally, no doubt. But realistically, if one can honestly come to grips with the inner agony of man, his terror, and his unbelievable primitiveness, it is all nonetheless "understandable."

Man Acts Out His Anxieties

Acting out is a technical term in psychology and psychopathology to describe a particularly dangerous and difficult mechanism of defense against anxiety.[34] What acting out describes is how human beings express or translate their passions and troubled feelings into destructive, overt behavior. Some people do so fairly regularly, for example, professional thieves, alcoholics, pimps, and cardsharps. Others do so when under great stress in order to get away from themselves. They do not trust themselves to deal with their stress as a process to be solved. In both cases, people are acting out their inner tensions in behavior that gets them away from their feelings. *A man runs away from his suffering in his marriage to drinking. He is afraid to confront his wife's bitter controlling of him, and he is also afraid to deal with his own weakness in needing to please her even when she demeans him. Instead of doing battle where battle is called for on these fronts, he flees to drinking.* Another very common escape is to run off into an affair outside the marriage, but not simply as a tension-relieving, enjoyable interlude (just as the harassed man in the previous example did not go off for just a few drinks or even for one or two nights of too much under his belt but took the full-blown alcoholic route). The affair becomes a full-time "escape" to drain off one's neediness and anger, and thus to escape feeling vulnerable at home.

As psychotherapists know, the serious problem with acting out is that so much of what one does via this defense is momentarily quite satisfying and pleasurable. Drinking and having affairs can be a lot of fun. The escapism is then reinforced by the pleasure that is derived from the acting out; worst of all, the underlying sense that one really is unable to cope with the real world of stress is reinforced each time one escapes from dealing with reality. Historically, psychotherapeutic methods have not been effective in cases in which acting out is a predominant part of the picture. Frequently, people who are acting out are forced to come to therapy because of their behavior and not because they recognize there is something seriously wrong deep in their emotions. The request for treatment is often to get rid of an unhappy symptom, not to deal with the underlying problem. Of course, the battle the psychotherapist then fights is to help the patient find the courage and strength to recognize the real problem; often this effort is not successful.

It would not be too serious a matter if the outlet of acting out were used with discretion, but this is not the case. Violence is an intense passion that can provide much satisfaction to people who need to run away from themselves. The toll of all acting out as an escape from real life issues is enormous.

Just how much acting out takes place is the result not only of individual predilection, but also, and crucially, of how much a given culture invites, allows, and even legitimates any particular form of acting out. For example, the extent of individual homicidal behavior varies drastically from culture to culture.[35] Even if we grant that by and large, people who engage in the actual killing of another human being are psychologically or psychiatrically ill, the fact remains that the prevailing expectations of a culture will determine in large part whether or not people who are extremely upset and unable to maintain normal mental judgment will choose the path of killing. In other words, the climate of expectation, even permission and facilitation, of violence in a culture (such as when a culture makes guns readily available or provides models of homicidal behavior through the mass media) determines to a very great extent whether people will choose murder as their way of acting out.[36] It is true that even in violence-prone societies, a majority of the people still will not turn to homicide, but when a process of *group* acting out gathers momentum, many people who themselves would never act out through homicide do take on the roles of killers and accomplices.

Escaping into Ideology

We seek meaning in our lives by participating in causes and championing ideas and purposes that are "bigger than us" and that will survive long after us. In many cases, these ideologies truly serve the cause of human progress. When people unite in common cause, marvelous cooperative efforts can result that enrich the lives of many. In a marvelous textbook on the psychological aspects of war and peace, psychiatrist and psychologist Jerome Frank writes:

> An individual human life is a momentary flash of experience squeezed between two oblivions in a universe that appears indifferent to human existence, or at least gives no universally convincing sign of caring. Since the full recognition of one's utter insignificance is intolerable,

everyone has some way of shielding himself from the awful truth. Most people accomplish this by identifying with some enduring and larger group and, beyond this, by viewing their lives as being in the service of some more or less permanent abstraction—freedom, democracy, communism, human welfare, or a religious creed.[37]

However, there is also a dark side to humans' joining together to support ideologies. Not only are there ideologies that are committed to evil, life-destroying purposes, but to the extent that human beings are driven by their terror and neediness to find a haven in ideology, members of a group may fail to note that their group is moving toward a destructive position with regard to other people's rights to life and is abandoning earlier justice-seeking, life-advancing values. To the extent that the major purpose of one's identification with an ideology is to spare one aloneness and dread of death, the believer is not likely to recognize or acknowledge that once-well-intended values are changing toward destructiveness. The "true believer" and committed group member often does not recognize or acknowledge that he or she is joined to an ideology that has become evil.

Everywhere in human life one sees this phenomenon. Again and again, the idolatrous need to conform to others and be one with them spoils once-great ideas. Thus, some great religious ideas become largely excuses for desperate, frightened clerics to gain control over other people; in truth, theirs is a self-serving godhead whom they wish to spare them anxiety. So, too, Freud's great breakthroughs into the depths of human psychology became rallying points for too many silly minded orthodox followers, who, for all their degrees in psychology or medicine, were no less frightened of aliveness than their patients. These superdevotees hid their real professional and personal selves in an idolatrous ritualization of Freud's ideas that often took the real meaning out of his remarkable innovations.

The story of how man has turned so many of his ideologies toward justifying every conceivable evil, cruelty, and death dealing is a terrifying tale. It is a story so often repeated that it would be virtually possible to write a history of human life around this dynamic. Commitment to an ideology is a two-edged sword; it expresses, on the one hand, man's finest search for ideals, but on the other hand, it expresses all that is pagan and serves man's most cowardly escapes from the terrors of unknowingness and mortality.

Several generations ago the philosopher Pascal wrote, "Men never do evil so completely and cheerfully as when they do it from religious conviction."[38] A contemporary philosopher, Lionel Rubinoff, writes:

Just as in the myth Satan is represented as playing out a role in the cosmic drama of good and evil, so the enactment of violence is often legitimized by being presented as the fulfillment of the cosmic destiny. . . . Just as the language of "I was only obeying orders" facilitates the mechanisms of projection, so the language of ideology—"it is our destiny," "it is our mission," "it is our national purpose"—introduces an external compelling force that is made to bear full responsibility for one's acts.[39]

Genociders make full use of this idolatrous process. The unquestioned justice of one's own ideology is combined with the devastating accusations (projections) of another people's infamy. Incredible as it may seem, virtually every genocide is defined by its doers as being on behalf of the larger purpose of bettering human life! In one case, it is to rid the world of infidels who prevent us from receiving the blessings of God; in another case, it is to improve racial purity; in still another case, it is to protect against economic enslavement by a people who allegedly want to exploit everyone else and gain total power. There are always words with which to attribute to ourselves only the finest ideological purpose and to another, the worst.

Immortality Seeking

The dynamic of seeking immortality normally does not appear in the standard lists of defense mechanisms in psychology textbooks, although in recent years this mechanism has been the subject of some very fine studies by psychiatrist Robert Lifton, beginning with his trailblazing work on the survivors of the atomic bombing of Hiroshima.[40] In truth, people do a great many things not so much for what they expect to achieve during their lifetime, but to link themselves to the next generation of their sons and daughters and, in fact, to the forever of immortality.

Throughout history, people have sought to escape the scourge of death. Men have sought fountains of youth, potions, and other guarantees of immortality. They have created magic rites and group ceremonials. And it turns out that a staggering number of seemingly nonmagical, rational human activities are fed by covert, symbolic efforts at immortality, which are hidden within the otherwise rational pursuit. For example, psychological studies have shown that many a prospective doctor unconsciously hopes to be able to gain some control over life and death (and this dynamic determines a good deal of the doctor's later faults as a person-physician). In many of the disappointments and conflicts of parent-child relationships, the demand for immortality plays a huge, silent role. It is as if the parents beseech and insist that the child eat, grow, or learn on behalf of perpetuating them, and what happens is that the young organism revolts against the intrusion of the parents' will and ambitions. And, of course, a good deal of the appeal and power of organized religious groups through the ages has to do with overt and covert offers of immortality.

We know that many individuals will do "just about anything" to save themselves from dying. Also, most of us are so frightened of the possibility that we will not feel really alive during our lifetime that we are prepared to do "just about anything" to ensure ourselves a sense of immortality.[41]

MAN LOSES HIMSELF IN GROUP EXPERIENCES

All human beings need one another. We have deep needs for support from one another in every sense of the word, ranging from cooperation in many tasks to no less important needs for emotional support. Yet we have known for a long time that the processes to which the human being is open when he participates in group experiences may also be extremely dangerous. Often they are virtually hypnotic and magnetizing. When human beings get caught in the grip of powerful group processes, they run a serious risk of accepting values that normally would not be acceptable to them in their independent judgment and conscience: "It is still frightening to observe in our democratic culture how the continuing relationship of one individual to his fellow through the common quality of altruistic surrender to a power creates, especially in time of any crisis, a chain reaction of hypnotic surrender which represents a *folie en masse* – a general abdication of critical judgments and an abandonment to self-esteem analogous to what happens psychologically in an orgy."[42]

One useful way of thinking about what happens to human beings in groups is to say that in the present stage of our evolution, we are vulnerable to losing ourselves in a group. This is the syndrome of the soldier who insists that he was "only following orders." I call the experience of being "taken away" from oneself or "losing oneself" in a group the "mass ego frenzy" of group experience. All of us know what it is to lose ourselves; each of us has had it happen sometime or another.

It was an innocent starlit night in the oar house of a summer camp. We were counselors to the campers by day and busy with our burgeoning teenage sexuality by night. It started teasingly, deliciously enough, with a dare that evening that any female counselor caught walking past a certain grove of trees would be subjected to the fullest measure of the law of the male counselors.

Several girls accepted the obvious invitation and to everyone's great delight were taken to the oar house amid peals of laughter mixed with mock protests.

However, once in the oar house, a strange process began to build. There soon arose from among us a leader to direct the unfolding drama. Interestingly, this leader emerged that evening as if from "nowhere"; his previous role in camp life had not been that significant or dramatic. Now the occasion of the imprisoned female counselors apparently brought forth a latent passion for leadership in this man—an Ivy League school law student, as I recall. With consummate concentration, he led the ceremony, and truth be told, the rest of us cowards and cheap thrill seekers piggybacked on the Leader's taking charge.

Before long, we had become Enjoyers of the Spectacle of our Leader commanding the Disrobing of the Lasses. The rule was that those girls who acknowledged the error of their ways in walking onto the male "campus" were to be set free but those who refused to throw themselves on the mercy of the court were to be subjected to disrobing. For awhile longer, there was still laughter, though now it was increasingly nervous and tension charged. Before long, the simple scene turned before our very eyes into a stark drama of stubborn pride, then increasing hurt, and finally even panic.

As the Leader continued resolutely in his methodical Prosecution of Justice, an increasingly ugly, sadistic beat began to pulsate in the Disrobing. More and more, the girls pleaded to be set loose, and a frenzy of hysteria and panic began to mount. Fortunately, the camp director arrived on the scene, and the episode was brought to an end, but not before all of us experienced a profound sense of shock that we had turned into groups of Oppressors and Victims. For we all sensed that, far away as they were, we too were on our way toward some kind of Auschwitz and Dachau.

Even if one has never participated in an actual group orgy, we have all been there at some time in our minds. We have all traveled through the pages of history with this conqueror or that. Americans have all walked the trails of comic book orgies and movie and television spectacles of mass lynchings and rapes. We have all traveled with Aaron and the people of Israel dancing raucously around the Golden Calf, and we have all been one with the Canaanites serving up their children—sacrifices to the Moloch god.

In the mass ego frenzy of a group, people are carried away toward violence that most would never choose individually. Sociologist Randall Collins has described how violence among animals involves "a building up of frenzies through an interchange of instinctual gestures. The pack of wolves or rats work each other up into sheer ferociousness which enables them to kill as a team." The team effect expresses itself in a whole patterning of arousal against the enemy, then in the "post-kill 'celebration' in the form of eating their victim together," descriptions that seem remarkably and tragically apt for human group orgies as well.[43] Several very powerful mechanisms seem to be at work in these situations, which deserve our further efforts at understanding: contagion, the atmosphere of the group as a shaper of experiencing, surrender of one's identity to the group, and ideology as group identity.

The Process of Contagion in Group Experiencing

In groups, experiencing is transmitted contagiously from one person to another.[44] A happy environment invites other people to happiness. An angry room filled with bitterness casts its shadow on all who enter. How much of what we are calling contagion resembles the contagion of physical illness is not exactly clear. Then again, neither is the phenomenon of physical contagion entirely understood. For example, many physicians and nurses who tend to the very contagiously ill do not contract their patients' diseases. One possibility is that these medical professionals build up an immunity to diseases through repeated exposure. If so, this notion corresponds nicely with what we understand to be the immunity value of emotional experiencing. People can be helped and trained to ward off much of the contagious hazard of emotional experiencing by being opened to their own normal passions and by being prepared to guard their individuality and not surrender to the group process.

The Atmosphere of the Group as a Shaper of Experiencing

Every group takes on its own special identity and tradition. Deeply powerful processes are at work in creating the highly idiomatic subculture of each and every group. Within the same community, one hospital differs from another. Within the same economy, two companies doing the same kind of business differ in their emotional environments. Within the same educational system, different schools take on their own identities and atmospheres. So far, the social scientists are far from having a language that is rich or precise enough to describe these different shadings. Nor do powerful literary descriptions of group events quite do the trick. No one as yet has learned how to describe the curious, decisive qualities of a group atmosphere, or how a given atmosphere comes about. Much of our language is limited to using words whose meanings are mostly relevant to the description of individuals, and although we know we are talking about something different when it comes to groups, we don't know how to express the difference. So we describe them somewhat the way we describe people: happy, bad, inviting, dull, profound, disorganized, capricious, irresponsible, productive, creative, disciplined, ennobling.

We especially don't know how group atmospheres first develop, although we certainly do know that once a tradition and spirit take hold in a group, they color and shape many of the group processes that follow. A very interesting, almost laboratory-like opportunity for seeing how groups develop differently, even when they begin under relatively similar circumstances and with essentially identical ideological commitments, is to look at the kibbutzim, or collective settlements, in Israel. There may be four kibbutzim surrounding a certain geographical spot, but a local might tell you that one collective is prospering economically and socially and enjoys a strong sense of morale; two of the kibbutzim are making it, but not as successfully—a fair number of members elect to leave those two settlements; and the fourth kibbutz is in very serious trouble—there is a pervasive shakiness about the community, no stable leadership group has emerged, many of the members who stay on seem to do so more because of inertia than because of enthusiasm, and a great many members leave. Just how each of these "group faces" evolves is surely a fascinating story, which a good journalist and/or social science researcher might try to describe.

Surrender of One's Identity to the Group

Groups provide something of an antidote to the terror of facing life all alone. However, so beguiling is this opportunity, so captivating the group experience as a way of relieving untold terrors of aloneness, that many people utilize the opportunity of the group process to try to bypass and do without the pain of being an individual.

It is true that much of what takes place in a group is beautiful and constructive. There is little doubt, in fact, that the cultures of many Western countries fail to emphasize many of the rich, constructive opportunities of group life, identification, and commitment. Studies of growing up in the USSR as compared to growing up in the United States show that Soviet youngsters have a much greater emotional strength as a result of their experiencing themselves as committed members of their collective. Soviet youngsters are responsible to the group for their actions, and in turn, they draw untold support from their responsibility to the group.[45] In a group, members feel much less alone in life, and they are also far less vulnerable to the hazards of instability in their nuclear families. In Israel, the collective settlement movement is well known for its disproportionately high yield of top-ranking military and civil leaders. The kibbutzim turn out many self-confident young men and women, who are notably more sure of themselves and make a stronger commitment to their people.[46]

The normal group process invites identification and solidarity with the collective identity of one's group. Thus, groups quite purposely take on names, insignia, protocol, and other forms of pageantry. It is to this group identity that members surrender some of their individual identity, and indeed, under normal circumstances, there are entirely credible reasons for putting aside some of one's identity in favor of a group identity. We worry about the mental health of those people who do not know how to join groups and enjoy "getting away from themselves" with others. However, in the intoxication of group experiences, many people virtually surrender their entire individuality to the group and practically blend themselves into the group identity. They are now no longer themselves, and, therefore, they are the more available to conformity to any instructions they are given just because those instructions come from a leader. Caught up in a mass group frenzy, those people are no longer emotionally experiencing, and, hence, they are no longer responsible for their decisions or choices (although I again emphasize that nothing of this effort to understand is intended to excuse the responsibility for one's choices). In a deep psychological sense, such people are no longer individuals.

Ideology as Group Identity

What I would add here to the earlier discussion of commitment to an ideology is how ideology extends the group process. The development of a group ideology ties people quite remarkably to their collective even when they are physically far apart from the collective. The committed believer is "with" his group in spirit whenever he conjures up the common belief system. In addition, one of the profound functions of ideology is to provide people with a sense of survival extending beyond their own mortality. "Although I in my mortal body will die, my group and its purpose will live on long after me." Clearly, the lure of such consolation is powerful, especially for people who fear they cannot find a sense of purpose for their own individuality.

The dynamic of needing to be committed to one's group ideology, whatever it is, is frequently a more powerful force than allegiance to the actual ideology. Thus, some good people who originally intended sincerely to support decent human values of liberation or freedom end up, almost without knowing it, staying with their group when it turns to guillotining, torturing, oppressing, and destroying – all in the name of liberty or freedom. No matter that the group process is moving toward destructiveness, those people are so mesmerized and paralyzed by their dependency on the group for purpose and continuity in their lives that they fail to notice or to be able to stand up to take action against the very destructiveness they once sincerely opposed.[47]

THE DYNAMICS OF SEQUENCES AND MOMENTUMS

Following the Momentum of an Activity

Whether we like it or not, a variety of banal, "meaningless" structural considerations also enter man's most crucial decisions. In other words, qualities that issue from the sheer momentum of the dynamics of a structure and situation can lead man to do things "just because" it is the natural thing to do next.

It seems so simple as to be beyond explanation, yet a critical force in human behavior is the natural tendency to continue in the direction one is going. To go on doing what one is already doing is easier than choosing a new course (and when we look carefully at the process of choice making, we find it also calls for a great deal of courage). Staying with the ongoing momentum of activity is perhaps also psychophysiologically the most comfortable; we can continue the forward thrust or flow of a sequence of our self-expression and do not have to call on braking mechanisms. Of course, following one's momentum also means not having to acknowledge that one is going in a wrong direction.[48]

The Need for Consistency

For whatever reason, but undoubtedly including a basic insecurity about being alive, people have a terrible need to be consistent, or not to be inconsistent with themselves, so that once a position or a direction is established, people need to pursue that same course. A great deal of research in recent years on what has been called cognitive dissonance has shown that people will go to great lengths, emotionally as well as conceptually, to "prove" and justify their initial choice of principles and course of action.[49]

This same need for consistency leads to polarizations and projections of evil qualities onto one's opponents. In an extraordinarily lucid discussion of the principles of community conflict, James Coleman presents the following sequence, in which an opponent to one's ideas is made to appear totally bad.[50]

1. Initial single issue
2. Disrupts equilibrium of community relations
3. Allows previously suppressed issues against opponent to appear
4. More and more of opponent's beliefs enter into the disagreement
5. Opponent appears totally bad
6. Charges are made against the opponent as a person
7. Dispute becomes independent of initial disagreement

Before it is all over, the argument or feud exists for its own sake, regardless of what set it off. In small instances, it becomes a bad joke; in larger instances, it becomes a historical process that can determine life and death outcomes for many centuries.

Momentum Seeking Its Maximum and Structure Seeking Its Whole

In addition to a tendency to go on with whatever one is doing, we saw earlier that there appears to be a tendency in all of us to want to let the throttle out and "go all the way" with the potential thrust of an energy force. This tendency to complete a pattern, especially as one approaches the "final" unity of that pattern, is what Gestalt psychologists taught us earlier in this century about the tensions that structures themselves bring to our experiencing of reality. The concept of going all the way also has its example in biology, as we are taught that it is natural for certain parts of the human machinery to "fire" on an all-or-none basis. This notion of all-or-none behavior also appears in clinical psychology to describe certain people who are impulsive, easily seduced by excitement, unable to delay gratifications, and go all the way in their emotions and behavior.

Those are not idle words from the point of view of managing everyday life. In government, for example, one might conclude that there is reason to appoint an ombudsman or comptroller to monitor the late stages of projects and processes and to reevaluate them before they are completed "just because" they are so far along the way. The same advice can be given on the levels of individuals and families as well. For example, it is not at all wise to have children just because one has been married for some time. It is far better to submit such a choice to testing one's real desires to be a parent.

These dynamics apply even when the goal of a behavior sequence is clearly ugly and unspeakable. Once people get away with a certain amount of whatever they are doing, they seem to have a tendency to go on doing more of the same, not only in terms of power seeking and getting away with something, but also in terms of fulfilling that apparently archaic tendency to go all the way that seems to be deep within us all. So, if there are already human beings massed behind barbed wire, if we already have gone the route of beating them and perhaps of inadvertently killing a few of them in the course of the beatings, and if we swing naturally into defenses that remove us from consciousness of and experiencing what we are doing, the next "logical" step is to go even further and go the whole way toward a "final solution." It takes great wisdom and courage to stop the fast-moving train to Auschwitz.

The Precedence of Negative Process

An impressive number of observers have noted at various times that in the never-ending flow of positive and negative processes within human beings, individually as well as collectively, a natural precedence may well be given to the negative, disorganizing, or destructive elements. To my knowledge, this principle has not yet found relatively systematic acceptance by psychological theoreticians and is often not treated in textbooks of human behavior, but if it is correct — or to the extent that it is correct — it throws a great deal of light on man's never-ending disruptions of whatever successes he does achieve, whether in individual equilibrium, love relationships and family units, or community and international relations.

On the level of individual drives, the psychoanalyst Wilhelm Stekel has written:

> I have long ago answered the important question, which is primary in man, love or hate, in favor of hatred. . . . Pleasure presupposes pain. It creates its greatest strength from the effect of the contrast. Indeed, pain is unconditionally necessary as a contrast effect for the heightening of pleasure. . . . Our need to hate is just as great as our need to love. At the beginning as there is no one that can live without love, so there is also no being who can live without hate.[51]

According to psychiatrist Helm Stierlin, who concentrates especially on the complex condition of schizophrenia, psychiatric illness is a condition in which "vicious circles" of negative processes reign and interfere with the differentiation and growth of the human being. Once triggered, the momentum of the process, whether negative or positive, tends to feed on itself, following the laws of momentum and repetition.[52] "Nothing succeeds like success" is a positive antidote to the negative process, and the goal of much psychotherapy is to reteach the struggling, self-destructive patient how to balance out and reconcile the negative elements that are dominating his living experience with the positive forces in his being. Throughout life, all of us must face recurring challenges from the negative sides within us and the priority they claim.

In his analysis of community conflict processes, James Coleman goes so far as to support a Gresham's Law of Conflict.

> The harmful and dangerous elements drive out those which would keep the conflict within bounds. Reckless, unrestrained leaders head the attack; combat organizations arrive to replace the milder, more constrained pre-existing organizations; derogatory and scurrilous charges replace dispassionate issues; antagonism replaces disagreement, and a drive to ruin the opponent takes the place of the initial will to win. In other words, all forces put into effect by the initiation of conflict act to drive out the conciliatory elements, replace them with those better equipped for combat.[53]

Jerome Frank describes the inevitability of the drive for power in human beings:

> Neither the drive for power nor the potential for violence can be excised from the human psyche, especially since they are the obverse and reverse of a coin. The drive for power keeps humans perpetually dissatisfied by creating a permanent gap between performance and expectations: since their reach always exceeds their grasp, they will eventually feel frustrated no matter how well off they are; and since as likely as not the source of the frustration will be another human being or group of human beings whose drive for self-aggrandizement might have led them into a collision course, no degree of affluence or self-fulfillment will in itself assure that humans will live peacefully together.[54]

The Comfort of Repetition

There is a strangely comforting quality to repetition. Certain Greek and other Middle Eastern music, for example, repeat the same sounds over and over again; at first, the Western listener may wonder at the boring endlessness of it all, but before long he, too, is likely to be caught up in the joy and relief of familiarity and the pulsating power of sameness. When we see a familiar landmark or face, especially when we are far from home, there is almost an exhilaration of "familiarity" that leaps inside of us. Is it that the familiar reassures us that we are still the same? That we are still alive? That life is not altogether unknown and hazardous? Whatever the case, whether it is for no reason at all or for huge symbolic reasons that lie embedded within the inner meanings of sameness and repetition to our still-primitive beings, human beings do have a tendency to keep doing the same things and to derive much comfort from such repetition. Whatever people get involved with, including — God help us — genocide, they are inclined to get into the rut of whatever it is and do it more and more.

Activity — Any Kind — As an Antidote to Death Fears

Experimental psychologists have taught us that (1) given a situation of anxiety or need and (2) given a response on the part of the living organism that reduces its anxiety or need, (3) that same response is "reinforced" and the probability of its repetition is increased. Therefore, if we agree to the proposition that all human beings are afraid of nonaliveness and death, it follows that anytime human beings feel they are alive because of some activity, whatever the activity in which the human being is engaged has a high probability of being repeated further simply because that activity has become connected with some sense of mastery over nothingness. Of course, there are many considerations that will enter into the fuller equation that determines whether or not an activity will be repeated. For example, an activity that causes discomfort or leaves a bad taste will be negatively conditioned and will be less likely to be repeated, despite the fact that it was, in its own right, an active process. But I am suggesting that over and above whatever other positive and negative meanings or reinforcements are generated by destructiveness, destructive acts are vigorous experiences of being active and alive, and the very fact of their vigor relieves people of their anxiety about not being alive.

In the commonsense language of everyday life, when one has something to do, one is less afraid. "Give me something to do," the child insists of his parents; it is called "occupational therapy" in our psychiatric hospitals. Tragically, in adult life, the emptiness-banishing "something to do" can also be all manner of "routine" activities, including deploying human beings into death transports.

History's countless examples of war demonstrate that we experience erotic, heroic excitement when our sons go off to war and that in bitter battle, many neurotic symptoms disappear. A nation joined in the common task of defense is a nation enriched with a sense of purpose that puts a spring in many a man's step; paradoxically, such a time is more enlivening than periods of prosperity and the haunting fears of emptiness and isolation that cloud our minds in the "good times." More than a few individuals actually relish war as it puts an end to their unbearable, unspoken inner terrors of nothingness and meaninglessness.

It is only when it is too late, and the full measure of the stench and decay and horror of war is felt, that men know they have erred. For the longest time, the excitement of being forceful, vigorous, and triumphant (much of this through bringing about the death of the enemy) narcotizes even would-be good men. The basic truth is that the more one activates oneself purposefully and commits one's energy to living, whatever the ends to which such energies are committed, the dread, shaking inner terror of nonbeing recedes.

That is another way in which even genociding comes to represent an antidote to the killers' fear of nonlife. Add this sense of vitality to the other reinforcements of triumph over loneliness through losing oneself in intoxicated identification with a group and the magic triumph over life and death that comes from controlling the life and death of others, and we see that genocidal actions can build into an enormously satisfying and powerful thrust for reasons other than the actual meanings of the behavior. It becomes increasingly possible to conceive of the fact that many genociders don't really know what they are doing, because in many ways they are busy doing things that come naturally to scared people who are searching for antidotes to the fears of nonaliveness and death.

EXPERIENCE-DENYING MECHANISMS

There still remains a final sense in which we must continue to ask, How can human beings allow themselves to be ghastly killers? No matter how powerful the momentum of a group moving toward genocide, seeing oneself in a group that is on the road to mass killing must be an unbearable human experience. How in the name of God do otherwise decent human beings turn into genociders or their accomplices? Why don't more human beings break away from their groups when those groups turn to mass killings?

The best answer, if there is any, is that from a certain point on, human beings no longer really know what they are doing. Once human beings allow themselves to be drawn seriously into genocidal events, once they have surrendered their ability to choose *not* to be among the destroyers, there also come into play powerful experience-denying mechanisms. Otherwise it would be unbearable to experience the humanity of the victims destroyed.[55] The experience of the victim's human identity is more and more blotted out, and the experience of destroying life is more and more blotted out. What remains in the consciousness is largely a sense of reordering objects and things in one's environment and doing what is required by and for some larger purpose or ideology. What also remains is a sense of elation at being all-powerful, of being able to order one's environment, including the forces of life and death. The ultimate reality of ending other human beings' lives is rarely allowed to register in a real way.

That human beings are capable of a massive denial of their experiencing we know without question. Man is capable of full-blown amnesia. Man is capable of denying his own immediately imminent death. Frightened human beings are forever denying all manner of facts about themselves. Many people blot out their simplest joy wishes. Some people seemingly deny that they have genital organs and desires. Many people refuse to love so as not to feel hurt if they do not succeed.

Few of us are strong enough to admit our failings to ourselves, lest we suffer an overwhelming confirmation of our worst fears. Thus, there are few doctors who can acknowledge that they did not treat a patient wisely. Rarely do teachers acknowledge that they did not do their best to reach a student. Few parents are able to acknowledge that they have been less helpful to their children than they might have been. Denial is a psychological narcotic that we literally lavish on ourselves. And so, too, human beings deny the violent destruction they permit themselves to do to others.

Now the drama's pace quickens to the point of virtually no return.

The normal structures of our thinking are of no avail.

We enter a time and place that are made of all the hells ever described.

It is like the sulphuric hell of Sodom.

It is the incarnation of Satan and the Devil.

It is the worst conceivable madness of the insane.

It is the ultimate moment of triumph of a malignant cancer eating away at living cells.

Perhaps we should choose not to "understand" how human beings actually live out the ugly moments of no return when they become genociders. Perhaps it is better to leave the butchers entirely beyond understanding so that we can rail at them relentlessly. On the other hand, are we too afraid to understand that it is people like us who commit genocide? Do we fear becoming part of them? Are we fleeing discovery of our own potential to become mass murderers? It is agonizing to approach the black zone of hell that is the actual point at which people choose to commit genocide.

Aren't all these words I am writing unreal?

Is not this whole book and its purpose unreal?

These events of which we dare speak in such trivial words are so bloody and grotesque that only a madman can bear to search their meaning.

I want to scream!

I want to burn all these words!

I want to burn this book in the ovens of Auschwitz!

I want to throw away all these words on the refuse heaps of Hiroshima, Buchenwald, and Biafra!

I despise these words.

No, I don't wish to understand!

I would rather hate, despite, and fight!

And yet I dread not understanding. I dread that someday I, too, might allow myself to become an agent of death because I did not know how to choose life.

It is a choice we must all learn to make.[56] We need to understand more about how a man comes to be a genocider, how there is an ultimate choice for each person, for each person within his collective, and for each collective through its leadership and through its people. Most of all, we want to understand how man can learn to choose to affirm life.[57]

Interlude

THE AUSCHWITZ OF EVERYDAY LIFE

The sun rises on a beautiful light-washed day. Cool morning breezes greet us, and the stunning green of nature delights our sight and smell. The birds sing their songs of morn. The day's rhythm beats an invitation to work/sweat/joy.

It is a long but good day, and finally evening falls. Tired children embrace tired parents. Each miraculously brings renewed life to the other: the rippling laughter of a hug; a tender touch cheek to cheek; a walk amid neighborhood people and pets; ball games in which bold young muscles flex against their still-playful seniors; shopping larks for little and big people in magic souks of fabric and color; fun and fatigue. Before long, the night begins to deepen. Still ahead are eat-to-gethers, read-togethers, talk-togethers, and think-togethers. It is a rich life.

Finally, the children are off to sleep, and the moonglow beckons a greeting to Adams and Eves of all ages. The night music begins. Some sit on porches quietly listening to the music of the night and drinking in the star-moon sky. They talk in small whispers of rest and letting go from the turbulence of another day of doing and tiring. Others hear the music beating stronger in an ever-mounting cadence. Their mouths cling hungrily and tenderly to one another's juice giving. Their arms and legs entwine around each other. Their bolero rhythm quickens to a crescendo in which sweat-sparkling bodies lace, enter, capture one another, then sadly, beautifully part to the full quietness of the night in last-minute fond farewells and au revoirs.

* * *

The trouble is that life isn't all that beautiful after all. He tires of her, and she of him. They don't want it to be that way, but it happens.

Worse yet, he can't stand her, nor she him. In fact, he is terrified of her, and she of him. Each seems to be the nemesis that threatens the other's very being.

They try. Oh how they try. Nowadays people go to therapists and analysts and teachers and growth leaders. Some lucky ones find the path, but there are so many who, even with helping counsel, only confirm their haplessness. So they move on to stand before cynical, bored justices of the land who duly confirm the dissolution of their marriage. "I've never been so happy in my life. It's like a terrible weight has been lifted from me," they say. But then there often follows a terrible loneliness, and the divorce is no longer a festival.

The therapists and analysts of the Western world try hard, for themselves no less than for others. They, too, seek their own gurus. The first idealized and disappointing therapist is followed by a second, and often there is a number three, and even numbers four and five. The seekers hope after hope that their own great men and women will lead them through the valley of darkness. But as the years go by, they are stunned to see many of their leaders grown fat and locked into their own patterns of rigidity and limitation.

At home, the children stop touching and hugging. Often they snarl and sneer. They attack. When they are big enough to be less afraid, they turn vengefully on their parents' most treasured beliefs and ceremonies. Bloodshot, tear-streaked parents' eyes look at their once apple-tender little ones and find little sweetness in them. The generations stand and look at each other across yawning chasms of disappointment. Each breathes, "You hurt me too much. I trusted you, and you hurt me too much." Now and again, children who wanted better see their parents' spirits die, and something in them dies too. Some tragic children spin desperately in an autistic world, cowering from the nothingness about them. "He was always such an easy baby. Never a moment of trouble; he would lie there in his crib quietly amusing himself for hours." Other children see the stillness spreading toward them and are wise enough to explode in a desperate protest. One parent says: "I don't know where he learns such things. In our home he never heard a cross word." The other says: "We are a devoted family. Everything is neatly in order in our home." Yet the child turns tough and cruel. He himself does not know that he is trying to defeat the sterility that threatens to rid him of energy and life, and the parents do not know what they did to him—for, truly, they had meant well.

It is not always bad, of course. For many people there are family festivals graced with heartwarming cheer and garnished capon. The beloved holidays and festivals come anew each year. New children are born, and family chains are lengthened. There are birthdays and anniversaries. There are also days of common tragedy to bring families together. Friendly generations meet one another in common rituals grown familiar over the years. For many fortunate people, the year-round calendar is blessed with embrace, conversation, and contact.

And yet, all too often, tragedy strikes even these happier family groups. Often, the tragedy is from without as if the devil fate mocks those who dared too much to be joyful. Everywhere on our planet, screeching automobile tires announce the shattering of just-now-alive human bodies. Everywhere freak accidents unpredictably fell good people. An electric circuit goes crazy and burns a man to death. A factory machine turns vampire and devours the man who was feeding it a moment before. An unexpected embolism chokes off the life breath of a patient at the very moment when he is being treated by an able physician. An otherwise life-saving remedy turns silent killer of some unfortunate patients.

All around, vulture-viruses sit perched on the ledge of life waiting to see who of us will fall. Many times, one senses that somehow people themselves are inviting nature to do its worst. People burn themselves up in fierce hates they cannot control. Others are so devotedly glued together in goodness that they do not gather the momentum to be alive for themselves, and, finally, brave muscles and nerves go flaccid and die. Still other potent tragedies are born directly of human acts, though often the people doing the acts did not mean to be destructive. They didn't know. Often they are trying to make the world more perfect. Sometimes they try so hard to make the world better that anyone who differs with them has to be eliminated, and they delude themselves that they are bringing death in the name of life.

Everywhere there are shattered life dreams and veritable Auschwitzes.

*   *   *

Below just about everybody's surface, there is a story of worry and agony. There are little expressions of this truth in our language—for example, "Everyone has his load to bear"—but the real truth of the process is far deeper than such expressions convey. One difficulty is that people generally don't acknowledge consciously the hell of their lives for fear of being overwhelmed with greater pain. Another difficulty is that people are embarrassed to speak candidly of their problems to one another lest they appear to be a failure in the eyes of others. Many unnerving experiences are kept private (or seemingly so), and the result is that each person then must deal with his painful problems and defeats relatively alone, not knowing that his neighbors behind their white picket fences are cut of the same cloth.

One result is that cultures often do not develop enough helpful folk concepts so that people can learn that it is best to anticipate deeply painful experiences throughout their lives. The prevailing culture motif remains that life is only or mainly beautiful. What gets lost in the pretend folk pictures of life is the lesson that all people need to yield to many deep hurts in their lives and then work back from their pain to win once again. Cultures that downplay life's hells weaken people because they are not prepared for the realities of life. People are not taught honestly that serious problems in life are inevitable. They also are not taught how difficulties are intrinsic to the creative process of life.

Consequently, many people panic at hurt and fright and problems and run away. Sometimes these are "easy" escapes. They simply get fat. Or dull. Or they earn thousands of millions of dollars and believe they are now happy. Or they accept some magic belief in some person idol or ism idol. There is a very real price for all of these easy escapes. No matter that the people look as if they are having an easy time; in the real inner worlds of the too fat, too rich, and overly assured, there is a sad loss of being and a failure to feel alive.

There are other escapes from life's pain that are even more serious and life shattering. Some people flee to the very arms of psychosomatic deaths. The emotions they cannot master surface in the form of diseases that corrode and explode their bodies, hearts, and brains. There are also millions of people who flee to madness and, in effect, kill their spirits. There are also many other people who "succeed" in turning their flight from life into a frenzied gallop of brutalities and death dealing to others. They sacrifice/murder the other as if to say, "Take him, not me!" All around us, man's world is a slaughterhouse altar on which desperate, primitive men sacrifice one another to the gods in the hope that they themselves will be spared nonaliveness and death.

Damn it!

Damn all life-killing cancers and heart failures!

Damn the idiocy of wars!

Damn the monstrosity of mental illness!

Damn all fatness, drunkenness, and stupidity!

Life is beautiful!

Life is worth living!

Is there anyone who knows the route?

Is there a passage from hell to hope?

Where, if at all, is there a map of life?

We don't know, yet for many of us a sense builds that there may be a path from Auschwitz to life and that the path begins whenever man dares to know the Auschwitz within him and about him.

We are all of us humans living in the face of death. In all our lives, death is behind us, around us, and ahead of us. We live even our finest hours amid the puzzle and mystery of nothingness and death. The staggering richness of the joy of life is always surrounded by grim, bleak Auschwitz camps. We are each on our own exciting, painful journey through life. Along the way we meet one another. Often we think and hope that one or another of us will know the way and will rescue us from the perils of our voyage. But the truth is that this is never so. No one really knows a sure way. The best we can do is walk together some of the way, sometimes holding hands and enjoying the pleasures of friendship, even loving, but still knowing that we must each walk our own path.

*   *   *

Is it possible that the Auschwitz of everyday life is a metaphor of which the real smokestacks of Auschwitz are a concrete representation?

Is it possible that Auschwitz casts into deadly real-life sculptures the hell that is each man's private living and dying?

I believe so.

I believe we need to understand the private concentration camp that makes up much of each person's life. Instead of pretending that life is good and then discovering at the ovens that it is not so, we need to know the facts of hurt and rage and revenge. We need to know the capricious and demonic nature of our being and how easily we turn cruel. Instead of avoiding our human agonies and hells until it is too late and the oven flames are leaping at us, we need to learn how to struggle with our demonic natures. We dare never forget our common roots in Auschwitz; then, perhaps, we shall begin to find the way out.

Part Two

WHEN DOES MAN COMMIT GENOCIDE?

The Massacres in Indonesia

On October 21 and 22, 1965, communist-controlled workers', peasants' and youth organizations began savagely attacking their enemies in cities and towns of Central Java. The military acted with speed and vigor to restore security.

They distributed arms to anti-communist groups to help in hunting down communists. In the foreign press, the ensuing savage violence in Indonesia has been likened to Stalin's purges in the 20's and 30's, to Hitler's pogroms in the 40's, to the communal violence in India and Pakistan at the time of partition (1947), and to the Chinese Communists' liquidation of landlords and bourgeoisie in the 50's. None of these parallels is appropriate, in my judgment, for the tragedy in Indonesia was partly systematized liquidation by government security forces.

What Happened?

How widespread was the massacre of communists in Indonesia? Reports indicate that it was not limited to Java, where communist strength was greatest, but took place in North Sumatra, Bali, Flores, Timor, Celebes and other areas as well. It was rampant in those areas where the rivalry and tension had been sharpest between the Indonesian Communist Party (PKI) and other parties, notably the Muslim (NU) and Nationalist (PNI) parties, in East Java and Bali for example.

In terms of numbers killed, it is impossible to give exact figures. In January President Sukarno announced, for foreign consumption primarily, the results of a government fact-finding commission: 87,000 people had been killed in what followed the October 21st events. Immediately thereafter the Armed Forces daily gave the figure 78,000 with a regional breakdown. As time has elapsed, the estimates have gone up. The *New York Times'* early dispatches spoke of 100,000. Later, in March, the figure was 200,000. And in his May *New York Times* magazine article, Seth King had little difficulty in accepting 300,000 as a moderate estimate. Stanley Karnow in his April 17 *Washington Post* report based on personal observation on Java and Bali, "calculates that the post-coup holocaust took at least half a million lives."

And more recently still, the Prime Minister of Australia visiting in the U.S.A. spoke of between half a million and a million casualties. This may include persons arrested and imprisoned as well as those executed or massacred.

In any case, it appears likely that some hundreds of thousands were killed and more hundreds of thousands imprisoned. . . .

> **Margaret Mead on Indonesia**
>
> Docile cultures may be deceptively peaceful in that they have not learned to deal with aggression. Case at point: The natives of Bali who rose up recently and Indonesia leaders who massacred 100,000 or more in recent riots.
>
> —Donald C. Drake
> *Philadelphia Inquirer*
> November 2, 1965

Not Only the Government Killed

Who did the killing? Again the situation is complex. At least four categories of persons were involved. First the army, particularly the Commando units were dispatched to the regions about the middle of October to "clean up" and "restore security." The military apparently supplied weapons to local anti-communists who then participated in the killing too. Much of the killing on the village level was done by groups of Muslim Youth, Nationalist Youth and others who used whatever weapons were at hand—knives, sickles, bamboo spears, anything. Finally, the police executed (and reportedly continue to execute) those turned over to them whom they judge to have been directly involved in planning the coup. There is no need to dwell here on the grisly details except to make clear that it was an incredibly cold-blooded, savage operation in which the victims were women and children as well as men.

One educated guess has it that about 25% of the total were killed by the army, 10% by local anti-communists armed by the military and the rest by the people and the police. . . .

Some journalists, notably in the *New York Times* and *Time,* have suggested that the massacre was a manifestation of "amok," a Malay word referring to an emotional explosion in which the actor strikes out blindly and murderously at any who crosses his path until he himself is subdued or killed. True, many Indonesians have felt heavy pressures—political, economic, psychological and moral—in the latter years of Guided Democracy. But the violent reaction was not blind and irrational. It was popular and collective, and directed at those who were felt to be threatening the nation. Explaining the event by suggesting that the nation ran "amok," is, in my judgment, both inaccurate and simplistic for a phenomenon as complex as this. . . . This response of eliminating the enemy in a situation of crisis is not at odds with the moral and religious sensibilities of Indonesians. Observers have noted how persons questioned about the violence and slaughter answered that the victims were evil and had to be liquidated. One notices the tendency to polarize good and evil. Many Muslims interpreted the affair as "jihad," or holy war against the unbelievers—"atheistic communists"—who, if they prevailed, would bring disaster to the community of the faithful. Catholics and Protestants too had no difficulty finding Scriptural support, especially in the Old Testament, for radical conflict to defeat and destroy those who oppose "God's law and his people." If one views this tragic event against the background of the "way-ang" or shadow puppet plays which play such an important role in Javanese and Balinese life and thinking, the struggle with the communists can be likened to the struggle of Ardjuna, the hero in the Mahabaratta, or Rama, the hero of the Ramayana, in their wars to vindicate the good and the right against evil and wrong. In both cases, the outcome is a great slaughter of the enemies.

—Frank L. Cooley, "The Massacres in Indonesia: How an Accumulation of Social Ills, Political Rigidity, and Religious Militancy Produced a Slaughter Without Parallel in Southeast Asia," *Fellowship,* September 1966

7

THE HUMAN BEINGS WHO ARE TO BE THE GENOCIDERS: THE INDIVIDUAL, THE FAMILY, AND THE GROUP AS WE KNOW THEM IN THEIR "BETTER DAYS"

I recognize in my children potential parricides as I recognize in myself a potential infanticide—especially when the going gets rough. I am keenly aware of those drives which, under radically altered conditions of living, could elicit from me the behavior of a Nazi Gauleiter or SS man. I have no illusions about human nature.

—Rabbi Alan Miller

The contemporary marriage and family structure . . . does not seem able to produce enough loving, caring, socially responsible citizens to reverse man's self-destructive course.

—Herbert A. Otto

London. Pandemonium halted a David Cassidy pop concert in London on Sunday night as thousands of screaming teenagers, most of them girls, crushed forward toward the stage. The besieged White City Stadium resembled a battlefield when it was over, witnesses said. Estimates of the injuries went as high as 1,000.

—Associated Press, May 28, 1974

When one or another genocide is all over, the rest of us twentieth-century moderns say to ourselves, "What kind of human beings could have done that?" The honest answer is, "Nearly all of us normal people," but that is so terrifying that the question is generally not pursued. We say instead: "They must have been madmen." "They must have been

139

unbelievable monsters." "What can you expect of a primitive people? Even their educated class is one step away from the jungle." "_____ (name of dictator) was crazy. People will suffer so long as there are madmen like him around." All of the answers in one way or another beg the central question of how it is that human beings like us, "born in the image of God" could allow themselves to be killers of masses of living people.

In this chapter, we want to look at (ourselves) the human beings who are going to be genociders before they become so. We want to see the human beings who are to be the genociders in the normality of their everyday lives as individuals, as they participate in the very special, ostensibly most loving collective that is their family, and as they undergo collective or group experiences. When we are finished, we want to emerge with a clearer, better-founded picture of the normal human being as he or she really is, not as he or she still appears in the texts of most present-day psychologies and ethics – an ostensibly "normal" person who is free of evil and madness.

THE INDIVIDUAL WHO IS TO BE THE GENOCIDER

The human being who is to be a genocider is deeply frustrated at all times. This might not be that much of a limitation were it not for the fact that much of the time he is busy denying his terror. In his "better days," he is energetically impressive at this or that brilliant invention, tantalizing commerce, exhilarating recreation, and disarmingly happy-appearing family life. Yet, the truth is that in those days, too, he is pounded deep within by waves of agonizing fright that remind him over and over again of the blackness and inevitable meaninglessness that is soon to come.

Many observers of infancy and childhood have concluded that even from the outset of life, the human infant carries a fair share of the human burden and challenge of anxiety. Along with the beautiful, red-cheeked, wholesome innocence of infancy, there is for every infant an enormous dose of fear, upset, and rage. Of course, whatever the infant feels is mediated to a large extent through his experiences within his family group, especially through the mysterious bonds of feeling between the infant and his mother and his father and also through the insistently powerful, silent connection between the father and mother. It turns out, in fact, that the infant's distressing experiences result not only from inner feelings of vulnerability or premonitions of mortal destiny, but also from the fact that the beloved human beings who are the infant's parents often turn out to be thoughtless, superficial, selfish, terrified, bitter, unstable, callous, cruel, or sadistic and to have any number of other variations of human weakness.

It is a sad and dangerous path the human infant travels. In the process, the infant suffers a series of painful "immunizations" to the truth of human experience. Slowly but surely, there grow within his heart and mind deeply felt traces of the truth that mother and all life speak with forked tongues, whip with forked switches, hurt, disappoint, and enrage in countless ways.[1]

Along this "trek" toward their own future adulthood, many children "die." Some children "die" of the dread mental disorder, infantile autism. The autistic infant appears to give up his very humanity and to spin endlessly in the space of his unformed person. Beyond the tragedy of each autistic child and his family, there is a larger meaning as to just how much damage a nurturing human being can do to another, without intending to do so and without knowing that one is doing so. Despite the present-day vogue of attributing autism to an unknown neurological defect and/or genetic weakness, no one who has ever seen the incredible phenomenon of lovely looking, well-educated, consciously well-meaning parents forgetting to pick up their infant for hours on end can ever forget that many human "deaths" to autism are wrought by other people.[2] Nor need it be unclear to any of us who have experienced at one time or another a strange skeletal coldness that can issue from otherwise beautifully shaped fingers and bodies that it is possible for people to transmit soundless psychological hurts. A parent's hands can touch the skin of an infant seemingly nurturingly, but if the hands are in truth ominous, cold talons, they will terrorize the child. Anyone who has experienced a cadaverlike iciness in an otherwise attractive sexual partner should be able to imagine how it would feel to an infant to repeatedly experience such a terror-frozen quality.

Erich Fromm has described graphically how much of the development of the human spirit can be tracked over a course that begins in a bloom of innocence and moves through a sequence of hurt, disappointment, and demoralization.[3] If at any point there are massive or traumatic hurts that are beyond the ability of the tender person to digest, the result is a burdening of the human heart with hurt and rage that will be expressed over the years in various unhappy outcomes, including explosions of retaliatory vengefulness and violence.

What is not always understood is that each and every human child is obliged to live through such a developmental sequence. It is not as if we might someday create ideal conditions wherein we will no longer need to burden children with any serious hurts to their innocence and trust. On the contrary, insofar as some parents or societies have attempted too much to protect children from experiencing themselves as the objects of frustration, hurt, and danger, those children have been denied the capacity to develop their fullest abilities.[4] They do not learn to trust themselves to be able to live through hurt and to be able to reorganize themselves from their own reservoirs of potential strength. Those children are also denied sufficient impetus for separating emotionally from their parents and from their child-dependent roles in their society. Often they do not learn how to experience themselves as shapers of their lives and of their society, and they remain slavish conformists to the existing norms that determine their lives.

A beautiful paper by the late British psychoanalyst and pediatrician Donald Winnicott discusses the naturalness and inevitability of every child suffering the hate of his mother.[5] On the simplest level, every mother at some point necessarily will find herself tired, depleted, and challenged beyond her resources to cope. It is an entirely natural fact that she, like all human beings, then turns to anger as a protest against being depleted and as a way of stirring her energy machinery to replenish her. How the mother and child then live out their experience of hating, being hated, and hating in return and how they reconnect their experience of hating and being hated to their loving and being loved become great dramas of the development of the human spirit. Winnicott argues forcefully that in many cases of serious emotional disturbances, the person we now see as a patient never enjoyed a constructive experience of being hated, he did not learn to link the experience of being hated with being loved, not did he learn to link his natural hatred with his also natural capacity and wish to love. Winnicott therefore proposes that one of the most important experiences the psychotherapist can give his patient (especially the very sick ones) is the constructive experience of being hated by the therapist. This way, the patient may learn of his undeveloped capacity to bear hurts and to bear his own hatred, and to link them to his wishes and readiness to love and be loved.

Psychiatrist Joseph Rheingold has described what happens as human beings unknowingly experience the unrecognized hatred of their own mother.[6] Rheingold also postulates that all mothers necessarily experience moments of hatred toward their children. However, his emphasis is on the particularly destructive consequences of the mother's hatred insofar as she seeks to deny her hatred to the child and to herself. Despite the mother's denial, the child incorporates her unrecognized hatred unknowingly within himself, but then makes every effort to maintain the illusion that mother only loves him and never wishes to hurt or destroy him. The end result is that because of his denied feelings of his mother's hatred of him, the child—and later the adult—becomes a "carrier" who transmits the same anger and hate toward others, such as his own children.

It is a proven principle of psychotherapy that people are better off when they can recognize destructive feelings directed at them and when they can acknowledge the destructive feelings they themselves have and direct toward others. People often go out of their minds because they don't dare define honestly to themselves how much they feel hated by someone else; when the truth is acknowledged, it doesn't change the facts, and yet they feel much better. Similarly, when people acknowledge their own murderous feelings and wishes, the likelihood of impulsive acting out is significantly reduced. The more one denies rage burning deep inside oneself, the more the relationship remains distorted and the more there is a likelihood of the rage's erupting in destructiveness or overt violence.

Earlier we saw that at our present stage of evolution, a majority of human beings are available to follow instructions to do serious, even potentially lethal, harm to a fellow human being. Milgram's so-called Eichmann Experiment and the follow-up studies in the United States and Germany confirmed man's incredible obedience to authority when instructed to be destructive, even for the flimsiest of reasons. So, too, we recall that penetrating observers of the human condition, such as the late Father Thomas Merton and Albert Camus, have grappled with the disturbing fact that the mass killers of Nazi Germany were for the most part not clinically abnormal. They were apparently versions of what many of us could be.

One important difference that did begin to emerge between the genociders and other people was that the killers seem to perceive other people as *things*, which need to be arranged and ordered, rather than as humans. However, the mechanism of "thinging" people, or seeing people as if they are not of our species, does not appear only in emotionally disturbed or immature people or only under conditions of significant emotional stress. The tendency to "thing" people and denude them of their humanity and membership in the human race is fairly easily evoked in most of us by any situation that, wittingly or unwittingly, makes it possible for us to relate to people in this way. Thus, psychologist Philip Zimbardo assigned college students role-playing tasks as jailers of other students who were given the role of "prisoner" and "locked up" on one floor of a university building, which was to be the jail.[7] The students who became the jailers of their fellow students were in no way distinguished beforehand for their toughness, meanness, or known emotional problems. Yet, within a few days, they had become increasingly dominating, cruel, and sadistic to a point where the experiment had to be prematurely discontinued, as much on behalf of the "humanity" of the student jailers as for the student prisoners. Given a situation in which there is inequality or one person has power over another, most human beings seem to be drawn into increasingly excessive aggression and exploitation of another's weaknesses.

Another interesting demonstration of how people are given to imposing their authority on others once they have gained a modicum of control over them comes from the work of David Rosenhan, who sent eight professional and lay people to mental hospitals with an initial report that they had been hallucinating.[8] Once admitted to a hospital, these emotionally healthy people refrained from any further complaints, yet, without exception, they were held for long periods in the hospital and were diagnosed as suffering from schizophrenia. The same experiment was repeated in twelve hospitals in five East Coast and West Coast states. When released, each and every one of the fake patients was diagnosed as "schizophrenia in remission." When Rosenhan's findings were shared with mental hospital colleagues, they were aghast, and in one case, the staff of an excellent teaching and research hospital argued that such misdiagnosis could not possibly occur in their institution. It was agreed that within the following three months, Rosenhan would send some of his "patients" to that hospital, and the bet would be whether the hospital staff would be able to identify those nonpatients among their admissions. In the weeks that followed, different members of the staff identified 41 phonies out of 193 patients who were admitted to the hospital during that time. In point of fact, Rosenhan had sent *no* pseudopatients to that hospital during the test period.

Psychiatrist-psychoanalyst Thomas Szasz has argued for many years that mental illness is a myth that serves the power needs of people over one another.[9] The new family psychotherapists of the past twenty years have demonstrated that many patients who previously would have appeared to require the offices of a mental hospital no longer require hospitalization if an immediate effort is made to treat the family as a group and to modify their ways of communicating their emotions to one another.[10] Clearly, human beings—including the mental health professionals—all too regularly and readily label one another as inferior, definitionally different, and unworthy.

The work of Rosenhan, Zimbardo, Milgram and many others also leads us to another critical conclusion that human beings easily fall into whatever roles are assigned to them by the given structure or situation in which they find themselves. Too often, too many of us do not know how to define ourselves from within, and unknowingly, we take whatever direction we are pointed in by others. If, moreover, those who point us are authoritarian and instruct us to mistreat others, many of us will be available to execute the destructive acts they prescribe, although acting on our own we would never have done such things.

People's responses to the actual destructiveness around them also raises serious questions. The tragic story of Kitty Genovese[11] once and for all puts an end to the rationalization that most people become passive bystanders out of a natural human fear of risking death at the hands of a murderer. It also puts to rest another partly true rationalization that people are afraid to intervene because under many state laws in the United States, good samaritans expose themselves to legal hazards for their courage and goodness.

Bystander studies in social psychological laboratories (many of which were specifically inspired by the Genovese tragedy) seem to indicate that whether or not human beings who witness hurt and tragedy will involve themselves depends to a great extent on whether they think of themselves as individuals who see another human being in trouble or as members of a group or crowd of onlookers. Too often, when people see tragedy from the perspective of an anonymous member of a group of bystanders, they deny themselves the experience of feeling individually involved with the humanity of the victim and his or her cry for help. When human beings do think of themselves as individuals in such situations, the odds increase significantly that they will take some meaningful action on behalf of the victim.[12]

Whether or not people go to help a fellow being depends on other psychological mechanisms as well. Psychologist John Darley set up a situation in which theological students on their way across campus encountered a groaning, coughing "victim" slumped in a doorway.[13] To add a touch of irony (and an important experimental variation) to it all, some of those same students had been asked beforehand to prepare a short, impromptu talk on the parable of the Good Samaritan, and a second or control group had been asked to speak on the neutral subject of vocations. The experimental drama took place when the students were walking across the campus to a laboratory where they were to tape their speeches. The experimental design also had the students subdivided further: At the time of the walk across campus and the encounter with the victim, some of the students had been told they were already late for their session, others had been told they were due at the lab at any moment, and others had been told they had plenty of time. Overall, 60 percent of the theological students passed the victim by. Of the 40 percent who did stop to help, only 10 percent were those who had been told to hurry because they were late. To be a real-life good samaritan evidently means having more time on one's hands; the majority of those who helped were those who had been told they had plenty of time. Thus, another consideration in viewing the history of indifference, selfishness, and tacit acceptance of hurt to other human beings is simply whether or not people feel they have the time to help. A person who is in a hurry does not have the time to help – even if he is on his way to preach to us all to be good samaritans.

The Not-So-Pretty Picture of the Individual of Our Species

We can conclude that man is in many respects selfish and harassed, so lacking in identity as not to be able to experience any connection to the tragedy of another. We can also conclude that even in his "better days," the human being who is to be the genocider is driven to relegate others to inferior status and to harass and exploit them. Whatever the established order, no matter how manifestly unjust, people agree to accept the authority of their society and to maintain the established status quo. The individual who is to be the genocider is easily led and available to conform to instructions to destroy others, even on relatively flimsy grounds. He is deeply suggestible and often takes his direction from a given situation instead of defining his course on the basis of his own values. It can also be concluded that human beings do not know very much about how to handle the sequences of hatred and being hated that are their natural lot, along with life's gifts of loving and being loved. Overall, the individual who is to be the genocider is a terrified human being, but he is largely unaware of his terror. In his unknown terror, he is available to do much harm to others, to assist others who are destructive, or to stand by during the destruction of others. It is not a pretty picture, but what may be reassuring is that it is not necessarily a picture of overwhelming meanness so much as it is a picture of tremendous weakness and unawareness at our present stage of human development.

THE FAMILY LIFE OF THE HUMAN BEINGS WHO ARE TO BE THE GENOCIDERS

Human beings by and large treasure their families – or at least want to. There is little else in life that offers so much reassurance and promise of comfort than connection to one's family. It has been remarked over and over again that at times of crisis and tragedy, it is our family relatives who give meaning and comfort at times of illness, death, natural disasters, and so on. Even anniversaries of sadness and loss bring family groups together in almost festive gatherings. Conversely, there is little in life that is as thrilling as the birth of new life; this happy event brings families together in grand celebration, and over the years, the family group gathers to celebrate and recelebrate the unfolding of its members' lives on birthdays and other milestone days. Strangely, no matter how prosaic and repetitive any or all of these gatherings become, they are savored and welcomed by most people as opportunities to repair one's courage to live on.

It is not surprising that in most cultures, the overwhelmingly accepted and conscious picture of family life is one of mutual devotion, caring, and companionship, if not love. And yet, we know that all is not at all well in family life. The rate of breakdown of family units seems to leap higher every day in the Western world, and as for families that do not actually part, it is no secret that many of them are riddled with bitterness, emptiness, and despair. Yet, the fact that the modern family is riddled by divorce and breakdown in ever-increasing, epidemic numbers has generally still not affected the prevailing image of family life. In the face of all the evidence of family misery and breakdown, we still believe in the traditional, idealistic picture of family life with remarkable tenacity. Indeed, an important contributor to family problems is the still widely supported illusion that normal families do not experience serious conflict and disappointment and that when serious conflicts are present, they are signs of disturbance and pathology.[14]

The real facts of human family life are that families are both sources of immensely positive experiences of joy and connection and arenas of painful, even murderous, experiences. Here again is the dialectic of life and death. The challenge of family life is very much like the challenge of life itself: a unique opportunity to seek the greatest measure of aliveness (family joy) along with an acceptance of the inevitability of vulnerability and loss (heart-breaking hurts and separations) as integral parts of that opportunity for aliveness and family connection and pleasure.

We do not have to go far to tie down our understanding of the capacity of a normal, everyday man for destructiveness within his own family group. If we turn to the classic document of Western culture, the Bible, we find ample records of family destructiveness. The allegory of Cain and Abel, for example, is a powerful harbinger of what is to come in all of family life. Here in the first family of human history, two of the principals lock in bitter role polarity and jealousy that ends in actual murder. We don't go much further before we encounter father Abraham, who is prepared to sacrifice his son, Isaac, to God's commands – and mother Sarah, who does nothing to intervene.[15] For people for whom the latter remark is too-heady heresy, it can be noted that there are actual legends in the traditional Hebraic folklore that say that Sarah was aware of what was happening; modern family therapy would argue that a mother could not help but be aware of such a dastardly plot against her child by her husband.[16] The Bible is full of murders and attempted murders. Parents banish and slay their children. Children banish and slay their parents. Spouses and lovers plot, condemn, and execute one another. If these are the *recorded* events of biblical family life, there must also have been innumerable unrecorded acts of violence, as we learn from modern evidence.

Family life is a never-ending arena of actual and symbolic destruction. For example, it has now been established that in several societies, a significant number of homocides take place within the family itself and a considerable, additional number take place within the family's extended network of relationships (such as triangular sexual situations). Marvin Wolfgang's landmark study in Philadelphia identified the nature of the acquaintance between pairs of murderers and their victims. They were relatives 25 percent of the time, paramours in 10 percent of the cases, close friends in 20 percent of the cases, and acquaintances in 14 percent of the cases. Only some 12 percent were strangers to one another.[17] A cross-cultural study by Stuart Palmer showed that in forty-one out of forty-four societies studied, murder victims and killers were rarely strangers.[18]

Recent years have also brought new information to light as to the high incidence of the battered child syndrome. These are matters that people do not like to talk about, and only in very recent years have such problems begun to receive scientific attention and public credibility. David Gil estimates that over 2 million cases of child abuse occur every year in the United States. "In most incidents of child abuse the caretakers involved are 'normal individuals' exercising their prerogative of disciplining a child whose behavior they find in need of correction."[19]

Emotional Murders in Family Life

Beyond actual killings and batterings, all observations of modern family life tell us that most people are having a very rough time of it. Certainly, in the United States of the last thirty or forty years, most family members fail to achieve emotional stability or a rewarding sense of themselves as being loving and joyous. Regularly cited divorce statistics are that now close to one out of every two marriages actually dissolves. Moreover, at least another third of the marriages that do last are far from satisfying and represent states of accommodation, surrender, indifference, bitterness, and muted rage.

Data from child guidance clinics concerned with the problems of millions of youngsters tell us that most psychological problems of children are linked to serious, unresolved marriage and family problems and hatreds, and that at least one major meaning of most children's psychological symptoms is that they are messages of family distress. From mental hospitals, where millions of Americans spend some time of their lives, and from the network of psychological and psychiatric services for adults, available in community mental health centers and through private practice, we learn that distressed and demoralized marital and family situations are the context for many emotional breakdowns, which then require treatment of the couple or family as if they were an individual patient. There is no end to the evidence of family turmoil in the background of many other human agonies. Many addicts are found to be fleeing from domination by their families. In the general practitioner's offices, as many as 75 percent of the patients appear in response to conditions that are intrinsically psychosomatic – that is, conditions in which the patient's worries predominate – and they are most often centered in the patient's family experiences.

Where and when are all these agonizing events taking place in families? If we look at the seemingly simple events of family life with our inner machinery for intuitive, symbolic comprehension of emotions, we discover that all through normal family life there are powerful hurts, antagonisms, rivalries, splits, attacks, and emotional murders. We gather at our family breakfasts and are seemingly occupied with the pedestrian tasks of having our eggs and sharing the small talk of the day – loving, angry, or indifferent. Yet there is a larger sense in which we are really busy living out the much more fundamental process of defining our deepest identities in relation to one another through complex maneuverings for position and power, and often actual threats and attempted attacks and invasions of one another's integrity. What is most deceptive is that the deadly side of this process is generally played out right alongside of, and literally within, the sincerely caring and loving exchanges. Even at happier and better-integrated times in family life, there is a continuous psychological stream of annihilating impulses and experiences being played on in the family.[20]

We see the destructive side of our family lives in each of the many situtions in which one family member presses another to supply or ensure meaning for the first member's experience of living. There are many ways to so trap another person's being: demands of obedience and conformity, attempts to trap another in return for overgiving, assuming too much responsibility for another's development, and so on. Too often, *giving* in family life actually is contaminated by fierce emotional demands for oneself, advantage seeking, gratitude claiming, or threats of attack and wiping out. "Eat, learn, love, grow – for me – or else!"

No less important is whether or not one allows oneself to be invaded, possessed, or annihilated. So often *taking* emotional support from another is not for one's own genuine self-comfort but for the purposes of trapping the giver into being obligated to produce more of the same or of working the giver around to being on the receiving end again. In addition, we should not overlook the series of decisions family members make as to whether or not to serve as accomplices or indifferent bystanders to trapping maneuvers and destructiveness between other members of the family.

These challenges cannot be solved by avoidance or by efforts to immerse oneself in unending family love and devotion. For many well-intentioned human beings, the solution to such issues has been to generate enough great love and caring to triumph over all hate and destructiveness. However, insofar as this well-intentioned strategy only to love leads to an effort to suppress all tensions that build around natural dominating, attacking, and annihilating feelings, the result is a kind of make-believe that actually saps the emotional vitality of family members.[21] Much of human strength comes precisely from mastering the challenges to be neither an annihilator of others nor a victim to be annihilated. Those who avoid the challenge end up pseudostrong.

Frequently, altogether nice parents give their child a far worse break by not giving the child someone to fight against. In adolescence and adult mental health work, we find that many children who were formerly too successful are unequal to the emotional challenges of their own separate lives. There is overwhelming evidence that the family group that doesn't live out conflicts fosters the worst kind of weakness in one or another of its members, and often sets itself up for an ultimate breaking apart that can be sudden and total and relentless.[22]

Family life affords basic training in touching and being touched by other human beings and enables us to learn to experience and enjoy a never-ending cycle of recurring attractions and repulsions, comforts and dangers – where each side of the experience always implies the potential of the other. It follows that for all of us, coping with destructiveness – what I might do to another, and what I fear will be done to me – is a central issue of life and one of the key purposes of family life is to provide an arena for experiencing and learning and learning to cope with destructiveness – our own and that of others.

**In Family Life, as in Larger Groups, Man Lives Out
a "Foreign Policy" for War and Peace**

It is fascinating, and I think useful, to extend these observations of the true transactions of family life to comparisons with the ways communities and nations develop their relationships and foreign policies in intergroup and international events. There appear to be many parallels. Consider the following sequences of complementarities in family life and in affairs between nations (see Figure 7.1).

FIGURE 7.1　　The "Foreign Policy" Needs of People and Nations Have Much in Common

PEOPLE
AND
NATIONS
MUST:

SEEK TO BE SEPARATE

YIELD TO NEEDING OTHERS

SEEK PEACEFUL ALTERNATIVES

*DEVELOP THEIR ABILITIES
TO FIGHT BACK IN SELF-DEFENSE*

SEEK NOT TO BE VICTIMS

NOT BECOME KILLERS

People and nations must seek to be separate and be able to define their boundaries, territory, and identity against threats of and efforts at hurt, attack, and invasion. Yet people and nations also must yield to needing others, for even the strongest people and nations necessarily are incapable of meeting all of life's challenges.

One way to diffuse would-be aggression is to convey to potential aggressors the deep sincerity of a person's or nation's peaceful intentions. A deeply principled persistence against being seduced into an escalation of conflict can stave off family wars as well as international wars. So often, people and nations who are would-be aggressors (spouses in marital wars, parents in intergenerational wars, and peoples in international wars) are in large part responding to their own fears of the other's aggressions. Many times, much can be gained from creative efforts to negotiate with, even love, one's would-be attacker and inviting the potential aggressor to a renewed effort at peace. Finding a basis for cooperation toward a common goal especially can bring belligerents together. At the same time, people and nations must also be prepared to confront overt destructive attacks that, in fact, do threaten them. Even though they may abhor violence, people and nations must develop an ability to fight back in self-defense. Deep within, there is an instinct for self-preservation that justifies fighting for one's own life.

In the very effort not to be victims, people and nations are confronted with the further challenge to not become killers as, all too often, sincere self-defense unwittingly escalates into the very destructiveness being fought against. There can be no compromise with being victims, yet one must be careful not to turn one's self-defense into an excuse for becoming equally destructive.

Linking the Family Experience with What Human Beings Do to Other Family People

Ultimately, we want to confront the question of how human beings can allow themselves to cold-bloodedly snatch others from their family lives and commit those fellow family people to death. In the blood-filled history of genocide, we routinely read about children's being literally taken from their mother's breasts and their father's arms to their deaths. Our hearts cry out; How can it be that the killers, who themselves are born of family love and who are still linked to continuing family ties, do not see their victims as family people just like themselves, their own children, and their own parents?

How we made them sleep and purified them
How we perfectly cleaned up the people and worked a big heater
I was the commander   I made improvements and installed a guaranteed
    system taking into account the human weakness I purified and I re-
    mained decent . . .
I was born into a Catholic family but as these people were not going to need
    a priest I did not become a priest   I installed a perfectly good machine
    it gave satisfaction to many . . .
Children of tender age were always invited by reason of their youth
    they were unable to work   they were marked out for play
They were washed like the others and more than the others
Very frequently women would hide their children in the piles of clothing
    but of course when we came to find them we would send the children
    into the chamber to be bathed . . .
Their love was fully stopped by our perfected ovens . . .
You would do as I did if you knew yourself and dared.[23]

Simon Wiesenthal, a Jew who has committed his life to bringing
Nazi genociders to justice, describes the paradox of the family ties of the
Nazi genocider:

> A letter from an SS Fuehrer described matter-of-factly how his unit
> had been ordered to repair a landing strip in Uman, near Kiev in the
> Ukraine, where a Russian bomb had torn a large crater. The SS mathemati-
> cians figured out that the bodies of 1500 people would just fill a crater of
> that size, whereupon they methodically procured the building material by
> shooting 1500 Jewish men, women, and children, and throwing their dead
> bodies into the crater. The bodies were covered with earth, a steel mat was
> placed on top, and the landing strip was as good as new. All this was
> described unemotionally, with much technical detail.
>   On the same page of the letter, the SS man inquired about the roses in
> his garden and promised his wife to try to find a Russian servant girl "who
> can cook and look after the children."
>   In another letter, an SS man describes how they killed Jewish babies
> by throwing them against the wall, and then he goes on to ask whether his
> baby got over the attack of the measles.[24]

The linkages between family experiences and human beings'
availability to be genociders begin with the fact that the human family
life is not an idyll of joy and peace but is riddled with murderous tensions, feelings, and acts. Therefore, there is at least the possibility that
human beings who have experienced much hurt in their own family
lives may be disposed to participate in and allow the hurting of other
people in the larger family of man. The genociders who previously ex-

perienced great danger and hurt in their own family lives perhaps take on the larger role of destroyer as if to replay and externalize their own very bad "dream" or inner experience memory. We know that such replays of the past serve many psychic purposes. There is first the "simple" explanation of doing the familiar once again, out of habit. There is also the deeper truth that we tend to re-create our traumatic pasts in an effort to rid ourselves of the terrors they have left in us. Externalizing earlier torments and agonies is intended to remove the problem from ourselves, to get rid of it or get it out of our system. We see this process within a family when once-children continue destructive exploitations they suffered at the hands of their parents by attacking their own child or children in much the same way. The last thing in the world that many parents consciously want to do is to end up "just like mother" or "just like father," yet they do exactly that. It is a familiar phenomenon in family life.

The replay of destructiveness toward others is also a vehicle for revenge, a desire that springs readily to the *lex talionis* instinct of the human animal. This notion has been developed impressively in an innovative study of family life by family therapist theoreticians Ivan Boszormenyi-Nagy and Geraldine Spark.[25] These authors emphasize the notion that people's family ties can best be understood in terms of what they call "ethical ledgers." As the story of family life unfolds, each person enters into his private ledger as credits and debits the justices and injustices that have been his lot at the hands of his loved ones. As the years go by, much of a person's behavior within and outside the family can be seen in terms of his efforts to "balance the books." Human beings also act upon the accumulated balance sheet of their family justice ledgers in their dealings with people outside the family. People who have been ill treated cannot but seek to discharge their accumulated hurt or rage in one way or another, including doing harm to others.

Nagy and Spark attempt to generalize even further to culturewide systems of justice ledgers: "We believe that the concept of justice of the human order is a common denominator for individual, familial, and societal dynamics. Individuals who have not learned a sense of justice within their family relationships are likely to have a distorted judgment of social justice."[26] They also link the doing of injustice with projection onto a third, innocent party. They describe how "the unsettled account that stands between a person and the original culprit can revolve and get between him and any third person. An innocent third person may be used (scapegoated) as a means for balancing the account. . . . We call this phenomenon the 'revolving slate.'"[27]

A critical linkage between family and larger group life is through man's repeated distinctions between his chosen in-group and a less-favored out-group that is to carry the burden of the projections of all that one cannot bear in oneself and life. "The definition of any social unit—family, nation, religion, or race—is inseparable from an intrinsically preferential, prejudicious definition of the in-group as superior to the out-group."[28] Nagy and Spark emphasize a deep abiding loyalty to one's original family, and therefore, "One may attack someone else or the whole world in the noble pursuit of returning one's loyalty by not blaming one's parents. The parents' alleged harmful acts get revenged in absentia."[29]

Some psychoanalytic and family therapy clinicians suggest that one of the key sources of destructiveness is the need of people to flee the murdering they might otherwise do within their own families. The intense hostility that builds in them within their own family experience is projected onto outsiders. This process can be seen in extended kinship groups when one clan turns all of its venom onto another clan and there develop long-standing feuds. At the very least, the feuds serve to organize much of the meaning of life for both parties, and the enmity and rage that might otherwise divide each clan within itself now has an outside focus. Psychoanalyst Louis Linn writes:

> At least three separate patterns for channeling intrafamilial aggression can be recognised. . . .
>
> 1. This pattern insists unequivocably and without exception "Thou shalt not kill." This may be called the Religious or Universal Brotherhood of Man pattern. In accordance with this point of view no outward expression of violence is countenanced in the family. . . . This superego structure sees suicide as an ultimate act of morality which prefers one's own death to causing the death of another.
> 2. This superego pattern may be called the Scapegoat pattern. This parental injunction reads "Thou shalt not kill any member of a family except the one chosen as the scapegoat or the sacrificial lamb."
> 3. The last pattern reads, "Thou shalt not kill any member of your own family. However, individuals who are not members of your own family are fair game."[30]

Another, even simpler, linkage between personal family experience and one's availability to destroy derives from the fact that family life can be so upsetting that people do not go forth from their families sufficiently protected from anxieties, so they are left desperately in need of magical defenses against their terror. We have seen that included in such defenses are projections onto others of one's own fears of being destroyed and projections of one's own destructiveness. "You are out to kill me, but I'll get you first. You die and not I!" The fact that the victims are helpless people busy with their family lives does not register in the killers' minds and hearts, for the killers are lost in their primitive efforts to escape overwhelming anxiety. Their own family lives did not strengthen them enough to fight off primitive, irrational ways of being human.

These, then, are three possible linkages between person-forming experiences in one's family and a subsequent murdering of other family people:

1. Man learns to be destructive in his own unhappy family life experience and then plays out the emotional destructiveness he suffered in the destruction and killing of others.
2. Man seeks to destroy others lest he destroy his own family.
3. Man escapes from the terrible hurts he suffers in family life by sacrificing others to the destructiveness he fears for himself.

However we work to refine and reformulate each of these linkages, each and all add up to a picture of a human family life that fails to protect people against the emergence of their evil potential because of the unbearable tensions and murderous feelings they experience in their own family lives and do not know how to process.

A further linkage between people's experiences in family life and their proneness to be destructive in the larger world has to do with self-defense within the family. Characteristically, every member of a family sincerely feels he is the victim of others' hurts, indignities, and betrayals and sees his own aggression as natural self-defense. These reactions then confirm the other family members' convictions that *they* are under attack. They swing into their self-defense procedures, so there are at least two processes of defending, counterattacking, and rearming in operation. It is an utterly incredible picture. Talk to an upset spouse or parent or child about the possibility that they themselves are contributing to a spiral of hurt, and almost always the response is one of pouting and rage. Often it is only the shock of almost losing one of the other family members (e.g., the spouse walks out or threatens divorce or a child becomes emotionally or psychosomatically disturbed) that makes us aware how little our feelings about the other's unfairness matters and that what does matter is building new bridges of cooperation and love.

It is from such "basic training" in the illusion and yet sincere conviction of fighting in self-defense that human beings go forth from their family lives to their relationships in the larger community and "family of man." Is there any doubt that people everywhere in the world are utterly convinced that they are exploited and terrorized by others? Before very long, the unchecked escalation process brings both sides to a point where it is objectively entirely true that each is the enemy of the other. Often it is only after a bloody war that people are able to break out of the cycle and see the utter meaninglessness of their conviction that it was necessary to make war in "self-defense."

The Not-So-Pretty Picture of the Family Life of Our Species

I conclude that the family lives of the human beings who are to be genociders are, in many respects, arenas of selfish harassment in which people engage in considerable destructiveness toward one another, while denying what they are doing. We human beings largely do not know how to handle the natural sequences of hatred and being hated that are our lot along with the deep love we feel in our family lives. Also, the family lives of human beings who are to be the genociders are replete with invasion, coercion, and scapegoating. In our family lives we are easily caught up in spirals of ever-mounting hurting and retaliation, and each of us justifies our own acts by the injustices and attacks of the others. It is not a pretty picture, but what may be reassuring is that it is not necessarily a picture of overwhelming meanness so much as it is a picture of tremendous weakness and unawareness at our present stage of human development.

THE GROUP LIFE OF THE HUMAN BEINGS WHO ARE TO BE THE GENOCIDERS

Long before tribal drums beat their call to genocide, people gather in groups for many fine collective purposes—for commerce, art, cooperation in science, or simply the fulfillment of fellowship. The power of the collective is enormous. Often a person working with another person will succeed in doing far more than he or she would have done alone. An amazing strength is released by the encouragement and support that take place among people, as well as by the silent modeling of one another that group experiences makes possible.

In groups, one is spared aloneness and also much of the objective vulnerability of being the only one to be for oneself. In twos, threes, fives, nines, twenties, fifties, hundreds, and thousands, people create building teams, research teams, surgical teams, sports teams, explorer groups, office staffs, parties and festivals, triumphant armies, religious movements, and national groups.

Group joy is contagious and fulfilling. There is something about the flow of good talk, the fun of dressing up, and especially being together at a celebration that can electrify people with an aliveness that would be hard for an individual to find within himself. Often there bubbles forth in social merriment a joy that leaves a warm afterglow for hours and days.

Yet groups can also be fickle, irascible, hurtful, and dangerous. Despite all social conventions, some fraternity gatherings turn into occasions that emotionally disfigure an individual whose weakness is seized on as an object of ridicule and exploitation. Despite so-called business ethics, corporations viciously attack and destroy people within the organization and without. A major corporation may dismiss its soon-to-be-pensioned workers a few years before they go on the pensioners' roster. Or a land-purchasing group squeezes a competitor's credit sources dry until the competitor collapses. Is this "simply business"? It seems that often something other than money is involved. The very same kind of thing happens in settings in which money as such does not appear to be the key issue. For example, the faculty group of one university department will squeeze out another department for a new graduate program or priority for a new building, or one faculty faction will push out another within a department. The very same power plays and prestige races occur within charitable organizations and foundation groups, even though there is no question that all concerned are committed to the same principle or cause. Group warfare also occurs within religious institutions; people divide against one another and assemble thundering, powerful attacks against a minister or a particular church faction.

What is it about groups? What is it about crowds and mobs? What is it about human beings when they are joined in groups? Le Bon described the crowd in 1903:

> Whoever be the individuals that compose it, however like or unlike be their mode of life, their occupations, their character, or their intelligence, the fact that they have been transformed into a crowd puts them in possession of a sort of collective mind.

> This explains how it was that among the most savage members of the French Convention were to be found inoffensive citizens who, under ordinary circumstances, would have been peaceful notaries or virtuous magistrates.[31]

Le Bon considered a crowd unreasoning, primitive, fickle, dictatorial, intolerant, and stupid. The crowd is an emotional and a stupid aggregate. Although individuals possess the potential for the behavior they demonstrate under crowd conditions, it is characteristically when they are in the mob that they go wild. Le Bon writes about the individual within a crowd or mob, "He possesses the spontaneity, the violence, the ferocity and also the enthusiasm and heroism of primitive beings."[32]

In old psychiatric books, one finds reports of "psychic epidemics" occurring in Europe from the eleventh to the seventeenth centuries. In discussing such "collective psychoses," Silvano Arieti and Johannes Meth go to some pains to point out that they were not psychoses but rather "psychoneuroses of hysterical nature which were induced by the effect the crowd had on the predisposed person."[33] At first glance, the distinction seems like a belabored point of semantics. The problem for mental health professionals is that if psychosis is an illness that strikes only a percentage of the population, and there are situations in which total or near-total groups of people act at one and the same time, how can it be that they are all psychotics? It is because of problems like this that the traditionalists in psychiatry have been having a hard time for some time now with once-vaunted distinctions between health and illness. More and more in mental health work, new concepts of problems in living are being accepted rather than the concept of illness.[34] When it comes to accounting for groups of people acting quite irrationally in concert, there is massive evidence that human beings in groups readily allow themselves to get lost in one or another orgy, intoxication, or pseudocertainty, which releases them from anxiety and the pressures of real living.[35] So many human beings behave in this way that it cannot be a matter of their being exceptional or sick. Rather, acting crazy in groups appears to be a natural weakness that lurks in all of us.

What is it that happens to human beings in groups? Is the group experience so different from the individual experience that the laws of human behavior that might explain what takes place are unique to the group situation? Is it the *same* human being who nourishes his children, swears allegiance to noble ethical values, and is kind to his neighbors that goes wild within a group's wildness?

My own reply, obviously, is that it is very much the same human being. We therefore need to recognize that within each of us, there is a potential for irrationality, stupidity (as Le Bon put it), fickleness, and madness and that potential may explode if and when we lose ourselves in group life. At the same time, the probability of our succumbing to our "irrational and ugly crowd-mob selves" is lower unless we are in group situations and there is the right mixture of certain collective conditions.

Political scientist J. David Singer has written of the importance of our developing cognitive maps that will bridge between the psychology of the individual human being and an understanding of the larger world of the dynamics of major political events. Singer acknowledges that most efforts to explain the psychology of large-scale events have left social scientists looking childish and amateurish in their strained, undisciplined efforts to magnify familiar, individual psychodynamic principles so that they will cover the forces of larger events. Yet, he insists, there are indeed linkages, and we must continue our search for them.

> Between the familiar regions of individual behavior and the dimly perceived ones of world politics lies a *terra incognito* into which few social scientists have yet begun to venture. Given the inadequacy of our maps, it is little wonder that we have given those regions a wide berth. While the behavior of men or of social systems may be *described*, and perhaps even *predicted*, . . . no satisfactory *explanation* is possible until we understand the psychological link which joins man to his socio-political environment, and through which each impinges on the other.[36]

Psychiatrist and international relations researcher Bryant Wedge has described the linkages among the individual, the small group, and the larger group as transactional in nature.[37]

Both Singer and Wedge are helpful because they go beyond a simplistic effort to reduce group experiences to the sum impact of the psychological processes of the various individuals within the group. Both are concerned with the larger patterns and processes that are generated by the structure of the group. Yet, that structure operates on and through people whom we otherwise know through the psychology of their individuality, so there is also a legitimate basis for looking at groups as collectives of individuals.

Each level of experience has its own identity, and processes on one level are not equivalent to processes on another level, yet they bear distinct relationships to one another on a ladder of development, enlargement, and progression. It is a human being who operates through the mechanisms of group behavior to do what he does to fellow human being, but it is the mechanism of group experience that potentiates, legitimates, operationalizes, and narcotizes the emergence of man's various and often unsavory selves.

Modern social psychological literature is full of experimental studies that show how people lose their individual identity in group life. Under the pressure of group experience, people literally see things differently than they do when they are acting alone. The extent of group suggestibility is so great that it can reach the point at which people are not able to be accurate in their perceptions of simple objects (which in themselves have no emotional or symbolic significance) if the people are pressured by fellow group members telling them that they are seeing something very different.[38] When excited, people in groups are transported "out of themselves."[39]

Yet, just as there is an idealization of the "normal individual" and the "average family" in general psychology and popular folklore, there is also an idealization of group life. The group is hailed as a cooperative and as an arena for warmth and encountering other people. Even when the possibility is recognized that crowds and mobs may grow wild and destructive, too little recognition is given to the fact that the same underlying processes of madness and contagion are latent in all group processes—including sophisticated, modern corporate organizations or groups of scholars in the universities. On the other hand, even when the group potential for madness is recognized, no further effort is made to probe *why* that is so. One result has been a considerable dissociation of how people behave in group experiences from the psychology of the individual human being. Although the psychological understanding of the individual is taken as a basis for understanding people in groups (e.g., humans need warmth and security and seek those in groups), what really happens in groups is treated as if the group were a world of its own and had no implications for our understanding of the normal individual human being. The individual human being who goes mad in group events is, of course, the same terrified person we saw when we looked at the nature of the individal of our species. He is the same selfish, harassed person, so lacking in identity as not to be able to experience his connection to the tragedy of another and protest the indignity done a fellow human being. He is also the same family man we saw unknowingly living out terrible invasions, hurts, attacks, and destructions in his family group. In short, he is a human who has a long way to go in learning how to handle the anxiety and challenge of being alive and preparing for ultimate death.[40]

Group events, in particular, seem to provide an antidote to death and loneliness, nothingness and anxiety. There is the illusion that if one moves with the swell of the group, one will discover aliveness and anti-death. To fuse with the meshing of energy that is a group of people is like pooling the life resources of all and thereby transcending one's own mortal limits. In a group, the individual is no longer so alone, no longer so terrified, no longer so confused. Being surrounded by living bodies, being a part of a mass, and taking on the purpose of the group give a feeling of direction. To be part of a group is such a relief that it hardly seems to matter that so many of its actions are at the expense of other people, even of their very lives.[41]

The Not-So-Pretty Picture of the Group Life
of the Human Beings Who Are to Be the Genociders

I conclude that the group lives of the individuals who are to be the genociders in many respects are arenas in which selfish, harassed people bring tragedy to others but do not experience the tragedies they foment. Even in the "better days" of his group experiences, the human being who is to be the genocider often hides his identity and individuality by blending into the group and its purposes. The individual largely uses group life to escape from the anxiety of seeking his own aliveness and of dealing with his own forthcoming death. The individual who is to be the genocider is easily led. He is deeply suggestible and often takes his direction in life from the givens of a situation. He is available to conform to instructions to destroy others, even on relatively flimsy grounds. It is not a pretty picture, but what may be reassuring is that it is not necessarily a picture of overwhelming meanness so much as it is a picture of tremendous weakness and unawareness at our present stage of human development.

A PROPOSED STATEMENT:
WHAT IT MEANS TO BE NORMAL
AT OUR PRESENT STAGE OF HUMAN EVOLUTION

Always we return to the question of how and why we are as we are: at one and the same time shallow, primitive, and obscene yet brilliant, beautiful, and decent. How do these two sides play on one another? Where do we find in ourselves both the light and the dark?

We want so very much to live, but we become overwhelmed and exhausted by life's travails to the point where we yearn for rest at any price. We know that we must die, and we want to prepare to die well. Yet we also hate the thought of not being anymore, and we strive desperately to stay alive and to perpetuate ourselves. We go off in unending searches for fountains of life, secrets of life, and triumphs of immortality. Yet, deep down, we know there is no way out. More than anything else, we want to savor life's opportunity to experience as much as we can. We hope we will be able to die at the end of our time satisfied that we have lived.

Unhappily, most of us falter along the way. Life is too much for us. Once so trusting and full of hope and ideals, humans are deeply hurt by their discoveries of life's hurts and hells. We are especially shattered when we discover that those whose love we need the most also turn on us. We are even more crushed when we find that we are also capable of terrible cruelty and destructiveness.

All through life, we know little of how to use our repertoire of emotion. We are forever getting into trouble with those we love the most. We hate too much or too little. We are shattered by being hated too much or weakened by being hated too little. We try to be tough with those with whom we should be more tender. We try to escape the cruelties of harshness by being tender, only to wake up to the fact that it would have been far wiser to be strong. We are terrified by the scale of our emotions and block out many of the feelings and options that are at play inside of us. We often are especially terrified that we will not be able to control certain feelings and they will spill out into actual behavior. We do not trust ourselves to experience feelings inside ourselves without actually acting them out.

Through it all, we are driven to try to feel alive. This need is so strong that often we turn perversely toward destroying life in a desperate seeking to feel more vital and alive. To feel, to move, to do – these are the antidotes to nonaliveness and death, so whatever it is that we find ourselves doing, the sheer activity is likely to make us feel good. Whatever the activity, we want to go on doing more and more of the same so long as we feel active, hence alive – even if the activity leads to the destruction of others.

In all things that we do, we are inclined to follow our leaders, no matter how mad they are. We are also inclined to follow the momentum and direction that already exist in a given situation or structure, almost disregarding what they are. We know little about facing up to choices. We do not understand that choices necessarily mean giving up something, even though we find joy in what we choose.

We say to ourselves that we are creatures of serious values. Yet, as we walk to and from our churches and synagogues and other value-homes, we devote ourselves to all that is opposite: We lie, steal, pillage, and kill and do not realize the staggering contradictions that exist between our declared values and what we are doing. We preach honesty to children, but we cheat one another in the marketplace. We build beautiful communities, but in the process, we are indifferent to the natural ecology that supports life. We call for family love, but behind the shutters of our homes, we are petulant, demanding, parasitic, and assaultive. Children are called sweet but often are, in fact, rowdy, petty thieves, and petty tyrants. Grown-ups talk of tenderness and mutuality in sex but are alternatively licentious, unfaithful, and insatiable. In our working relationships, we are competitive, combative, and exploitive.

Our leaders and statesmen are pride seeking, control seeking, two faced, three faced, and war mongering.

The more destructive we are, the more we must block out any awareness of what we are doing against life. Many of us drink or otherwise narcotize ourselves so as not to bear the pain of our failure in what was originally a sincere search to be fully alive. We lie to ourselves increasingly. We ritualize our attacks on life and call them by ceremonial names so that they appear different from what they really are. War is called making peace; destroying people is described as helping; dictatorial cruelty is referred to as love; indifference and abandonment are disguised as permissiveness. We are still largely ignorant of how terrified we are. We tend to run away in panic or to give up. Often we flail so wildly and madly in making our escape that we leave a bitter trail of death behind us.

In our terror, we call on ancient magic rites. Most of all, we seek to cast out the weaknesses we fear in ourselves and to lay them on the heads of others. This we do within our family to certain "bad" members or "weak" ones. This we do outside the family to people who are different in color, manner, appearance, or affiliation, hence, not deserving to be protected from hurt and death.

In time, enough of us assign the major responsibility for all that is dangerous and destructive in our lives to a particular group of hapless people, thereby setting the stage for the ultimate ritual of sacrifice. We seize those people whom we hold responsible for all our ills, accuse them of seeking our annihilation, and proceed to annihilate them instead. The greatest deception of all is that we call our hate and destruction by other names. We claim that our enemies are the enemies of life itself. Always our destruction is as if called forth by the gods of life.

> Nature has let us down. God seems to have left the receiver off the hook, and time is running out. To hope for salvation to be synthesised in the laboratory may seem materialistic, crankish, or naive; but, to tell the truth, there is a Jungian twist to it — for it reflects the ancient alchemist's dream to concoct the elixir vitae. What we expect from it, however, is not eternal life, nor the transformation of base metal into gold, but the transformation of *homo maniacus* into *homo sapiens*. When man decides to take his fate into his own hands, that possibility will be within reach.[42]

Whether we waken to our madness before the time of our species runs out is not yet clear. At the moment, we are trapped in the Auschwitzes we ourselves have created. There is some hope, but we do not know how much.

Mass Grave Found in Cypriot Garbage Dump

Nicosia — Turkish forces have uncovered a new mass grave containing up to 75 charred bodies in a small Turkish Cypriot village, a civilian Turkish Cypriot spokesman said yesterday.

The Turks said they believed the victims were Turkish Cypriots reported missing before Turkish forces reached the area, north of Famagusta, in their second offensive on August 14.

But Greek Cypriots said the bodies might well belong to some of the hundreds of Greek Cypriots reported missing from this area.

The Turkish Cypriot spokesman said the bodies in the mass grave had their wrists wired together and had been riddled with bullets. He said some had been beheaded.

The burial site was in the same area where a mass grave, which the Turkish Cypriots said contained 57 bodies, was found a week ago.

The spokesman said the Turkish soldiers had so far dug out the remains of 35 bodies from under a pile of garbage that had been bulldozed over them in a quarry near the now abandoned village of Maratha. Survivors of the village's onetime population of 90 said the killers were gunmen from nearby Greek Cypriot villages.

The corpses were so battered and decomposed that they crumbled to pieces when soldiers lifted them from the garbage with shovels, and an accurate count of the dead was impossible.

"I have counted 21 skulls so far," said Chief Inspector Lars Hakansson, a Swedish UN policeman who was at the graveside on Sunday when the bodies were discovered, and again yesterday.

At least another half dozen corpses could be seen sticking grotesquely from the earth. At least two of them were women holding babies in their arms.

A Government statement broadcast by Cyprus Radio did not deny the massacre, but noted that hundreds of Greek Cypriots were missing from the same region. The statement claimed that an article from the body of a woman in the grave showed she was Greek, not Turkish.

A UN spokesman said the Swedish troops at the mass grave had been invited only to observe, not to make identifications. He added that the bodies of two elderly Greek Cypriots, one a woman, had been found on Saturday near the village of Akheritour, west of Famagusta, an area now controlled by Turkish forces. He said they had been blindfolded.

Meanwhile, the International Press Institute in Zurich said yesterday it had been told by Cyprus President Blafkos Clerides that a soldier responsible for fatally injuring a Turkish journalist had been arrested and was under psychiatric observation.

Adem Yavuz, a reporter with the Ankara news agency, died in a Turkish hospital last week after being airlifted out of Cyprus in critical condition. The Institute said yesterday that Cypriot President Blafkos Clerides had expressed his condolences.

—United Press International, September 3, 1974

8

THE TRAGIC ILLUSION
OF SELF-DEFENSE

We make up stories to prove that things are going the way they should be going, the way they started going in our minds when we began firing. Mountains of the plainest evidence can't convince us of the truth. But in the real world the arbitrary distinctions by which we sought to justify our actions have broken down once and for all. Our people have actually done the thing we accused their people of being ready to do. And our people and their people lie together in a common grave, brothers in death as they were brothers in life, had we only known it.

— New Yorker

Earlier we discussed man's terror of dying and his terror of not succeeding in feeling alive, and we saw how people erect powerful defenses against these terrors. We also saw that human beings are forever terrified of real threats of annihilation and that they must mobilize defenses to protect themselves against their terror of being destroyed by other human beings. Moreover, we saw that people are terrified of their own desires and inclinations to destroy others; they then flee those impulses by projecting them onto others and then defend themselves against their own projections. Thus, there are several powerful, interlocking threats of death at work in man's natural experiencing and they drive him to fight back in what he feels is self-defense.

ILLUSIONS OF FIGHTING IN SELF-DEFENSE
OFTEN ARE SINCERE

Some people might argue that to solve one's fears of death and of one's own destructiveness by projecting them onto others is really a Machiavellian or a consciously calculated effort to terrorize and tyrannize others. You call another what you fear in yourself because this is

167

your strategy to get the best of the other. Such self-defense, therefore, should not be considered the same as acts of self-defense against bona fide threats of annihilation.

With no little sense of sadness and tragedy, I suggest that the experience of fighting back in self-defense is often sincere even though it is an illusion. Of course, there are times when the claim of self-defense is a downright lie born of a calculated strategy to blame others for our own worst intentions. And yet even some of those Machiavellian claims of self-defense can also be largely sincere. For many of the claims of self-defense that are conscious lies are also true insofar as they genuinely derive from a deep terror of dying and a feeling that one must exaggerate and manipulate the truth in order to survive.

Groups, Too, Enter into Illusions (As Well As Lies) of Self-defense

In many cases genociders, too, sincerely see themselves as fighting in self-defense. To understand this bizarre state of affairs is to understand the infinite ways human beings become terrified that they may lose "everything." It is not enough that people fear their actual death or even that they fear not feeling alive. Many of our terrors about dying and feeling alive are lived out through symbolic representations of ourselves, and we experience ourselves as vulnerable not only on the level of our physical identities, but also on the level of our symbolic identities. "I will be destroyed if something important that I believe in is destroyed." People are endowed with an enormous capacity for symbolization, and though many great ideas, inventions, and works of art result from this gift, the same capacity can be committed to the service of primitive mechanisms as well. For example, we know too well how parents project onto their children their wishes for immortality. Many serious psychological problems in children or in adults have to do with the demand that the child reduce the parent's anxiety about immortality through some achievement or service. We also extend the symbolism of surviving our earthly existence to the works we leave behind – our books, music, buildings, inventions. Those, too, are "our children." We commit ourselves to ideologies and group causes from which we seek emotional support and, in effect, a sense of immortality through the fact that the group's belief system or purpose will continue far beyond our mortal time. Thus, individuals' anxieties about their deaths and their projections of such anxieties onto others also take place through their identification with causes and groups and their projections onto those groups.

People cry out to be worthwhile and important forces on this earth through their groups in order to satisfy their deep-seated needs for immortality. They then fight in self-defense against whatever other groups or ideologies they see as would-be destroyers of their identities. A group also "decides" to extend its power over others, as if to prove the group's invulnerability. And groups unconsciously project their destructive wishes onto other groups. *Christians must destroy the antiChrist. The purebreds must destroy their genetic contaminators. God-fearing people must destroy the devil worshipers. Freedom lovers must destroy the aristocrats. The people's revolutionaries must destroy the imperialists. Touchables must destroy the Untouchables. Thus could it be that someday Believers in such and such psychology or education will seek to destroy those who oppose their methods of "training" or "socializing."*[1]

The critical point is that people see their ideological enemies as no less dangerous than their actual physical enemies. In fact, the passion of killing in self-defense often is greater when a threat is felt against one's ideological survival and immortality. People kill quite readily to protect their desperate efforts at some sort of symbolic continuity and immortality. Although in history books the large group events often appear as coldly calculated Machiavellian politics, I believe that those historical processes often build from the same deep human terror over death that we see in individuals, now amplified and channeled through group processes.

TRACKING THE SUBJECTIVE EXPERIENCE OF FIGHTING BACK IN SELF-DEFENSE

A remarkable opportunity to see how two parties can simultaneously believe they are fighting in self-defense is to look at the eternal battles of spouses. Again we need to note the danger of analogizing. One level of human experience is not simply a magnification of the other, but there are continuities and transactional linkages among levels of human experience, so that some aspects of battling spouses can help us also understand battling peoples and nations.

The pivotal generalization is that each and every spouse feels that he or she is the victim of the other and so feels justified in fighting back in self-defense. The drama of marriage characteristically has its original deceptive beginnings in the emotional period of courtship and much of the first year of marriage. During those stages, both mates still enjoy an idyllic fantasy that their love will banish, or at least atone for, any big hurts and disappointments in life. Each lover will be so good to the other that henceforth there will be little pain or distress. If there is pain, it will soon pass through mutual understanding and comforting.

Before very long, there explode terrifying hurts, demoralizations, and rages. "How can you do this to me? I am so good to you, and this is how you treat me in return!" There now follow searches for new ways of dealing with the inescapable reality that the beloved one is many times a very hurting other. Each spouse experiments with old and new devices for the management of threat. Some try to be nicer. This method may help for a while, but often enough, spouses who try to be nicer end up being hurt, and then they are much more upset, confused, and enraged. Some attempt to express how hurt they are. Even if that method helps for a while, almost inevitably more serious hurts follow. Other spouses invoke retaliatory anger when they are hurt. Some do so relatively fairly and maturely, others less fairly and less maturely. In either case, it still remains almost inescapable that the beloved spouse will continue to inflict bitter disappointments and provocative hurts.[2]

The one noteworthy exception to all of these variations on the discovery of hurt concerns those spouses who agree to act largely as if there were no differences between them and to do everything possible to smooth over all potential areas of conflict, difference, and irritation. But that pattern of denial of natural conflict has been shown to be, in the long run, a breeding ground for serious psychological illness because of the intrinsic dishonesty of avoiding natural clashes.[3]

Now we have the typical marital situation, in which two hurt and angry people each think of the other as the hurting and unfair one and themselves as responding in justified self-defense. When one spouse speaks up in protest against the other's unfairness, most mates automatically turn off the criticism, because in their minds they are entirely justified that they are doing whatever they are doing in self-defense. Even if they acknowledge that they are hurting their spouse, they say to themselves that they are not *really* hurting their mate, in the sense of *trying* to cause hurt, because whatever they are doing is "just self-defense."

Despite the sincerity of feeling that one is fighting back against the terror of the other, each spouse actually provokes, invites, initiates, and escalates the hurting and attacking. Although the concrete complaints of each spouse often are objectively accurate descriptions of what the other actually has done or is doing, the intrinsic claim that the other spouse is the sole or predominant aggressor is, of course, not correct.

The only way through this maze of illusion is to learn how to appreciate the legitimacy of our own and our spouse's feelings of fighting in self-defense, to learn to regard with self-critical humor the self-justifying and self-beguiling conviction that what we are doing is tit for tat and an eye for an eye, and to learn how to cut the vicious circle of fighting each other in self-defense. The spouse who learns how to accept his or her legitimate anger and how to appreciate the other's hurt and anger has a chance of becoming a constructive leader for peaceful conflict resolution. Freed of the illusion that one is fighting a solely evil other, one is emotionally free not only to fight unfairness but also to express positive feelings, invitations to anger-dissolving communications, and invitations to loving (including, of course, especially happy reunions in love-making).[4] Note that this kind of approach toward positive feelings and peace is altogether different from a consistently pacifist insistence on being good no matter what the provocations of the other. Marital therapists know only too well that pacifist perfection in marriage actually demoralizes and enrages spouses, because of the intrinsic dishonesty and unnaturalness of not standing up against unfairness and because if one does not get angry, one cannot then harness the same aggression in pursuit of renewed and better loving.

The Psychotherapy of Spouses Fighting in Self-defense

For a long time, therapists did not know how to put together the claims of battling spouses, and the prevailing tradition of psychoanalytic treatment was to exclude the reality of the spouse of the analysand.[5] The therapist would advise whichever of the two spouses it was who first appeared to seek help for his or her marital plight along these lines: "You need psychotherapy to work out your problems, including your contribution to the upset between the two of you. You need to do so regardless of what your spouse does and whether or not your spouse will also get involved in therapy." Of course, there was an important truth in the point of view that a good deal of correction of the conflict lay in the patient's maturing, but there was also a ludicrous denial of the realness and interests of the other spouse and of the marriage as such.

As the therapy developed, the therapist would often begin liking and identifying with the patient, whose hurts were obviously real and sincere. Much of the job of the therapist then involved encouraging and guiding the patient to learn to stand up to the unfairness and badness of their mate. Therapists would soon tell the patient that their spouse was obviously quite "sick," and the therapist would admonish the long-suffering patient, "You shouldn't take such abuse." Various strategies for confronting or limiting the nonpatient spouse would be constructed during the treatment hours. Some of these strategies were very helpful. A mate who had been accepting the other's tormenting behavior passively, for example, would learn in treatment how to call a halt to the punishment. Whatever the counsel, the building of a program of thoughtful, well-planned responses to the stress of the marital situation brought significant improvement to a certain number of marriages. But what also happened, too often to be ignored, was that the one-sided, subtly adversary advice did not relate to the pain and suffering of the unknown mate or to the simultaneity of the goading and provocation between the two

172 / WHEN DOES MAN COMMIT GENOCIDE?

spouses, each of whom saw himself or herself as a victim. As a result, there often followed escalating sequences that built toward unsparing showdowns and ultimatums, and ultimately to divorces that were more than subtly encouraged by the therapist on the grounds that the other mate was obviously "too sick" to change.

It was in the world of marriage counseling that many counselors first made an effort to see spouses together and to understand their interlocking problems (to this day there are psychoanalytic purists who refuse to see a patient's spouse).[6] Many marriage counselors did intelligent and helpful work in showing each spouse the role their basic immaturity played in the marital relationship. However, a disturbing motif pervaded much of the work, as counselors labored valiantly to prove the immaturity of each spouse. Rarely was there an appreciation of the fact that even essentially mature people necessarily have to struggle with a complex system of conflicts in the intimacy of marriage. Moreover, the counselors would call on each spouse to be mature enough to forgive and compromise, almost regardless of the provocation.

Only in recent years has it become clearer that the real challenge in marriage is not only to correct one's own immaturity and to accept the other person as a human being with limitations, but also, and at the same time, to expect and challenge the other person to grow as a person. Played out properly, spouses learn to accept the natural spiraling upsets and provocations as useful ways in which to set healthy challenges to their own and their spouse's unfinished growth. The result can be a healthy *system* in which love, affection, and cooperation are accompanied and supported by a network of ambivalences, hurts, and conflicts. Each spouse has a chance to learn about his or her own limitations and also to challenge and provoke the other spouse to the growing she or he needs to do.

Seeing Mutual Provocations in Large Group Events

We return now to link up with our larger concern about serious conflicts and violence between peoples and nations. The usual sardonic image of history is that nations are led by scheming manipulators who cold-bloodedly plot the takeover of another people's land and then systematically spread rumors of attack by the enemy to justify a cynical claim of self-defense. But is it possible that just as people can't help seeing themselves as victims in their married lives, some leaders of nations can be essentially sincere when they see themselves and their people under attack by others?

As in marriage, nations focus their experience on what they are doing to us. Rarely is there appreciation of what the other people are experiencing. Even more rarely is there an appreciation of what we are doing to arouse their fears. Rarest of all is there an effort to perceive what we both are doing to one another. *The Israelis feel threatened by the Arabs who surround them and who have proved their intentions of destroying the Jewish state through repeated wars and terrorist attacks. The Arabs see Israeli society as an alien, expansionist military presence in their homeland and therefore feel justified in attacking the invader in any way possible.*

The world is still far from developing interactional concepts of how people mutually provoke one another. Analyses of large-scale conflicts generally are written in adversary terms, and only rarely are conflicts seen in terms of how each side triggers and confirms the other's fear of annihilation. Were the latter type of analyses to become the basis of negotiations and peacemaking, the possibilities would be quite remarkable. For example, as an alternative to adversary negotiations and their inevitable escalations, psychologist James H. Craig and his wife, Marge, a public relations consultant, propose that intergroup conflicts be mediated by a method they call All-Win. "The All-Win process allows people on both sides to discover that their former enemies are fellow humans with fears and dreams like theirs."[7] The purpose of this approach is not to pretend that there is no threat, but to turn admitted enemies into cooperative allies. The method is based on the concept of seeking maximum power for all conflicting parties, as opposed to methods of resolving conflicts that seek power for one party over the other.

Needless to say, there comes a point when it is too late to seek peace. Groups and nations, like individuals, get to points where they have no alternative but to fight back (no matter how correctable the tragic escalation might once have been). If thousands and millions are marched off to death camps, the time has passed when one can think of the original causes. The real victims of the moment have no alternative but to fight back as vigorously as they can in self-defense. And yet, there is the possibility that thinking in terms of "interactional analysis" rather than in terms of "adversary analysis" may offer a basis for earlier interventions "next time." It is at least a creative exercise for students of human events to consider what possibility there might have been for arresting various acts of violence, war, and genocide in history if the mounting violence had been approached from the frame of reference that both parties were suffering distress before the final crystallization of their respective roles of destroyers and victims.

THE PROBLEM OF "JUST WARS"

The idea that some wars simply *must* be fought goes back to the time-honored concept of the "just war." The notion of the just war was an important formulation in very early religious thought and has been given considerable attention and development by numerous religious, philosophical, and political thinkers through the ages.[8] The doctrine attempted to define what conditions of "just cause" would give rulers the right to take up arms: A just war was to be fought to protect one's natural rights or to reclaim a violated right. In addition, a just war was to be fought only by means approved by the doctrines of justice to be followed by nations. Unfortunately, "The just-war doctrine . . . was of little avail. At best its rules were ambiguous exhortations, not laws."[9]

Nonetheless, despite the practical failure of just-war codes, the very effort to differentiate just and unjust wars represents an important symbolic milestone in the historic and evolutionary process of man's search for peace. In effect, the just-war doctrine is an effort to formulate moral and legal conditions for the exercise of self-defense, and as we understand more of the psychology of self-defense, it should be possible to formulate better definitions of just and unjust fighting. Even now, with only fledgling social science tools, it seems possible to look forward to the time when it will be possible to apply social science methods in international law to objective evaluations of claims of self-defense.

In a modern treatment of the just-war concept, Theodore Weber proposes the following principles:

- The belligerents need to accept the fundamental truth of the common humanity of all parties to the conflict.
- The opponent's right to exist politically must be recognized. Unqualified and unlimited violence against the opponent's person and property is not legitimate. The goal must be for the belligerents to develop a *modus vivendi* within a common set of political relationships.
- War must not intend at vengeance against the enemy nor at his dispossession; in particular, war must not intend to destroy the enemy society.
- War must be conducted in such a way as to point towards the restoration and development of peaceful political relationships.
- The mixed religious and political character of international conflict must be reduced to its basic political elements. Where ideology does reign over politics, there needs to be a "dethroning" of ideology.
- There needs to be a constant renewal of sensitivity to the human suffering and deprivation which create the conditions of war and which war itself imposes.
- Belligerents need to persevere in searching for means to transfer

the conflict from violent to non-violent and from military to legal modes of resolutions.

- Questions of just cause for the use of force in international politics must be looked at within the framework of managing the power relations of the larger international system, and not only within the smaller framework of the right of national self-defense.[10]

Of course, if we think about the psychology of self-defense, the problem with those attractive and important concepts still is that people are so easily given to self-deluding, self-deceiving judgments. It takes little effort to talk oneself into believing one's cause is just. The problem that has never been solved is how to help people know when they unwittingly stimulate and confirm one another's terror and drive one another to battle.

Justification for self-defense takes many deceptive forms. Psychologist William Blanchard has written of the historic weakness of the United States to engage in disguised imperialism and oppression of others under the (sincere) guise that the other people require U.S. help in their self-defense. Blanchard believes that the U.S. character is marred by a fierce desire for achievement and a "desire for virtue which makes it necessary for us to deny the aggressive aspects of this achievement motivation." He continues:

> On first consideration it would appear that the desire for virtue would mitigate the intensity of our ambition, i.e., that the two needs are in conflict and each one would restrain the excesses of the other. There are no doubt times and situations when this is true. However, it often happens that the need for virtue is fused with ambitions in such a way that the total thrust is intensified into a kind of Messianic zeal—the ambition to be more virtuous than anyone else. It is under these circumstances that one hears such themes as "making the world safe for democracy," "coming to the aid of free people everywhere," and other glorious phrases which imply that America can be a savior of the world. . . .
>
> If an American leader manages to engage in aggressive acts without being aware of the provocative aspect of his behavior, he will be forgiven and supported by his people. One often has the feeling that innocence and guile are working so closely together that it is impossible to determine when one leaves off and the other begins.[11]

A good example of how claims of self-defense are invoked on behalf of violent murder is found in the Palestinian National Covenant, adopted in 1964 at the establishment of the Palestinian Liberation Organization (PLO) and amended in 1968. Over the years, the PLO has been responsible for a variety of killings of civilians, including school children and air travelers of various nationalities, and its covenant calls for the "purge" of the Zionist presence (i.e., the State of Israel) from Palestine:

> Article 5: The Palestinians are the Arab citizens who were living permanently in Palestine until 1947, whether they were expelled from there or remained. Whoever is born to a Palestinian Arab father after this date, within Palestine or outside of it, is a Palestinian.

> Article 6: Jews who were living permanently in Palestine until the beginning of the Zionist invasion will be considered Palestinians.

> Article 15: The liberation of Palestine, from an Arab viewpoint, is a national duty to repulse the Zionist, imperialist invasion from the great Arab homeland and to purge all Zionist presence from Palestine. . . .

> Article 18: The liberation of Palestine, from an international viewpoint, is a defensive act necessitated by the requirements of self-defense. For this reason, the people of Palestine, desiring to befriend all peoples, looks to the support of the States which love freedom, justice and peace in restoring the legal situation to Palestine, establishing security and peace in its territory, and enabling its people to exercise national sovereignty and national freedom.

> Article 24: The Palestinian Arab people believes in the principles of justice, freedom, sovereignty, self-determination, human dignity and the right of peoples to exercise them.[12]

Although it is obvious that the terrorists are murderers, that fact does not mean that many of them are not sincere in their belief that they are fighting justly in self-defense. The same terrible human process is at work in many walks of life. In psychiatry, for example, we find especially troubling illustrations of how treatment procedures that are sincerely intended to help patients nonetheless carry within them the serious dangers of oppression and brutalization. The Academy Award winning movie of Ken Kesey's *One Flew Over the Cuckoo's Nest* portrayed brilliantly for millions of aghast viewers how entirely sincere psychiatric professionals can beat patients into submission, even through mind-destroying lobotomies.[13] In recent years, there have been increasing protests against the vicious acts that go on in some so-called mental health institutions: beatings, injections of the patient with his own urine, electric shock, far-reaching psychosurgery and so on.[14]

Ultimately, the problem seems to be man's age-old tendency and need to project onto somebody else what they cannot bear in themselves. "I blame you, my spouse, for the misery in our marriage." "The Jews are responsible for the breakdown of our economy." "The blacks are causing the deterioration of our society." It does not seem likely that people can be taught to fight only in genuine self-defense until we learn much more about how to control and reduce our tendency to attribute to others responsibility for our own problems and worst weaknesses, as well as our ingenious ways of blaming others for our own destructiveness. Even when claims of self-defense are largely valid, if the psychology of people is largely directed toward blaming others rather than toward a genuine search for reconciliation, a projection process is set in motion, and the odds are that no lasting solution will be found to the conflict. It is as if people say to one another: "Thanks for starting the war with me. Now I can blame you for the war as well as for all the troubles of my life."

Objective Justification for Fighting in Self-defense

We live in a fairly insane world in which both innocents and killers cry out in sincerity that they are being attacked and must fight back in self-defense. Before long, trusting people become demoralized and cynical in the face of the true lack of meaning of the claims of self-defense issuing from all quarters with equal passion. People who choose to see the situation cynically insist that there are clear-cut differences between the innocent and the guilty and that we ought to be able to tell when Machiavellian people lie and call their murdering "self-defense" in order to throw everybody off their trail. The situation is more complicated for the people who are prepared to see the credibility of the unbelievable; namely, that in most cases, even murderers' claims of fighting in self-defense are not entirely cynical. Sometimes it seems that mankind is forever doomed to walk a tightrope between claims of self-defense that are, in fact, true and claims that, though essentially false, are rendered with a sincerity that invests them with a quality of truthfulness.

We also have to differentiate between the initiation of destructive attacks and all that happens later on. If Party A is the original aggressor but actions taken by Party B in self-defense are used to justify and confirm claims of self-defense by Party A, a system of circular events soon develops. The later events in the sequence create a new reality, which almost inevitably justifies the positions of both parties that they are acting in self-defense. Anatol Rapoport points out an ultimate absurdity in the definition of self-defense in natural life. The original predator destroys his prey only incidentally to fulfill food needs, but the prey in turn might try to destroy the predator with the intention of being destructive. Carried to its logical conclusion, the label of aggressor falls not on the original predator or conqueror who destroys people because of a need for land, but on the people who resist, in self-defense, because their intent, clearly and decisively, is to destroy the foe.[15] *Arab terrorists attack an Israeli school bus, and many children are killed. The Israelis react with an attack on the terrorist base from which the attack was launched. For obvious reasons, the Arab terrorists maintain their headquarters and training camp adjacent to a civilian refugee camp. Although the Israeli soldiers take care not to harm civilians and even provide emergency medical services to civilians who are hurt, a price in innocent lives is paid. The next day brings pictures of dead and wounded civilians, and the Arab world is confirmed in its conviction that the Israeli attacks are cruel, murderous assaults on helpless people.*[16]

Is it never possible to objectively differentiate the degrees of validity of claims of self-defense? In criminal law, there are established criteria for examining a claim of self-defense. When an individual claims that a killing was done in self-defense, the legal system seeks to examine objectively the extent of the threat to which the person responded, how the defender perceived or experienced the threat, and the true nature of the defender's motivation at the time—including his behavior preceding the act of self-defense. The total configuration of these different elements is then considered by the judge and jury before they render judgment.

There is no reason why the same standards cannot be applied to affairs between nations and peoples. However, before that can be done, there must be an acknowledgment of and even a respect for the sincerity of the experience of self-defense that is claimed by all people. Evil men, too, can and do feel that they are killing in self-defense, and this fact needs to be registered in legal, historical, political, and social science analyses along with the rest of the objective research on the extent to which a nation or a people plan, initiate, express, and revel in their destructiveness.

USING OUR UNDERSTANDING OF SELF-DEFENSE
TO CREATE NEW TOOLS OF CONFLICT RESOLUTION

We have seen that in marriage an awareness that the hated other is suffering just as we are can lead to better marital relations. So long as a spouse sees only the other's "evil," there is little basis for anything but more hostility. But something can shift if and when one becomes aware that the agony of one's mate is no different from one's own. In marital therapy, we teach spouses to respect the other's genuine hurt while protecting oneself against further assault. We teach techniques of communication that aim both at self-defense against further abuse and at opening the door to mutual reconciliation. We teach mates how to express their anger to one another without acting on those feelings in overt ways; to recognize that even their hate is part of a larger whole of caring and wishes to love again; to communicate clearly and effectively the key emotional issues; and to invite and respect their mate's similar communication of feelings. We teach spouses how to seek the help of a therapist (a conflict-resolution consultant); how to involve other members of the family and even friends in the conflict process so that a larger "community" helps deal with the conflict; how to deepen one's love of one's self while riding out the worst conflicts; and, most of all, how to extend crises over a period of time rather than to expect solutions immediately.

These various prescriptions for bettering marital relations work only when one spouse is not too angry and not too consumed by the "legitimacy" of his or her self-defense to be able to realize the worthwhileness and humanity of the other spouse. The same is true in affairs between nations: Breaking the grip of the notion that another nation and people are forever and totally evil is necessary if the door to the corrective processes that may save lives on both sides is to be opened.

So much unnecessary violence results from misperceptions of another people as an entirely cruel enemy that deserves only to be destroyed in self-defense,[17] and some of the great moments of history have come when leaders of nations have dared to take the initiative to make contact with dreaded enemies. Although the final outcome is not yet clear, Anwar Sadat's remarkable initiative in going to Jerusalem after thirty years of war between Egypt and Israel is a heartwarming example of a peacemaking effort.

Unquestionably, the who, how, and when of courageous initiatives to stop violence between peoples requires far more than idealistic hopes. In recent years, there have been exciting, though fledgling, efforts in the social sciences to experiment with new ways to bring conflicting people into contact and communication with one another. Morton Deutsch has shown experimentally that communication is useless in highly competitive situations unless people are taught how to cooperate and that the best overall strategy for eliciting cooperation from an adversary is to reward cooperative behavior while continuing to maintain an adequate defense against the threat posed by that adversary.[18] The same theme has been developed in greater detail by peace researcher Alan Newcombe in an exciting review of various models of behavior for developing foreign policies – as individuals and as nations.[19] A growing number of efforts to develop new models and techniques of communication, negotiation, adjudication, and conflict resolution are reported in the social science literature. Many of these innovative models aim at the possibility of considering the interests of all concerned parties rather than resorting to traditional legal structures, which attempt to justify the rights of one party over another. In group dynamics and communication labs, exciting procedures have been developed to teach people how to separate fact from perception; how to seek to empathize with one another; how to separate criticisms of another person's means and goals from attacks on the totality of that person's right to exist; how to identify and respond to the similarities of otherwise opposing points of view; how to effect significant social change by beginning with units of behavior that are small enough to be changed before tackling larger goals; and how to deal with immediate practical problems instead of entrenched ideological viewpoints.

Optimal Self-defense Is Victory for All Concerned

Earlier we considered a proposal to conceive of solutions to conflict as no-lose solutions. In a no-lose model, the aim of negotiation is to arrive at a solution that is seen by both sides as honorable and as satisfying their important goals. Under no-lose ground rules, any proposed solution that is not seen in this way by both parties cannot be considered. If this no-lose principle is accepted by both parties, neither party tries to wear down their opponent until the opponent gives in to their pressure. Instead, both parties must – which really means are free to – search for marvelous, undreamed of new solutions (or dialectical syntheses) that promise to satisfy and encourage both sides. No effort is made to bargain – "I'll give you this if you'll give me that" – to strong-arm – "Unless you give us such and such we'll destroy you" – or to wear out – "We've been through this again and again; in the meantime, people are suffering, so why don't you see it our way?" Rather, the emotional and procedural focus of no-lose negotiations is to discover mutually winning solutions, no matter how long it takes. No-lose thinking takes people away from their polarized convictions of what they must have and opens the door to new, innovative ideas for cooperation. If working on a problem in this way leads to entirely new definitions of what is needed for the good of all concerned, so much the better. "We thought we had to keep business competition out of our area, but now we find that a cooperative promotion of our products is paying off for both of our companies."

Obviously, it isn't easy to arrive at no-lose solutions. Nor is it easy to rechannel one's natural feelings of fighting in self-defense. To the best of my knowledge, actual applications of no-lose thinking to serious war-peace, revolutionary, or terrorist situations have not been reported. However, there are reports of a meaningful use of no-lose concepts in family situations, organizational development, and a variety of laboratory studies of conflict.[20] The point is that the no-lose concept is an example of the possibility of developing new tools for solving conflicts if and when we accept the truth that virtually all people feel that what they are doing is in self-defense.

The no-lose point of view means that victory in any conflict situation is a victory for all, whereas the traditional concept of successful self-defense means you destroy the other party before he gets you. In traditional thinking about self-defense, we are encouraged, even if inadvertently, to seize, wound, or kill the other—in effect, to confirm his vulnerability before he can do so to us. We are now saying that really optimal self-defense is to build a new climate of respect for all parties to the conflict—in effect, to erect defenses against a projection of our vulnerabilities onto one another. Optimal self-defense is an effort to help all parties triumph over terror. We seek for all of us to feel better, stronger, more equal, more competent, and more open to real aliveness for whatever time we have on this earth.

The effort at such optimal self-defense requires that at least one of the principals seeks to do everything possible to contain the immediate conflict process and to try to develop a momentum toward long-range, no-lose solutions, which will strengthen the self-interest of all parties to the conflict. Such a concept of self-defense is patently far more attractive and life saving than are the empty triumphs of murder and subjugation of other peoples, claiming large land areas, or imposing one's religion or ideology on others. Such cooperation can also often lead to agreements to join forces in a common battle against the mutual enemies of disease, pollution, and want. It should also be acknowledged that nothing in these remarks is intended to speak against shooting in self-defense when a blazing gun is firing at you. However, it is far better if one can manage to say before the guns blaze away, "Don't shoot, we're also earthlings!"

Fighting Against Seductions of Power

Proper self-defense involves a circular process, both for individuals and for nations. Take, for example, people who have been weak and have not known how to fight for themselves and inspire them to grow in their dignity and self-reliance; now watch excitedly as they raise themselves up so they are no longer available to be victims. They grow strong and proud of their new-found ability to stand in their own self-defense when they must. But now these newly strong people are also faced with perplexing new choices as to when and how to use their power. Even if they develop a long tradition of guarding against destructiveness, eventually their power will lead to potential corruption, and they stand to lose the integrity of fighting only to protect themselves.

As we have seen, any and all uses of power are self-reinforcing, because the very thrust of activity is a welcome antidote to anxieties about nonaliveness and nonbeing. Without knowing it, people are drawn to seek more and more power. There is also the banal tendency to repeat whatever one has been doing, in increased proportions. Sadly the process of power begetting more power appears to be an inexorable process, that after gaining a sorely needed strength, the former victims will face the same possibility of being drawn to a misuse and an immoral exercise of their power that their former oppressors faced. Furthermore the now-powerful, former-victim people will continue to have a sense of fighting in self-defense for a very long time, and that feeling will justify even inappropriate decisions to exercise power.

Our whole tragic-comic world is fighting in self-defense. There are the powerful ones among us who are still fighting against long past histories of victimization. There are small but proud peoples trying to stand up to the giants. There are weak and desperate peoples ready to fight to the last man in a heroic, martyred self-defense. There is never an end to starry-eyed revolutionaries fighting for new freedoms, unaware of the bizarre irony that when the dust of their revolution settles, they will be leading people to the same execution sites their current oppressor takes his victims to.[21]

A touching *New Yorker* piece, written at the height of the U.S. struggle over the morality of the war in Vietnam, captures the tragedy of man's illusion of fighting in self-defense.

> Why, we keep asking in bewilderment, are the people on our side always getting themselves mixed up with the people on the other side? Why are the hostages mixed up with the prisoners? Why do the friendly villagers wear the same kind of clothes as the unfriendly villagers? Why are our own children marching with that disorderly mob? By blinding and deafening ourselves with our own gunfire, we get past these confusions and create a temporary, false simplicity. We are never so sure of the identity of our enemies as when we see the dim figures running through the tear gas in the sights of our rifles. After all, if they aren't our enemies, why are we shooting them? We override the disorderly variety of the world with an indiscriminately uniform type of violence. When we go in, all thought breaks down, and we can speak of saving villages by destroying them and of saving hostages by killing them. We begin to kill our own allies, to kill our own people who are being held as hostages, to kill our own children. For a moment, we forget who they are and forget who we are, and forget what it is we're trying to do to them. And when the violence is over, we remain trapped in the fictitious world that was born of our fears and our violent impulses.[22]

Peasant Woman Stomped to Death by GI's at My Lai, Sergeant Writes

Portland, Ore. — A former member of Capt. Ernest Medina's company, in a letter made public today, said some men in the unit had turned into "wild animals" two days before the alleged My Lai massacre in Vietnam, beating children and stomping a friendly peasant woman to death.

"Why in God's name does this have to happen?" Sgt. Gregory Olsen, 20, of Portland, asked in a letter mailed to his father on March 14, 1968. "These are all seemingly normal guys, some were friends of mine. For a while they were like wild animals."

Medina's company entered the My Lai area on March 16, and according to participants and eyewitnesses, deliberately killed as many as 370 men, women and children.

In his letter, Olsen said the woman was killed after one member of his platoon was killed and four others severely injured when a booby-trapped artillery round exploded. The letter scrawled in pencil on standard GI field stationery, continued:

"On their way back to 'Dotty' (Landing Zone Dotty, the company's support base near My Lai) they saw a woman working in the fields. They shot and wounded her. Then they kicked her to death and emptied their rifle magazines in her head. They slugged every little kid they came across.

"Why in God's name does this have to happen? These are all seemingly normal guys, some were friends of mine. For a while they were like wild animals.

"It was murder, and I'm ashamed of myself for not trying to do anything about it.

"This isn't the first time, dad, I've seen it many times before. I don't know why I'm telling you all this. I guess I just want to get it off my chest.

"My faith in my fellow man is all shot to hell. I just want the time to pass and I just want to come home."

William Doherty, 21, of Readville, Mass., now stationed in Texas but who then served with Medina, recalled it this way:

"It happened right after we had a couple of guys killed and injured by a mine. . . . we started shooting at her, she fell down.

"I ran there. I was the first to get there. I kicked her, and then I saw she was a woman, so I stopped. But some of the other guys kept on."

Moments later, he said, she was shot.

Mike Terry, another member of the company who now lives in Utah, gave this account:

"Several of us spotted her . . . we ran and chased her . . . she fell down . . . a couple of guys were kicking her . . . then all of a sudden it happened.

"They were just standing around, kicking her. . . . I saw it happen and yelled as I ran up, asking why they were doing it. Then another member of the company walked up and shot her."

After that prelude came the My Lai incident.

Olsen remains convinced that there was no direct order from Medina to destroy the village and kill the people, as others in the company have told newsmen.

—Seymour M. Hersh, Special Correspondent, *Philadelphia Bulletin,* December 2, 1969

9

SACRIFICING OTHERS TO THE DEATH WE FEAR OURSELVES: THE ULTIMATE ILLUSION OF SELF-DEFENSE

The Nazis ran closed bids for the construction of the gas chambers:

1. *A. Tops and Sons, Erfurt, manufacturers of heating equipment: "We acknowledge receipt of your order for five triple furnaces, including two electric elevators for raising the corpses and one emergency elevator. . . ."*
2. *Vidier Works, Berlin: "For putting the bodies into the furnace, we suggest simply a metal fork moving on cylinders. . . ."*
3. *C. H. Kori: "We guarantee the effectiveness of the cremation ovens, as well as their durability, the use of the best material and our faultless workmanship."*

— Harry H. Shapiro

The more I think of it, the more it appears that the intelligent, the just and the really good people who come after us will find it hard to understand how this could have happened; to comprehend how the very idea of murder — mass murder — could begin in the dark recesses and convolutions of the brain of an ordinary human being: one born of a mother, fed at the breast, educated in a school. An ordinary human being like millions of others. . . . A normal human being, at the sight of another's suffering, even at the thought of it, will, in his imagination, see it all happening to himself, or will, at least, feel spiritual pain.

— Anatoly Kuznetzov

What brings people to the state where they become gruesome murderers? We know that most "everyday" murders take place within a context of intimacy. Unpardonable as the crime of murder must always be, there is at least some sense to what takes place, for example, when a deeply upset man or woman is enraged by a mate's betrayal. In the agony and madness of the moment, it seems as if there is no way out but to rid oneself permanently of the torturing presence of the other. Indeed, a murder committed because of sexual betrayal by a spouse has long been recognized by courts of law around the world as "justified homicide." Yet, most of us know deep inside ourselves that even when our hearts are breaking in agony and rage, we remain solidly committed not to become killers. We may very well *feel* like killing, but we know that we will not actually do so.

The most maddening paradox is that many people who would never allow themselves to be drawn to murder even in the passion of domestic agony nonetheless are counted among that terrible majority (the "nearly all of us") who are available to be a genocider. What inner psychology can possibly bring people to that state? What inner experiences can allow otherwise good people to murder, not in a moment of passion or self-defense, but in a cold-blooded, systematic extermination of helpless people?

THE UNIVERSALITY OF PROJECTION

There are few human settings in which the device of projecting one's feared weaknesses onto another is not encouraged, rehearsed, and reinforced. Apparently, the natural temptation for all of us to put onto someone else whatever we fear most in ourselves is enormous. Knowing how to select a scapegoat and how to unload our feared weaknesses onto another seems rooted in our very being.

Even very young children show an intuitive knowledge of how to lay their own feelings or behavior at the doorstep of someone else — a doll, a pet, a sibling, a parent, or even an imaginary friend. In how many households around the world do we hear an "innocent" young child attribute his own impulse to bite mother to mommy herself or charge the family pet with the unwelcome bowel movement that didn't quite make it to the toilet? As life goes on, every human being becomes a "jailhouse lawyer" and learns how to draw rapidly on the defense that someone else did whatever it is that he or she is charged with doing and does not want to acknowledge. Before very long, this style of defense becomes so beguiling and self-deluding that we end up not being able to distinguish when we are using it. Even when we really do want to know the truth, we discover that we no longer know how to discern it. Thus, the ludicrous situation can arise in which we feel more guilty than we should. Take an automobile accident that really was caused by someone else. Since everyone's first instinct invariably is to blame others when we are at fault, those of us who are aware how readily we project responsibility for our actions onto others may end up questioning ourselves even when we are "sure" the other party was at fault.

In married life, the most frequent reason for arguments turns out to be the unconscious projection of one's denied weaknesses onto one another. Often, one spouse harbors the same inner weakness of character the other one does but shows that weakness in a different way. For example, a man may rail against his wife for her poor housekeeping. He himself is a well-organized, successfully functioning executive. However, when it comes to the organization of his emotions, his inner state is very similar to the disarray in which his wife keeps the house. His fury in attacking her housekeeping is testimony to his own deep shame and fear of how unkempt he is in his own emotional housekeeping.

In every mythology and folklore, there are numerous symbols and devices for projecting what we fear in ourselves onto others. In the Bible, there are actually explicit instructions as to how to go about projecting one's burdens onto a substitute. One is advised in Leviticus to cast all of one's sins and transgressions onto the hapless animal that is sent as the scapegoat into the wilderness; the explicit purpose of this ceremony is to lighten the load of guilt borne by people in their everyday lives and to relieve their dread of punishment by God. The whole era of the Bible, of course, was characterized by an intricate pageantry of sacrificing animals, and we are told by cultural historians and students of religion that those animal sacrifices represented a developmental substitute for the sacrificing of children.

In the prayers, ceremonials, and myths of ancient peoples, efforts to gain good fortune for oneself are coupled with prayers and incantations beseeching that all manner of woes, misfortunes, and plagues befall one's enemies. A people generally asks their gods to be blessed at the expense of their enemies. Almost universally, the underlying mythology is that it is either them or us, hence, we pray for our good fortune and the destruction of others. We curse our enemies with the blights and tragedies we fear may befall us.

The same mechanism is at work in human beings' never-ending revenges against enemies, real or fancied. How much of life is spent in "getting even" or "getting back" at some other person or group? Many revenges are not only efforts to even a score of some sort, but vehicles through which we transfer all of our vulnerability onto the subject of our revenge. "Thanks for giving me such a hard time. Now I'll be able to fight back and use you as my whipping post. I can accuse you of causing me to feel bad and not have to challenge myself for how poorly I am managing my own life." Nations do this all the time. Often an outside enemy is welcomed as a means to get away from the serious problems in one's own government, economy, or society. Whatever ails a people, they find another people to blame. Ronald Laing, who is remarkable for his understanding of interplays both in family life and in the larger flow of the family of mankind, writes: "As war continues, both sides come more and more to resemble each other. The uroborus eats its own tail. The wheel turns full circle. Shall we realize that We and They are shadows of each other? We are They to Them as They are They to Us. When will the veil be lifted? When will the charade turn to carnival? Saints may still be kissing lepers. It is high time that the leper kissed the saint."[1]

Back and forth it goes. I blame you for blaming me. You blame me for blaming you for blaming me. We lock horns in feuds, hates, and non-forgiveness.[2]

DEFINING ANOTHER PEOPLE AS NOT-HUMAN

In group life, the mechanism of projection seizes on the differences between people. From the very beginning of life, human beings are aware of the difference between the strange and the familiar. The infant develops a warm, joyful relationship with the familiarness of its mother. However, the very joy of such familiarness is accompanied by considerable anxiety about the possible loss of the mother. The process of handling separation anxiety is one of the critical processes in an infant's early development. It is the fortunate human being who learns to trust his inner experience that mother is with him and caring for him even when mother is not in fact physically present. For too many infants, unfortunately, the challenging-enough natural process of separation anxiety is further complicated by insults and hurts of actual maternal rejection and abandonment, which scar the inner psyche so that a great deal of patience and courage is required to overcome those insults and hurts in later years. Paradoxically, infants who are not left sufficiently alone also suffer, because they are not able to practice mastering their separation anxiety and to build a conviction born of experience that mother can be counted on to return.

In addition to building self-assurance to bear aloneness, the infant also has to master a normal anxiety about strangers. Beginning somewhere toward the end of the first year of life, the stranger becomes a frightening presence for an infant.[3] Sometimes a warm, loving infant will embarrass its family by being obviously frightened of an aunt or a grandparent who has not been to visit for a while. The fear of strangers is naturally linked by the infant to its basic anxiety over being separated from its mother. It is the capacity of the mother and the familiar to offer a comforting presence and reassurance in the face of the unknown that allows the infant to trust its ability to survive the tensions of the stranger and of strangeness itself. Of course, what strangers actually do to the infant also has a good deal to do with shaping the infant's mastery of this anxiety. The ability to separate from mother and the ability to bear the tension that strangers engender are processes that a child develops stage by stage. As the years go by, a child can enjoy longer and longer periods of being without his or her parents and can make more and more venturesome sallies into life to deal with its challenges.

It is amusing to see just how deep man's yearning for the familiar is when neighbors or acquaintances who never really enjoyed one another back home meet far away from their home terrain. The remarkable warmth that flows between them in such reunions bespeaks the great comfort that people find in one another simply because of their familiarity with one another. In some parts of the world, it is a foregone conclusion that commerce, politics, and avoiding bureaucratic hassles are best accomplished by going to a person one has dealt with previously. Often there need not have been any special experience of emotional connection; what makes the difference is no more than the simple experience of two people meeting and recognizing one another as familiar. The wave of "familiarity warmth" that is set off by such reunions is remarkable, and it is little short of incredible how this feeling leads people to want to be helpful to one another. It almost seems as if a reunion with a familiar person or object offers an unconscious reassurance that one is still alive.

The stranger, on the other hand, represents all of people's fears of aloneness, vulnerability, and ultimate death. For most of us, it takes a considerable amount of experience to learn to trust those who are very different from us and to experience our common humanity with them. If we read in the newspaper that a neighbor has been killed, we are startled and upset; among other things, we immediately begin thinking about ourselves and the possibility of our sharing the same fate. But if we read about the death of someone further off, it is only to the extent that we experience some symbolic identification with the other person that we feel some measure of concern and involvement. Thus, if our religious or ethnic compatriots across the sea are slaughtered, we are likely to experience a reaction to their fate. But if people who are very different from us are slaughtered, we are not likely to have any sense of emotional involvement. As a matter of fact, there are many sensitive people who are upset by the realization that they can't care very much about some far-off victims when they really wish they could feel more.

From time immemorial, the stranger has been seized on as the object of projections of what people fear and dislike in themselves. Ultimately, this means people's fears of their very mortality. Projection onto strangers is a process that can be tracked through several stages. In some instances, the projection stays pretty much on the level of an awareness of difference. "They are so different from us, and we don't feel the same in their presence as we do when we are with our own kind." In itself, this level of projection is not especially damaging, but too often this beginning level of projection is escalated until we categorize the other people as less valuable.

In a further stage of the projection, the other people are defined not only as intrinsically less valuable, but as not of our kind, even as not of our species. This is a critical point in the sequence of escalating the projection. Representing another people as if they were a nonhuman species sets the stage for possible violence to them. As ethologist Konrad Lorenz has pointed out, it is not characteristic of most animal species to do violence to members of their own species (intraspecific aggression) except under specifically provocative conditions, such as overcrowding.[4] Violence is characteristically directed at members of other species (extraspecific aggression), and even then largely for "sensible" reasons, such as food needs. For Lorenz, the fact that human beings do not follow this rule is a disturbing indication that something has gone wrong in man's very evolution. However, the fact is that the natural process Lorenz has observed does hold for humans far more than he imagines. What human beings do through the enormous power of symbolization (or ideology) is to redefine another people as not of our species and then set them up as subject to that natural aspect of animal life that permits violence against strangers or members of another species more readily than against members of one's own family or species.

Throughout history, man has erupted viciously against the stranger in his midst or against the stranger at his border. North and South seem to be almost natural images for civil and neighbor wars, for example. Religious differences have led to countless bloody killings over the centuries. Men divide up according to their political labels and find in those distinctions ample justification for murder. And names for the accused others always spring into use—for instance, kikes, niggers, gooks.

Natural differences between people readily cause projections of weakness, vulnerability, and mortality onto those who are different and weaker than we are. Often groups seize on one another as objects for the projection of their deepest dread of dying. This is one of the main reasons that people have never been able to stop the terrible recurrences of war and genocide. It may very well be that unless and until we have tools for containing projection processes, most of the heroic efforts we make toward world justice and peace will be to little avail.[5]

DEATH: THE ULTIMATE VULNERABILITY

We know that many individual acts of murder represent efforts to rid oneself of a tormenting inner presence. It isn't simply that the ever-demanding wife is so exasperating that she drives her husband to murder. It is much more that the husband feels so controlled by his wife's nagging that he becomes desperate to rid himself of his weakness. If not, he could just put cotton in his ears, walk out of the room, or pretend to go along with his wife; or, if we dare think of genuinely healthy solutions to the problem, he could put his foot down firmly and tell her that the nagging is unwelcome. Similarly, it isn't simply the fact that a husband made love to another woman that drives one aggrieved wife to wield a knife (and others to the symbolic murder of instant divorce), but rather the wife's inner sense that her worst fears of not being able to hold on to her partner have been confirmed. It is to rid herself of this terrible fear come true that the wife plunges the blade into her husband's breastbone. The murder is essentially an effort to kill her own fears of weakness. The same situation exists in cases of battered infants. Generally, it is not only that the parent can't bear the child's crying, but the fact that the child's crying manages to set off the parent's own unsatisfied inner cry. The parent, in effect, hits out at the intolerable sound of his own inner anger when he mistreats the child.

The same dynamic that determines so much of what people do in individual self-defense is also significantly at play in large-scale events. Men are driven to kill in self-defense not only because of very real life threats, but because of their own inner dread of their vulnerability and mortality, which they cannot bear. History has shown over and over again that, characteristically, it is when individuals and groups are most terrified of their own possible destruction that they seize on another as the object of their fury.[6] The joy so many feel going into battle lies not only in standing up in real self-defense against the enemy, but also in their sense of triumph over feeling impotent and vulnerable.

Once we ask what fear can possibly drive human beings to feel they must drive a mass of other people to their death, the answer seems clear. Once we frame the question in this way, we are able to realize that the genocider is seeking to put off his own deepest fears of death onto others. It is no accident that the fate commanded for the other is death, for it is that fate the genocider himself is fleeing.

It is not difficult to see the deadly process of projection at work in genocidal violence, even when to all outward appearances, the genocider may be going about his business dispassionately. The guiding motif of the genocider is a proclamation to his victims: "Better you should die than I!"

Much of the incomprehensible cruelty of genocide issues from the gripping power of the genocider's own fears of death, which are projected onto his victims. The genocider does not feel cruel when he puts other people to death, because he believes he is justified in sparing himself death. Ernest Becker writes: "No one explained this dynamic more elegantly than Rank: 'The death fear of the ego is lessened by the killing, the Sacrifice, of the other; through the death of the other one buys oneself free from the penalty of dying, of being killed.'"[7]

In everyday life, people project onto one another all manner of weaknesses and their own serious fears of not feeling alive. We assign one another our fears of not being able to learn well, succeed in business, or enjoy sexuality and every other known desire at which we fear we might fail. We call the kettle black, our spouses frigid, our children stupid, our associates incompetent, our neighbors malicious. Is there any wonder that ultimately we seek to project onto one another our ultimate dread of death?

The real "demon" inside us is the *aggression* that stems from man's inability to escape awareness of his limitations of control over his destiny. Such aggressions, when dissociated, become duly projected onto the uncanny trigger agent who comes to represent this "demon." . . . It is not surprising, then, that man, in some instances, allows charismatic leaders to offer him a legitimate outlet for all the murderous impulses tied in with this complex, a license to destroy the uncanny agents—whether they be the infirm or the aged, a particular race of people, or scholars and intellectuals—who by their probings might cast some doubt on man's claims to autonomy and control.[8]

Human beings are terrified of death. True, we have seen that when we imagine our death, a part of us does accept and even looks forward to death's promise of rest and apparent wholeness. But these wishes for death are also frightening in their own right, because, most of all, we do not want to die. When we find ourselves edging toward the precipice of nothingness and face the prospect of time ceasing to exist, we are filled with a deep, horrifying terror. Much of what we know as anxiety in our everyday lives is an echo of this terror of death's nothingness. Is there any more powerful demand than a human being's crying out, "I don't want to die"?

* * *

It is the night of the full moon. The people gather to the muted beat of drums. A hush falls over the tribe. The leader raises his hands in what is at once a prayerful thrust toward the heavens and a quieting gesture to his people to announce the beginning of the rite. A young child is brought forth toward the roaring flames of the goddess.

* * *

They march past on a country road, tattered, disheveled, and broken. The stamp of approaching death is on them, and it is as if they are no longer of us humans. Yet, somewhere inside us we know only too well and remember that they have been of us. We try not to look, at least not to see. Somewhere inside of us we approach the edge of knowing that we too could have been among those disheveled nonhumans. At the same time, something in us also leaps alive with excitement at the feeling that these people are going to the mystery of the death we ourselves dread. Thank God it is they and not us. A strange beat of excitement grips us as well as a terrible shame at being so excited. The silent mixture of excitement, pleasure, shame, and terror sickens us. We are the neighbors everywhere — along the roads to Dachau, Auschwitz, and countless other places whose names we know and don't know.

* * *

THE ROLE OF LEADERS: INITIATING, SPEARHEADING, AND AUTHORIZING DESTRUCTION

If and when people talk about genocide in our culture (which is not too often), they are wont to say that such and such economic, political, or social circumstances brought about a particular genocidal event — if it weren't for those conditions, it could never have happened. Often the historical tradition of a people is faulted: "They were always a war-seeking people. Another people could not have done what they did." In most cases, the personality of the genociders' leader is seen as the prime cause: "If only Hitler hadn't been born," they say. In effect, humans continue to explain genocides as the acts of madmen or mad cultures.

The notion of the Bad Leader especially is so pervasive and such a disarmingly simple view of human holocausts that people flee to its "comfort" over and over again. But so long as one accepts the view that it is the leader who largely or exclusively determines genocidal violence, there is little that can be said about the choices of millions of us who are far removed from the leadership function.

Stated epigrammatically (and I hope not offensively), there is a "Hitler" in all of us, and Hitler himself was human too—so were Robespierre, Caligula, Cambodia's Pol Pot, and the many anonymous human beings in killer squads all over the world. The capability of being a genocider is in all of us, and a humanness beats in the killers' hearts as well. We were all with the U.S. military force in Vietnam that destroyed a village and its inhabitants. We were all on a deadly march with a Gestapo squad in the Jewish ghetto of Warsaw. There are far too many instances in human history of genocidal violence for us to dare to be content with seeing genocide as the act of only madmen or a mad nation.

How much of a role do the leaders of a people have, after all, in the inception, launching, execution, and legitimation of the destruction of another people? Much of history has been written around those focal personalities who demanded the death of masses of another people. Obviously, they did exercise enormous power, and in many cases, history itself gives us a clear picture of those leaders' personality styles as they ordered the death of others. Sometimes it is as if the leader were acting on a whim to remove inconsequential specks of humanity; other times, testing the blind obedience of men to him alone; still other times, removing the weak and ill as a matter of "convenience," because they were a burden to efficient administration. What is common to most of the styles of leadership for genocidal destruction is a psychology of power seeking. The act of delivering another people to death is used by the leader to prove his omnipotent position or emotional superiority or to serve the convenience of his power plans and needs. Often the leader will cast the motives of mass murder in a larger frame, which claims that the purpose of the destruction is to bolster the power of an entire people or an ideology. But in these instances, too, the basic mechanism is to gain power for oneself through obliterating another's power, and the leader who inspires or authorizes these plans is still serving his own personal psychology of power.

Some mass murders bespeak the actual madness of a given leader, although even this explanation avoids many serious issues, including the question of how those leaders get to be mad. They are not always mad when they start out. One question that has always intrigued scholars and laymen alike is whether the people who get to be great leaders and then turn to genocide were consumed all along with disastrous power needs. An entirely different possibility is that even well-adjusted people who mean to lead well might be driven by the enormous anxieties of leadership into the hands of the power dynamic as it corrupts people and makes them "crazy with power."

Some genocidal events in history have been a direct outcome of the psychology of a particular satanic leader who was consumed with a desire to destroy masses of people. History has produced an inordinate number of Genghis Khans, Napoleons, Hitlers, and Stalins. There is no question that such leaders wreak enormous damage, owing to the command or authority structure in which they operate. The worst problem of all in any society is that the majority of human beings are sheeplike in their obedience and conformity to authority, even when they are instructed to commit heinous acts that go against their real values and beliefs. In addition, even in a democratic society, where there are significant checks and balances against the excesses of leaders, it takes some time before the society's corrective machinery is mobilized to contain the badness of a duly vested leader. This age-old problem of a leader's power for destruction has become more and more overwhelming as methods of destruction have become more and more grotesquely powerful, easier to launch, and increasingly anonymous and mechanical. The fact that technicians thousands of miles away from their victims can destroy thousands, millions, of people with little or no warning means, increasingly, that a leader needs to command only a few underlings to wreak massive destruction.

And yet, it would be a grave error to focus exclusively or even primarily on the leaders of a people as responsible for mass destruction. The main problem with that view of history and life is that it adds to the illusion (projection) that the potential for meting out cruel death to large numbers of people is borne by only a few people and not by all of us. Morever, it is not clear whether the leader really operates as independently as it appears. For example, we might say as follows about Hitler and Germany:

1. The charismatic mad leader
2. captured the leadership of a people at a point of
   a. deep frustration in the historical pride of the people
   b. that was the more bitter and extreme because of mounting economic want.
3. The leader exploited the people's readiness to act violently as a mob
4. and exploited the traditions of compulsive efficiency and cruel militarism that are integral to the Germanic tradition.

That is not an unsophisticated analysis. As a beginning "systems analysis," it goes well beyond the childlike folk picture of the single bad man (Hitler) who was the sole author and executor of a dastardly policy. The flow of events I have sketched includes something of the processes within a society that lead to a people's readiness to rely on a charismatic leader because of a severe attack on the pride and stability of that society. There is, furthermore, a recognition of the basic traditions and processes of the culture that invite and authorize the leader to command the society to undertake various degrees of destructiveness. In this analysis, it is clear that although the leader stands out as the person most dramatically responsible for the destruction, the leader's power rests on the people's availability to violence. Such a systems analysis says, in effect, that the leader is the person who is responsible for deciding whether or not to activate available violence in the society but the society, too, is responsible for its interest in and propensity for violence. This is different from what is generally implied in the bad man theory, namely, that a given leader plants and cultivates violence and evil in an otherwise innocent society.

In his exciting history of the end of World War II, John Toland writes:

> Hitler did not spring from a void; the excesses perpetrated by him were a culmination of a straight, relentless line of persecution that had been going on for centuries, from the time of the Crusades through the First Reich—the Holy Roman Empire—in the Middle Ages to the Second Reich of Bismarck and Kaiser Wilhelm the II, when a strong belief in German racial superiority was developed. He was the logical heir to the bloodthirsty prophets as well and, like them, he was dynamic and ruthless, obsessed by apocalyptic fantasy and completely convinced of his own infallability.[9]

In his powerful study, *The Denial of Death*, Ernest Becker compares the role of the leader to a hypnotist and then links that role to the role of the people who respond to the leader through their urges for power, especially their readiness to sacrifice others in order to spare their own lives.

> The leader takes responsibility for the destructive act, and those who destroy on his command are no longer murderers, but "holy heroes." They crave to serve in the powerful aura that he projects and to carry out the illusion that he provides them, an illusion that allows them to heroically transform the world. Under his hypnotic spell and with the full force of their own urges for heroic self-expansion, they need have no fear; they can kill with equanimity. In fact they seemed to feel that they were doing their victims "a favor," which seems to mean that they sanctified them by including them in their own "holy mission." As we have learned from the anthropological literature, the victim who is sacrificed becomes a holy offering to the gods, to nature, or to fate. The community gets more life by means of the victim's death, and so the victim has the privilege of serving

the world in the highest possible way by means of his own sacrificial death.[10]

However, this analysis still does not account for the terrible fact that there are almost always bad men around to fill the role of such leaders.

The deeper truth may well be that in any collective power system, there is a standing invitation for charismatic, dictatorial, and brutal leaders to emerge and there will always be candidates for the position. The fuller test of what happens in a society is how the collective system is structured to deal with the emergence of such would-be leaders for destruction.[11] Even when we grant that in modern times, a mad, destructive leader can wreak terrible damage in a short time before the corrective forces of society can stop him, the question remains whether there is any kind of collective responsibility in a society. Certainly one can observe human life on a grand scale, but the question goes even deeper: To what extent does the ongoing historical process of a people make it likely or possible for their leader to become madly destructive in the first place? Students of German history point out that the brutality encouraged by Hitler's grim megalomania was entirely consistent with the long-term compulsive-militaristic traditions of the German people.

Similarly, some observers see various forces in the culture process in the United States that line up for and against the possibilities of a U.S.-made genocide. On the one hand, there is the enormous vitality of the system of checks and balances within the structure of the U.S. government, and there is an electoral process that is largely responsible to the collective power of the people. The history of the United States shows that the people are capable of stopping massacres and are capable of bringing about the removal of leaders from office. On the other hand, in many ways the U.S. tradition continues to be frontierlike and therefore tends to accept power and violence as everyday facts of life.[12] Everyday violence continues to dominate much of the life in the United States, amid the grandeur of plenty and creativity. The U.S. tradition is also overwhelmingly committed to the values of pragmatism or efficiency, which often compete against the people's needs and humanistic values. In the previous chapter, we noted William Blanchard's observation that the United States is given to a self-righteousness that gives rise to a seductive rationalization of violent power.[13] These various trends in the collective U.S. experience make possible periodic genocidal campaigns against other people: the war in Vietnam (seen as a whole or in events such as My Lai); some would say the use of the atomic bomb; the campaign against the Philippines earlier in this century; and certainly, the early—and, strangely, still-celebrated—history of the white man's subjugation of the Indians.

In other words, there are processes at work within cultures that make it possible and even likely that leaders will arise who will call for a campaign of destruction. The leaders do so because of their own personality needs, of course, and they trade on the dynamics of the power that their position brings them, but they are able to strike out in the direction of mass murder because their culture makes it possible for them to express power in that way.

The same process is at work in determining how violent "everyday disturbed people" will be in different cultures. There are cultures in which it is expected, and therefore likely, that people will kill in the anguish of great passion and rage; there are other cultures in which even when you "go crazy" with the very same kind of anguish and rage, you are expected not to kill, and, therefore, even very upset people generally find other ways to vent their rage and passion.

In a wide-ranging survey of contemporary violence, A. S. Barram proposes that in the long run, society is the critical factor in determining the play of oppressors and victims. He suggests that there will always be extremists who are in authority, and there will always be people selected for the role of victims, but the third force, which has the power to determine "to what extreme of classification or abuse any minority can be taken is entirely dependent on . . . the audience, in which case this becomes a matter of personal concern to every man."[14]

If there are processes at work within a culture that make it possible, probable, and even "psychohistorically necessary" for the leaders to move toward the "triumphant" destruction of other peoples, then we should not accept simplistic versions of history that do not go beyond the stories of individuals who lead their people to genocide. We need a more sophisticated and complex picture of the dynamic forces that are at work within each society or cultural tradition as a whole, along with the dynamics of its leader as a person, as well as the historical picture to which the leader and the society are subject in a given era. It is not enough then to say, "Hitler was mad." At the very least, the capacity of a Hitler to move up the political ladder, consolidate power, and mobilize a campaign of genocidal destruction of another people has to be a function of the readiness of the people to go in that direction. From this point of view, if there had not been an Adolf Hitler, another John Doe Hitler would have arisen, who would have given expression to that particular society's thirst for war and sacrifice-hunting folk psychology. To the extent that a people rejects scapegoating another people in their everyday life and in their society's social and political institutions, it is doubtful that a leader can lead that people to genocide.

It seems more correct that we seek both to assign responsibility to each leader for the choices he makes within the flow of events that swirl around him and through him and to understand the processes of the collective events that make up the context in which the leader makes his choices. Even within the flow of deterministic historical events, the leader, and all people, are able to make choices. We know that each of us can go mad, for example, because there is a well of madness in us all, but most of us choose, even if unconsciously, not to go mad. In modern psychotherapy, we seek to teach people who have chosen to live out the mad side of their beings how they can and should choose not to do so. We do so even as we see how those unfortunate people are led by the events of their lives to madness. We say to them nonetheless, "You can throw off the chains of your background (determinism) and exercise new choices (freedom) so as to be in charge of your life."

The historical view that emphasizes the role of the leader leaves out the contributions of key aides and decision-making assistants, who do or do not agree to authorize and carry out murder of the victims. In today's United States, Canada, or England, for example, it is reasonably doubtful that any police force would carry out the order of a chief of police to line up a group of prisoners and execute them; in a totalitarian country, policemen would and do do this kind of thing all the time.[15] Irving Janis has documented how the small-group method of governing through a governmental elite often creates a strangely unreal atmosphere in which the participants do not experience the human significance of the decisions that are made. Without their knowing it, their critical capacity is dulled, and they ratify each other's ideas in an unconscious desire for group consensus and unity that pushes all other considerations ruthlessly aside.[16] Even in a democratic society, elite decision-making groups operating in this kind of atmosphere are capable of initiating totalitarian or reckless ventures, such as cloak-and-dagger conspiracies to assassinate rulers of other countries and decisions to undertake an undeclared war on an enemy. Anyone who has ever participated in committees knows the strange feeling of unrealness that can take hold of a group and how one can accede to resolutions and decisions that are far from one's true convictions. Almost without realizing what is happening, one can be pulled toward rubber-stamping whatever idea it is that somehow got going in the group. Often such decisions are mercifully lost in the minutes of the meeting and never get off the ground, but it is also a fact of life and history that many of these unrealistic, ill-begotten decisions do launch devastating sequences of events.

Granted, in a society that is openly committed to totalitarian values and the basic model of decision making invests enormous power in the chairman of any decision-making group and in the power elites of the decision-making bodies, it is overwhelmingly dangerous not to join in a majority decision. But the real dynamic is essentially the same in a democratic society: All the assistants, associates, and administrators, let alone the "simple" soldiers, policemen, or citizens "doing their duty," are responsible for making up their own minds—and too few do. In Nazi Germany, the Holocaust was the product of a complex process of many decisions by many national leaders, policymaking groups, and field commanders, all of whom slowly but surely extended the policies of brutality and local extermination to a more and more intricately organized "final decision" to destroy the Jewish people in a more terrible and methodical way than history had ever known. It is childish to think that this whole process was the work of the one madman leader, Hitler.

At the same time, it is true that the focal leader does play a critical role. In fact, the power that people vest in their leaders in a gathering historical process toward a campaign of terror and death means that, at any given moment, the very leader who is expected to authorize the killing can decide not to do so and to save the intended victims. The same people who would have blindly executed orders to kill now will stop short of killing if ordered by their leader to stop. It matters not how or why the leader comes to this out-of-character decision. Perhaps it is a whim; perhaps it is an attack of conscience; perhaps it is falling in love with someone from the victim group—all of these scripts can be found in human history. There are many tales of kingly and princely choices to rescind imminent executions. It is little known, for example, that when the Allied powers in World War II systematically refused the entry of Jewish refugees from Nazi Germany, dictators Franco of Spain and Trujillo of the Dominican Republic, who had not hesitated to massacre their own people, both offered the Jews sanctuary.[17] Another illustration of the decisive role of leaders is found in the positions taken by the different leaders of Hungary. At first, there was enthusiastic cooperation with the Nazis and at least one massacre of Jews and others, but later in the war, under the leadership of Prime Minister Kállay, the Hungarians refused to cooperate with the Nazis' extermination plan.[18]

Thus, there is much to be said for remaining aware of the important role of the leader of a genociding people. S. M. Silverman makes a cogent analysis of the victimizer in a systems analysis in which he strongly insists that we must understand the crucial role of the victimizer as well as the relationship between the vicitimizer and the victim.

> It is my contention that human nature in the mass need not be changed in order to make progress, but rather that the pathological extreme in the small group must be dealt with. In practice the difference is one of either changing human nature, an enormous and possibly impossible job at this time, or learning to recognize and deal with the pathological extremes in the nature of Everyman, a difficult but more hopeful task.[19]

Silverman believes victimizers have a number of common char-acteristics: a sense of alienation from others and from society; a deep sense of loss or deprivation; a need to control and dominate a situation; a constant need to justify one's actions on "moral" grounds; a belief that deprivation or loss is always the result of actions by persons or forces outside of the individual; the ability to use provocation techniques; needs that can never be satisfied (if the victimizer's demands are met, a new set of demands is forthcoming); a belief that language and all other communications are to be used to influence the actions of others rather than to communicate information or exchange ideas; a need to be a hero and a charismatic leader.

Silverman links his analysis of the victimizer to the availability of victims and thus avoids the oversimplification of a bad man theory. However, the leader is seen as the critical figure to whom responsibility is assigned for the key triggering role. This is an appealing, comprehen-sive analysis that combines several levels of understanding, including knowledge of primitive personality processes, interpersonal strategies, and the interacting influences of victimizer and victim.

Essentially the same conclusion is advanced by Vahakn Dadrian, one of the leading researchers of genocide, although Dadrian carefully directs his observations to decision makers rather than to the single charismatic leader. Understanding the role of the perpetrator group in general "has paramount importance," states Dadrian.

> Among the components of the initiator, the first rank is occupied by the decision-makers, the central authorities. Their chief contribution lies in their supplying the three essentials for such perpetration, namely, legitima-tion, authorization and rationalization. . . . The decision-makers are not only crucial in terms of conceiving of genocide, but far more importantly, in terms of motivating the rank and file of their cohorts as instruments of design and execution of genocide.[20]

Still, the danger that remains in any assignment of responsibility, even to an admittedly key leader or leaders, is that we are drawn to denying the potential in all human beings to be genociders, whether as leaders or as followers. I prefer, therefore, to focus on the leader as the key figure in a people's movement toward genocidal destruction but to see the leader's life as a study of the choices of good or evil that all of us must make.

THE BYSTANDER AS ACCOMPLICE TO EVIL

The relationship between leaders and followers brings us to the need to define the role of all those people who are not leaders, active followers who actually participate in executing the destruction, or victims. These are the bystanders to destruction and genocide.

Numerically, bystanders make up the majority in our world (notwithstanding the incredible numbers of people who constitute the victims and destroyers). Ostensibly, the bystander has little to do with the terrible events that take place around him, and in many cases, the bystander pretends to himself that nothing remarkable is happening, certainly nothing that requires his response, and he may actually achieve a conscious state of unknowingness. In some instances, the state of unknowingness is seemingly honest, considering that the killers take extraordinary steps to obscure what they are doing. And yet, all reports and all logic tell us that no matter how hard the killers work to conceal what they are doing, as the Germans did with malevolent skill, the smell of death is in the air, the facts filter out, and in the final analysis, knowing or not knowing is more a function of one's inner choice to dare to know or not.

Elie Wiesel deftly taps the bitter truth that the bystander, though neither executioner nor victim and apparently wanting only to live in peace, chooses to play his role of the unknowing one *after* he has, in fact, seen the hell about him. "He, standing behind the curtains, watched. The police beat women and children; he did not stir. It was no concern of his. He was neither victim nor executioner; a spectator, that's what he was. He wanted to live in peace and quiet."[21]

We have already seen the bystander up close in individual situations, such as the murder of Kitty Genovese, and we have followed some of the findings of contemporary laboratory experiments that describe what conditions tend to lead people to be seemingly unaware of the suffering that is happening to others about them. Two main conclusions seem to emerge from these various observations. The first is that if an individual experiences himself as being related to the victim, he is more likely to act on his awareness and intervene or call for help. Whenever a person is part of a large group of onlookers, the odds are greater that he will allow himself to not get involved with the victim on the grounds that others will undoubtedly become involved instead. The second major conclusion is that the greater the price to be paid for involving oneself with the victim, the more even good people, or people who strive to be good and otherwise identify themselves with the better values of humanity, allow themselves to go on with their own selfish activities and remain oblivious to their fellow human being's plight.

A further element determining the posture of the bystander is a sense of hopelessness, a sense that there is nothing anyone can do. The bystander, in effect, gives up in the face of the enormity of an evil or a tragedy. This hopelessness is akin to what Robert Lifton describes as "psychic numbing" in his study of the survivors of Hiroshima.[22] Lifton emphasizes that psychic numbing came to characterize the entire life-style of the survivors. He notes that the same phenomenon was observed among concentration camp victims (what the prisoners themselves called *Musselmänner* or "walking corpses" or "living dead"—people who had given up the effort to feel alive and then often died shortly thereafter) and is a feature of any general disaster syndrome (where people are seen as "stunned" and "dazed").[23] Lifton emphasizes that the process of psychic numbing is related, ultimately, to man's universal "death encounter." One gives up trying to be alive because the anxiety about the inevitability of death has become too overwhelming. In people who have been exposed to the brutal trauma of mass death along with the threat of their own death, psychic numbing is an immediate, altogether understandable response to an unbearable hell. But psychic numbing or escape from anxiety about death into nonaliveness is a response pattern that beckons to all of us, even when we are not traumatized by actual experiences of death. "Psychic numbing poses constant paradoxes for general issues of autonomy and survival. A way of maintaining life when confronted with unmanageable death anxiety, it threatens always to snuff out the vitality being preserved. Our deadly contemporary technologies surround the paradox with ultimate consequences, and make certain that this aspect of the survivors' struggles envelops us all."[24]

The role of the bystander is, in effect, a compound of several forces: the unknowingness of people who easily surrender their identity to whatever groups they belong to; the selfishness of people who choose to protect their own interests even in the face of a degree of tragedy and evil that, objectively, must raise in every decent human being's heart the question whether one dare stand by uninvolved, even if there is risk to one's life and limb; and a despair and helplessness about the extent of the evil and tragedy with which one is confronted, to a point where it is humanly impossible to feel anymore.

Sociologist Leon Sheleff has studied the bystander role more in the context of "everyday" criminal events than in the context of the massive violences with which we are concerned, yet he, too, comes to the conclusion that there is a powerful larger meaning to each individual's choice of the bystander role and the values that each society assigns to that role.

> In the final analysis, it is the total value system of a society which dictates whether or not the innocent bystander will respond or not. . . . Each . . . event, marginal in itself, becomes—in conjunction with a host of other similar situations—a reflection, as faithful and precise as any other measure, of the true nature of man and his society.[25]

In a larger sense, given the interdependent, open, mass media oriented world of today, we are all bystanders of the events of our society. There is no escape in the final analysis from the role of bystander. What we need, then, is greater awareness of the meaning and implications of this role—in moral, social, legal, and practical terms.[26]

THE CHOICES WE MUST ALL MAKE

All of us are faced with the possibility of turning toward the potential destructiveness that is built into us from the outset as part of the mystery of life joined with death. We are all likely to turn toward our destructive potential without consciously intending to do so. We do so in an unknowing response to circumstances and processes from within and without, such as painful threats of personal loss or being placed in situations in which we have too much power over others. In all of us, there is a continuous interplay of forces of determinism as well as of free will, so that the wrong choices we make so often in life are to be understood both as unwitting outcomes of forces "larger than us" and as our own choices and responsibility.

Most of us are all too susceptible to be drawn into being genociders, their accomplices, or their victims. From this point of view, it is almost inevitable that a Robespierre, Hitler, Stalin, or Amin will arise in any community in which the play of forces and the prevailing structure of the society invite the madness of genocide. The wishful fantasy that if only Hitler had never been is a fool's fantasy. The idea that only a Hitler's personal choices of evil determined the historical flow of his era is a very small part of the truth. Irvine Schiffer concludes his penetrating study of the charismatic process thus:

> Without the initial free-floating creative thrust of a people at large, perhaps some of the most brilliant as well as some of the most malignant of public figures of any era might have never risen so high or reaped the harvest of their particular charismatic qualities. I make the further contention that certain individuals, not particularly blessed with either special skills or significant ideologies, have received, under certain conditions of human crisis, a call to the charismatic role. Such a call has not simply emanated from an intrinsic inspirational force within their individual personalities, but came as well from a rescue-hungry people, prepared in their distress to invest a leader with charisma.[27]

It is true that we need many legal, political, and sociological devices to check and turn back the nefarious plans of leaders who call us to the destruction of life. But in the longer historical run, it seems that we need even more something we can barely imagine at this point in human consciousness, namely, ways to be aware of, control, correct, and indeed replace our primitive defenses of blaming, projecting onto, and delivering others to the death fate we fear so desperately ourselves. For this is the truly central dynamic that makes it possible for both leaders and group processes to initiate and authorize the mass destruction of others. Lionel Rubinoff asserts, "To recognize and accept the extent of one's own complicity in the drama of evil that was Auschwitz is to undergo substantial not merely accidental change and to act in a manner commensurate with that change."[28]

Learning to Choose

Nature's grand design has afforded us a remarkable faculty for experiencing that includes the ability to weigh and choose between variously desirable options. Ultimately, this ability is probably our single most important tool of change or evolution. The ability to choose is an active expression of the human's gift of consciousness,[29] and it is man's machinery for mapping and shaping his unfolding future. Unfortunately, most people have not been trained in the art of making choices. Many people do not understand that each time we choose something, we are also giving up something that we desired in some part – or there would have been no choice to make. As a result of the choice to give up another somewhat desirable alternative, we enjoy what we do choose the more; our preference becomes the more valuable when it is considered against the background of what we gave up. However, many people are inexperienced, frightened, and angry when they are faced with giving away or giving up something they want. As a result, they may seek to keep both alternatives for themselves, even when the alternatives are mutually exclusive, so that in the end they enjoy neither. There are also many people who balk at making any choices at all, so they lose out on many of the deepest experiences of life and on many of the opportunities to progress.[30] The latter condition is so widespread that it has been given the name of decisionphobia by some students of human behavior.

The ability to make choices pays off not only in pointing people in a clear-cut direction and in building enthusiasm for what they are doing, but also in an overall strengthening of the personality. People who know how to make choices feel stronger and surer of themselves. Some psychotherapists consider the choice-making process the most important aspect of treatment.[31]

The implication, of course, is that we all need to learn how to choose among being genociders, victims, or champions of life. Each of these roles has its attractions, and we must learn to choose among them. The art of making choices among enticing alternatives is probably the most important tool humans can use to find a solution to the dilemmas of good and evil.

However, the concept of choice is not a simple one. The problems of choice making go beyond the necessity of relinquishing one desirable alternative for another. In many cases, the ability to choose requires an ability to accept a partnership of contradictory and seemingly antagonistic alternatives. When we choose to love a mate or a child, we also open the door to disliking, hating, and hurting that same person and being disliked, hated, and hurt in return. We need to know how to be prepared to live out the opposite side of hating and hurting whenever we make our choices to love. Also, we often discover that we need to be prepared to love when we choose to hate. In matters of emotion, along with yielding or giving up something when we make a choice, we often also have to prepare to return to what we gave up, as another undeniable side of the choice we are making. If, despite our present anger, we choose to love our spouse, we need to give up our anger as we choose to love anew — yet we must also prepare to be angry and hate once again in addition to loving. It is a complicated process, and there is no cheating on the real inner truths of how well we take each step in the sequence.

So, the choice-making process as to whether or not to be genociders, victims, or champions of life includes many built-in contradictory processes. There is an undeniable victimizer part to all of us, a victim part, and, of course, a life-champion part. We genuinely need to choose to affirm life, but we must accept the subtle play of impulses in us to be victimizers and victims or else those secreted parts of us may grow to overwhelm us.

DEHUMANIZATION, OR KILLING THE HUMANITY OF ANOTHER TO SPARE ONE'S OWN

The underlying ideology of or "justification" for delivering another person to death is dehumanization, and the mechanism of dehumanization operates every time one person takes away a quality of the living experience or aliveness from another in order to spare himself from his own dread of not feeling alive. Dehumanization is at the heart of the destructive process; it provides the necessary rationalization for the destruction.

The common denominator of racial persecution, witch hunt, experimentation on human beings, all "scientifically" justified, is the devaluation of human life. Once a human being is classified, labeled as inferior, he becomes fair game to those who reduced him to sub-existence. The power and the law are on the side of the oppressor and these derive from the authority that sanctions him. The consequence of the devaluation of human life is always violence, the exploited, the victim.[32]

The dehumanization process extends along a continuum to the ultimate of removing the other person's opportunity to live. The "little" everyday dehumanizations we practice on one another are stations on the way toward the ultimate act of one person taking away another's life. It is not simply the insult that we do to another that is at stake in everyday dehumanizations. It is the fact that we are learning a devastating process, rehearsing it, deriving gratification from it, and perhaps preparing ourselves to one day participate in the removal of other people's lives.

Years ago, people were excited by the trailblazing clinical and social psychological studies of the authoritarian personality and the prejudiced person. We learned then that people who demand the humiliation of other people and claim that they are their superiors are, in truth, frightened, rigid, cowardly people who are seeking to make themselves feel better at another's expense.[33] We also saw earlier in this chapter that ethologist Konard Lorenz teaches that it is not characteristic of animals to destroy members of their own species, for in nature's design, animals who attack one another are generally from different species.[34] However, dehumanizing other people effectively redefines them as not being of the human species. Dehumanization aims at a redefinition of the other person as not deserving the protection due members of our species. Hence, anything and everything that is destructive of the other person, even killing, does not violate nature's design. "Because I am afraid that I will be nothing, I see you as nothing. I say that you are not human because deep within myself I fear that I am not. Once I see you as not human, I can attack and kill you without fearing that I have done harm to my own kind."

More than anything else, it is men's projections of their fears of death and nonaliveness that lead to "nearly every one of us" being available to participate in genocide or to support genocidal acts. Ultimately, the killers are every one of us who is afraid of our own death; hence, the conclusion that many of the killers are not madmen, nor people deliberately setting out to do harm to another. Driven by nameless, overwhelming fears, men turn to the primitive tools of self-protection, including the belief that they may spare themselves the terrible fate of death by sacrificing another instead of themselves.

I also want to speak very frankly about an extremely important subject. Among ourselves we will discuss it openly, in public we must never mention it. . . . I mean the evacuation of the Jews, the extermination of the Jewish people. This is something that is easy to talk about. "The Jewish people will be exterminated" says every member of the party, "this is clear this is in our program: the elimina-

tion, the extermination of the Jews: we will do it." And then they come to you—eighty million good Germans—and each one has his "decent" Jew. Naturally, all the rest are pigs, but this particular Jew is first-rate. Not one of those who talk this way has seen the bodies, not one has been on the spot. Most of you know what it is to see a pile of one hundred or five hundred or one thousand bodies. To have stuck it out and at the same time, barring exceptions caused by human weakness, to have remained decent: this is what has made us tough. . . . This is a glorious page in our history which never has and never will be written.[35]

Learning to Withdraw One's Projections

Many people think that if a pattern of behavior is "natural" or "instinctive," it won't ever be possible for mankind to do much about changing it. Actually, the opposite is true, for the more we understand a natural process, the more we open the door to mastering the process. Take, for example, the many destructive natural diseases that man has conquered. Generally, the first harbinger of progress is the scientists' ability to describe the natural sequence of a disease, and that is followed by successful treatment techniques and techniques of prevention. The same is true for other destructive processes in nature, such as weather catastrophes—the more we learn about the forces of nature, the more we learn to anticipate, circumvent, and even prevent bad situations. It will obviously take time before we learn to translate any understanding of projection and dehumanization into new devices that will contain man's destructiveness, but it is to be hoped that the social scientists are at least ready to develop a first-stage understanding of how human beings turn to genocidal violence.

Behavioral psychologist Albert Bandura describes simply and clearly several mechanisms used by human beings to make inhuman behavior legitimate. In effect, he defines a number of natural but highly undesirable psychological reaction processes that we must learn to identify and restrain in ourselves and others.

> One device is to make inhuman behavior personally and socially acceptable by defining it in terms of high moral principles. People do not act in ways they ordinarily consider evil or destructive until such activities are construed as serving moral purposes. Over the years, much cruelty has been perpetrated in the name of religious principles, righteous ideologies, and regulatory sanctions. In the transactions of everyday life, euphemistic labeling serves as a handy linguistic device for masking reprehensible activities or according them a respectable status. . . .
>
> A common dissociative practice is to obscure or distort the relationship between one's actions and the effects they cause. People will perform behavior they normally repudiate if a legitimate authority sanctions it and

acknowledges responsibility for its consequences. By displacing responsibility elsewhere, participants do not hold themselves accountable for what they do and are thus spared self-prohibiting reactions. . . .

Attribution of blame to the victim is still another exonerative expedient. Victims are faulted for bringing maltreatment on themselves, or extra-ordinary circumstances are invoked as justification for questionable conduct. One need not engage in self-reproof for committing acts prescribed by circumstances.

A further means of weakening self-punishment is to dehumanize the victim. Inflicting harm upon people who are regarded as sub-human or debased is less likely to arouse self-reproof than if they are looked upon as human beings with sensitivities.[36]

If it is difficult, even farfetched, to hope for a control of processes like projection and dehumanization on the broad plane of international relations, the good news in marital therapy, at least, is that some people can learn to identify and stop making projections onto another. Some of the most exciting growing and loving times in marriage occur when one spouse stops blaming the other. *The husband is so afraid his wife will hurt him that he goes out of his way to look for a fight with her.* What he is doing is projecting onto her his conviction that he is bound to be hurt, and by getting her to be "bad," he can be angry at her before she hurts him. In marriage therapy, we try to teach the husband to face his fear of being hurt in love and to stop picking a fight with his wife. We also try to teach the wife how not to allow herself to be lured into a fight. These are often quite manageable goals. We are also sometimes able to teach parents to examine whether their need to punish a child has anything to do with a problem they aren't able to stand in themselves—for example, a child's poor sportsmanship infuriates the parent because of his or her own feelings of inadequacy in sports. There is no intrinsic reason why people cannot learn how to give up projecting their fears onto others in other areas of life as well. It is a difficult task but not an impossible one. Are there ways, for example, in which we can train people to test their hostile and accusatory perceptions of other people?

Who knows how the creative human mind will find new ways to control and reduce projection. Perhaps we will be able to develop a method for controlling projections that is akin to the medical process of vaccinating against disease. Vaccination involves the introduction of an illness-producing agent, but in controlled doses so that the organism's natural potential to overcome the condition is stimulated. Perhaps it is similarly possible to teach children to expect experiences of ambivalence, mistrust, and projections toward the strangers in their lives and to teach them to restrain and overcome their natural tendency to hate the stranger. Today, there are exciting educational programs around the world that aim at teaching children positive feelings of respect for and interest in peoples of far-off lands, but few efforts have been made to prepare children for their inevitable negative reactions to people who are different.[37]

Must it be beyond our imagination that someday we may find ways to teach human beings not to take their troubles out on somebody else? Every day, teachers and other human growth leaders are learning how to teach people to be less afraid of their various problems and weaknesses. We know that when people learn to respect their problems and limitations as challenges to growth, they are less in need of compensating maneuvers such as scapegoating and dehumanizing others. Perhaps someday the resources and inventiveness of our vast educational and communications industries can be devoted to teaching people how not to project their fears into a hatred of others. Some advertising agencies already devote some of their resources to promoting respect for human life. Is it conceivable, for example, that advertising and public relations professionals can someday "sell" the world an image of leadership that would make leaders who dehumanize people highly unpopular? These are idealistic, impractical, and sophomoric ideas at the moment, but that does not mean that there is no possibility of someday reducing and controlling disastrous human projections.

We Are All Responsible for Our Choices and Actions

Again it needs to be made clear that no matter how much we don't know about how to make choices at this point in our evolution, we are still responsible for what we choose to do, knowingly or unknowingly. If only from the larger perspective of the evolution of human consciousness, people must accept responsibility for what they choose and what they elect not to choose.[38]

There is exciting evidence in psychotherapy that even when we do things unknowingly, inwardly – deep in the unconscious – there is an awareness and an experiencing of the choice even though we do not know it. We live with all the implications of our behavior, even though in many instances we did not mean to do what we did. That is true for each of us who discovers that unwittingly and unknowingly, we have been destructive of this or that loved one, this colleague, or that associate and that we are responsible for what we have done. Our inner registers of truth do not easily forgive us for the unnecessary wrongs we do in life – even though it is often right that we should also accept ourselves as decent people who couldn't help themselves at the time.[39] Many times we can and should forgive ourselves for much of what we did not know we were doing, but we must simultaneously accept responsibility for what we did and the fact that we will have to foot the bill. Our children whom we hurt, for example, will not so readily forgive us, nor will our colleagues and associates whose fortunes we have damaged. We will have to live with these "accounts," and we can best live with them if we accept our responsibility but do not overwhelm ourselves with self-hate.

On the level of genocide it would be too insulting to talk in terms of forgiveness for those who have been the mad killers—whether forgiveness by society or them for themselves. Human progress demands that we cannot be complacent or forgiving of murder in any way and that history not be written to accept such events. Yet, on some nth dimension or perspective of the human tragicomedy, there is some sense of humbly seeing the killers of our species as unwitting players in a swirling system that was more than they—or we—knew how to handle.

Even when we understand that nearly all of us are available to be genociders, it is also true that some of us, to some extent, are *not* available to be genociders. In our still so-primitive history as a species, some fortunate people have reached a more advanced point in the evolution toward a respect for life. For example, some people are touched deeply and meaningfully in their upbringing by the traditional Judaeo-Christian emphasis on the dignity of life and the sinfulness of killing.[40] Some people are touched by the lilting beauty and tenderness of their nurturing experience in childhood, and those fortunate people have a love of life imprinted deeply within them and are far less inclined to project their own vulnerabilities onto others. Still other people will develop a deep intellectual conviction as to the necessity of peace and non-violence and will draw from that conviction the courage to stand against the violence of their culture. Some people's struggle with disappointments in their lives leads to a deep conviction about standing up to life's hurts and terrors and not exploiting the weaknesses of others. If we think of cultural and national groups as a whole, it is also true that some peoples have been fortunate enough to develop more of an awareness of the choices of becoming genociders or victims or neither.

The fact that genocidal violence springs naturally from the many complexities of the human condition in no way contradicts the fact that demands for peace and decency also spring naturally from our human condition. The present sad state of man does not mean that we may not yet discover ways of arresting the sequences that presently culminate in the destruction of life.[41] That discovery is the challenge each of us must attempt to meet in our individual experiences, marriages and family experiences, and relationships with others—in our work and communities, our group identities, and our large-group national and international relationships.

South Africa Accused of Massacre

Stockholm—A Swedish freelance journalist said yesterday that South African Government troops recently wiped out a whole village in Northern Namibia, the former Southwest Africa now under the Pretoria regime's rule.

A total of 105 black Africans were killed, he said.

Per Sanden, who appeared in a Swedish television programme, said he had recently returned from a journey in Namibia and South Africa where, he said, he met the only survivor from the alleged massacre.

He brought a film which showed the location of the alleged massacre. At least five human skulls were seen in the grass of the alleged village, which was said to have been razed to the ground by the troops.

The village, he said, was situated in the Kalonga District in the Caprivi Strip in the Northeastern corner of Namibia.

The film contained an interview with a man identified only as Aaron, 44. The man sat outside a hut and said that South African troops, chasing Swapo guerrillas fighting the Pretoria Government, arrived in his village looking for resistance fighters.

"All villagers were chased up and ordered to gather in a line in front of the troops," Aaron said. He said that one soldier told him what would happen and advised him to run. "So I did. But my children and wives were killed. The troops poured gasoline over the bodies and set fire to them."

He was later seized by South African troops, who, he said, tortured him to get information about alleged Swapo strongholds. He showed marks of knife stabs and rope burns on his body.

Sanden said he met Aaron outside Namibia but did not give the location. He said he would appear as a witness in a UN Committee hearing on Namibia next month.

South African Defence Minister Piet Botha said yesterday the report "is absolute nonsense."

"I can only admire the reporter's imagination," he said.

—United Press International, July 26, 1974

10

THE HUMAN BEINGS WHO ARE TO BE THE VICTIMS

Most grievous is the sorrow surrounding those "oppressed ones" who as still sucklings are taken from their mothers' breasts. On their account, truly, the whole world weeps. The tears that come from these babes have no equal. Their tears issue from the innermost and farthest places of the heart.

— Zohar: The Book of Splendor

If there are to be victimizers, there must also be victims, and this chapter concerns the other side of human violence, the victim, and the extent to which the victim contributes to his or her own tragedy. It seems cruel and insulting to call down on victims a further burden of incompetence and shame by suggesting that they bring injury and death to themselves. It also seems, in the simplest sense of the words, unfair and illogical. After all, it is the victimizers who do the hurting and killing. If they did not do what they do, there could be no victims.

Nonetheless, there is also a great deal of evidence indicating that when there are no available victims, there are far fewer victimizers. Both victimizers and victims appear to be necessary conditions for tragedy; each contributes to defining the reality of the other.[1] Victims are essentially the tragic innocents of another's evil, and they can be unknowingly swept into their roles by powerful natural forces they do not know how to monitor and master. Yet, often there is some sense that the victims are also involved in their fate. The mixture of victimizer and victim roles varies all the time. Elie Wiesel has written, "Between victims and executioners there is a mysterious bond; they belong to the same universe, one is the negation of the other."[2]

* * *

It happened so suddenly. One of the sports cars competing in the race blew a tire and crashed into the lower grandstand. Two of the spectators up front were killed instantly. "Every week they went to the speed races. They insisted on seats along the front rail where there was no safety barrier. They said they wanted to feel the race, that staying behind an artificial barrier took too much away from the excitement. Well, it finally happened last week. One of the cars careened madly out of control and broke through the fence where they were sitting."

*   *   *

A plane crashes in darkness against a mountain peak, and all aboard are lost. "He was quite a guy, always flying. He loved every minute up in the sky. Whenever he could, he would fly with local charter outfits instead of on regular commercial flights. The little planes were his air taxis, he liked to say. He knew that the safety record of these small private lines was very poor and that their accident rate was even worse than automobiles. Nonetheless, he insisted on flying any charter plane he could find. Well, last week, he was out West, and weather conditions were pretty bad, but he took this small private flight. Nobody knows exactly what happened, but they never made it over the mountain ridge."

*   *   *

War breaks out suddenly. The unexpected enemy air attack on a town leaves many people dead. "It's fantastic how these people keep up their spirits under the grueling punishment of the air raids. They are a proud people who won't go down. Smith was one of the best. Even when the sirens sounded, he would insist on staying in his own house instead of going down to the shelter. 'I'd rather die in my own bed,' he would say heartily. Well, when this bomb hit the Smith flat last week, he and his family were all in there. There's nothing much more I can tell you."

*   *   *

At 3 A.M. he was mugged in an elevated subway train going through Brooklyn. "We talked about it many times. I told him he had a wife and children to take care of and it just didn't make any sense for him to come back so late at night from his job in town by subway. But he insisted. He wasn't about to take our car into Manhattan and pay those crazy prices every night for parking. He also said he couldn't see spending a huge amount on a taxi either. So I told him he ought to change jobs, ask for more money, or something; it just didn't make any sense in this day and age to endanger himself the way he was doing. Well, last week, he was on the subway going into Brooklyn when this big man got on his car . . . ."

*　　*　　*

One telling way of looking at human interactions is to think of them as power transactions. When two people meet, they observe how each presses against the other with a certain force or strength, and whether it is for the purpose of taking advantage or not, there follows a subtle kind of testing and measuring of one another. It may be to make a sale or to complete a trade; it may be an attempt to gain emotional control; it may also be a good-humored interest in sizing up a possible colleague, friend or lover. If we look carefully at seemingly routine pleasantries and conversations, we will see that rich exchanges of "power information" take place, in which each party conveys how much power he feels he has, what his hopes and ambitions are, and so on. This process also includes tantalizing messages as to one's "foreign policy" and "defensive strategy" vis-à-vis the power of others. Some people communicate a healthy pleasure when they meet well-matched fellow human beings. They radiate a conviction that the other's power is not so much a threat to their own as it is an invitation to mutual sport of one sort or another—be it commercial, sexual, or what have you. Others put out messages of blustering competitiveness, or, in effect, of fright and volatile resentment of another's strength. Still others make it clear that they will back off from any contact with energetic, powerful people, because they want only "safe" relationships that bypass all power considerations. (Since issues of power ultimately are inescapable, these "nonpower" players often are actually setting themselves up to effect devasting behind-the-scenes power plays.) *Two women meet cordially; their smiling eyes calculatedly check each other up and down. Two veteran professionals are exchanging the latest gossip; obviously having fun, they are also soberly checking out what professional gravy train they may have been missing recently. A man and woman share cocktails laughingly as they play the game of sizing up each other's sexual appetite. A salesman and customer "dance" around one another—observing, calculating, plotting.*

An exchange of power messages also includes each party's signaling the extent to which he will or will not be vulnerable to the other's power. Contemporary philosopher-novelist Kurt Vonnegut, Jr., deftly satirizes one mistaken assessment of a victim's vulnerability, in this case, that of Jesus.

> The Gospels actually taught this: *Before you kill somebody, make absolutely sure he isn't well connected.* . . . The flaw in the Christ stories . . . was that Christ, who didn't look like much, was actually the son of the Most Powerful Being in the Universe. Readers understood that, so, when they came to the crucifixion, they naturally thought . . . *Oh, boy—they sure picked*

the wrong guy to lynch that time! And that thought had a brother: *There are right people to lynch.* Who? People not well connected.[3]

There is also the phenomenon that people often let one another know that they are available to be victimized. At first glance, such a concept strikes us as outrageous. Who in his right mind would ask to be hurt? This idea frequently arouses a great deal of protest and anger, especially in people to whom one suggests that they are available to be hurt, because people who are really "asking to be victims" don't like to admit such foolishness. They also resent the accompanying implication that they must be psychologically sick, since obviously no one in his right mind would submit to punishment and victimization. Most would-be victims also do not want to look weak — hardly a flattering portrayal of oneself.

Yet, there is no question that people unknowingly do ask to be hurt. There is a great deal of rich, conclusive psychological and sociological literature on this subject. In recent years, a new scholarly discipline has been born, victimology.[4] Psychologists, psychiatrists, sociologists, criminologists, jurists, and others join together to study how, when, and why human beings are chosen, choose, or allow themselves to be chosen as victims. The facts amassed by victimologists in recent years point increasingly to the fact that victims play a considerable role in their own downfall.

The victimologists also seek to understand what conditions lead people to be selected by the victimizers, for at no time is it implied that all victims choose their role or that victims alone determine their roles, even when they do play some part in inviting the attack. A magazine article on urban violence some years ago noted that people who walk aimlessly down U.S. city streets are more likely to be mugged than are people who carry themselves with a steady, vigorous alertness and look about them as they move. The same article also suggested a variety of other simple protective behaviors and devices that citizens might adopt to reduce the likelihood of becoming victims of violence, such as walking near street curbs, rather than buildings and alleyways, and carrying a police whistle.

One area of victimization that has been the subject of considerable research is rape. Rape victims often cue, seduce, attract, and "allow" the rape without knowing (or being able to acknowledge) they are doing so.[5] Many of the victims are furious if this point is called to their attention by a professional observer who has studied the incident carefully. Unfortunately, it is also true that in a good many instances, rape victims have been unfairly accused and even mocked and abused by investigating police as well as in the court process. One reason for such abuse is that rape and the victim's vulnerability unconsciously trigger the latent sadism of policemen and court officers. It is important to know that not all rape victims invite their situation, but there are many cases in which, to a greater or lesser extent, the rape victim plays a role in soliciting or allowing the assault.[6]

Marvin Wolfgang's studies of the relationship between murderers and their victims have already been mentioned.[7] Some of the findings of those studies also bear out the provocative quality of many of the victims, not just that the victims are often involved in ongoing relationships with their killers. The data as to when and how murders are likely to be committed also imply there are various preventive steps that life-seeking people can take. For example, husbands are well advised to stay out of the kitchen during heated marital arguments, and during such times, wives are well advised to stay out of the bedroom.[8]

Another expression of unconscious wishes to be victimized is psychosomatic illness, some of which are fatal. A wish to die or a lack of will to live are too often seen at the bedside of sick patients who do not fight hard enough against their illness. In Chapter 3, "The Cancer of Human Experiencing," we saw that the wish to die or not to live often invites or allows the onset of illness.

S. M. Silverman has emphasized that an adequate model for understanding genocide requires a recognition of the interrelationship of victimizer and victim.[9] Silverman emphasizes the seemingly simple truth that no matter what the dynamics of the potential genocider are, genocides do not take place unless the killer can get away with it; stated otherwise, if the cost to the genocider outweighs the gains he achieves in acting out his superiority over a victim people, he will not commit genocide.

Everywhere in life there are instances of people participating in being hurt and cheated. *"He's a nice little boy, but all the kids seem to pick on him. The teacher says that he is always being teased. He comes home from school and talks about how the kids beat him up. I've tried keeping him home and choosing his friends for him, but that doesn't seem to help."*

"Your Honor, this scoundrel sold Mrs. Jones a roof improvement job. We won't deny she needed the work. But first he told her that it would cost $6,000, and of this amount $4,000 had to be paid in advance. After he had collected the $4,000, he tore the old roof off and then told her that he couldn't continue unless she paid him the balance of $2,000. She didn't like the idea, but she felt she had no choice and gave him the money. A few days later, he came to her again and said he was charging her another $2,000 because the price of materials had gone up. She tried to refuse, but he got tough and said it was either his way or he would leave the roof the way it was."

WHY DO PEOPLE ASK TO BE VICTIMIZED?

What is it that leads human beings to ask for hurt, humiliation, and even death? How can it be that people ask not to be alive? I believe that the key is to be found in the same existential processes we discussed earlier that find all of us both wanting to live and tiring from the stresses of life to the point of wishing for nonaliveness and even death.

Contending with life's challenges overwhelms all of us at various times, and we then understandably yearn to surrender to nonaliveness and peace. What we do in most cases, of course, is to rest, not to die. If our wishes to rest lead us too much toward the boundary lines of wanting actually to die, a natural alarm is triggered inside of us to take heed and to fight for life. However, there is in all of us some measure of wishing to die. Death is an experience we are all preparing for, and there is at least a kind of rehearsing, getting ready, or wondering how it will be and also a certain desire to get it over with.[10] For many people and cultures, there is also a mythology about an afterlife.[11] If and when we are truly miserable and hopeless in our lives, our wishes to rest and to be as if not alive link up with those wishes to die that are also natural in all of us, and the call of death can grow, gain, and take over.

People Flee to Deaths, Little and Big

Slowly but surely, we have been learning in the world of psychotherapy how people flee from life to self-hurting and death. In one of his earliest works, *Man Against Himself*, the psychoanalytic teacher Karl Menninger details instance after instance of self-hurting.[12] It turns out that there are many paths to self-destruction.

Studies of people who attempt suicide reveal that they have an underlying conviction that it is possible through death to be united with a force greater than oneself and no longer to feel so alone and vulnerable. In inner images, this reunion is experienced as if with mother, earth, or nature—that is, an embryonic peace and reattachment to our mother source.[13] It is also important to know that many people who have attempted suicide report that even while planning to die, they did not experience themselves as slated for death. Indeed, they imagined that somehow nothing would change very much in their own sense of existence as living creatures.[14] The mechanism of denial works so powerfully that people are able to move toward destroying life, in this case their own, without knowing what they are doing.

One important route to self-punishment derives from what psychoanalyst Anna Freud has described as identification with the aggressor. This is an utterly fantastic process in which the victim turns about to identify with the very person who has been hurting him or her. This process is reconstructed regularly in the psychobiographies of many adults who once hated a parent who victimized them but discover in adulthood that they have incorporated so much of that parent that they are just like him or her. This mechanism often involves inflicting the same kind of punishment onto someone else, but it can also mean turning the punishment against oneself. One amazing facet of identifying with one's aggressor is well known to interrogators and prison officials, who know that mocking helpfulness and simulated sympathy can be mixed with cruelty toward a prisoner to the point where the prisoner will love the jailer and torturer. Writing about Indians who are subjected to cruelties, Chaim Shatan has described the process vividly.

> Like a child playing dentist, or children in a schoolroom, the victim learns to impersonate his victimizer, and to imitate his cruelty and aggression. . . . He learns that surrender to the mores and standards of his manhandler may lead to approval and reward—even to acceptance. . . . Once he sheds his old identity, the victim's personality becomes *transfigured*: He adopts the behavior patterns of his tormentor. . . . He is reborn as a white man. He is no longer embedded in the cohort of his ancestral dead, but—like Jewish police in Nazi ghettoes—his identity is submerged and absorbed into the corporate identity of a vast encircling host, an almighty presence, partaking of the limitless power of his conquerors and their traditions.[15]

The fact that human beings punish themselves mercilessly was discovered in early twentieth-century psychoanalysis, which showed that learning to recognize one's self-punishing ways in itself could be very helpful. For some people, seeing how they are hurting themselves triggers a spontaneous outburst of protest and pride, and they rally and fight to stop their self-hurting. However, for many other people, knowledge in itself is not enough, and many refuse even to acknowledge that they are hurting themselves. There are also people who make an effort to fight against their self-hurting, but their drive toward being stronger or better to themselves does not gain enough potency and momentum. So the question becomes, How does one go about helping people to stop hurting themselves?

The Pleasures of Pain

The question of why human beings hurt themselves so was an especially troubling one for early psychoanalysts, since so much of psychoanalytic thought emphasized that man seeks pleasure, relief, and impulse satisfaction above all else. How could the same creature who wanted so to please himself also be drawn to self-hurting?

For a long while (and to an extent it is still true today), psycho-analysts tried to solve the problem by discovering that sexual pleasures could be found in punishment. There are, of course, many human beings who link their sexual-sensual pleasure with macabre rituals that involve using whips, truncheons, or high boots or who incite sexual pleasure by submitting themselves to hurtful actions. So it stood to reason that other forms of self-hurting might also involve concealed sexual pleasures, and this formulation seemed to solve the problem for those devotees of early psychoanalysis who sought to prove that just about all behavior derived from the pursuit of pleasure. Only slowly did the titillating notion that there was sexual joy in being a victim yield to broader concepts that are rooted in the deeper existential truths of living and dying.

For one thing, pioneering studies of psychosomatic conditions made it clear that many people "eroticize" pain so that it gives them pleasure that goes far beyond the sexual pleasure. What that finding means is that pain enables people to care about themselves more. The ache, hurt, bleeding, draining, or wasting that is overtly their burden of sadness or worry secretly offers a haven and refuge from life's deeper agonies. The psychosomatic process is a hidden treasure room for feeling sorry for oneself. It is a way of having a kind of love affair with oneself or turning oneself into the object of one's own attention and pity. It is a way of being less alone, adrift, or vulnerable.

Wilhelm Stekel, an early psychoanalyst, established an important connection in the history of many children who provoke their parent's emotional rage: The rage, distressing as it is, represents a gift of emo-tional involvement or energy directed at the child, which is preferable to being left alone. "Even blows and the anger of the person who ad-ministers them become evidences of love. . . . The effect of the one who strikes becomes the touchstone of this love, and even the pain is pleasure-toned, for it becomes a sign of the love. The overcoming of one's own resistance is then felt as pleasurable and awakens the will to subjec-tion."[16]

Another important aspect of self-hurting is that a great deal of it results from turning powerful forces of rage and hate inward. Often peo-ple are afraid that they will end up more destructive than they truly want to be, so they turn their hate against themselves to keep from being destructive to others. The original basis of this process, of course, is that we all have more than enough reason to be terribly angry at the frustrations and injustices we suffer in our lives. In our upset, we naturally respond with anger. We want to take revenge by hurting others: those same loved ones who have broken our spirit; those same business and professional associates who have tricked, cheated, and reneged on agreements; ultimately, everyone—in fact even God himself for all the fathomless cruelty He expends on man. In itself, such anger, even when intensely felt, is no problem. On the contrary, we know from mental health work that anger is good for all people who know how to accept and enjoy their inner experiences of angry feelings. It is also healthy to translate some of the anger into an appropriate communication, self-assertion, and toughness in the real world.[17]

The problem for the largely unevolved human mind is that all angry feelings are necessarily pointed toward their fuller potential as acts of actual destruction and killing; and many human beings have not learned how to differentiate their angry feelings and wishes to hurt others from overt acts of hurting. Whatever the cause, call it "an inner decency" or primal feelings of regard for life, human beings basically recoil from becoming agents of death. Many of the people who actually go mad can be seen, on closer examination, to be defending themselves against their overwhelming wish to destroy others. They take themselves out of circulation by being mad. Similarly, we have learned that many people who hurt themselves by developing psychophysiological or psychosomatic conditions are taking their rage at others out of circulation and recycling it through their own bloodstream, lymph glands, and organs.

We also find that suicide is often a defense against homicide. In many ways, homicides and suicides are two sides of the same coin. Sometimes in the history of people who commit homicide, there is an earlier, serious suicidal effort that was aborted. Often, too, homicides are so constructed as to lead to a "sure-fire" death for oneself—in effect, suicide. In a little-known but worthwhile book, *The Urge to Mass Destruction*, Samuel Warner constructs a larger-scale picture of how genocide plays out this murder-suicide dynamic on a grand scale.[18]

But Still, Why?

Still, we continue to ask ourselves what is it about us that makes us so inclined to hurt ourselves? One "simple" answer is that many of us have not learned how to care for ourselves. Many of us are the recipients of so much unfairness and cruelty and destructiveness in our critical emotional experiences that we do not learn to love ourselves. These hard knocks can mount up to overwhelm and break the human spirit, so that people can hate themselves far more than they love their right to life.

And yet, still we ask, Why? Why don't more people rebound to love themselves even under stress? After all, we do see many instances in which human beings stand up with great dignity and self-regard under difficult, even terrifying, conditions. "You may kill me, but you cannot kill my own love of myself." A great deal of psychotherapy is an effort to excise or reduce self-hating and to replace it with self-loving. Many therapists and patients have witnessed marvelous recoveries of self-regard. It is a beautiful experience to see people recovering from disabling depression, invalidism, and all manner of self-defeat. And yet, why is it that so many people turn against and remain turned against themselves? Why is man often his own worst enemy?

The Fear of Pleasure

One of the first people to break through to a deeper understanding of why it is that people go to such great lengths to hurt themselves was Wilhelm Reich, the brilliant, beleaguered, and ultimately mad psychoanalytic pioneer.[19] Reich was especially perplexed at how some people in therapy would begin to allow themselves greater pleasures but would then suddenly become very anxious and spoil their newly found joy. The maddening paradox was that such renewed self-punishment often was unleashed just as people were approaching the point of being able to love better, achieve, and win.[20] It was like the classic tragedy of Moses: The long-sought Promised Land is at hand, but actual entry cannot be achieved. Reich asked himself how it could be that people became more anxious and surrendered themselves crazily to self-induced suffering just when they were getting closer to the pleasure they had fought for so courageously. Was there pleasure in the suffering, Reich asked? Hardly, he concluded. What was being achieved in the suffering was safety. The experience of being alive to pleasure proved too dizzying to bear. After years of an inner conviction that one did not dare enjoy oneself, the taste of freedom was too vivid and awesome. The pleasure of success was too frightening. By hurting oneself, one escaped the pain of a pleasure that could not be tolerated.

The Fear of Winning and Then Losing;
The Fear of Trying and Failing

Some people are overwhelmed with the fear that their pleasure will soon be taken away. It is incredible how many people go through much of their lives with the dread that whatever or whoever is precious to them will, at any moment, be taken from them. Needless to say, this dread interferes considerably with enjoying what one does in fact have. People who live with the expectation of future loss often have difficulty in enjoying present pleasures. In fact, they often experience a good deal of suffering amid otherwise pleasurable feelings. For example, some people experience a sense of distaste or emptiness or panicky anxiety following what otherwise appeared to be, and might actually have been, an enjoyable sexual encounter. The pain of these experiences can be so great that some people understandably flee to actual loss or seem to welcome loss when it finally comes, because now at least the terrible tension of waiting for the expected disaster is over. Not infrequently, these people unconsciously set up a loss when there need not have been one. For example, there are instances in which there is a divorce because one of the mates is tired of living with the constantly agonizing feeling that their spouse, sooner or later, is bound to leave. It is as if this mate finds a way to say: "Okay, then, I want a divorce. I've known all along that you're not going to stay with me."

In addition, an enormous amount of human suffering and unnecessary incompetence has to do with people's fear of trying for pleasure and success lest they fail. "Why should I bother?" they ask in effect. "Why should I study hard for the test?" asks a schoolboy who has lost confidence in his ability to succeed. "Why should I make the effort to go out with anyone?" asks the deeply hurt young woman who can't break out of her feeling that no one will be attracted to her. Of course, not trying means certain failure. "But it is my choice to fail that I bring on myself, and I can still hold onto the fantasy that were I really to try, I would succeed." To not try at all is certainly less agonizing than trying and then suffering the bitter pain of losing. Much hurting of oneself is caused by not trying enough for oneself: not succeeding in business by not trying for promotions; not making a team by not playing hard enough; not keeping one's love by not standing up courageously enough to bad moments. Is it laziness? Sometimes. Being spoiled and looking for the easy way out? Often enough. But very often, it is primarily a habit of quitting before trying. Psychotherapist Albert Ellis, the originator of rational-emotive therapy, notes the prevalence of this pattern of fleeing from failure.[21] He emphasizes that underlying many fears of not succeeding is the distorted assumption that one must be perfect; one not dare be ineffective or incompetent. Thus, people fail to apply themselves to learning, improving, and developing themselves because they cannot allow themselves periods of not knowing, making errors, or not being sure.

On a deeper level, existential therapists see in such fears of failure a phobia of risking. That phobia is a lack of faith in one's natural recovery cycle or ability to spring back. It is a fear of vulnerability and incompleteness. It is a fear of not being able to stand up to pain or loss. It is not knowing and not trusting the enormous fun there can be in living out the natural down and up cycle of all aliveness.

In general, the whole process of coming to the end of an important experience has much pain to it. Is there anyone who doesn't know the tense, intoxicating experience of approaching a finish line? It is almost as if there were a magnetic pull to the finish line that draws us more and more powerfully as we approach it. That pull can be felt when building a bookcase, writing a poem, doing a paper for school, working on a sales project, working up an experiment in the laboratory, opening a new store, or coming to a sexual climax. "How terrible if I fail now. What if I can't make it? Do I dare believe in myself that I can really go 'all the way?' I'm scared to death." The final thrust toward pleasure requires enormous courage, for one must be open to the possibility of loss and failure just as one is trying the hardest.

SELF-HURTING IS NOT KNOWING HOW TO BE ALIVE

By now, we have assembled a reasonably respectable array of dynamic explanations for man's self-hurting. Perhaps self-hurting is not loving oneself enough. Sometimes self-hurting is a turning inward of the destructiveness people are afraid to unleash. In other ways, self-punishment is a regressive, safety-seeking infatuation with oneself in lieu of taking risks; to hurt oneself seems less painful than trying for what is perhaps unattainable. Certain self-hurting is bound to be based on an inner hope of fusing oneself with an outside force in order to be spared aloneness and vulnerability. Hurting oneself is also a fear of unaccustomed pleasure, as if we do not deserve to be successful and enjoy ourselves. Self-punishing is often a flight from trying, lest one fail after mustering up the courage to try.

All of us are alone in the face of the mystery of life and death. Often the burdens of life become intolerable. We are terrified of not feeling alive, and we are terrified of dying. We are desperately afraid to be alone with ourselves on the always-lonely voyage through life to death. So we reach desperately for something, anything, whatever, wherever. It is then that so many of our unholy misalliances with self-hurting are born. "Do anything to me, just don't leave me alone to myself," we seem to cry out—to alcohol and opiates, to fads and cults, apparently even to microbes and viruses. "Even beat me, and I will be excited and happy," we seem to say to all manner of oppressors.

Victims and oppressors give themselves to one another, fuse with one another, and exploit one another—anything not to be alone with their own life and death. In Virginia-reel fashion, people pull to their respective roles as oppressor or victim, each serving the other. The masochist turns himself into part of the stronger personality beating on him, grateful to no longer be alone in facing the terrible anxiety of being alive for himself. The sadist-oppressor extends himself to dominate the other, and now he, too, is no longer alone. The sadist's cover-up is perhaps the more impressive, for the sadist acts as if from a position of power and assurance, but the truth is that the oppressor, too, is living out a nightmare of fright about being alone and is desperate for linkage and fusion with another. Little wonder, then, that the sadistic and masochistic roles are so often interchangeable or even are both present in the same person.[22]

Do people really derive pleasure from hurting themselves? We are now answering this basic question in a fairly commonsense way: People hurt themselves because they are afraid to try to be alive and to face the essential aloneness of life moving toward death. When people hurt themselves, they are protecting themselves from their fear of failing to win aliveness despite their trying, and they are protecting themselves from the deep hurt of winning aliveness but then having it taken away. Better not to try. Better to lose on one's own terms. The protests heard from many self-hurting people that they are not really finding pleasure in inflicting pain on themselves are, in fact, true. In most instances, they are finding safety from greater pain, hence the pleasure of safety, but not pleasure for pleasure's sake.

A GROUP'S AVAILABILITY TO BE VICTIMS

Is it possible that groups and cultures as a whole also become unconsciously self-hurting and available to be victims? If we come to understand the self-hurting of individuals as a way of trying to reduce terrible fears rather than as a direct effort to get hurt, can we also think of groups of people trying to flee life's risks together? The civilized world was shocked in 1978 by the mass suicide of hundreds of Americans who lived in a cult community in Jonestown, Guyana. A careful reading of the story illustrates very clearly that the ultimate tragedy of mass death was rooted, from the outset, in the people's surrender of their identities to the collective cult.

Is it possible that an availability to be victims can find its way into the very fabric of culture?[23] One simple linkage between our understanding of individuals and of groups is the extent to which a people's leader turns himself toward self-hurting, and his people along with him, so that even future generations of the group are affected by the tradition or historical precedent. The rules of a historical repetition of precedents can take hold, and future generations will continue a way of life that is largely self-defeating. If we look at a given organization, say a hospital staff or a sports team, we can find distinctly clear traditions of winning or losing in the group. To a great extent, these traditions can be traced to the psychology of the organization's leader as he shapes the atmosphere for his workers or players. Even good ball players do poorly on a losing team — presumably that is why managers of ball clubs are replaced when their teams lack spirit and fight. History, too, is not without examples of weak, self-defeating leaders whose influence and precedent-setting impacts on their peoples were toward being available to be victims.

There is some intriguing psychiatric speculation that many great leaders are driven by a psychology of risking death. In a discussion of how much great leaders themselves contribute to their proneness to assassination, David Rothstein, who was a consultant to the President's Commission on the Assassination of President Kennedy (Warren Commission) and the National Commission on the Causes and Prevention of Violence (Eisenhower Commission) observes:

> There do appear to be some indications in the observable behavior of these leaders of what one might view as unconscious fantasies of omnipotence or counterphobic elements aimed at mastering man's mortality. These could inadvertently elicit the very fate which they seek to master.
>
> In one way, this could be viewed as evidence for an unrealistic belief in their own indestructibility which would allow them to take unwarranted risks, unwarranted because the leaders remain, after all, mortal men. It even appears in some cases as if there may be a tendency to take a risk for the sake of the risk — to challenge or dare death — combined with an air of fatalism. All of this would both mask and reveal an underlying fascination with death.[24]

Another interesting way of looking at the historical process of a group or a people is to trace the evolution of a group's philosophy of strength or weakness. Groups vary markedly in their definitions of strength. In some traditions, martial strength, conquest, and domination are the expected historical goals against which people measure their success or failure. Other traditions emphasize excellence in commerce, excellence in learning, or the cultivation of a pastoral way of life and correspondingly avoid and possibly denigrate the use of physical power. Groups also vary markedly in their definitions of how violence against them should be managed. There are cultures that call for compromise and accommodation until an invading force will have spent itself. Other groups mobilize for tenacious grass-roots resistance against alien powers.

There are some nations that deem themselves above considerations of power and prove to be remarkably successful in remaining neutral while wars and holocausts rage around them. Other peoples see themselves as committed to peace but ready to fight fiercely to protect themselves whenever necessary. Some groups define themselves as largely powerless and available to whatever their destiny might be.

Sociologist Vahakn Dadrian is pioneering major penetrations into the structure of genocide; especially noteworthy are his studies of the terrible massacres of his own Armenian people. In an intriguing comparative analysis of the holocausts of the Armenians and the Jews, Dadrian shows that both future victim-people remained distinct minority groups without political power. "In the Armenian and Jewish cases, a unique combination of *vulnerability* and *definability* served to reinforce the criteria of selection and targeting." Throughout the process, "the targeted victim remains a conditioner of the end product of the actions and responses of the perpetrator."[25]

The group tradition also affects the leader's psychology to a considerable extent. To the extent that a people's collective morale and style at any point in history already highlight certain traditions—say of appeasement, surrender, incompetence, or suffering—a leader will find fertile ground for strategic decisions to appease or surrender to an enemy.

Note, too, that the dynamics are not necessarily straightforward and visible on the level of group tradition any more than they are on the level of individual psychology. For example, a group may overemphasize virility, strength, and superiority at any cost, even annihilation, if total power over others cannot be achieved. A leader of such a warlike people would find ready responses to his decisions of state to be bellicose and Napoleonic, even if all the people sense that the potential price for the nation may well be total defeat and destruction. Was there anything of such a pattern at work in Hitler's leadership of his warlike people?

The group experience should also be seen as a vehicle for one or another of the various pent-up emotional patterns that lie latent in all of us. Whatever pattern is reinforced by a given leader, it is in a direction that amplifies the personality traits of various people, who then emerge as the active supporters of the regime. If we all have a part of us that wants to rest, give up, and die, then a leader and a general cultural climate that head in that direction will serve to powerfully reinforce this personality orientation in those of us who are most inclined to die. The same is true for our universal latent impulse to erupt in mad, defiant, omnipotent-seeking rage (that is often at the same time a covert prelude to rest or suicide). *Past and present-day Napoleons will be welcomed and supported by those elements of the citizenry who most want to be Napoleonic.*

The psychopathic brown shirts are loyal "starters" for the Nazis before the broader recruitment of supporters. Note, too, that choosing which of our several potential selves we should be is one of the most difficult experiences of our lives. People often feel no little relief at having a decisive leader who chooses a style of life for them to emulate, even if the result could turn out to be disastrous. According to Irvine Schiffer, even a leader who is known as a heroic loser will sometimes be welcomed by the people. "It matters not for charisma what may be the ultimate fate awaiting such a figure; the key element is that he symbolize, in his image, someone who is taking an active stand, taking one side against another. His personality, in fact, may have all the markings of a heroic loser; and just because of this, he may fit the ideal image of followers who look to project the heroics of their own polarized stance of losers."[26]

Another useful way of seeing how groups and cultures as a whole may turn unknowingly toward an availability to be victims is to follow the historical impact of crushing defeat and humiliation in a people's history. In the wake of a crushing defeat, a people's traditions may turn toward escapism, passivity, and servility, and in time, historical and cultural elaborations of these trends can cement a style of availability to be victims. It becomes understood that enemies are to be appeased and not fought. The culture may even develop elaborate rituals for surrender and suicide as the preferred and honored responses to domination.

Both groups and individuals who suffer overwhelming experiences as victims may develop a long-term tradition of being victims in the future. For example, an enslaved people often learns to submit to its role to the point where members of the group even turn against their own members who call for revolution. Groups, like individuals, may suffer such a deep insult to their self-confidence that they become fearful of trying and failing again. In professional life, for example, certain lower-status professions may resign themselves to accepting a second- or third-class status for a long time, notwithstanding their considerable tension and anger over being devalued. The same is true of religious, cultural, and national groups, as they can become unduly self-hating and obsequious.

Groups, like individuals, are also prone to defend themselves against the agony of terrible cruelty by identifying with their aggressors and turning on themselves a good deal of rage and cruelty. Witness the self-destructive behavior of various American Indians or the Nazi-like brutalities of Jewish *kapos* in the concentration camps. Like individuals, collective groups also "choose" to be servants, slaves, and victims in unconscious or symbolic maneuvers to gain advantage over their competitors and enemies. "We rejoice in dying, for we go confidently to our Maker."

Just how these processes are experienced by a whole group (or a large number of the members of a group) we don't know how to express exactly, since our descriptive terms for experiencing are largely intended to depict individual experiencing. But whether or not one works with the literal or metaphoric meanings of concepts, such as Jung's racial unconscious or archetypes, we do know that groups build up self-reinforcing and self-perpetuating traditions.

* * *

Who knows how it happened originally? They were overpowered by an invading people. Many of them were taken into captivity, and they and their children were sold as slaves. The old temples of their culture were destroyed, and the inner momentum of the growth of their pride as a people was dealt a huge blow. In the years that followed, there grew a new tradition of submission and obeisance to more-powerful people. Of course, deep within their spirit, they still searched for new ways to feel strong and proud. Even in their slave songs there beat rhythms of hope and drive mixed longingly with the wails of captivity and weakness. Still, their destiny now was to be everybody's slaves and servants, easy marks, and victims. It would be a long bloody while before they would recover.

* * *

They turned fiercely to their learning. That was to be their pride. That was to be their private world, where no other person could be their master. What matter that the Temple had burned? What matter that they were in exile? True, time and again the ruling group would invade their communities and kill their people en masse in heart-breaking "pogroms," but what mattered most was learning the Holy Book and being one with one's God. The fuller triumph would yet come in the next world where, Lord, Thy enemies will cower before Thee, and the righteous will be rewarded. Over long years and generations, the people perfected their style of "fighting back" through prayer and self-righteous resignation. They made excellent victims until one day they learned to build an army and stand straight.

* * *

THE JEWISH PEOPLE AS FORMER VICTIMS

It is somehow "unpardonable" to speak of the complicity of victims after thousands and millions of decent people have gone helplessly to their death at the hands of others. Speaking of a people once having been available to be victims after the same group or culture has finally turned the corner of history to become more capable of self-defense is also a problem. To recall a past tradition of servility is almost to insult the fledgling potential of a people now seeking to be strong. Inevitably, when observations are made of how a certain people once was weak, the leaders of the newly striving group will turn bitterly on those who dare to recall the past.

The case of the Jewish people and the Holocaust, of course, is dramatically representative of such a people. The Jewish people have come a long way in reorganizing themselves a healthy, life-defending national group. In the wake of the Holocaust, the State of Israel might perhaps be considered the largest-scale "psychotherapy" ever in the history of man! In Israel, the most incredible variety of people has gathered in what is probably the most unusual experiment in history to return a people to their onetime home and especially to reshape their once-overwhelming availability to be victims: bearded, black-robed Hasidim and Talmudic scholars; fireball-intense reformers seeking to establish a socialist utopia; uneducated, dark-skinned peoples from remote Jewish communities in Arab lands, where the clock of civilization has stood still for centuries; countless survivors of that most dreadful destruction in the history of man, the Holocaust; sophisticated, freeborn Westerners come to join in the rebuilding of a people – these and all others constitute the largest group in "psychotherapy" ever.

One of the serious problems of the new Israeli society is how to learn not to brandish the newly developed strength cockily with a chip-on-the-shoulder attitude, whether conscious or unconscious. (Interestingly enough, this same quality of cockiness was discerned years ago in the early graduates of psychoanalysis, in an era when psychoanalysis was characterized by an almost single-minded emphasis on self-assertion as opposed to today's emphasis on a broader spectrum of emotional maturity, including a capacity for humility and a capacity to love.)

Understandably, as the Israeli national strength is still evolving, criticism of the past tradition of the Jews' having been available as victims runs afoul of all that is oversensitive, overcompensating, and unsure. Israel is a country in which a significant number of the Jewish population are survivors of the Holocaust or their descendants, and the very meaning of the state's existence is inescapably tied to the Jewish people's effort to recover from genocide. Under these circumstances, it appears unspeakably insulting to refer to the Jews as having been available to be victims.[27] Much of the Holocaust consciousness in Israel is directed toward affirming (indeed "proving") the many remarkable feats of resistance to the Nazis on the part of the Jews, let alone the dignity, courage, and spiritualness with which the Jewish people lived out their last days in the Nazi death camps.[28] When a Hannah Arendt dares to describe the passivity of the Jewish victims or a Bruno Bettelheim speaks of the failure of the Jews to fight back, they are attacked almost hysterically.[29] Still, the fact remains that in many ways, the Jewish people of Europe, like the black slaves of Africa brought over to the New World, are an example of a people who unwittingly developed traditional patterns of thinking and behavior that made their people available to victimization. In their original innocent development, their acts were not the acts of national weakness. They were the curious and unconscious turns of historical events shaping a national group, just as so many curious, unconscious turns of events shape individuals and families toward destinies and fates they do not see ahead of them in time.

Once a people recognizes their conditions of weakness, the very tradition of self-hurting can set up a dramatic challenge to new growth. In time, a once-weak people can achieve a more wholesome strength than may commonly be found in a culture that has enjoyed a less unbalanced psychohistorical experience. The ironies of history and nature decree that peoples who have been strong may take their strength too much for granted and without knowing it, become lazy and weak; peoples who have been too weak and available to be victims may turn toward remarkable new wholesomeness. In any case, whether in groups or in individuals, the process requires attention and effort.

VICTIMS AND VICTIMIZERS MEET IN THE SAME "CANCER WARD"

What has been said about an availability to be victims is much the same as what was said earlier about people who are the victimizers. In both cases, victimizers and victims lose the ability to be alive for themselves. In defense against their anxieties, they seek to fuse with an identity or power outside of themselves.

The genocider, ridden with cancer of his humanity, tries to destroy others to confirm his own potency. The victim, ridden with cancer of his humanity, makes himself available to be subject to the power of others. Psychiatrist Joost Meerloo writes in his study of suicide and mass suicide, "Self-destruction is the last image of power: it is the last means of maintaining a feeling of being valuable and potent."[30]

In both cases, people lose sight of the optimal fusion of strength and weakness, or the correlation of life and death. Genociders fight too much for life against death; they unleash a too-intense aggression in order to gain life. Victims fight too little for life and too openly for death; they allow great aggression against them as an ingenious strategy not to be as hurt by life as they believe would be the case if they were to try to live more fully. Both groups fail to successfully channel their natural aggression in support of life. Victimizers commit their energies to bringing about death. Victims resign themselves to an inability to harness sufficient life energy and allow themselves to be absorbed by the power of others. In the end, victimizers and victims meet in the same "cancer ward" of distorted human experiencing, as both have surrendered their rights to build, love, and create to a rampaging cancer of destructiveness.[31]

THE PSYCHOETHICAL IDEAL THAT ALL PEOPLE SHOULD BE NEITHER OPPRESSORS NOR VICTIMS

Having followed the trails of both victimizers and victims, we can see that there is a rich psychoethical ideal for all of us, both as individuals and as collectives, to know how to avoid being either a victimizer or a victim; to know how to fight in self-defense, yet also know how to yield and deescalate conflict; to know how to fight hard to live, but also know we must not deny our vulnerability, no matter how strong we become. In short, we must know how to reconcile strength and weakness, or affirmation of life and acceptance of death. Both too-little strength and too-much power open the door to cancers of destructiveness.

Those people who would be strong need to be able to stand up for themselves; challenge, confront, even threaten others; fight back in self-defense when necessary; and, yes, also kill in self-defense – this despite the fact that we know in advance that sometimes in the heat of battle, they will end up being more destructive than was necessary. We need to affirm our right to live in our mad world. At the same time, those people who seek to be strong in affirming life also need to be aware that many times they will be seduced by the deceptive belief that they are fighting legitimately in self-defense and will be drawn into unwitting escalation toward violence that need not be.

Victim persons or peoples, on the other hand, need to learn to recognize their unwitting and unconscious surrenders to "the pleasure of pain" and to the safety seeking that comes from being too afraid to fight to win one's share of aliveness. Victims need the courage to give up the secret gratifications of martyrdom and self-righteousness and to break out of the cowardice of appeasement and fusion with others. Victims need to learn to be bad, destructive, and evil in the sense of daring to own and use their basic life energy to insist on not being exploited, enslaved, or annihilated. Once successful, victims need to know how to guard against becoming victimizers as they get stronger. The proper development of a person or a people who has been weak requires an awareness of the dangers of arrogance, excesses of power, and seduction by the new ideology of strength lest the onetime victim emerge before too long as a new oppressor.

It is an intriguing, ever-repeating process to be neither a victim nor a victimizer. The challenge for us to overcome the potential destroyer and the potential victim that are in all of us is at one and the same time a grand jest of nature and a brilliant invitation to life.[32]

Part Three

WHY CAN THERE STILL BE HOPE?

Soviet Charges China Killed 12,000 Tibetans in 1972

Moscow—The Soviet Union's major literary weekly has accused China of killing more than 12,000 Tibetans last year and said "with flame and sword" the Chinese have suppressed minority uprisings in six regions in recent years.

The new charges against the Chinese were in an article by M. Barnabekov in this week's edition of "Literaturnaya Gazeta." In it he apparently was replying to a charge printed in the Chinese press that the Soviet Union "is a colonial empire of a Czarist type."

Praising the Soviet policy toward minority nationalities, Barnabekov said the Chinese attacks on the Soviet Union are to distract attention from the fact that "national minorities inhabit more than 60 percent of the territory of the People's Republic of China."

He said the Maoists "imagine themselves as the inheritors of the empire of Genghis Khan . . ." and would like to acquire 44,000 square kilometers of territory east and south of Lake Balkhash in Soviet Kazakhstan.

He said "several dozens" of peoples and tribes conquered by China have already been "wiped off the face of the earth, either totally executed or totally assimilated."

Barnabekov said in the 1967–72 period the Maoists suppressed uprisings in Sinkiang, Inner Mongolia, Tibet, Kwangsichuang Autonomous region, Kainan Island and Yunnan province. . . .

"It is known that during the suppression of a new uprising of the Tibetans in 1972 more than 12,000 people were killed, thousands upon thousands of people were thrown into prisons and sent into penal servitude," he said, adding: "They have done the same in Inner Mongolia, using tanks and artillery against them."

—Associated Press, November 11, 1973

11

NONVIOLENT AGGRESSION AS AN ANTIDOTE TO DESTRUCTIVE VIOLENCE

The line separating the war professions from the peace professions can no longer be drawn. The once encapsulated system has defused throughout its environment, like a solute in a solvent, like a cancer in a body. Surgery is useless. Successful chemotherapy presupposes a substance lethal to the cancer but not to the host.

— Anatol Rapoport

The average book on the psychology of the normal human personality doesn't say much about healthy aggression or energy. If anything, one is apt to find negative statements about aggression. More often than not, the concept of aggression is used interchangeably with the notion of anger or destructiveness, and what is emphasized is that the healthy human personality should not be too angry.[1] The normal, mature human being is seen largely in positive terms — as loving, caring, relating, able to enter into warm and cooperative relationships with other human beings, and so on. The humanistic psychologists who have been extending our picture of the human being's potential at his best or healthiest also paint a pretty picture of the normal, emotionally whole individual growing to experience himself as a beautiful person, entering into joyful touch and embrace of other people, and expanding his gifts of mind and experiencing through meditation and fantasy. However, in these romantic pictures of man at his presumed best, little, if anything, is said about strength of aggression or spirit or energy for toughness in the face of life's problems.[2]

Yet, many discussions of the psychological treatment of people with problems do relate emphatically to the problem of aggression. Nearly all therapists speak of the desirability of some kind of strength of purpose, will, self-expression, ability to fight for oneself, and other aspects of aggression energy. It is evident that a great many of the people who turn for psychological help show either too little or too much aggression.[3]

Those who do not mobilize sufficient aggression tend to be browbeaten and exploited. In their marriages, they are belittled, harassed, and betrayed. In their everyday work, they are the fine reliable people who carry too much responsibility too seriously, or they are so self-effacing that they do not rise to positions of significance and authority. In matters of health, they suffer psychosomatic disorders that say for them that they are overwhelmed and angry at being controlled. In the world of mental health, they are the people who break down and become neurotic or worse, and the critical problem is not the symptom but the style of resignation and abdication of the right to stand up for oneself. In short, there are many variations of nice guys and good guys who finish last. The goal in treatment is to help these people learn to fight, be angry, and press for their rights.

On the other hand, it is also true that many people who seek psychological help are too driving, attacking, and aggressive. They are characteristically filled with hate, rage, or an enormous concern with power. In their marriages, they insist on "owning" their spouses, or they are "Virginia Wolf fighters." In their businesses or professions they are overly competitive or contentious and seek to dominate others whenever they can. In matters of health, sometimes they are too healthy and among the last to appear in physicians' offices (but it is also not uncharacteristic for some of them to "go down with a bang" and succumb to a sudden serious illness). A good number of these aggressive types do go to physicians for treatment of a lingering pathology, such as ulcers or colitis, which is a secret cry for the tenderness and closeness that are otherwise denied. For these people, the treatment goals are to reduce their aggression and to learn to experience softness, needing, and caring.

Actually, the extremes of too much and too little aggression have a great deal in common. The truth is that both people who begrudge themselves enough spiritedness in life and people who seemingly are cocksure in their power lack a real belief in their basic right to exist.[4]

These extremes also alternate in one and the same person. For example, sometimes a person who is unduly passive in his marriage bullies his children; or a person who overpowers his marriage partner is unduly solicitous and indulgent of the children; or a man who bosses his peers and subordinates at work is unable to stand up to his own superiors. It is clear, then, that a lack of basic power or belief in oneself can be expressed either in undue passivity and retreat from life's challenge or in exaggerated uses of power and attempts to dominate others.

Reports of successful psychotherapy also underscore the importance of healthy aggression and self-assertion. Therapeutic growth is demonstrated by such behavior as speaking up for oneself, the ability to express one's anger (but to discipline and reduce rage), the ability to fight for one's beliefs and to pursue challenging goals, the courage to stand up for one's ideas or desires under unfavorable circumstances, and many other expressions of man's exciting spirit and energy in ways that say, "I believe in my power and in my right to be strong without abusing the rights of others to be strong too."

FEARS OF AGGRESSION

Why is there so little about healthy aggression in the standard psychological texts and books about normal living? The obvious answer is that people are frightened of their aggression and power because they have seen so many terrible detonations of destructiveness and violence. In their hope for a more peaceful world, people have sought to emphasize the positive qualities of love, goodness, tolerance, responsibility, mutuality – qualities that appear to be as far away as possible from any destructive aggression. However, no matter how sincerely people may try to love and relate creatively to life, denials of aggression do not stem the relentless tide of power and violence in human affairs.

Some years ago, serious-minded pacifists designed an exciting experiment on Grindstone Island in Canada to test the theory of nonviolent resistance in a mock "war game."[5] The script called for the defending force to utilize nonviolent methods of resistance against the invading force. Needless to say, all the participants in the experiment hoped to demonstrate the effective power of nonviolent resistance, yet the results were little short of disastrous. Not only was it soon apparent that the aggressors were unmoved by the nonviolence, but before long the aggressors began "killing" off the "defenders" who resisted them so idealistically.

On the levels of individual and family experience, it has been observed by many psychotherapists that those gentle dear people who seek to avoid anger in their lives or to deny their children aggressive games often work themselves into boxes of dammed-up aggression to the point where they cause themselves and their families considerable damage. A Quaker psychiatrist, Robert Clark, writes:

Quakers deplore violence. We believe in being at peace with ourselves and encourage others to be just as peaceful as we are. When we give way to our own aggressiveness and express hostility toward others, whether in actions or in words, we are very concerned. . . . We Friends often neglect or overlook the importance of aggressiveness or hostility among ourselves. . . . We must face these differences and the hostility resulting from them rather than try to avoid them, gloss them over or deny them. . . . [In family life] it is better to express one's anger and other negative feelings, temperately or intemperately, and when one first feels them, rather than keep them so bottled up that they may burst out in an explosive way later on and do much more harm.[6]

Paradoxically, it may also be that so little is taught about the management of aggression because we are afraid to extinguish the "fires" within us that we know make possible our enormous creativity. We have always known instinctively that building the world calls for brave frontiersmen, not pacifists who would be impotent under fire. The good pacifist may know how to fell trees, but unless he also knows how to shoot attacking "Indians" (of all sorts), he cannot stand up to the realities of life. Granted, a pacifist makes an enormous contribution to his community, because he never stops exploring any and all creative possibilities for making positive contact with the "Indians," but when the arrows are about to fly, a good pacifist is a dead pacifist unless he shoots first and surest.

When it comes to everyday life and gauging peoples' energy or aggression for tasks, most of us have a sense of what the optimal range of aggression is. We look curiously at other human beings and unconsciously listen for the "hum" of their aggressive energy or level of basic vitality. People with weak handshakes do not impress us. People who don't carry themselves with a measure of erectness, attractiveness, and personal assurance neither attract us nor win our respect. Conversely, people who pulsate with too much energy or bristle with competitiveness strike us as forcing themselves into an unnatural state of aggression that rests on very insecure foundations.

If People Do Not Wish to Be Destructive, Should They Hold Back Their Aggression?

Many of this century's finest thinkers in the mental health sciences have sought to solve the problems of human destructiveness by emphasizing the importance of disciplining, reducing, and finding alternatives to aggression and expressions of hostility. Leon Saul, a brilliant contributor to the evolution of modern psychoanalytic treatment, has written a great deal about the devastating role of hostility in emotionally disturbed people.[7] He argues that people who want to be free of personal torment and vicious interpersonal problems with loved ones or associates must stop feeling intense hostility.

Psychologist Thomas Gordon has pioneered an important approach in what he calls parent effectiveness training.[8] In his best-selling book by the same title (which is widely used in parent study groups around the United States under the direction of instructors trained by Gordon), he insists that parental anger is invariably a statement of emotional bankruptcy and failure to utilize alternative methods and tools. Gordon successfully teaches parents several valuable alternatives. He emphasizes active listening—listening to what the child is saying and recognizing that it is an expression of a feeling that deserves to be recognized and acknowledged no matter how much the parents disagree with the child. Overall, Gordon places great emphasis on a method of no-lose negotiations with the child, in which differences and angers are to be resolved by the parents' and child's searching together for mutually acceptable decisions and goals.

Earlier in the century, a pioneering psychoanalyst, Trigant Burrow, courageously subjected himself and his colleagues to a probing analysis of group life and found that underlying the outward appearance of good-will, there were powerful undercurrents of self-centeredness, hostile oppositeness, competitiveness, aloofness, and resorting to prerogatives of status—in short, all the qualities that tear our emotional health to pieces.[9] It was Burrow's conclusion that such self-centeredness evolved as a "social neurosis" that masked man's earlier, more natural state of "organismic feeling" for himself and his fellow human beings. Burrow then formulated a method for teaching groups to detach themselves from the immediacy of tension and ambition to achieve a warm organismic feeling. In recent years, there have been fairly similar descriptions by humanistic psychologists of "oceanic feelings" of oneness and respect for life. All of these approaches have in common the stated or unstated implication that given the ability to connect to one's natural joy and respect for life, human beings will no longer need to resort to hostility and destructive aggression.

An important semantic problem that complicates this and most discussions of aggression is that many people use the words *aggression, hostility, rage,* and so on interchangeably. Most of us agree that it is desirable to reduce and remove a great deal of our hostility and rage. The more difficult question is what we think about the overall well of man's aggression once we define aggression as a basic life force that may or may not be turned to destructiveness—with aggression being both the source of our necessary power and the source from which anger, hostility, and destructiveness spring and are fueled.

A sizable number of mental health thinkers emphasize the importance of experiencing and expressing aggression as the wellspring for all self-expression, aliveness, and being. However, within this framework of an appreciation of aggression as a positive force, there are two alternative opinions. Some mental health thinkers like the idea of teaching people aggression in the sense of encouraging self-expression, exploration, learning, creativity, joy, sexuality, and so forth, but they propose avoiding all negative aspects of aggression such as anger, hate, violence, and rage.[10] On the other hand, a considerable number of other mental health thinkers advocate expressions of anger, hate, and even rage, but they emphasize that the expression of these negative emotions must be differentiated from any and all *acts* of destruction and that negative feelings need to be balanced by emotions of caring, respect, and fellowship.

Finally, there is an emerging viewpoint that healthy aggression is, in fact, both loving and anger, friendship and hate, the ability to assert oneself and the ability to criticize and fight against unfairness, all balanced together and flowing inseparably with one another. It is this point of view that we should now study in greater detail.

HEALTHY AGGRESSION AS A BALANCED THRUST OF POSITIVE AND NEGATIVE FEELINGS

The approach that healthy aggression is a balance of positive and negative feelings is consistent with the now familiar assumption that from the very beginning, people are given to both positive and negative expressions of themselves, that is, they love and build as well as tear down and destroy. Both types of expression are natural parts of the symphony that is aliveness.

The critical point in a modern psychological approach to integrating positive and negative feelings is to put together opposite processes in a single flowing dynamic. When we put together our experiencing of love and hate, liking and disliking, wanting and rejecting into integral unities, we enjoy thrusts of greater strength, satisfaction, release, and achievement — in short, greater aliveness. But when we split our loving and hating, or goodness and badness, there develop the serious distortions of life that we know of as emotional illness, cruelty, and destructiveness. Ronald Laing writes poetically:

> When violence masquerades as love, once the fissure into self and
> ego, inner and outer, good and bad occurs, all else is an infernal dance of

false dualities. It has always been recognized that if you split Being down the middle, if you insist on grabbing *this* without *that*, if you cling to the good without the bad, denying the one for the other, what happens is that the dissociated evil impulse, now evil in a double sense, returns to permeate and possess the good and turn it into itself.

When the great Tao is lost, spring forth benevolence and righteousness.

When wisdom and sagacity arise, there are great hypocrites.

When family relations are no longer harmonious, we have filial children and devoted parents.[11]

But many people hope that in their family life in particular, one can be wholly committed and loving toward one's dear ones. Religiously oriented philosophers of family life especially tend toward that idealization. Yet the bulk of the evidence shows that families require both deep commitments to one another and an honest processing of conflict. In an excellent treatment of love and conflict in family life, a Protestant minister writes: "Most families today need more honest conflict and less suppression of feeling. . . . We cannot find personal intimacy without conflict. Intimacy and conflict are inseparable in human life. This is true in the relationship between God and man. It is true in human relationships.[12]

Among the ancients, we find delightful pointers in the same direction, though, as noted earlier, the overall tradition could not escape entirely the prevailing dualistic separation of good and bad. Psychologist Sheldon Kopp observes of the Jewish Hasidic tradition:

> Even the urge to evil is a kind of vitality, a life source to reclaim rather than reject. We need to be in touch with and hopefully to own every part of ourselves so that we are not at war within ourselves. . . . Our own willful impulses can renew our imaginative powers. We can transform our stubbornness into determination and our struggle with others into intimacy. Each of us must confront himself to accomplish this turning of the self. What is the proper time for this turning? *If not now, when?*[13]

The problem for well-meaning people, of course, is that it can never be exactly clear when or how much aggression should be released. At any given time, we most likely either undershoot or overshoot in expressing our aggression. Moreover, what is appropriate or best in one's own psychology is often not acceptable to another person. It is not surprising that decent people are so often drawn to the fantasy of living without any aggression and well-intentioned philosophies are constructed to accomplish the ideal of shaping people and societies to be entirely wholesome. British psychiatrist Anthony Storr has written about the impossibility of this dream thus:

To imagine that, if only we had all had ideally loving parents and the serenest of possible childhoods we would not be aggressive creatures, is to be totally unrealistic about human nature. . . . Men think that a world without war would be a world without aggression. . . . Such visions are based on the idea that we can somehow get rid of our aggression. If only, these prophets allege, inequality between nations was abolished, or capitalism overthrown, or Esperanto universally spoken, or birth control everywhere adopted – then, at last, we should be able to live at peace with one another, and our true nature, pacific, gentle and loving, become universally manifest.

The idea that we can get rid of aggression seems to me to be nonsense. . . . Man's aggression is more than a response to frustration – it is an attempt to assert himself as an individual, to separate himself from the herd, to find his own identity.[14]

THE NATURALNESS AND NECESSITY OF PUTTING TOGETHER POSITIVE AND NEGATIVE FEELINGS

Of course, all quotations, even those from learned sources, are no more than observations by human beings, no matter how high their professional standing. There is a no less impressive array of observations that can be cited from spokesmen of the other camp, who believe that oceanic feelings and loving do not require a base in aggression. The argument rages.

Spokesmen for the "goodness camp" produce evidence of instances in which aggression is destructive of human relationships and should be changed to positive feelings and love. Likewise, spokesmen for natural or creative aggression produce evidence to show that an improved refining of aggression frees many emotionally sick people. What many therapists teach, which seems to make a lot of sense, is to experience and to express natural anger, when necessary, but also not to be unduly angry. We are to stand up for ourselves, insist that we will not be exploited, be proud of our identities, and press to win love. We are instructed to gain relief from the various demons of psychosomatic illness by "getting feelings off our chests," "taking a load off our backs," "standing up to problems," "letting go," and so on. But we are also to learn not to fume and rage incessantly and not to give vent to our natural feelings through acts of actual violence and destruction. The most effective process seems to have at its base a love of life and of oneself. There are "troops" of loving and caring to heal, cheer, and cultivate new warmth and love. These "troops" of loving remain on the scene, but along with them there are standby "troops" of anger to form a balanced force. In winning friendship and love, for example, loving coupled with an ability to be angry usually brings more rewarding, exciting, and enduring interpersonal relationships.

The process of separating from any close emotional bond seems to necessitate healthy doses of anger.[15] Teenagers busy with the developmental task of separating from parents show bursts of such anger. So, too, do young professionals who are getting ready to move on from a beloved teacher and mentor and husbands and wives when they need to define more of their own "space" or independence.

When it comes to marriage, several important studies conclude that a maximal return on the marital relationship calls for a continuous flow of honest criticism, expressions of anger, and challenges of each other's weaknesses – all to be distinguished from blaming, carping, and raging. In his seminal work, *The Intimate Enemy*, George Bach writes: "The notion that a stress- and quarrel-free emotional climate in the home will bring about authentic harmony is a preposterous myth, born in ignorance of the psychological realities of human relationships. Fighting is inevitable between mature intimates. Quarreling and making up are hallmarks of true intimacy. . . . Intelligent fighting regulates the intensity of intimate involvement by occasionally creating relief from it."[16]

Bach's emphasis is largely on the verbal and overt methods of fighting between couples. He proposes a variety of gamelike rules that people can use to exchange their negative feelings. I emphasized a different side of the experience in my book *Marital Love and Hate*, in which the focus is more on experiencing within oneself the naturalness of anger at one another and how to connect one's anger to wishes to love, so that together, couples can enjoy a sincerity, forthrightness, and even humor about their positive and negative feelings.[17]

There is also evidence of the naturalness of parental anger and even hatred of one's otherwise beloved children, and there has long been evidence of how otherwise loving children experience deeply hateful feelings toward their parents. Some of the most significant psychological-psychoanalytic work on these questions is that by the psychoanalyst Melanie Klein, who pioneered brilliant probes into the basic cycling of experiences of anger in the child toward the parents.[18] Klein takes as her point of departure the inevitable dissatisfaction of the child with certain aspects of the mothering experience. She sees the child dividing the mother object into two sides, a "good breast" and a "bad breast." However, she emphasizes that each of these images are not only responses to the mother's acts but also projections of the child's own love and hate of the mother. The "good breast" is, of course, that side of the mother that loves her child – but it is also an image born of the child's love of the mother's nourishing; the "bad breast" is the child's experience of the mother's hatred—but this image is also formed by the child's hatred of the mother for one or another deprivation or frustration.

What happens in increasingly complex sequences is that the child "internalizes" or takes in the very object images he himself has created. *The good-breast mother I created as a reflection of my love of mother now "resides" in me as an inner image, upon which I draw for a sense of being loved. The bad-breast, wicked mother I created becomes an object that "resides" inside of me, from which I experience renewed expectations of being hated.* The future of the child's emotional health depends to a large extent on its handling of these internalized object images. There can develop benign spirals of experience that lead to an increasing sense of well-being, or there can develop vicious spirals that lead to an increasing sense of persecution. The child reprojects onto mother, and onto other people as well, its internalized images of both loving optimism and expectations of renewed destructiveness.

This is one reason why in later years the offer of good mothering or loving to many disturbed children and adults in itself does not heal, and even incites, renewed provocation and anger. Until the internalized bad feeling is brought under control or released, the too-angry person recreates time and again a hating environment that "confirms" an inner expectation of being hated.

The process is very similar to what can happen when one acts in self-defense: One's own responses to the other party can trigger the other's aggressive behavior, and this aggressive behavior, in turn, confirms the projections we attribute to the other party. The correspondence between Klein's picture of the basic emotional interaction between the child and its mother and the ways in which people and nations behave toward one another on far more complex levels of interaction is, to say the least, impressive.

According to Klein, to be emotionally healthy, the child must maintain the *wholeness* of the inner good object. The child's greatest anxiety is the fear that its own destructive and greedy impulses will destroy the goodness of the "breast," or mother, and then its larger object world. In Klein's construction, the way to pass through this danger successfully is for the child to accept responsibility for the damage it has done via its hating. In less idiomatic language, children (and throughout life, all of us onetime children) need to become aware of their angry feelings and learn how to regulate the destructiveness these feelings can unleash. In short, the powerful perspective developed by Klein speaks of an inherent universal sequence of rage on the part of children toward their parents. The child projects it rage onto its parents regardless of what the parents' actual feelings are toward the child, and then the child responds to its own projections with still further hate. The major challenge for each human being is to master and control this hate and to integrate it with loving feelings lest the hate destroy the loving connection to others. According to this analysis, it would be impossible for a human being ever to work out a relationship to others by emphasizing only loving feelings. Hatred inevitably exists, and the challenge is to deal responsibly with feelings of hate rather than to try to avoid them.

Klein's theoretical constructions have led to highly effective applications in psychotherapy, as well as to further exciting elaborations of theory by other clinician-researchers. Earlier we saw the intriguing contributions of British psychoanalyst-pediatrician D. W. Winnicott as to the desirability, as well as the inevitability, of parents' hating their children.[19] These feelings are inevitable, if only because of the inescapable frustrations and exhaustion parents are bound to experience in the face of the child's continuing and intense needs. In Winnicott's view, this is just fine, because angry parental feelings provide a base for the child's unfolding individuation from the parents. The parents' angry feelings toward the child are part of nature's grand design to make possible flows of mutual angry feelings, which ensure the child's developing an independent identity. The implication of this natural process is that in psychotherapy, it is desirable that the patient enjoy a healthy experience of being hated by his or her therapist. Like the child, the patient in psychotherapy needs to learn to be able to stand up to anger and hatred, because these emotions are natural in all relationships, including relationships that are basically caring and supportive. The alternatives are no relationship or an unsatisfying relationship. There is no way out, because there is no way of avoiding, denying, or substituting for angry feelings in a whole relationship.[20]

Other observers have noted that children, and people in general, do not make a real connection with other people insofar as they are unable to process negative feelings. The process of linking with another person requires an interplay of both positive and negative emotions. Selma Fraiberg, author of The Magic Years, is an astute and gifted observer of the inner world of young people.[21] She explains lucidly how the negative side of feelings between a child and its parents provides the grit or tacky surface for the concomitant experiences of genuine caring and loving.[22] The same observation has been offered by Konrad Lorenz in regard to those animal species that display definite evidence of intimate relationships.[23] Lorenz insists that only animals that express aggression to members of their own species show bonding and love relationships. Lorenz also concludes that love and hate, or positive and negative feelings, are two sides of a single, larger dynamic of relating and connecting between creatures.

A young adult woman in psychotherapy complained that she was largely "dead" and unfeeling, except for periodic outbursts of rage, which puzzled her and embarrassed her. She was the daughter of two Holocaust survivors, whom she depicted as people who didn't dare to feel emotions. She realized that she had also resolved not to feel anything, lest she betray and hurt her parents by becoming more alive than they were able to be. In the course of therapy, she wrote her therapist the following vivid description of how she was forever too nice and friendly to people, at the expense of her real self and pleasure.

> *I'm everyone's friend, yet have no lovers. I care for no one, yet have no enemies. I'm incapable of feeling anything but frustration, anger, and self-pity. I can no longer feel anything. I don't feel passion. I don't feel richness. Even this stinking letter is a cop-out, because the few petty things I do have to say, I relate to you on paper, not face to face, eye to eye. That is my real talent—having complete conversations with faceless people. I'm afraid of them. Intellectually they exist, but physically they don't. Or maybe it's like the ostrich—if I hide my head, they don't see ugly me—I don't exist. . . . I want to fight, to feel, to really be able to make love, to touch something and feel it, but the darkness, blandness, takes over and I find myself too tired to move. How can I get rid of the dark?[24]*

British psychiatrist John Bowlby has argued for some time that aggression is important in maintaining affectional bonds. One function of aggression, he notes, is to attack and frighten away intruders. Another is to punish an errant partner, be it wife, husband, or child. Indeed, Bowlby concludes that "much aggressive behavior of a puzzling and pathological kind originates in one or another of these ways of seeking to maintain an affectional bond one fears losing."[25]

A heartwarming story of the importance of aggression to the general well-being of infants is reported by the pediatric psychiatrist Albert Stolnit in a report of medical treatment of infants who were severely ill with diarrhea.[26] Stolnit describes a case in which, despite all the usual medical procedures, one infant died. There were several other children in the hospital with the same symptoms at the time, and the staff doctors urgently sought to understand everything they could about the first child's death. Observing the sick infants, Stolnit noted that whenever the babies would swing into a period of irritability or aggressiveness, the nurses interpreted their behavior as expressions of distress and made every effort to restrain them. Stolnit proposed that the infants' displays of aggression should not be restrained but should be welcomed as an indication of their active effort to recover from their illness. All the remaining infants were treated in this manner and recovered successfully.

HOW TO INTEGRATE POSITIVE AND NEGATIVE EMOTIONS TO GENERATE HEALTHY AGGRESSION

How can we best go about integrating our positive and negative feelings into dynamic unities? If the natural human energy drive or aggression is built of an interplay of coexisting loving and hating feelings, it is the interplay itself, more than either component, that is the primary source of natural human energy.

One effective way to put love and hate together is to concentrate the power of our consciousness on activating both sides of feeling in close proximity to one another—better yet, simultaneously whenever possible. Thus, even when one is living out either the positive or the negative emotion in a relationship, preparations are in readiness for experiencing the reverse emotion shortly. Even better is to be able to parenthetically experience the reverse emotion along with whatever is the major emotion at the time.

Loving times are then what they are, but they include a wry awareness that one also is angry, has been angry, or will again be angry at the other person. Among other things, this awareness protects us against too-devastating "falls from high places," so we are less vulnerable to later disappontments and the rages that bitter disappointments can set off. Loving that is linked to an awareness of present, past, and future hate is no longer so innocent and vulnerable but is linked to a strength that enables one to stand up and fight future hurts.

Many of the worst moments in people's lives follow peak experiences of loving and intimate connection. In married life, it is often not too long after wondrous moments of loving, including high points of sexual joy, that couples wake up to discover a strangely painful distance and anger between them. Experienced couples soon realize that these sequences are almost "without reason"—although there is always some ongoing or latent thread of difference or conflict between spouses to spark the process. This natural sequence allows spouses to separate to their own selves for recharging. Unfortunately, the process is not recognized by enough married couples, so many people panic and then tumble into painful, deepening complications. The disappointment and anger of the moment are bitterly magnified against the background of the loving that immediately preceded. "How can you do this to me? I loved you so deeply and now you take advantage of me and hurt me this way!"

Some of the worst moments for married people come with the discovery of infidelity, an issue in married life that can be viewed as almost decisive opportunity for training in the handling of hurt.[27] Obviously, many affairs are expressions of disappointment and rage at one's spouse, but sometimes it is actually after high points of loving that spouses discover to their utter horror that their mate is betraying them. Something of the same pattern is sometimes seen following a couple's engagement. Two people are happily betrothed and committed to one another. All is joy and anticipation of the milestone event, and yet one of the betrothed goes on a "last fling" that is, in fact, an unconscious antidote to the too-much loving and happiness they fear will smother them. What hurts a betrayed mate even more than the concrete act of infidelity is the fact that the person they loved is capable of inflicting so much hurt.

But if spouses arm themselves in advance with the knowledge that their mate will inevitably hurt them, turn on them unfairly, and betray them, they have, in effect, prepared some measure of an antidote to much of the pain. Preparing to be angry ahead of time and knowing in advance that we are going to hate our beloved ones brace us against the demoralization that follows a total surrender to loving.

Clinical experience shows that the mixture of angry and loving feelings is also a tonic that generates more vibrant loving and heightens the delights of sexuality. As we saw in Chapter 4, symptoms of sexual dysfunctioning, including impotence and frigidity, can issue from too much positive feeling that is not linked with a sufficiently tough, attacking, or emotionally separate quality. The treatment task becomes to increase the ability of a person to be separate from, and angry at, the beloved spouse.

The same process is true in other human relationships. It is good to know in advance that our children will hurt us. It also strengthens children to accept that parents hurt them. At the least, children who have survived the "vaccinations" of parental hurting will be more prepared for the realities of life, for the fact that other people will surely hurt them and not just love mama's boy or girl.

Similarly, times of anger are accompanied by an awareness that one also wishes to love another – in fact, does love, has loved, will again love. One critical result is that the anger one experiences is no longer as raging, so that one is already somewhat protected against the potential for becoming destructive. Hating that is simultaneously linked to one's loving is no longer a brute force that is aimed at the destruction of the other but is linked to loving wishes to protect, care, and build.

We know only too well how many acts of destructiveness derive from the engendering of a violent hate because of wishes to love that prove desperately unattainable. The hate then surges forth to destroy the person one cannot reach in love; in a way, the hate aims to possess the other through destruction since there is no other way. However, if one maintains a steady connection between positive and negative feelings, love guards against hate flowing unmitigated and unchecked. Even when one is deeply hurt over a failure to win the other's love, one guards especially carefully against giving up the experience of loving that is, was, and, one still hopes, will be. The continuous interplay of loving and hating feelings means that it is possible to hate because of being hurt, abandoned, or attacked, but at the same time it is possible to stay connected to one's deepest wishes to love the same object or, if necessary, other objects in place of the unattainable one.

Hating that is linked with one's wishes to love means one does not surrender to passions of destroying—either of oneself in the suicidal despair of a person spurned in love or of the would-be beloved. Such hate is more humble, muted, wistful, and even tender. It is no longer a brazen, total, and escapist wipeout.

Buddhist Nhat Hanh offers the following instructions among his "recipes in mindfulness":

THE PERSON YOU HATE THE MOST: Sitting quietly, breathe and smile and then half-smile. Picture the person who has caused you the most suffering. Regard the person's features. Continue with the person's feelings. Examine what makes this person happy and what he or she suffers in daily life. Imagine the person's perceptions; try to see what patterns of thought and reason this person follows. Examine hopes, motivations and actions. Continue until you feel compassion rising in your heart like a well filling with fresh water. Practice the exercise many times on the same person.

SUFFERING CAUSED BY WAR: In the case of a society suffering war or any other situation of injustice, try to see that every person involved in the conflict is a victim. No person, even those in the warring groups and opposing sides, desires the suffering to continue. See that it is not only one or a few persons who are to blame. See that the situation is caused by the clinging to ideologies. . . . See that the most essential thing is life—and that killing and oppressing one another will not solve anything. Meditate until every reproach and hatred disappears and compassion returns. Vow to work for awareness and reconciliation by the most silent and unpretentious means possible.[28]

A great deal of the integration of loving and hating can and should be done entirely inside of ourselves and does not need to be expressed directly to others. Certainly that principle is true in intimate love and family experiences. At the height of a marital fight, there can be a dramatic and delightful turning point if one of the angry mates concentrates inwardly on his or her wishes to love. The same angry sentences of the fight continue, as they should, but there is now a delightful and winning mellowing, which tones the experience of the fight. The eyes are angry, yet also tantalizingly soft; the body is poised in fight, but there is also a subtle body gesture that invites touching and renewed positive contact. Experienced couples testify to the fact that a marvelous warmth and affection can flow from such battles. The same technique is equally applicable in other relationships. Many people who have learned to put together their loving and hating report that they are able to approach their bosses or business and professional colleagues with remarkable effectiveness by linking their expression of anger with an inner concentration on positive feelings.

POSITIVE AND NEGATIVE IN THE FOREIGN POLICIES OF PEOPLE AND NATIONS

It is fascinating to see how the same principles we have been discussing are also useful on the levels of larger groups, peoples, and nations. There is a considerable similarity between the choices individuals make in handling anger and hate and the choices groups of people make that lead to intergroup and international policies.

Canadian peace researcher Alan Newcombe has developed a beautiful analysis of the choices that are open to nations in their foreign policies.[29] His descriptions of the various strategies are cast in a charming play on words drawn from the game of chess, as well as from the history of monarchy prior to nineteenth- and twentieth-century nationalism.

The Bishop's Strategy (in Newcombe's dry-witted humor, a play on the chess piece as well as on the clerical figure) is to meet hostility by turning the other cheek; to return love for hate and friendship for hostility. The problem with this approach, of course, is that a hostile power may not return friendship for friendship and may take advantage of the expressed goodwill. In fact, the Bishop's Strategy may actually induce aggression on the part of the other power.

The Knight's Strategy in international affairs is a hawk's strategy that argues that people should respond to hostility by arming and preparing to defend themselves against attack. This hawkish strategy is appealing when it is entirely clear that one faces a leader and a people who are bent on war, but it leaves much to be desired in many situations in which a very hostile response will actually confirm the other people's fears and will lead to mutual escalation. The Knight's Strategy can, in fact, induce aggression and provoke war when no violent confrontation was in the offing.

The King's Strategy (Newcombe takes off here on the relative weakness of the nonetheless critically important chess king, and he also deftly touches our memories of the great contributions of Martin Luther King) is one of nonviolence. This strategy does develop an important definition of how to respond to hostility, but the nonviolent strategy is not without serious risks in the face of a warlord or warring people; hence, it cannot be a basis for shaping an overall approach to international relations.

"The difficulty in finding a foreign policy that will turn hostility into friendship (a state that may be related to peace) is to find a policy which is self-adjusting to the situation. What is required is a policy which will allow an Adolf Hitler to reveal himself in his true colors and which, on the other hand, will not compound a minor hostility into an arms race, with its subsequent increase in hostility, and produce a war which might have been avoided."[30] Such a self-adjusting policy has now been found, Newcombe announces excitedly, in the Queen's Strategy (the most powerful piece on the chessboard, of course), which is to meet hostility with strength but to move on to seek and develop initiatives for peace.

> The Queen's Strategy suggests that when the other nation is perceived as sending a hostile signal (either by word or deed), then one should respond with an equally hostile signal; and if one finds that one is locked into an exchange of hostile signals one should, at some frequency, determined in advance by oneself . . . make a friendly initiative. If, after several attempts (or perhaps 7 times 70 as the Bible suggests), the other side has not reciprocated, then one could conclude that you were faced with an Adolf Hitler and should proceed at once to arm in order to defend oneself. If, on the other hand, the . . . initiative was reciprocated, one should continue with such initiatives until a friendly state was reached. This aspect of the policy would fit in with the testament that one should love one's enemies, and the over-all policy approach would not leave one vulnerable to those people who would take advantage of the Bishop's Strategy.[31]

Newcombe finds considerable backing for his analysis in a social-psychological experiment. When a laboratory confederate played a strategy of militarism in response to highly militaristic subjects, the latter cooperated only 6 percent of the time. When the confederate played the equivalent of the Bishop's Strategy in response to the others' aggressions, 50 percent of the militaristic subjects cooperated all of the time, but 50 percent of the subjects still persisted in their militarism. When the confederate was instructed to play a tit-for-tat strategy, that is, to return good for good and evil for evil, the level of cooperation rose to 85 percent.

The problem with this tit-for-tat strategy is that it is limited entirely to the initiatives of the other player. The other party has the full say as to whether it will opt for peace or war. This is why the Queen's Strategy includes not only a tit-for-tat strategy but also a strategy for initiating peace seeking. The effective peace seeker needs to reach out in peace-probing alternatives and peace-offering behavior, even to apparently hostile opposites. Note how this is not the same as the Bishop's Strategy—which is to turn the other cheek at all times—nor is it an effort to respond with nonviolence under conditions of actual attack. The Queen's Strategy is a tit-for-tat strategy for responding to the other party's behavior and initiatives that is combined with a policy for initiating one's own peace moves.

Newcombe cites psychologist Charles Osgood's development of a strategy for Graduated Reciprocation in International Tension (GRIT).[32] The point of this strategy is that one of the players unilaterally communicates an initiative that he believes the other side will perceive as conciliatory. By and large, the GRIT approach has stood up well to experimental testing, but its noteworthy failing shows up when the other party is definitely intent on militarism. In such a situation, Newcombe's Queen's Strategy has the advantage over Osgood's GRIT. The queen is a tit-for-tat player, and she will fight staunchly against out-and-out militarists. Newcombe's queen is an outstanding exponent of the process we have been studying of integrating positive and negative approaches as the best way to generate and maintain healthy power for oneself.

Unquestionably, surrender, cowardice, long-suffering masochism, and other failures to stand up to another's hostility do not contain an enemy, in fact, they invite even more hostility and excite sadism. It is vital for all people, individually and collectively, to be able to stand up against the attacks of others. This is the only possible road back to friendship. By the same token, to stand up only angrily and violently (the Knight's Strategy) leads to an escalation of hostility.

According to Newcombe, the point of making peace is to arrive not at friendship and love, but at a state in which the parties can live together in peace, even while they experience considerable hostility to one another.

> This idea is quite real, for we have numerous examples of neighbours who are quite hostile to each other who live together in peace because each has essentially renounced the violent expression of hostility and each has decided to resolve conflicts with the other by recourse to law. . . . Meeting

hostility with hostility and . . . meeting hostility with a friendly response is the response of civilized and disciplined men. Using this strategy, one finds that one can love one's enemies to death . . . to the point at which they cease to be enemies and become friends, (that is, to the death of enmity).[33]

AGGRESSION AS LIFE SEEKING AND LIFE LOVING

It is time for social scientists, philosophers, students of ethics, and people of goodwill everywhere to adopt a new model of human behavior that honors aggression as life seeking and life loving. Many good people have made an effort to find alternatives to destructiveness by emphasizing goodness, peace seeking, loving, and avoidance of all aggression (lest it lead toward destructiveness), but nature will not honor the splitting off of one side of human naturalness from the other. To be only selfless and peace seeking is to deny the realities of the toughness and attacking tendencies that are in all of nature. Granted, serious risks come into play when we turn on the "atomic reactor" of our full energy and are both tough and caring, loving and hating. It is obvious that we have a long way to go in learning how to use our fullest energy safely and effectively, but the burden of evidence seems to be that natural aggression is the source of the best of our human potential.

Aggression is life seeking and life loving, as well as a source of strength for attacking and counterattacking when we need to fight for life. Aggression that builds from an integration of loving and attacking offers the greatest flexibility for moving back and forth in response to the unfolding realities of life. This is what psychologist George Bach calls creative aggression.[34] For centuries, this is what men have called courage. In many ways, this is also the stance of the Old Testament God, who is alternatively loving and wrathful.

The human species needs to learn to trust aggression as the great miracle of human energy. We need to understand that peace and non-violence are best forged from a joyful and disciplined experiencing of our natural energy, not from escape from ourselves. Aggression is the power to be. It is the hum of life.

Shame of Switzerland

That neutral, humane Switzerland, with its thousand-year tradition of democracy, could not be trusted by the persecuted Jews of Europe will come as a shock to many. Yet even after Hasler has given full credit to the humanitarian deeds of individual Swiss, the chief contention of his book cannot be waved away. During World War II Switzerland abandoned its traditional role as a refuge for the politically persecuted, and tens of thousands of Jews fleeing from Germany were turned away at the Swiss border to end up in Auschwitz.

In July 1942 Eduard von Steiger, the Swiss Federal Councilor, compared Switzerland to an overcrowded lifeboat. If any additional refugees were taken aboard, he said, the boat would capsize. Official Swiss policy was clearly reflected in von Steiger's remarks. A confidential bulletin sent to all cantonal police departments states the case bluntly: "Refugees in flight solely because of racial reasons—Jews, for example—do not qualify as political refugees."

At the time von Steiger made his speech, there were only 8,300 Jewish refugees in the entire country, yet the 12,000 at the border pleading to get in were forcibly turned away to face certain death. Not only were tens of thousands refused entry into Switzerland during the course of the war, but many hundreds who had somehow managed to sneak into the country were rounded up by the Swiss police and handed over to German agents at Customs points.

It may distress those who have always believed that European writers traditionally took liberal positions to learn that the Swiss Writers' Union succeeded in its efforts to keep famous Jewish authors from entering the country.

Despite government policy, a sizeable number of Swiss citizens violated the national passion for law and order and helped smuggle Jews into their country. Hasler gives them full credit in his book.

Yet the puzzle remains unsolved: Why was the Swiss government opposed to saving Jewish lives during the war years? Hasler feels that the chief reason was a dread of inundation by foreigners, a fear of a kind of stockpiling of the victims of inhumanity. Perhaps Dr. Guido Muller, a prominent figure in the Swiss Social Democratic Party at the time, was much closer to the truth when he said: "In each of us, somehow, a smaller or larger anti-Semite is lodged."

—Harold Flender, Review of Alfred A. Hasler,
The Lifeboat is Full, Hadassah, November 1969

12

STRATEGIES FOR NONVIOLENT AGGRESSION IN DESIGNING THE SOCIAL ENVIRONMENT

I have told my sons that they are not under any circumstances to take part in massacres, and that the news of massacres of enemies is not to fill them with satisfaction or glee.

I have also told them not to work for companies which make massacre machinery, and to express contempt for people who think we need machinery like that.

—Kurt Vonnegut, Jr.

The concept of aggression as a natural life force has many implications for designing less violent social environments. To a large extent, the behavioral sciences have swayed impotently between two conceptions of violence, both of which tend to paralyze constructive action. The concept that destructiveness is built into the human race does not offer much practical relief to anyone—except perhaps to teach one to stay off the street when one senses an urge to be destructive coming on (either in oneself or in others). On the other hand, not much progress has resulted from the other explanation of destructiveness as entirely the outcome of environment. If violence is entirely a matter of environment, we need to think about global programs of social justice to free people from becoming hostile and destructive—something that no society ever seems to achieve.

A new way of generating ideas for the reduction of violence, based on a theory of aggression as a natural life force, can be developed. The concept of nonviolent aggression opens new doors, because it calls for steps to eliminate violence without suppressing the spirit of healthy aggression.

FOUR BASIC CONDITIONS FOR REDUCING VIOLENCE: A STRATEGY FOR NONVIOLENCE ON DIFFERENT LEVELS OF HUMAN EXPERIENCE

Some of the conditions we should seek to develop when differentiating between desirable nonviolent aggression and violence are as follows:[1]

1. *Aggression should be encouraged on all levels of human experience, including reasonably modulated angry feelings and wishes but not overt acts of destructiveness.* Too little aggression means too weak an expression of our aliveness. We have reason to believe that too little aliveness opens the door either to violence (the desperate aim of which is to overcome one's nonaliveness) or to availability to be victims. On the other hand, unrestrained aggression leads to explosive chain reactions of violence. Human beings do need to experience a steady flow of aggression, including angry feelings and even violent wishes toward others, but angry feelings must be restrained and carefully differentiated from overt acts of attack on or injury to others. Destruction of others is hardly a basic necessity of life, except in clear-cut cases of self-defense.

2. *The quality of aggression needs to be continuously monitored and corrected for excesses and insufficiencies.* An awareness that one is too intensely energetic or trying too hard to be alive calls for more letting go and letting be. An awareness that one is too full of hate calls for reducing the hate and making an effort at greater loving. Seeing that we are not fighting hard enough to feel alive calls for trying harder and engaging more of our willpower to be vigorous. Realizing that one is too innocent and intent on too-positive relationships calls for becoming tougher and giving greater expression to protest and anger.

3. *We need to guard against projecting onto others responsibility for our own feelings of vulnerability and our own destructive wishes. We need especially to guard against dehumanizing other people as if they were not us, hence, nonhuman and therefore not deserving of life and protection.* We seek safety in projecting any and all conditions of vulnerability and our deep dread of dying. We also take refuge from our fear of being too destructive by attributing our hostility and destructiveness to others. Worst of all, we build images and definitions of others as not the same as us, less than us, and ultimately, not human; therefore, outside the pale of the traditional moral imperative, "Thou shalt not kill."

4. We need to guard against being drawn into escalating conflicts based on a misperception of one another's efforts at self-defense. Especially under circumstances of conflict or incipient police or military measures, we need to be wary of a mutual escalation toward more serious destructiveness resulting from each party's viewing the other's efforts at self-defense as a confirmation of destructive intentions. We need to learn to cut these cycles without rendering ourselves impotent in the face of real threats.

In sum, four of the basic conditions that should underlie efforts to reduce violence are these:

1. Encourage nonviolent aggression
2. Monitor aggression for excesses and insufficiencies
3. Guard against projection and dehumanization
4. Stop escalation of conflicts

These conditions are obviously applicable to individual relationships,[2] but it is very important to see that they can also be generalized to other levels of human behavior.

Strategies for Nonviolent Aggression in Family Life

The concept of nonviolent aggression fits the major findings that are emerging from the new family therapies. What family therapists, in effect, are now advising is the cultivation of family life as an open system or cooperative for the mutual expression of healthy aggression. Each person is encouraged to stand up as a naturally aggressive individual to be both fun for and trouble to everyone else, so long as there are ground rules and boundaries of fairness for the exciting transactions that follow.[3]

Encourage nonviolent aggression. Each family member should be encouraged to be healthily aggressive and to be his or her own self. Powerful angry feelings and wishes that arise are entirely natural and should be expressed in appropriate ways, but not in overt acts of violence.

Monitor aggression for excesses and insufficiencies. Family members should be neither under- nor over-aggressive, and they should make continual corrections of both excesses and insufficiencies in their love and hate of other family members.

Guard against projection and dehumanization. Family members should guard against blaming one another for their own weaknesses and

failures and for their own angry feelings. Family members especially need to guard against scapegoating one family member and
turning that person into the sick, disturbed, or incompetent one for
the whole family group.

Stop escalation of conflicts. Family members should exercise great caution
not to be caught up in escalations of destructiveness. Each family
member needs to learn not to misperceive another's sincere efforts
at self-defense as efforts to attack or destroy them.

Strategies for Nonviolent Aggression in Group Life

In groups, too, nonviolent aggression and the democratic process
are best served by providing for the "negative" processes of criticism, dissent, protest, competition of ideas, and political struggle, along with
group structures that call for a positive commitment and a sense of
responsibility to the group. Conflicts are, in effect, very much encouraged, in sharp contrast to violence, which is outlawed.

Any group that is built around the legitimation of violence against
another subgroup or against society as a whole (generally in the name of
some great ideal) brings untold misery not only to its target victims, but,
far more often than is realized, to its own members as well. This problem
is heightened sharply in the case of revolutionaries, who often set out in
quest of sorely needed justice but, because they fail to control the process of violence, often turn on large segments of their own population
before it is all over (e.g., the French Revolution and the Chinese Cultural
Revolution). The revolutionaries justify the "legitimacy" of their "purging"
antirevolutionary elements as necessary for the common good, but the
real result of terror is that many ordinary, innocent people suffer greatly.
For example, few people know that Arab rioters in Palestine in the
1930's, when that country was under British mandate, killed more Arabs
than they did Jews and Britons together.[4] The same is true of victims of
murderers in the black community in the United States, as the number of
homicide victims is far greater among the blacks themselves than among
the whites.

Some groups, including certain revolutionary societies that tire of
their purge, succeed in limiting violence by imposing a rigid political
ideology and harsh legal sanctions to enforce the strict obedience of all
members. Other societies, such as those built around a religious system,
also prescribe a highly ritualized way of life that does not allow for individuality or for openness to change. Such groups can persist for considerable periods of time, and sometimes they succeed in meeting their

people's needs far more satisfactorily than some democratic societies. However, in the historical process of these groups, there is characteristically a breakdown point at which the irrepressible internal pressures of difference, dissent, and opposition explode.[5]

The optimal political conditions for nonviolent aggression are, of course, part and parcel of a democratic society. The points of pride of any democratic group are the provisions for free speech and the processing of differences. However, a democratic society also suffers from a serious hazard, namely, the exploitation of its freedom for demagoguery and subversion. Without a structure that commands responsibility, defines the limits of personal freedom, and punishes those who actively seek to destroy the system, the flow of aggression in democratic groups turns increasingly violent, pulling toward a breakdown of the society.[6] Many observers fear such a process may be happening today in the United States.

The goals of an effective democratic society must be, simultaneously, the freedom to express and serve oneself and a commitment to the larger purposes of the society. Ruth Benedict has written, "Societies where non-aggression [viz., nondestructiveness] is conspicuous have social orders in which the individual by the same act and at the same time serves his own advantage and that of the group."[7]

In sum, the same conditions for reducing violence exist in group life as on the levels of individuals and family relationships.

Encourage nonviolent aggression. Groups should encourage all their members to stand up for their ideas and interests. Inevitably, powerful hostilities and conflicts will erupt, and these must be processed in lawful ways that do not allow for overt acts of violence or for destruction of the group.

Monitor aggression for excesses and insufficiences. Groups need to monitor the quality of aggression within the group to ensure that there is an ample representation of differences and expression of conflicts in group life, while preventing demagoguery, subversion, and overt violence.

Guard against projection and dehumanization. Group members need to guard against blaming one another for their own weaknesses and failures. Group members especially need to guard against projecting their own hate and rage onto one another and against splitting into "good" versus "bad" and "we" versus "they" factions that define certain subgroups as less than, and alien to, the group.

Stop escalation of conflicts. Group members and factions need to guard against escalatory sequences, in which expressions of differences and efforts at self-defense are misperceived as attacks on the group as a whole and its continuity.

Strategies for Nonviolent Aggression in Intergroup and International Relations

The same conditions apply to the intergroup and international process. What is perhaps least familiar in this case is the notion that nonviolent aggression should be encouraged in the intergroup and international spheres, even as violence as such is discouraged, but this is the conclusion that emerges from responsible studies of the international process. Paul Wehr, former executive director of the Consortium on Peace Research, Education, and Development, has described how conflict can be viewed as a potentially creative process to move social relationships toward peace and justice.

> Social conflict can be both *creative* and *directive* if a conscious and systematic effort is made to insure such outcomes. By creative here, I mean the use of those techniques and the reinforcements of those dynamics which bring parties in acute conflict to new and healthier relationships. This involves new methods of conciliation, mediation and crisis intervention. Creative conflict would, by definition, be limited in intensity and nonviolent.
> Directive conflict refers to those longer-term conflict processes aimed at the transformation of a society into a peaceful and just social order. Like creative conflict, directive conflict has built-in capacities of self-limitation. It minimizes violence and maximizes productive confrontation around basic issues. The two conflict types are complementary. The Ghandian dialectic is one historical example of the creative and directive aspects of conflict integrated in a single movement. For *satyagraha*, in both its mediating and confronting functions, just and peaceful human relationships—truth in the social sense—are the projected outcomes of the conflict.[8]

Aggression between groups needs to balance real power for self-assertion and self-defense with serious peace-making and peace-protecting efforts. This is the strategy we saw in Alan Newcombe's delightful analysis of the Queen's Strategy, in which tit-for-tat power is marshaled against out-and-out attack while peace making and initiatives to deescalate conflict are constantly promoted.

Johan Galtung, an international relations researcher and former head of the International Peace Research Institute in Oslo, Norway, has made a detailed study of how conditions of conflict, disorder, and flux are more conducive to peace than are conditions of consistent stability and lack of conflict. Galtung works with the concept of entropy, or the extent of disorder in a system.

> In a high entropy system the world is more complicated, more "messy." . . . The possibilities at any point in the system are more numerous; the range of interaction-patterns and chains of interaction much broader. Conflicts are absorbed locally; they may be numerous indeed but their consequences are slight. There is a generally high level of trust, or if not of direct trust at least of feeling that the system works, that there will be no major discontinuities in the near future. . . .
>
> By this is not meant that the system is stable, that there is no dynamism. On the contrary, precisely the high entropy system is the system that permits more change at the local level. But these changes are less likely to be of the devastating kind that are associated with large-scale group violence, i.e., with war. . . .
>
> The general formula is: *Increase the world entropy, i.e., increase the disorder, the messiness, the randomness, the unpredictability—avoid the clear-cut, the simplistic blue-print, the highly predictable, the excess of order.* Or in other words, if somebody tries to form the world according to one clear blue-print, then initiate a contra-blue-print that will see to it that the level of total order is not excessive.[9]

Thus, a guiding principle of nonviolent strategy is not only to protect against violence but also to foment constructive or nonviolent conflict. The aim of the nonviolence is both to deescalate mounting violence and to attack and destroy the opponent nonviolently. As Gandhi has written: "Passive resistance, that is, soul-force is matchless. It is superior to the force of arms. . . . Physical-force men are strangers to the courage that is requisite in a passive resister. . . . Passive resistance is an all-sided sword, it can be used anyhow; it blesses him who uses it and him against whom it is used. . . . Wherein is courage required—in blowing others to pieces from behind a cannon, or with a smiling face to approach a cannon . . . ? Who is the true warrior . . . ? Believe me that a man devoid of courage and manhood can never be a passive resister."[10] On the level of intergroup or international relations, it can therefore be concluded:

Encourage nonviolent aggression. Groups and nations need to stand proudly in their collective identities and to press for their group needs and goals. In their relationships with other groups and nations, powerful conflicts are inevitable, as are feelings of deep enmity and anger. The processing of collective anger must be carefully channeled in nonviolent politics and not in overt violence, which, in effect, threatens to destroy one or both people's rights to their identity.

Monitor aggression for excesses and insufficiencies. Groups and nations must monitor their aggression so as to be neither too submissive and vulnerable, nor too power seeking and warring. Groups and nations need continuously to balance strong stands on behalf of their self-interest and self-defense with peace-searching and peace-strengthening initiatives.

Guard against projection and dehumanization. Groups and nations need to guard against scapegoating other peoples for their own weaknesses and failures. They particularly need to guard against projecting their own attacking, violent tendencies onto other peoples or nations and against dehumanizing another people as if they were not of the same human species, therefore not deserving of protection, and ultimately, eligible for extinction.

Stop escalations of conflict. Groups and nations need to guard carefully against escalatory spirals. A concentrated effort should be made to understand other peoples' efforts at self-protection by examining what appear to be policies of attack or war for their possible meanings as efforts at self-defense.

SOCIAL PLANNING FOR NONVIOLENT AGGRESSION

The rest of this chapter presents several illustrations of designs for nonviolent aggression on the levels of group life and the international community. The purpose of these descriptions is to illustrate realistic applications of the preceding principles, but the material in each case is necessarily too brief to treat any of the subjects in depth. My purpose is to show the possibilities of policy planning to reduce violence in our social environments.

Design for Nonviolent Aggression in Communications and Mass Media

An increasingly serious problem that plagues modern democratic societies is the role of the mass media in inadvertently stimulating, spreading, and educating for violence.[11] The various mass media teach violence through (a) news reports of current violence, which provide a great deal of information on how to be violent, arouse latent violent impulses through excitement and sensationalism, and generally convey a depressing and demoralized message that we are getting nowhere fast in our ability to control violence, and (b) fictional programs of violence, which also teach us—often very innovatively—how to be violent, excite vulnerable listeners, and confirm for one and all that violence reigns everywhere.[12]

For many years, a strange alliance of scientific purists and media spokesmen have argued that it is scientifically impossible to prove the influence of media programming on the subsequent aggressive behavior of viewers, listeners, and readers. In my opinion, even the scientific evidence is by now unambiguous, let alone the fact that the contagious effect of media violence is obvious on a commonsense level that should never be denied while we wait for science to provide objective "proof." There was similarly a long period before it was proved that cigarette smoking contributes seriously to fatal disease. It is clear that the media are transmitting over and over again information about how to be violent, an excitement and pleasure in violence, and a message of despair about our ability to ever control violence. Margaret Mead has written of

> the collusion of the mass media in celebrating every sort of violence, including putting the picture of the murderer of the President of the United States on the cover of a national magazine and permitting his mother to rejoice in his deed on television. Publicity becomes a sort of sanction within which violent behavior previously forbidden is expected. This effectively undercuts the education of children in which they were taught to control socially unacceptable impulses.[13]

The education offered by the media on how to do violence is often highly advanced, and there is dramatic evidence to confirm this commonsense conclusion. In the definitive U.S. Public Health Service report on the impact of televised violence, there is one story that in itself proves the point. In 1969, NBC broadcast a Rod Serling film, "The Doomsday Flight," concerning a man who places a bomb on an airliner and then phones the airline repeatedly to give hints about where the bomb is. Before the broadcast was over, one airline had received a bomb threat. Within twenty-four hours, four more threats were reported. By the end of the following week, with continuing publicity via news reports, a total of eight bomb threats had been phoned into airline offices—twice as many as in the entire month before the broadcast. In May 1971, the TV film was rebroadcast in Australia. Several days afterward, Qantas Airlines paid $500,000 in ransom to protect 116 passengers on a flight to Hong Kong.[14]

Similarly, during the urban riots in the United States in the late 1960s, clear-cut evidence shows that the media lured more people into the streets to join the excitement that was being described to them on their radios and television screens. In several cities, some members of the news industry created new codes for a voluntary self-regulation of broadcasts during riots to avoid fanning the contagion of violence.

There are complex dilemmas in the handling of media violence. The basic problem in the realm of newscasting is the principle of a free press. The right of the public to know the entire truth is, after all, central to the whole structure of a democratic society. Centuries of bloody struggles for freedom have won a free press for some few nations, but it is a freedom that is still denied the majority of the people on our planet. Where precious freedom of the press does exist, people must guard carefully against encroachments that will chip away at their hard-gained right, but there is also another side to the issue. Democratic societies have to recognize that freedom cannot mean license to say anything at all if the result endangers human life or the continuing structure of a free society. No one can be permitted to exploit the principle of freedom of speech to incite people to riot, terror, or revolution. To the extent that the media incite to violence, there need to be restraints on media activity.

The dilemma, obviously, is how to set constructive restraints on incitement to violence without destroying freedom of the press at the same time. Attempts to develop approaches that will satisfy the two objectives of accurate news in a free society and protection of the public from incitement to and education for violence have thus far met with little success. Elsewhere, I have described how newscasts of violent events in our lives unconsciously build a despairing refrain for all of us, as if to say, "Well, folks, it's happened again; it always happens this way, and it's always going to be this way."[15]

The dilemma in the realm of media fiction is, again, to control against the destructive effects of unrestrained portrayals of violence while not allowing undue censorship in a democratic society. Moreover, it is important to recognize that fictional portrayals of destructiveness and violence serve natural functions:

1. People have an urge for excitement and adventure.
2. People are glad for the opportunity to rehearse in fiction the challenges and dangers that they face in their real lives.

3. If we are psychologically honest, there is a relief in seeing others trapped by tragedies one fears for oneself.
4. There is a pleasure in identifying vicariously with a fictional character's violence as he or she goes about doing what we feel like doing.

It is little wonder that fictional violence pays in audience interest and satisfaction. On the other hand, to portray violence repeatedly, blatantly, matter of factly and crudely is to surrender to the inevitability of violence, incite emotionally susceptible people, and educate and rehearse those who are looking for training in violence.

The concept of nonviolent aggression suggests a new direction for solving these media dilemmas. The object should be to portray the naturalness and tension-releasing functions of aggression as it really exists in our lives (both in our inner mind and as a fact of real life) and simultaneously limit the extent of the destructiveness shown, the incitement, and the message of indifference to human life. Moreover, much of the aggression that is shown and emphasized should be aggression that is expended on behalf of life.

A set of guidelines could be developed for conveying the news of human destructiveness in ways that do not demoralize and pander to violence, *without* changing the basic news-reporting function of journalists. Newscasters should convey the news of violent events in a subdued tone of voice, they should use their mood to project the truly tragic effects of violence – the real "human interest story" – and they should counterbalance reports of destructiveness with stories of human efforts to improve life. For example, reports of violence and destructiveness should not be juxtaposed callously with breezy, cheerful commercials or with the routine news of government, community life, or sports; instead, they should be preceded or followed by news of new advances in medicine or science, progress in community life, efforts at peace, and so on.

Insofar as there is a natural excitement that is generated by reports of destructiveness, the newscaster should subtly express the dramatic excitement of the story, but he or she should also link this natural excitement with a tonal communication that what has happened is tragic. All these devices can be implemented by the newscaster, as a professional who uses his or her skills both as an editor and as a dramatic artist, without introducing demands for any additional broadcast time and without interfering with the basic objective of reporting all the news.

Moreover, the immense power of the worldwide newscasting facilities could be turned into a powerful preventive force if broadcasting professionals—perhaps an entirely new international news service—took upon themselves the task of reporting instantly news of violations of human rights, massacres, and genocide all around the world. At the very least, it should never happen again that people are led to death in a world that does not even care enough to *know* that such events are happening. At best, such reporting might mobilize protests and intervention against the killings (see Chapter 13, "Toward a Genocide Early Warning System").

The principle of nonviolent aggression also lends itself to a new solution of the problem of fictional violence on television. It would be an intriguing task for responsible media executives and disciplined writers to create fictional formats that would provide viewers with the release, relief, and pleasure of violence but at the same time turn the script responsibly toward the potential for nonviolence. There is little problem, for example, in turning a story of war, past or fictional, toward the human suffering it causes and its inherent wastefulness (even when the war is just) and toward creative efforts to solve the issues of the war on behalf of all the peoples involved. This, too, is exciting drama. It is also no great loss to media showmanship to refrain from overdetailed prescriptions for violence that are likely to invite repetition by people who are hungry for incitement and available to education for violence. For example, a drama can refer to an act of murder rather than show a detailed portrayal of the act itself. Emphasis on solving the problems that led to the violence and on ending the violence can replace emphasis on the violence itself. Portrayals of a Sherlock Holmes type of cleverness, the frontiersman courage of a peace offer, or an army genuinely fighting for the safety of its people are no less exciting than stories of criminal or terrorist acts or wars of conquest. The same skyjacker story could center on the drama of ending the skyjacking rather than on the skyjacker and how he perpetrates his deed. Police and army agencies can be portrayed as representing the morality of genuine self-defense rather than as parties to the escalation of violence. It is not so much a matter of whether a given act of violence should or should not be shown, but rather a matter of the patterning and weaving of the story's message and the opportunity of the viewer to identify with peace-seeking heroes and motivations.

Religion and Education on Behalf of Nonviolent Aggression

There are few sensitive human beings who have not been bitterly disappointed by established religious and educational institutions, which they once trusted to offer leadership toward justice and peace. It is shattering to realize that all people in our world go off to war and destruction in the name of their gods, and that these gods are mightily unaware of the humanity of other peoples. With the few noteworthy exceptions of some religious groups that have maintained their commitment to respect life, the history of church complicity in war and even in blatant genocide is pitiful.

In public education, the majority of the educational institutions in almost all cultures fail to take a stand against violence that is authorized and perpetuated by their own governments. It seems to be characteristic of most educational administrators in most societies that they play safe and keep a careful distance from "radicals" who dare to oppose the establishment. Frequently, educational institutions actually aid by identifying "undesirable" students and teachers to the government authorities and acquiescing in their removal. Educational programs that treat the learning process as a fact-gathering or thing-gathering activity instead of as an opportunity to learn how to experience and safeguard life are, in effect, handmaidens of violence. Educational programs that agree to cooperate with any program that classifies some human beings as "things" to be ordered and disposed of are blatant allies of violence.

Together, religion and education often teach blind adherence to tradition, conformity to social mores, and unquestioning obedience to authority, all of which open the door to violence. Ultimately, the goal of all education and religion should be to inspire and equip people to fight for life — for themselves and for all people.

The concept of nonviolent aggression lends itself to a great many educational programs. The basic principle to be emphasized is the inherent right of human beings to be alive and feel alive. Classes in history, political science, or international relations can relate to the movement of peoples across the pages of history not only in terms of broad social-political-economic forces, but also through the meaning of events of heroism and tragedy for the human beings of the time — who, like ourselves, were seeking first and foremost to stay alive. The study of history can also be turned toward a psychohistorical understanding of the terrifying choices made by leaders in various cultures, not only as representatives and shapers of massive social-political-economic forces, but as human beings who were strong and weak, good and bad, and cursed with the poorly understood burdens of great power and the need to make decisions — just as we do in our everyday lives in our families and communities.[16] In our own small way, we face the same issues leaders do when we are involved in decisions about unfairness in our families, medical management and the mismanagement of a patient, or adjudication of rights in a local zoning dispute. How well we know the frailty, irrationality, and seductions of primitive passions and defense mechanisms that stamp so much of our decision making.[17]

There are infinite possibilities for focusing religious and educational experiences on the positive values of humans' striving for peace and humanity. Many fine efforts to teach international understanding and friendship are being made by world bodies such as UNESCO, religious groups such as the American Friends Service Committee, and countless individuals and organizations of goodwill.[18] Bold new approaches to peace education exist on every level of the educational curriculum, from the university level, where there are programs in peace studies for future peace practitioners and researchers; down through the high school level; and into the elementary schools, where children are taught to appreciate the humanity of all peoples.[19] For example, Bradford University in England has initiated a program of research around the theme of how "unpeaceful" relationships on all levels of human experiences can be transformed. The Institute for World Order, based in New York, is committed to a program of world order values, including peace, ecological balance, economic security, and political rights. The institute also promotes new curriculum development on the high school and college levels, as well as important projects in international law. A few college communities are attempting to transform their own campuses into "peace communities." A number of research institutes are devoted to the issues of institutional violence as underlying causes of later overt violence in society.[20]

Far less developed to date are methods for teaching students to prepare for and to handle their natural and inevitable experiences of ambivalence toward others, the inescapable impulse to project unwelcome fears onto scapegoats, problems of dealing with power, and all of the horrible traps that lead well-intentioned people to define some others as less deserving or undeserving of life.[21] But these are tasks that can be undertaken.

Here and there, some educators have begun to deal with these issues in exciting new ways: projects designed to teach children about their angry feelings and how to manage them; experiences to make students realize their prejudices against other peoples; instruction in group dynamics to develop skills for conflict resolution; and simulations to teach disarmament and peace-seeking initiatives in situations that are escalating toward violence and war.[22] In an interesting report of a school program for peace in Heidelberg, West Germany, Herman Roehrs makes the point that I have previously emphasized—that peace education is not simply education toward positive emotions and an absence of conflict.

> There exists also a way of seeing conflicts and resolving them which considers conflicts as a type of basic element necessary for the illumination of one's conscience and therefore striving only for a partial overcoming of conflict in order to secure its use as a continuous driving force for social development. In this manner an attitude comes into being which actually affirms conflict and aggression as a kind of social therapy which teaches the individual how to live with that humanly unavoidable phenomenon of conflict and how to keep this situation under control. Against this background, education toward consciousness of conflict implies that conflict is regarded consciously within education for peace as a basic condition of life and is to be accepted within this context as an educationally rational solution.[23]

The largest challenge of all would seem to be to teach all of us how not to allow a buildup of personal and social images, definitions, and institutional and legal codifications of any other people as so different from us that they are less than we, not of our species, or not human. We know that when these definitional structures take hold, the target people are set up as potential objects for attack and annihilation.

Educating for positive feelings of friendship, world citizenship, and even the universality of mankind does not seem to stem the tide of dehumanizing projections onto other people when pressures to scapegoat and victimize build in a group or culture. The challenge of developing educational methods and programs that will teach us not to be drawn to dehumanizing others is clearly a major task that has not yet been solved. How remarkable it would be, for example, if each church were to teach honestly the history of its bigotry, exploitation, and destruction of other peoples and instruct its members that we are all responsible for the deadly wrongs each of our respective faiths has perpetrated against other peoples and the sanctity of life.

An interesting example of a group that has turned acceptance of responsibility for destructiveness toward a commitment to help fellow human beings is the Aktion Suhnezeichen (which means, literally, "action, sign of Atonement"), an organization founded by Germans of different religious and political backgrounds. In announcing their purpose, the group declared:

> We Germans began the Second World War and have thereby caused, more than any other people, immeasurable suffering among mankind. We still do not have peace largely because there has been too little reconcilia-

tion. . . . But we can still work to overcome the bitterness and the hatred if we ourselves forgive, ask forgiveness, and practice this conviction. As a sign of this, we ask those people who have suffered through our violence . . . to let us with our hands build signs of reconciliation . . . in their countries.[24]

Over the years, the group has sponsored thousands of young adults as unsalaried volunteers in short- and long-term projects in Israel, Poland, and some fifteen other countries. Since 1968, such service is accepted by the German government as an alternative to military service for conscientious objectors.

It may be that we are at a transition point and that an exciting vanguard of human minds and institutions is pioneering significant projects and technologies to educate for peace. However, most religious and educational institutions around the world continue to this day to inadvertently train for a nonexperiencing of humanness.

The Machinery of Government for a More Effective Control of Violence

The notion that governments should seek peace more than they should defend against war (and, of course, should not embark on wars of conquest) is still a relatively new and undeveloped idea in human history. There are not yet many instances in which governments concern themselves with institutionalizing the search for peace and alternatives to conflict along with their time-honored machineries for self-defense and war.[25] In the United States, for example, legislation has been introduced in Congress to create a cabinet-level department of peace. The proposal for this department is a serious one that provides for a many-faceted program of international strategy formulation, arms control and disarmament, peace research and education, and more. (In 1978, President Carter signed into law a proposal to create a National Peace Academy.)

From the long view of history, the emergence of a motif of government as seeking initiatives toward peace is an exciting step in social evolution, and perhaps someday this idea of governments' being responsible for furthering peace will prove to be one of the great ideas in the history of man. As of today, however, most governments are still largely oriented toward war or, at best, toward defense rather than toward peace.

One of the problems of talking about peace is that the concept is so global that it has become increasingly difficult to define. An important theoretical advance in a new discipline known as peace science has been to differentiate between states of peace in which no war is raging but there is a great deal of injustice and oppression and states of peace in which, in addition to the fact that there is no war, there is reasonable justice and equality. Many peace researchers agree that there are some conditions of nonwar that are so undesirable that one must question whether the necessity of major social changes may even justify revolution or war. In the inaugural lecture of the University of Bradford program previously mentioned, Adam Curle made the point strongly.

> There is some confusion about the word "peace." To my mind the study of peace is not the study of pacification, of suppressing dissent, of maintaining the status quo however painful it may be to the less privileged. Some would maintain that peace was simply the absence of overt violence, but . . . the student of peace, for example, would not attempt to reconcile the master and the slave without having first worked to abolish the practice of slavery. . . . Even if wars are brought to an end, many of the conditions associated with war continue throughout large areas of the world; people are driven from their homes, unjustly imprisoned, separated from their families, flung into detention camps, virtually enslaved, exploited by landlords, victimized by the police, oppressed by the government, starved and malnourished because of official neglect or official policies; they are humiliated and have their deceptions distorted by propaganda; many in fact die because of these conditions. Circumstances such as these inflict such damage on human life, health, capacity for creative and happy existence and work, and for the development of potential, that I find it impossible to refer to them as peaceful.[26]

Another limitation to the notion of peace is that even when a people means well, their natural instinct for self-defense sets off sequences of misperception and escalation of conflict through projection, threats and counterthreats, attacks and counterattacks. Many times governments that sincerely sought peace failed to monitor accurately the intentions of another people or were unable to discipline and pace the sequences of their self-defense maneuvers, with the result that war erupted and raged far beyond what should have been. It is in this context that some of the great political paradoxes of history can be understood. It has happened more than once that leaders who were known to desire peace led their nations into war after they gave up in outrage on efforts to achieve a fair and just peace with the adversary, lest the latter exploit their good intentions. On the other hand, there have been leaders who were initially identified much more with the spirit and sound of war but somehow found a way to stop escalatory spirals short of full-scale war because they were doubly careful not to be led into unnecessary wars and because they did not have to prove that they weren't innocents who might be vulnerable to the subterfuges of the adversary.

Guarding against projection and escalation is obviously central to any effort to curtail international violence, and it is also obvious that we know very little about controlling these natural tendencies. Is it conceivable that someday there could be governmental machinery aimed specifically at checking and testing intelligence reports, policy formulations, and action plans from the point of view of the dangers of projection and escalation? Most of us are largely unsuccessful in our own family lives in stopping our projections onto one another, and it would certainly seem we are even more millenia away from being able to deal with these processes on a broader scale. Yet, it is possible to conceive of some efforts in this direction: for example, introducing into the decision-making process of a Department of Defense or Foreign Ministry or National Security Council a "desk" that is responsible for analyzing and reinterpreting information and policy recommendations specifically in the light of the dangers of projections and escalatory spirals.

The role of government involves efforts to curb violence within a society as well. One might think of building into the operation of government specific machinery, such as the office of an ombudsman or a regulatory commission, that would be responsible for reducing violence in the same way that governments monitor other health and environmental menaces. Following the concept of nonviolent aggression, this would mean not only countering violence but encouraging nonviolent controversy and conflict. A commitment to encourage nonviolent aggression in a society would mean supporting a healthy diversity of opinion in the communications media. It would also mean issuing invitations to dialogue and dissent in the highest forums of government. Say members of a thorny minority begin to speak, in the rhetoric of self-determination, of their intent to take up arms and spill every last drop of blood until the homeland is free and their legitimate rights are recognized. Are there ways in which the national government can respond that would alleviate the minority group's suspicions and conviction of the necessity of violence? The principle of nonviolent aggression suggests various possible strategies on the part of the national government, such as demonstrating respect for a minority culture, invitations to minority group leaders to participate on higher levels of national leadership, and policies that would enhance a minority group's identity in the nations. If and when violent protests or terrorist actions take place, the principles of avoiding projection and checking escalation would call for firm police action (carefully avoiding brutality or reprisals against a minority group), restrained media coverage, and an intensification of efforts at and invitations to dialogue and mutual planning. Most important would be efforts to counter the dangers of mass projections onto the minority. *The mayor of the city appoints a deputy mayor from a minority group; together they visit minority residences, businesses, regional schools, and so on. The president sponsors a cultural festival built around a treasured holiday of a minority group. Ethnic-conscious educational programs are launched in the schools.* It is admittedly an arduous process, and a process that goes against so many natural responses, but if efforts such as these spare upheaval and bloodshed, they are worthwhile a thousand times over.

There are many other ways in which government efforts can regulate destructive violence and foster nonviolent aggression, just as there are many serious festering souces of violence in modern society. In legislating against drug usage, for example, government power for nonviolent aggression means accepting people's rights to turn to all tolerable drugs within reason (e.g., the traditional use of alcohol) while controlling against intoxication, driving under the influence of drugs, exploitation of supplies by profiteers and criminals, and, of course, fighting the traffic in hard addictive and lethal drugs. Problems of social inequality and poverty in a modern society mean that provision must be made for encouraging protests by the underprivileged peoples and stimulating class consciousness, pride, and ambition to overcome inequality. There remains the exciting and enormous task for political and social scientists, together with government executives, to explore innovative ways of promoting nonviolent strength in all elements of a society.

International Agencies for Nonviolent Aggression

Many international agencies in our modern world are seeking to advance the struggle toward peace. A large number of them are barely beginning efforts, which require much strengthening before they can move from essentially symbolic functions to a level of practical effectiveness. Some remarkable beginnings have been made in this century toward disarmament agreements, for example, yet many of these efforts are attended by hypocrisy, and overall our world bristles with more and more dangerous weapons. Although to date the nuclear threat has made responsible leaders of the great nations more aware of the dangers of escalation to nuclear conflict, it is obvious that the threat of nuclear war hangs heavily over us all the time. Moreover, despite the welcome fact that since World War II no nuclear battles have been allowed, the world seems to have turned more than ever to limited zone wars and revolutions. Most major powers use small countries as "laboratories" for military observers, mercenaries, and outright armies, as well as for weapons testing. Most major and even second-level powers are up to their necks in munitions profiteering. Thus, there has been hardly more than a bare beginning — and largely a symbolic one — toward disarmament to date. A concept of nonviolent aggression calls for a far more uncompromising morality about armament production and sales, so that weapons are produced only for purposes of self-defense and are not exploited for commercial or power reasons.

With massive weapons systems looming over us, it is difficult to think of other processes in the international system, but it is important to look at how representatives of different nations meet with one another and negotiate the fate of peoples. The present and historically accepted model for negotiations between nations is based essentially on a notion of getting as much as we can from the other party while giving in return the least that is necessary to make our own gain possible. It is, in effect, sharp, competitive trading. Today, international relations experts are beginning to realize that the diplomatic negotiating process can be designed in a variety of ways and that social science theory and research can be applied to the creation and testing of a variety of new negotiation models.[27] The concept of nonviolent aggression supports the development of new models for the negotiating process that bring negotiators together to achieve and safeguard genuine power for all concerned parties as opposed to negotiations that aim at gaining power for an us at the expense of an other.

James and Marge Craig propose acceptance of a model that would have both parties agree, and be helped by a trainer and facilitator, to seek only those solutions that are acceptable to both parties as promising to meet their genuine needs constructively.[28] This means discarding at the outset all those goals that are totally unacceptable to either party and putting the energy of negotiation into creatively searching for new solutions rather than into pressing, bargaining, strong-arming, seducing, dealing, and double-dealing toward one's original goals.

No-lose negotiations about the Old City of Jerusalem, for example, would begin with acceptance of the following contradictory assertions:

The Israeli Position	*The Arab Position*
The Old City of Jerusalem must be in Jewish hands.	The Old City of Jerusalem must be in Arab hands.

It is intolerable that the Old City of Jerusalem be in Arab hands.	It is intolerable that the Old City of Jerusalem be in Jewish hands.

In traditional negotiations, the aim would be to achieve one's own position, or as much of it as can be secured. In no-lose negotiations, the central assumption is that a solution must be created that is satisfactory to both parties. The commitment to search and create the shared solution is what makes the impossible possible.

Many other possibilities exist on the international level. Overseas cultural programs of various nations offer opportunities for reducing fear of other peoples. Veteran peace theorist and researcher Theodore Lentz has suggested an international agency for assessing technological developments before their implementation.[29] Our modern-day mammoth international corporations represent unprecedented international bodies. Perhaps some forward-looking corporations could bring together executives of different nationalities for training in the resolution of conflicts among peoples of different cultures. It was business corporations in the United States, after all, that pioneered many of the early techniques of group dynamics. Is it too unrealistic to imagine group dynamics session, leadership labs, or sensitivity training sessions for executives of different nations in which participants would work on simulations of the tough issues of international commerce, such as establishing the price of oil or negotiating the admission of a new nation to a common market area, and in which a major focus would be on experiencing the human consequences of the decisions to be taken?[30]

Airline, travel, and tourist interests already work toward promoting a greater awareness of diverse cultures and folklores. As international travel grows for business, personal, and recreational purposes, any number of moments in travelers' journeys through one another's space could be utilized for bringing people into contact with one another as fellow human beings.[31] Airline entertainment might include human-awareness films. International air terminals are natural settings for creative displays, exhibits, distribution of reading material and mementos, and an introduction to local eating customs and delicacies. Far more direct interventions in the international conflict system are also possible for the transportation industry. The skyjackings and terrorist attacks on planes in recent years make it clear that the people directly involved in the business of taking human beings across the globe, such as pilots associations or mechanics unions, have the power to demand that more be done to protect travelers from violence. Unfortunately, these powers so far have been exercised only minimally. The airlines themselves have similar power. One wonders what the outcome would be if a number of air carriers refused to fly to and from countries that allow air terrorism, or if several nations refused landing rights to those countries, and even refused entry to their citizens by way of other carriers?

International agencies, by their very definition, are communicators among peoples, and each international body represents a wealth of opportunities for work toward nonviolence in international affirs. Conveying food and medical supplies to developing countries is a fertile opportunity for conveying messages of our common humanity. International health agencies, environmental regulatory commissions, and trade associations all have a visibility that can be purposefully tapped for creative messages against the dehumanization of peoples or escalations of conflict. International professional associations are beginning to emerge as newly significant forces. Although their contributions to world peace are meager to date, there will be an increasing opportunity for such guilds to stand up, in action and not only words, against governments that oppress human life. Internationally linked religious groups are a powerful humanitarian force that has been shamefully neglected. Religious images continue to have an intensely powerful pull on the masses of the world. To this date, they have been invoked all too effectively on behalf of revolutions and war and far too seldom in the name of human rights values.

There is no doubt that international agencies will grow apace in the years ahead, and many of them have an enormous potential for advancing the prospects of peace. There are also possibilities of new agencies. One exciting strategy would be the development of national and international "disaster armies" which would intervene directly in disaster situations whenever many people were dying.[32] The International Red Cross and other voluntary rescue agencies that mobilize medical assistance are the welcome beginning of such international machinery, but a fully developed international rescue agency would be less dependent on immediate political considerations before acting and could undertake a broader range of actions on behalf of human rights and dignity in addition to fundamental life-saving medical tasks.[33] Such an international rescue army could include teams of trained technicians that would be ready to move immediately into any area in which a certain number of people had died in a mass disaster. Different units would be responsible for issuing food supplies, providing emergency health services, bringing in mobile communications, setting up emergency transportation services, and so on.

A theory of nonviolent aggression suggests still other functions. One division of a disaster army could have as its function the initiation of so-called pro-social or positive interactions between people. For example, in a community that had been devastated by a flood, a pro-social team could mobilize the survivors to engage in active reclamation efforts on their own behalf, not only as a practical matter but on the basis of studies that have shown that survivors of disasters fall into lingering depression and develop health problems unless they are actively engaged in the process of rebuilding. A pro-social team could set up "rumor clinics" to stem the momentum of the rumors and projections that inevitably attend disasters. At the time of a natural disaster, blame can be viciously projected onto entirely innocent people. In the Middle Ages, for example, the Black Plague was attributed to the Jews, who were then subjected to terrible death raids and pogroms. A pro-social team's concerns could include education toward nonviolence in situations in which violence has erupted or is threatening: in urban areas where a poor or discriminated-against class of people is rioting, on college campuses where students and troops clash bloodily, wherever religious or racial groups turn violently against one another.[34]

Of course, it is premature to expect that in our lifetime a world government will have the authority to automatically send such teams into a disaster area where people are dying en masse, not because of floods or starvation or disease, but because of racial strife or mass murder or genocide. At this point in history, it is virtually impossible to imagine disaster teams being allowed into the very situations where they are needed the most. The whole exercise breaks down into utter foolishness whenever a totalitarian power is involved, and few nations of any persuasion would agree to allow an international disaster team within their boundaries to counteract riots, persecution of minorities, counterrevolutions, and so on.

But that is the whole point. We know we are terribly limited at this time in history, but too often we do not realize that we limit ourselves even further by failing to dare to dream of new concepts and new motifs that in time might change human consciousness. It is at least an intriguing exercise in social design to consider such potential innovations. It is conceivable, for example, that a future Nazi regime would not allow itself to go as far as the Nazis of our century did were there a significant tradition of international intervention in the face of mass death. As it was, the Nazis did go to severe lengths to dress up the Theresienstadt concentration camp for Red Cross visits, and some lives were saved by the necessity of that exercise, but the basic definition of the Red Cross role was too limited, and uninspired, to result in a real exposé and international pressure. It is also conceivable that an international "army" could at least render some kind of assistance to victims from afar, mobilizing resistance by broadcasting the truth about extermination camps, smuggling in weapons, and more. One might even dream that one or another international agency that was committed to life saving might have prevailed on the United States or England to bomb the Nazi death camps—which the allies did not do, despite many appeals to do so.[35] Again my point is to illustrate, even if in simplistic ways, the possibilities of our dreaming of and designing new control systems to intervene in the agonizingly repetitive cycles of destruction that dominate the human experience—and I hope there are such systems before the cancer of mass destruction metastasizes and spreads beyond repair.

A Fascist Regime Which Stood by the Jews

Whatever one says of the Franco regime, it must be admitted that from a Jewish point of view the Franco era has been one of the few pleasant surprises of our time. True, this is a comparative finding, for judged by liberal Western standards, Spanish Jews have still far to go to achieve full rights. But the surprise was engendered not a little from the negative initial expectations.

Here was a Fascist regime established in a land of long-standing anti-Semitism as a result of the intensive activities of the Nazi-Fascist axis. One anticipated the worst. But in fact Spain was the only Fascist country which did not introduce anti-Semitic measures and even made considerable efforts to save and protect Jews during World War II. Granted she could have done much more, but her record was superior to other neutral countries inasmuch as she never turned back Jewish refugees who reached her frontier.

Once Franco triumphed, the new regime cancelled secularist laws and moved back to a Catholic regime. Recognition of non-Catholic religions was revoked and synagogues were closed. The whole atmosphere was pro-Axis. When World War II broke out, Spain seemed to offer no rescue potentialities.

Yet in the first couple of years, about 30,000 Jews escaped via Spain. This was a period when it was still possible for Jews in France to get exit permits and all of these were granted transit visas by Spain. Even those whose documents were patently forged were accepted, as long as they did not stay too long on Spanish soil — and this was guaranteed by Jewish organizations, notably the Joint Distribution Committee.

In the second half of the War, when other routes of escape were closed off, the Spanish route was increasingly important. Now it became difficult to cross France and the Jews were smuggled over the Pyrenees. Altogether an additional 7,500 Jews reached Spain after 1942. There was sometimes a certain ambivalence in official Spanish attitudes but U.S. pressures and the obvious indications as to which way the War was going guaranteed decisions favourable to the refugees.

One praiseworthy story is the efforts made by Spanish diplomatic representatives to save Jews, who could somehow claim Spanish nationality, from deportation to the death camps.

Avni relates remarkable stories of the devoted efforts of Spanish chargé d'affaires and consuls in Salonica, Athens, Bulgaria and Hungary who in various ways saved over 3,000 Jews after Germany allowed Spain to withdraw its nationals from occupied countries. The numbers could have been higher if Spain had not insisted that each group of such repatriates leave Spain before another was brought in.

– Geoffrey Wigoder, *Jerusalem Post,* November 6, 1975

13

TOWARD A GENOCIDE EARLY WARNING SYSTEM

I came home a little afraid for my country, afraid of what it might want and get, and like, under pressure of combined reality and illusion. I felt—and feel—that it was not German Man that I had met, but Man. He happened to be in Germany under certain conditions. He might, under certain conditions, be I.

— Milton Mayer

Ideas, even simple ones, have remarkable vitality, even propagate themselves and spread to new areas. History is full of examples of ideas which seemed at first too naive to be taken seriously, developing finally into movements of great power. Any voice raised against evil is better than no voice.

— Anna W. M. Wolf

Frequently we read in the *New York Times* or its counterparts around the world that in such and such a place on our planet, groups of people of such and such color, nationality, or religion have been murdered. Those of us who care sigh and worry a moment, but soon return to our immediate concerns. Were we to track the process of our inner experience during such moments, we would probably find that we feel a deep sense of impotence mingled with sadness and concern. However, since it is painful to continue to feel a deep sense of helplessness, with rare exceptions we turn the experience off, and it is all over in a flash of a few minutes. Once we feel that there is really nothing we can do about what is happening, it is maddening to continue feeling so deeply. We turn off our emotion and return to the small and large

This chapter was prepared jointly by Israel W. Charny and Chanan Rapaport, director of the Szold National Institute for Research in the Behavioral Sciences, Jerusalem.

events of our lives about which we feel we can do something. We turn our energies to areas of our living in which we can continue to feel alive, and we turn away from a problem of death about which we feel so helpless that it might draw us further toward our own death.

Now and then, journalists pick up news of genocidal events and provide some degree of continuity of coverage in their reports to their newspapers or broadcast stations. These are not "big stories," generally speaking. Sometimes a story is covered in an in-depth feature in a Sunday newspaper section or magazine, but reports of genocide are not treated with the electricity that is accorded to news reports of other types of societal upheaval or disaster. Nor are reports of genocide treated with a sense of immediacy or urgency. For the most part, the tacit understanding is that the peoples and nations of our world do not react to news of genocidal events with any great emotion, and certainly they are not going to take any collective action to stop a slaughter.[1]

There are some public groups, sometimes organized as quasi-governmental or quasi-international agencies, that do take a professional responsibility for following and reporting the facts of genocides that erupt in our strange world. However, these groups do not represent a major force in the shaping of world public opinion or of the responses of international agencies. To our knowledge, no such agency is significant by way of its reputation for accuracy and comprehensiveness of information or by way of its actual or symbolic status in the spectrum of agencies that represent man's efforts at international organizations, although the fact that the Nobel Peace Prize was awarded to Amnesty International in 1977 for its reporting and efforts on behalf of the imprisoned and tortured is an indication that some significant progress has been made.[2]

In the last twenty or so years, after the Holocaust of the Jewish people in Europe and the explosion of the atomic bomb on Hiroshima and Nagasaki began to be assimilated, there have been some indications of a growing concern about genocide. However, if such a concern is to build a meaningful momentum, new organizations and institutions will be needed to translate the concern about genocide into effective international law, communication, and action.[3] In December 1948, the United Nations drafted a Convention on the Prevention and Punishment of the Crime of Genocide (see Appendix C). This extension of international law gained sufficient signatures to go into effect on January 12, 1951, but it has never been tested as a legal reality.[4]

At this point in its evolution, mankind is deeply limited in its readiness to experience and take action in response to genocidal disasters. Most events of genocide are marked by massive indifference, silence, and inactivity. Some isolated events are followed by a measure of concern, outcry, and protest; but even those genocidal events that do trigger some degree of awareness and protest are rarely followed by any significant efforts to correct or limit the genocidal process by people who are not connected to the events by reason of kinship or geographical closeness.

THE SYMBOLIC AND PRACTICAL SIGNIFICANCE OF A GENOCIDE EARLY WARNING SYSTEM

In the treatment or correction of many human problems, there are fairly long stages in which the most that can be done is to observe systematically how and when a problem begins, the way in which it unfolds, under what conditions it is naturally arrested, and under what conditions it gathers momentum. Even this process of carefully monitoring the problem can begin to bring a certain amount of relief to the suffering. Even though real treatment of some diseases does not yet exist, the caring and involvement of a physician can bring the patient some relief from terror. Over and above the humanitarian meaning of such relief, the patient is also assisted in this way to gather new strength for however much of a fight for life he or she may be able to make. We also know that there are rare instances in which people survive even killer diseases, although no one seems to know exactly why. Some cancers, for example, even severe ones, have been known to recede by themselves. It is interesting for our concept of a Genocide Early Warning System that some cancer researchers suggest that these recoveries signify that the organism has recovered its natural ability to recognize the cancer cells as its enemy and so is able to successfully redirect its powerful immunologic "troops" against the enemy.[5] The efforts of organized medicine also try to provide for the comfort of the patient and the protection of the community from contagious diseases. Thus, although there may be no treatment for a specific disease, these side measures can help reduce the toll of a disease even as man awaits the breakthrough of new knowledge and the development of directly effective therapies.

There is little question that mankind as a whole would enjoy at least some sense of relief if there were a designated institution to monitor and report the terrible events that destroy so many human lives. As an official activity of such a responsible institution, an established Genocide Early Warning System would represent a new statement of concern about human life.

An early warning system would mean that some effort was being made to combat the primitive madness that has killed millions of people in every period of human history. Even if at the outset the tools and pro-

A Human Environment Ombudsman

Specific recognition . . . needs to be given to the function of national and international . . . "look-out" institutions which, through their specialized interest and sensitivity:

- identify *new* threats to the human environment at an early stage;
- mobilize support to draw public attention to the nature of each new threat;
- encourage governments to take legislative action to counteract the threats to the environment;
- help to generate the political will without which governments cannot act;
- support government agencies by providing a pool of experts to monitor the problems and steps towards its solution, and to advise on legislation;
- supply a non-political forum in which the problem can be discussed before it is handled between governments in a political setting.

Statement of the Union of International Associations of the Preparatory Committee for the United Nations Conference on the Human Environment, Stockholm, 1972

cedures of an early warning system were to inevitably suffer the weaknesses and limitations of most beginning programs and technologies, and even if an early warning system were to initially result in very little practical aid to the victims, there would be a profound evolutionary meaning to the development of such an agency.

Such an agency would speak not only to the immediate present, but to the long flow of human history as well. A Genocide Early Warning System would announce to all of us that mankind was gaining a new awareness of the widespread tragedy of mass murder and was seeking to develop new processes to control and remove this terrible cancer.

Admittedly, there is always some danger that the spotlight of world public opinion would impel some genociders to do their work with even greater haste and ruthlessness. But it seems far more conceivable that the major impact of the spotlight of world public opinion would be to reduce the number of fatalities. Ultimately, in a long evolutionary process, it should be entirely possible to turn the concept of mass extermination into an odious, unacceptable relic of man's onetime primitiveness, much as cannibalism is almost universally inconceivable today. The possibility that an insistent world public opinion would turn humans away from genocide is, after all, also based on our built-in wishes to respect and advance life. Our natural life-seeking side would be strengthened by the pressure of information from a worldwide early warning system and its representation of human caring.

The basic principle of an early warning system is to create an information feedback system. Just as biofeedback has shown us that a person can exert control over his body—rate of heartbeat, blood circulation, muscle tension, and so on—when informed of the current levels and told what level to strive for, social and cultural systems may have untapped adaptive capacities as well. Ervin Laszlo has proposed an "ecofeedback system". "Ecofeedback is the principle that the existing states of the world system can be measured, evaluated in terms of preferred states, and the pertinent information fed back to the population directly concerned in maintaining or changing the given states."[6]

LEVELS OF INFORMATION IN A GENOCIDE EARLY WARNING SYSTEM

Our concept of a Genocide Early Warning System involves at least three different levels of data collection, which are to be put into operation at different stages of the system's development.

1. A genocide warning data system begins by assembling the facts of ongoing genocide around the world in a comprehensive and systematic way. Incredible as it may seem, there is no such integrated data source anywhere in the world today—neither for current reports of genocide nor for past genocides. Moreover, a genocide warning system not only treats the data of genocide as facts in themselves, but it organizes the information into meaningful patterns and sequences that add to our understanding of how these events unfold and gather momentum.

2. A second level of information in an early warning system concerns the wide range of human rights violations that fall short of genocide, such as murder on a smaller scale, concentration camps, torture, imprisonment without due process, and a denial of rights to emigrate. In recent years, there has been an increasing amount of information about such human rights violations and suggestions for global information systems, but the need for such systems has not yet been met.[7] This level of human rights data in the genocide warning system not only

treats information about violations in their own right, but also connects those violations to predictions of the likelihood of a buildup of momentum toward mass murder.

3. The third level of information in the early warning system branches out to track a broad spectrum of social indicators. First, some social indicators cover a variety of societal and cultural processes that are not immediately related to overt violent behavior or to the ideology of genocide, but they are nonetheless considered potentially relevant to the unfolding of possible tendencies toward genocide. These indicators include the valuing of life in a society, the valuing of the quality of life, a culture's orientation to the distribution of power, and so on. Second, other indicators are specifically connected to the subsequent emergence of genocide. These indicators include the development of an ideology of genocide, patterns of dehumanization, legitimation of violence in a society, and so on. Unlike the first two levels, which could be put into operation at once, this level of information gathering and analysis would require longitudinal studies to develop and test the relevant indicators.

Level 1: Monitoring Ongoing Genocides

The major function of a Genocide Early Warning System is to report ongoing events of genocide anywhere on the globe. Such an early warning system means developing a worldwide, computerized data bank to collate, according to nations and other groupings such as tribes or religions, all allegations, reports, and investigations of genocidal events. The basic charge of the early warning system is to develop the best possible means for gathering and verifying information about mass exterminations. Of course, a true megalomaniac won't simply open the doors of his extermination camps to visiting investigators or otherwise stop his determined plans to remove a victim group just because an international agency makes inquiries, but it is not inconceivable that dedicated, relentlessly effective investigative reporting would at least hamper the course of an ongoing genocidal process.

The potential impact of authoritative, insistent reports on world public opinion is becoming greater and greater in our day and age as the penetration of an already incredibly powerful mass media continues to grow apace all over the world. An international Genocide Early Warning System could be expected to change considerably the continuity of coverage and the impact of information about mass murders when they are revealed to the world. It is no longer a matter of haphazard, short-lived journalistic reports that are dropped when a story is no longer "news," but a process of systematic reports, rendered at regular time intervals in addition to emergency alerts, followed up by careful investigations and verifications by an institution that represents a significant public or collective authority that news reports alone do not. Many outlets are used: the mass media, reports to national governments and international bodies, reports to scholarly organizations and publications, the development of learning and information resources for university and high school curricula, and so on.

Under a world spotlight, the momentum of at least some genocidal processes could conceivably be slowed. Many genocidal campaigns do not reach their zenith for some time and usually not until it has become clear that it is possible "to get away with it" in an unknowing and uncaring world.[8] Within the ranks of the genociding people, more dissidents might be emboldened to fight the genocidal policy. The role of "ignorant" bystanders to the genocide would be made far more uncomfortable by the glare of the international spotlight. In addition, the insistent reality of reports in the international news media might help a potential victim people recognize the danger to their lives so they could flee in time. Under certain circumstances, such publicity might also lead to the organization of more effective campaigns of self-defense and counterattack.

Incredible as it may seem, there not only have been (and are) genocides that were ignored by an indifferent world, but there have also been genocides that were not "at all known" until many years later. Robert Conquest describes how it was not until 1966 that it became known that during World War II, 200,000 Meskaji, a Turkish people of Islamic faith in the Georgian Soviet Socialist Republic, were deported by the Soviets from the geographic area of Mesketia and sustained heavy casualties during that deportation.[9]

A genocide data warning system will report events of mass murder as quickly as possible and carefully follow up all reports of genocide. The immediate life-serving purpose of such an information system is apparent. At the same time, the information bank should also be developed to include systematic data of past events of genocide and to organize past and current data in meaningful categories so that researchers can study how genocides have unfolded in different cultures and eras.

Level 2: Monitoring Violations of Basic Human Rights

The Genocide Early Warning System also gathers, evaluates, and reports informations on human rights violations that fall short of actual genocide, as well as on trends toward possible new genocides. Such data constitute a critical information mass as to present human suffering and also provide indications of possible momentums toward genocidal events in the future. Even in the current stage of mankind's "humanistic consciousness," it is possible to specify a large variety of actions that constitute clear-cut violations of basic human rights. The United Nations Universal Declaration of Human Rights (see Appendix B) lists certain violations of basic human rights, such as slavery, torture, and imprisonment without due process. Although there are always problems of interpretation, such rights and their violations are, relatively speaking, objectively definable.[10]

When combined with the data on actual genocide, this second level of information in the early warning system data bank provides a comprehensive picture of actual, overt events that deny human beings their fundamental rights—first to stay alive and second to be secure from torture, abuse, and denial of basic liberties. When analyzed and categorized in meaningful ways, these data provide a basis for seeing the pattern and sequential development of abuses of human rights, up to and including the occurrence of actual genocide. The following are categories for information assembly:

1. *Events: Reports of Genocide and other Major Human Rights Violations.* Information is collected on current reports of mass murder around the world as well as on other major human rights violations that fall short of genocide: murder, detention in concentration camps, torture, imprisonment without due process, slavery, denial of the right to emigrate freely, denial of free speech, and so on, according to categories selected from the United Nations Universal Declaration of Human Rights.

2. *Peoples.* The above events are recorded as to the nations or peoples involved, both as initiators and as targets. The classification also includes power blocs such as NATO, Warsaw Pact countries, and the Arab League and religious groups such as Jews, Protestants, Catholics, Hindus, and Moslems.

3. *Stages.* Events are analyzed according to a sequential classification of stages.

00 Historical events and transitions
01 Psychological events and transitions
02 Economic and cultural events and transitions
03 Political and geographic events and transitions
04 Legal events and transitions
05 Social events and transitions
06 Communication events and transitions
07 Ideological events and transitions
08 Religious events and transitions

09 Nationalistic and racial events and transitions
10 Formulation of genocidal fantasy
20 Precipitating factors or context
30 Mobilization of means to genocide
40 Legalization and institutionalization of genocide
50 Execution of genocide
51 Denial of commission of genocide

4. *Reported Causes.* The overt causes, precipitating events and background causes that are reported to have led to the events are classified. The data and explanations of these causes are provided by the same data sources that provide the information concerning genocidal events and human rights violations.

5. *Data Sources.* Initially, the data sources are news items gathered by those news agencies around the world that are judged as achieving relatively high levels of objectivity and accuracy in their reports. Data are also received from specialized agencies that investigate and report serious cases of genocide and human rights violations when they are brought to the agencies' attention. At a much later stage in the development of the early warning system, there are direct investigative procedures to supplement these data, especially for purposes of systematic follow-up reports.

Level 3: Predicting Buildups of Possible Genocidal Violence.

The further development of an early warning system concerns information about social indicators within a national group or culture that are known to be linked to the possibility of future genocide. These social indicators include attitudes such as defining other peoples as inferior or not deserving equal rights; defining people or minority groups as dangerous; and taking a ruthless attitude toward national warfare rather than accepting humanitarian principles of combat under international law. There are, of course, many complex problems to be solved before such a prediction system can be developed. First of all, there is no existing social science methodology for forecasting future events of genocide, and social indicator researchers, in general, are in a very beginning stage of development.

Nonetheless, until such research is done and actual predictions can be attempted, the collection of data about societal processes is useful in its own right. Thus, weather information that "a heavy cloud cover is seen over Kansas today" is useful even when no effort is made to predict the probability of precipitation in the next two twenty-four-hour periods. Similarly, it is useful to have observations such as "a certain head of state

FIGURE 13.1   Levels of Information to Be Monitored in a Genocide
Early Warning System

	Current Operational Feasibility	Appropriateness of Reports to World Public
1. *Monitoring Ongoing Genocides*		
multisource information-gathering and investigative system; e.g., collation of available news-service reports; reports from international health, environmental, and legal agencies; mobile teams for interviewing international travelers and refugees; and official field-investigation teams dispatched to scenes of reported mass murders	requires development of reliable data-gathering system; does not pose major conceptual or technical problems given adequate resources	appropriate on completion of reliable system of gathering, verifying, assembling, and retrieving information; calls for creative development of effective ways to deliver information
2. *Monitoring Violations of Basic Human Rights*		
expansion of information-gathering and investigative system to include a wide range of human rights violations such as torture, imprisonment without due process, denial of right to emigrate, and denial of free speech, according to rights defined in United Nations Universal Declaration of Human Rights	*yes*, as above	*yes*, as above

FIGURE 13.1   Continued

	Current Operational Feasibility	Appropriateness of Reports to World Public
3. *Monitoring and Predicting Buildups of Possible Genocidal Violence*		
further expansion of information-gathering and investigative system to track a broad spectrum of social indicators that are seen in the buildup of potential genocidal violence, e.g., cultural attitudes toward human life as expendable, prejudices and dehumanization of a minority, societal allowance of violence, acceptance of a fantasy or folk theme of genocide	*no*; requires long-range research program to develop and test relevant social indicators and to formulate a valid approach to prediction of possible future violence	*yes* as to description of ongoing, objectively defined social processes that are public knowledge, following research demonstration of linkage to buildup of genocide; *no* as to statements of predictions of possible buildups of genocidal violence until research confirms reliability and validity of such predictions

is demanding a variety of tributes from citizens on pain of punishment, including the requirement that shopkeepers wear clothing made of fabric on which the president's picture has been printed" or "The government in a certain country has announced the suspension of civil liberties for all members of a certain tribe or subpopulation."

Social psychologist Herbert Kelman emphasizes the importance of studying the conditions under which genocide occurs. Kelman discusses what he calls sanctioned massacres, or violent events in the context of a genocidal policy, that are directed at groups that have not themselves threatened or engaged in hostile actions against those who do violence to them. In contrast to other violent events, Kelman suggests that "the psychological environment in which such massacres occur lacks the conditions normally perceived as providing some degree of moral justification for violence. . . . [the] question for the social psychologist is: what are the conditions under which normal people become capable of planning, ordering, committing, or condoning acts of mass violence?"[11]

The observations collected will increasingly be based on research showing which indicators are historically relevant to the buildup of genocidal acts of violence. However, it is important that this level of data collection not be turned prematurely into prediction statements. Any concrete information that a responsible early warning institution would choose to make public would carry considerable weight, and a public reporting of social indicators by an international agency committed to the monitoring of potential genocide would in itself constitute a kind of prediction. An early warning agency carries a heavy responsibility for evaluating the kind of information it is proper to report publicly. Premature reporting could easily destroy the potential of such an agency. However, in principle, it seems both entirely proper and feasible for an international agency to identify a wide range of events that are linked to actual and potential violations of basic human rights and to release this information to the public.[12]

There is also a danger that one or more ideological blocs will seek to politicize the early warning system so that it will attack other ideological groups. In recent years, terrorist groups have justified their murderous actions against innocent citizens as self-defense against alleged genocide—a justification that has been aptly called the rhetoric of genocide. Historically, there have always been groups that subvert man's finest concepts to serve the purposes of the satanic; thus, once-profound religious ideals have sometimes been invoked to justify killing some "heretics," and the concept of democracy is regularly appropriated by dictatorial states, which then condemn free nations as fascist. No doubt efforts would be made to use the authority and prestige of an early warning system for the very purpose of dehumanizing other people. In fact, the machinery of the early warning system could be taken as a basis for rationalizing repressive measures against one population group or another. The data of a system that purports to identify the potential mass murderers might even be taken to justify the murder of some people as potential killers.[13]

It is therefore essential that a Genocide Early Warning System be established as an independent scientific agency that is safeguarded, as much as possible, from political entry. One way of doing this, which also suits the requirements of scientific development, is to encourage the development of multiple, independent early warning systems around the world. This procedure will make possible a healthy cross-checking of information and stimulate a variety of creative efforts toward the development, testing, and refinement of a "genocide meteorology." Strictly from the point of view of effective data gathering, it seems wisest to develop a variety of regional centers that will focus on the regional "climate" of their more immediate geographical or cultural zones. Today, for example, Westerners hardly know about the extermination of peoples in remote areas, such as Indians in Brazil, the Kurds in Iraq, or Christians and other non-Moslem Africans in southern Sudan. Regionally based centers can be staffed with knowledgeable, local behavioral scientists who are close to the pulse of the local peoples, can observe events at first hand, and are more sensitive to local symbolism and cultural indicators.

The same principle applies to the professional setting of the agencies. No doubt it would be good to see an early warning system within the framework of a legal international agency such as the United Nations. However, a strong argument can be made for the simultaneous development of early warning systems in a variety of settings, such as major universities and research institutes. University campuses today include a great many innovative centers that seek to apply traditional knowledge to the frontier problems that face human beings. All over the world, there are centers for the study of international relations, world law, social planning, peace, conflict resolution, world health, environment, and strategic matters. Any one of these settings could appropriately take on the project of monitoring and recording genocide and other violations of human rights.

For many years, my [Israel Charny's] fantasy has been the establishment of a center for the study of genocide, human rights, and the potential for peace. About 1966, I came to a deeply felt decision that I wanted to study what was known about the psychology of man's ability to engage in mass murder. I wrote to Yad Vashem, The Heroes and Martyrs Remembrance Authority, in Jerusalem, to inquire what information they had assembled in their archives on the subject. The brief and courteous reply I received stunned me: "There is very little material." In many ways, I owe to that reply a good deal of my resolution to work harder at the possible contribution of the psychological sciences to our understanding of how human beings can be so incredibly destructive – a crucial question in my opinion.

In such a center, people would link the study of all that takes place in the terrible holocausts with the study of the human potential to be peaceful and nonviolent. The center would invite groups of scholars from a variety of disciplines – psychology, sociology, political science, international relations and international law, anthropology, economics, communications, and other fields – to work together in a collaborative search for and study of the causes and treatment of cancers of human destructiveness. An effort would be made to seek to understand scientifically the causes, processes, and sequences that lead to genocidal destructiveness, and, at the same time, the tools of science and ingenuity would be used to create new designs for human evolution toward the potential for peace.

Understandably, the Nazi Holocaust has generated a good number of memorial agencies and traditions–the most significant being Yad Vashem. But these memorials–like the memorials to other peoples who have suffered genocide–generally fail to project a particular tragedy as a universal tragedy of the many peoples who have suffered, and will yet suffer, extermination. Moreover, the intent of the memorial basically does not go beyond a pious hope that the simple act of memorializing or remembering events that took place will make people more aware of the past and thereby reduce the possibilities of genocidal brutalities in the future. Although it is essential that we be aware of the past, there is nothing that says that historical awareness and heartfelt memorializing alone will correct man's ways. There is little hope of ending genocide until we truly learn to understand the sequences and processes that lead to genocide.[14]

RESERVATIONS ABOUT THE PROPOSAL FOR AN EARLY WARNING SYSTEM

There are many problems involved in setting up a Genocide Early Warning System. A system that in no way showed promise of development into a meaningful, practical instrument would not only fail to lead to a new sense of symbolic hope and aliveness, but conceivably could set us back. The fact that even when we tried, we were nothing more than naive fools railing against the prevailing realities of life would be another demonstration of man's utter impotence. Inaccuracies of reporting and prediction would be a serious problem and, in some instances, would touch off painful national and cultural sensitivities. The actual operational beginnings of all levels of a working early warning system would need to be very carefully planned, tested, and developed to a point of significant technical success.

Finally, it has to be clear that such a system in itself cannot be expected to bring about any immediate major changes on this mad globe. Only people who are naive and innocent about power and human life could subscribe to the illusion that just having the "weather reports" and "weather forecasts" of a Genocide Early Warning System will change the reality of life on earth in any immediate way. One might also say wryly that a world that has seen millions die for so many centuries will not be in much of a rush for early warning information. Nonetheless, even a beginning effort to build a genocide early warning system as a tool of future international process could arouse hope and other positive actions by various people. Although no "messianic" changes can be expected because of a genocide data system, mankind's taking responsibility for new levels of knowing and reporting how people treat human life could represent a step toward a better future.

THE EARLY WARNING PROCESSES

LIFE EXPERIENCE PROCESSES AS A FRAME OF REFERENCE FOR AN EARLY WARNING SYSTEM

In the long-range development of a Genocide Early Warning System, beyond reporting information about present genocides and other major violations of human rights, we want to look at those social forces and processes in a culture that predictably generate genocidal momentums and bring them to a head.

We have chosen very specifically to begin with a series of statements about basic life experience processes of individuals, families and groups, and society. These experience processes are, to our minds, universal attributes of the human condition, and all people must encounter them, constructively or otherwise. They are the basic conditions of being alive, staying alive, and feeling alive. However, these same conditions can be turned toward destructiveness, and then these processes can combine to build increasing momentums toward violence and can culminate in genocide. These processes are detailed in Appendix A, which shows how the basic life experience processes are sources of life satisfaction but can also be turned toward destructiveness. The negative restatements of these basic processes as destructive processes constitute the early warning indicators on the societal level.

Note that these concepts of the life experience processes generate terms that refer at one and the same time to specific behavior and to underlying human values.[15] Another advantage of this approach is that behavior on the larger societal level is linked to processes on the other levels of individual, family, and smaller group experiences.[16]

Other researchers of early warning systems may choose to define their categories strictly in terms of the behavior of large groups vis-à-vis human rights and life, and it may well be that the "weather predictions" that someday issue from those other early warning systems will, in fact, prove more effective. However, our own preference is to try for concepts that will be useful to us both along the roads to Auschwitz and Hiroshima and in relation to many everyday events. We are fascinated by pedestrian, everyday power plays, such as in an academic community when an entire department is eliminated or a department chairman is squeezed out, or in a family that scapegoats one member of the family into the role of a victim-patient to suffer a condition that represents a larger family problem. Other early warning studies may focus exclusively on concrete behavioral acts, without reference to their intrinsic value or experiential meanings, and not use concepts that can be applied to levels of human organization that are smaller than large groups. But the whole thrust of this book is to attempt to link genocidal events to the underlying sources of such behavior, because we believe that, ultimately, genocide takes form through a series of processes that extend across the whole continuum of human experience.

We believe not only that eventually there must be legal and institutional processes to outlaw discriminatory and life-destructive behavior, but that it is crucial that people's underlying value processes evolve toward a basic commitment to life. We therefore prefer to work from concepts that encompass the psychophilosophical principles (weltanschauung) of a culture or people and descriptions of actual behavior toward other human beings. An analogy in psychotherapy is that psychotherapists attempt to correct both the behavior and the underlying psychophilosophical processes. For example, they not only teach a family member the specific behavior of not being abusive to another family member, but they attempt to teach the larger principle of not trying to gain emotional security by putting down someone else.

This simultaneous approach to human values and behavior provides us with more linkages between the issues of a society's madness and the day-to-day problems of individuals, families, and small groups. Much the same dynamics are at work when people defend themselves against the terrors of life within a family that unwittingly "murders" one of its members emotionally as when a nation of people chooses to murder a "lesser" race. If we were to build our warning system more exclusively in behavioral terms that referred only to the political and power forces at work in large groups, the concept would not be so readily translatable into a framework for looking at individuals, families, and small groups as well as larger societies.

Nothing in what we are saying is intended to equate one level of human experience with another. The same mechanism of defense — say, projection of one's fears of inadequacy onto another — is not exactly the same in individual psychology, between members of a family group, between persons in a mob, or between persons in mobs heading en masse to kill their victims. However, there is a continuity of the human experiencing process, or what has been called transactional connections, from one level to the next, and we can learn a great deal by understanding the continuities of behavior from one level of human experiencing to the next.

This frame of reference also makes it possible to focus on positive, life-respecting values and behavior of a people, not just on destructiveness and violations of human rights. Such a frame of reference also makes it possible to record a society's positive values and attitudes toward the right of human beings to experience their life without harassment as well as to record a society's infringements of human rights.

Defining Early Warning Processes

Early warning processes represent a society's methods for managing certain basic life experiences or basic value processes that all societies have to contend with, e.g., the people's orientation to the value of human life, the importance placed on the quality of the life experience, or the people's orientation to power. These societal processes are extensions of universal life issues that we must grapple with on all levels of individual and collective experience.

The early warning processes are grouped under four headings:

1. *Devaluing humanness:* how people devalue human life; also how people devalue the experience of aliveness, seek power over others, and resort to overt violence and destructiveness
2. *The illusion of self-defense:* the absence of control machinery for monitoring and managing escalations of threats and the application of excessive force in self-defense
3. *The ideology of victimization:* how human beings utilize natural defense mechanisms in response to the inevitable anxieties of life — especially the universal tendency to project onto others qualities of nonhumanness and dangerousness and then to legitimize their victimization; also the corresponding degree of availability of a group to be victimized
4. *The cancer of genocidal destructiveness:* tracking the sequences of the actual buildup of genocidal destructiveness as it moves from stage to stage in a society

DEVALUING HUMANNESS

Early Warning Process 01: The Devaluing of Human Life

Although we have assumed that from the beginning of life all people experience a basic desire to live and have a reverence for life, many events and influences are capable of leading people away from valuing life. Moreover, there is also a natural side of human experiencing that moves in the direction of death. As a result, people develop vastly different attitudes toward the value of human life.

In gathering data about a culture, we ask, Does the culture speak to the sanctity and dignity of human life? or Does the culture teach capriciousness or a callousness toward life? Some cultures insist on the value of life even under highly problematic conditions such as war. Other cultures are indifferent to or depreciate the value of life, or readily define many conditions under which life may be taken without regret.

How does the value assigned to life compare with the value assigned to achieving power over others? Which does a culture value more? Is power always so important that it justifies eliminating lives? To what extent does the pursuit of power become the dominant value of life?

A people's perception of the relationship between life and death also enters into their valuing of life. Some cultures link preparation for death with accepting life's challenge to honor life until the time to die comes. Other cultures separate the reality of death from any linkage with the challenge of life, and death awareness is denied in every possible way. We know from clinical studies of suicide that very frequently, the suicide's unconscious conception of his death is that death will not *really* occur, that he will really continue to live after he "dies," and that he will be able to reap the pleasure of his vengeance against certain intimates whom he is seeking to punish through his death.[17] This individual psychological experience is quite similar to the larger ideological teaching of some cultures or religions that death, in effect, is not real so long as one gives up one's life on behalf of one's people or ideology. Such cultures or religions may teach and encourage a cult of suicidal missions against one's enemies on the grounds of the enormous rewards that will follow to the true believers. One psychologist has found a crucial link between suicide and murder and argues that the suicide-homicide linkage is the central dynamic of mass murders and genocide.[18]

In the cruel course of life peoples and cultures are likely to have to choose between their values of life and other values more than once. The question then becomes, How does the valuing of human life stand up under the competition? For example, in certain religions or cultures, death will be so highly valued that it can even win out over life. Or at various times, the value of life must compete against money—How deeply will a people value life when billions of dollars are at stake, say for new agents of chemical warfare?

Early Warning Process 02: The Irrelevance of Human Experience

How does a society relate to the quality of the human experience? Which is ultimately more important, production standards and efficiency, no matter what the human cost, or a combination of efficient production and decent work conditions and satisfaction? How a culture values the natural environment and ecology as a whole has a good deal to do with that people's approach to the quality of life. Respect for the environment means concern with how an environment will support human experiencing. It also includes concern with the public health of not only the present generation but future generations as well. A people that is oblivious to present and future human suffering caused by illness, blight, or pollution is not likely to care much about any loss of human life because of violence. On the other hand, a stated concern about the quality of the ecology and environment can also be taken, and has been taken, as a basis for the extermination of a people who are said to be a blight on the environment or to the genetic purity of the race. This fact illustrates what is emphasized elsewhere: Any ideology that is considered to be more important than human life necessarily becomes a possible basis for rationalizing the destruction of human life.

Another aspect of the quality of human life involves the way pleasure and responsibility are viewed. Are both joy in living and responsibility seen as necessary to human integrity? Is responsibility presumed to be the one overriding source of meaning in life? Are pleasures treated as entirely separate from responsibility, thereby inviting orgies and sadism?

In collecting data about the quality of human experiencing, we are often far from the actualities and tragedies of violence. However, by examining a group's attitude toward the quality of human experiencing, we seek to identify those group processes that, in time, may conspire to permit the emergence of violence. We would like to believe that, overall, those people who truly succeed in loving the opportunity that is life would not countenance genocidal violence.[19]

Early Warning Process 03: The Pursuit of Power over Others

All human beings need to attain a reasonable degree of objective control over their own destiny and a sense of their power over the flow of life's events. We are forever living with an awareness of our mortality. Without a sense of present and potential power over our environment, we would be doomed to total terror. It is not a matter of whether or not to have power; it is a matter of how to go about having power, how to exercise one's power, how to safeguard one's power, and how to express one's power in relation to the equally legitimate needs of others. Both excesses of power and insufficiencies of power are to be seen as dangerously supporting possible sequences toward destructiveness.

The early warning indicators that have to do with the development of power essentially probe the question, For what purpose is power sought? When power is intended as energy for people to experience their

---

FIGURE 13.2   Illustration of Early Warning Process 03: The Pursuit of Power over Others

	Supporting Human Life	*Moving Toward Destruction*
Use of power in conflict resolution	1. Society maintains pride in its power to face and resolve problems	1. Weaknesses and problems of society are handled by compensatory effort at power over others, such as through scapegoating

	2. Serious chronic problems are acknowledged and processes toward solution are initiated	2. Major weakness in society is likely to stimulate compensatory efforts to power
		
		a. Tangible loss of power
		  1. Political instability
		  2. Loss of significance in international affairs
		  3. Loss of national purpose, confidence or pride

---

own aliveness more fully, power is a tool for fulfilling human potential. The focus of life is one's own experiencing and not control over another person or people. On the other hand, when power is seen as vested in controlling another people, the focus of life is not the richness of one's own experiencing, but taking over, possessing, and dominating others. We are interested in gauging the extent to which a given culture seeks the further development of its own power potential and the extent to which a people turns its cultural and governmental destiny toward the fulfillment of power ambitions at the expense of others.

In any society, no matter how much a people tries, there inevitably arise enormous inequalities of power. How does a society relate to its inequalities? Are the inequalities taken as a challenge to social change, or does society tolerate and exploit the emergence of inadequate, excluded, or fringe groups? What kinds of checks and balances exist to prevent an excessive use of power?

It is also important to note any situations of national weakness that may lead a people to compensate by attacking a scapegoat victim. We look to see whether a people has recently suffered any tangible loss of power to which it is still reacting, whether there is any significant threat to the internal stability of the nation, or whether the society has experienced a sense of loss of significance about itself and its purpose.

Finally, the ways in which a society defines its intentions to other peoples are crucial. Although some societies are drawn, despite sincere and good intentions, into destructiveness, others define their power as strength at the expense of others and see the legitimacy of their power as justifying any means, regardless of the cost to human life. The latter societies will very probably become great destroyers, whereas a people that makes a commitment to equality and cooperation with other people at least has a fighting chance of containing the carnage.

Early Warning Process 04: Overt Violence and Destructiveness

In the psychology of the individual personality, we have known for a long time that the greatest potential for violence is in both those who are too removed from their natural rage and potential for violence and those who are too readily given to an impulsive expression of violent impulses.[20] The same seems to be true of societies in general. Whereas a society's momentum toward genocide is often marked by increasing violence, a society that fails to make provision for a sufficient discharge of violent impulses is also a prime candidate for a sudden eruption of genocidal violence (see the news report of a mass murder in erstwhile

FIGURE 13.3   Illustration of Early Warning Process 04: Overt
              Violence and Destructiveness

	Supporting Human Life	Moving Toward Destruction
Availability of tools of violence	1. Sale of weapons carefully regulated and minimized	1. Weapons easily, even promiscuously, available with little or token regulation
	2. Official use of weapons discouraged and subject to careful regulation following indoctrination re use of weapons as tools to preserve life	2. Official use of weapons automatically justified by position of authority; weapons intended to impose and protect reign of authority
	3. Arms development limited according to existing international conventions and active effort made to extend scope of disarmament and weapons-control conventions	3. Arms development is maximized and efforts are made to subvert existing international conventions
	4. Culture educates against use of weapons except in self-defense	4. Culture glorifies use of weaponry

peaceful Indonesia preceding Chapter 7). In developing an early warning system, therefore, we look at the extent to which violent impulses are accepted as natural and universal on various levels of human experience or, conversely, the extent to which they are denied and suppressed. By the same token, societies that condone, officially sanction, and encourage the spread of armaments and localized warfare are societies in which fuller onslaughts of mass murder are likely to take form.

What happens when a society must resort to violence in response to a realistic threat? To what extent does a culture seek to limit its official violence, even at the risk of some degree of error? Is violence in the name of self-defense sanctioned largely unquestioningly and even relished? Is the destruction of an enemy or oppressor gleefully sought? Are retaliation killings sanctioned and celebrated? Is the destruction of enemy civilians considered justifiable? Is a systematic large-scale destruction of the enemy people allowed to become the goal of the war response?

THE ILLUSION OF SELF-DEFENSE

Early Warning Process 05: Absence of Control Machinery for Managing Escalatory Spirals

It is certainly a natural requirement of life that there must be a machinery for the management of threat, for we live in constant threat as to our immediate future and the unknowns of the powerful natural forces around us and within us. However, the basic problem in all threat-management machinery is that of graduation of response.

The early warning data begin with the extent to which provision is made for some way to respond to threat. An absence of machinery to deal with threat is no more to be valued than are excessive responses to threat; both characteristically stimulate the escalation of a crisis. The important question is whether a people and their leadership accept the necessity and responsibility for monitoring and checking their management of threat, which also includes the necessity of evaluating the impact of any steps taken in response to threat. Monitoring is required at any and every step of managing the escalation of a threat, not just at the beginning and not just when critical action-decision points are approached, but at every step along the intricate system of communication and response to another frightened people.

There is the great danger at every step of a sequence of responses to threat that an uncontrollable process of escalation and counterescalation will be unleashed. It is proper to meet serious threat courageously and directly with appropriate strength, but just how is that strength posed, and to what extent is the show of strength linked to creative offers and invitations to find a way to remove the threat?

In the early warning indicators of the handling of threat, we include such information as whether or not there are monitors and ombudsmen within a government whose job it is to check undisciplined counterthreat behavior and to develop peace-encouraging initiatives as well as alternative, nonviolent responses to conflict. Similarly, we want to observe whether and to what extent societal institutions influence government policy through their monitoring and criticism (e.g., watch-

FIGURE 13.4	Illustration of Early Warning Process 05: Absence of Control Machinery for Managing Escalatory Spirals

	Supporting Human Life	*Moving Toward Destruction*
Societal responses to threat	1. Group conscience and individual conscience within group encouraged; negative group passions discouraged and limited by leadership	1. Contagion of negative group passions encouraged a. Loss of individual identity and conscience encouraged and accepted b. Projection of natural weakness onto outsiders encouraged c. Controlled media used to indoctrinate for hatred and rehearsals of violence d. Crowd experiences staged to inflame passions
	2. Decision making mediated by process of checks and balances	2. Authority-dominated decision making a. Machinery of government does not readily allow for differences of opinion b. Lack of centers of influence on government in society c. Major power in hands of military d. Dictator or dictatorial elite

dog foundations, labor and business interests, the communications media, and public opinion).

We also ask if the already existing channels of communication, such as diplomacy and mediation, are being utilized fully to try to ascertain the other party's intentions. Perhaps most important, to what extent is a people prepared to reach out directly to potential enemies to seek common purposes and interests that might be served by cooperative activity?

When it is felt that the time has come for overt power, what alternatives to out-and-out military or even quasi-military actions are sought? If and when actual military means are applied, what further decisions as to control and limiting of the military means are made? Are there efforts to negotiate? Are the military means withdrawn as rapidly as possible?

As the escalation of threat builds, the basic orientation of a people toward peoples other than themselves is subject to the most critical tests and pressures. At this time, a society that had previously maintained a climate of relative respect for other people may begin dehumanizing and scapegoating another people. One of the trends that we look at most carefully in a serious threat situation is whether natural passions of hate and vengeance seeking are fanned and encouraged, or whether the fighting back and natural rage of war are contained and focused on the immediate threat. Throughout history, an almost surefire solution of a present threat seems to have been to turn the flaming excitement of prejudice and hate onto an outsider. How many people are prepared to forgo this cheap solution?[21]

Early Warning Process 06: Applying Excessive Force in Self-defense and in Solution of Conflicts

In the course of history, a few societies have managed to maintain a noncombatant role, almost no matter what the circumstances around them. Just how this is best done or how this status can be developed is not entirely clear. One way seems to be for a nation to be useful to all the combatant parties, say, as a financial repository for the combatant countries (and for their leaders). Some peoples seem to take on a noncombatant status after they have lost a great deal at war and subsequently choose to withdraw from further "games" of conflict, perhaps by decisively reducing military expenditures or by withdrawing from an active striving for leadership or a visible role in international affairs. Another way to develop this status is for a people to choose purposefully to stand for peace and to build a noncombatant tradition. Of course, such peoples' lack of military strength can be exploited by a stronger and violent nation, but there have been instances in which the essential dignity and principle of standing for life in this mad world have survived even invasion and occupation.[22]

The issue of how a people can strive for peace when all peoples face enormous forces of destruction is extremely complex. The immediate purpose in the data system is to collect information about a culture's orientation toward force and violence. We begin with the prevailing motif of a people. Is peace or force valued? Is the major ideal to live cooperatively with neighboring peoples, or is there pleasure associated with the use of force and violence? Cultures that idealize force are often characterized as cultivating "hypermasculinity." There are many societies with military elites; there are others in which the military is valued but kept in check lest the values it can represent become too dominant.

If and when a society does find itself at war, what choices are made in the execution of that war? Is the nation's philosophy of war to take the least possible action consistent with self-defense? Are all possible efforts made to protect human life even in wartime? When the war is won, are the occupation policies humane or harsh and exploitative?

Within each society, there are many choices to be made concerning the use of force in solving ethnic and religious differences, economic rivalry, and political competitions. How does a culture instruct people to solve conflicts? Are conflicts to be worked out essentially through some version of the doctrine of survival of the fittest or in a more orderly fashion within the framework of the law? Does the legal tradition allow and encourage the triumph of raw power, or is the law developed more as a tool to help people solve problems equitably?

One of the crucial tests of a culture's stand on violence is how its members relate to force and acts of violence against those people within the culture who represent the least desirable elements, hence potential scapegoats, of that society. There have always been societies that enforce laws against wanton crime, excessive force, and murder except when those acts are directed against the Jews, blacks, heathens, sexual deviants, or who have you of their time.

To our knowledge, no people to date has successfully achieved an ideal balance between a commitment to peace and the ability to stand up to the evils of the world. It may be one thing for the Swiss to use their skills as world financiers as a hedge against being involved in international conflicts, but some still question the rightness of that country's serving as a financial prostitute for a killer nation such as Nazi Germany. So, too, if for many generations the Jewish people cultivated a commitment for peace by leaving themselves weak and available to pogroms and forced marches to gas chambers, that was not a satisfactory solution to the quest for peace. These collective processes raise profound philosophical and political questions we do not presume to be able to answer. However, within the framework of an early warning system, data about a culture's orientation to force and violence may indicate whether that culture is or is not likely to produce genociders.

THE IDEOLOGY OF VICTIMIZATION

Early Warning Process 07: Dehumanization of Potential Victim Group

The underlying machinery for the dehumanization of a potential victim group is housed in the attitudes of a culture toward differences between people. Even cultures that do seek to emphasize some sense of man's equality or godliness—that all people are God's creatures—still have to deal with the powerful realities of differences between people and the natural processes those differences set off in human beings. Some of the provocative realities surrounding man's differences are these:

1. People are remarkably different from one another—in color, build, and appearance, let alone in tradition and culture
2. Human beings naturally tend to react very strongly to differences—with fear, distaste, and repugnance
3. People who are different become likely objects of projection

No matter how humanistically oriented a particular culture is toward the brotherhood of all human beings, the fact remains that each culture must also provide ways for dealing with natural experiences caused by differences. Only in a relatively few instances are people educated toward accepting and enjoying differences. The exciting philosophy of such a positive approach to experiencing people who differ from us is that differences are the other side of the sameness and universality of man—both should be taught simultaneously. However, the prevailing situation in most cultures has been and is to make people feel that the differences are disturbing and problematic, so people who are different are assigned one degree or another of not-being-the-same-as-us-ness and, progressively, less-than-us-ness.

In the data of the early warning system, we seek to define the attribution of less-than-us-ness along a continuum from arousing distaste and/or disapproval to virtually lacking humanness, being as if not of our species.

FIGURE 13.5	Illustration of Early Warning Process 07: Dehumanization of Potential Victim Group	
	Supporting Human Life	*Moving Toward Destruction*
Definition of potential victim	All people are like us, one of us, equal to us, deserving of life like us	Definition of another people as not of our kind, not one of us a. Alien, different b. Unattractive, distasteful, not valuable c. Repulsive, repugnant d. Less than us e. As if not human, as if not of our species

Early Warning Process 08: Perception of Potential Victim Group as Dangerous

One of the important elements that spark the eruption of violence against a potential target group is a perception of the victim group as a source of serious danger to one's actual survival. This is a paradoxical situation. On the one hand, the victim group has been defined as so seriously lacking in quality and value that they are less than us. They are not human as we are. Yet these same people are also endowed with characteristics of such great power that they are literally seen as threatening our annihilation.

Annihilation is defined in many different ways, from the simple threat of conquest and death to a more symbolic threat to a people's racial, religious, and/or cultural survival. What is so striking is that people treat threats of the destruction of their symbolic continuity as virtually the same as, if not more dangerous than, threats of actual physical annihilation. Historically, we have been all too ready to kill those other people who threaten to wipe out our names, our God's name, our flag, our economic system, and so on.

It is, of course, possible to believe that another people is threatening us with massive annihilation without that enemy being also regarded as less than us or as not of our species. When fear is not linked with

FIGURE 13.6   Illustration of Early Warning Process 08: Perception of Potential Victim Group as Dangerous

	Supporting Human Life	*Moving Toward Destruction*
Perception of victim group	Potential victim group not perceived as threat	Potential victim group perceived as threatening actual annihilation

a. Physical annihilation
 1. Military
 2. Other territorial expansionism
 3. Population invasion
 4. Aiming at retaliation
b. Racial annihilation
c. Economic annihilation
d. Religious annihilation (heresy)
e. Other spiritual or psychological annihilation
 1. Weakens our culture
 2. Destroys our customs and way of life
 3. Infects our culture with evil
 4. Destroys our continuing identity (symbolic immortality)

dehumanizing another people, genocidal campaigns are not as likely. However, human weakness being what it is, projections of nonhuman status are likely to form with relentless suddenness if and when war erupts. Once such projections of not-us-ness and nonhuman take hold, the door is open to cruelties, atrocities, and genocides.

Early Warning Process 09: Legitimation of Victimization by Leadership Individuals and Institutions

The sequence of the early warning processes, which defines the buildup of a momentum of genocidal violence, is now nearing its tragic climax of manifest events of killing. Yet even now, the likelihood of genocide depends to a large extent on the basic cultural and legal definitions set by the leaders and societal institutions as to whether or not killing the victims is legitimate. When the idea of genocide begins to take form in a culture, the issue of whether or not violence and genocide will be legitimate, approved, and legal becomes supreme.[23]

Many levels of social organization are involved in the decision as to whether or not to legitimize victimization of a target people. In addition to the leaders, whom most people will follow, we look in our early warning system for individuals, groups, and institutions that might challenge the legitimacy of deliberate, officially sanctioned violence and perhaps check the government's excesses.

It is true that even major trends toward violence can be initiated and established by relatively small groups of "brown shirts" before a society wakes up to the danger. William A. Westley sees the legitimation of violence as a three-stage process: initial support by the public for mild violence by a special group, support for extreme forms of violence by that group, and support for systematic extreme violence—which often is executed by the same small group of people. Given the permission of society, the perpetrators become their own supporting audience and allow deeper and more fanatic kinds of violence on the part of their sick members. At the same time, the public can dissociate itself from responsibility for the violence done by that small group; in fact, the small group can even initiate a sequence of violence despite the official disapproval of the society's leaders.[24]

If and when a tragic full-scale policy of genocide is launched by a society, there is still a final choice for each person and each institution in the society. Even when an order comes from on high, each army commander has to decide whether to send his troops to commit genocide, and even then the troops must decide whether or not to execute the order. Even when a policy of genocide is well under way, each person

FIGURE 13.7   Illustration of Early Warning Process 09: Legitimation of Victimization by Leadership Individuals and Institutions

	Supporting Human Life	Moving Toward Destruction
Social approval and legal definition of victimization	1. Victimization is socially unacceptable and to be prosecuted under the law	1. Victimization is socially acceptable (even when there are laws against it)
	2. Leaders and institutions stand personally and through the law against victimization	2. Leaders and institutions sanction and progressively legalize destruction of victims
	3. Persecution of a group, overt or covert, direct or indirect, is to be exposed and stopped, and the persecutors and their accomplices are to be prosecuted	3. Persecution of a group is pursued as a legitimate and major goal of the society

and group within the society must elect whether or not to fight, directly or indirectly, against the policy. The legitimation of genocidal violence is a function of all segments of a society—the leaders, institutions, and people.

Early Warning Process 10: Availability of Victim Group

In order for the definitions of a given people as less than human and as highly dangerous to take hold, a certain compliance, acceptance, or tacit support of the definitions on the part of the victim group itself seems to be required. In our early warning data, we look to see if definitions of availability to be a victim are rooted in the culture. To what extent do the folklore and traditions of a people identify them as historic victims? Does the culture place tangible values on the status of being victims? "We shall remain valuable despite their attacking us. We shall become the more valuable because they persecute us." Granted, there

FIGURE 13.8　　Illustration of Early Warning Process 10:
　　　　　　　　　Availability of Victim Group

	Supporting Human Life	Moving Toward Destruction
Expectation of potential victim	Expectation of not being victims	Expectation of being victims

Under **Moving Toward Destruction** — Expectation of being victims:

a. Value in being victims
   1. We shall remain valuable despite their attacking us
   2. We shall become the more valuable because they persecute us
b. Honor extended to victims as serving group's destiny of martyrdom
c. Tradition of preparing to be victims

can be in such a spirit a beautiful and courageous stand in the face of real danger, but there often are also a kind of self-righteousness and a sense of martyrdom, which are unconsciously enjoyed for their "secondary gains." Although there may be great heroism on the part of certain victim peoples, the idealization of survival as the persecuted ones can become a way of life, through which people unconsciously find meaning for their existence and/or for their spiritual eternity after death. There is, we know, a deep magnetic pull to the apocalyptic-messianic images in the folklores of peoples.

How does a people honor its members who are the victims? Over and above the caring for those who have fallen, are the victims regarded as heroes and martyrs who, in effect, represent the group's desire for martyrdom? To what extent does a people's tradition prepare its children to be victims—even to intimating that the punishment is deserved because of their sins—instead of concentrating on teaching new generations how to avoid being victims?

Training to be victims often includes a tradition of denying the reality of a mounting threat. It is true that human beings can exaggerate the extent of a threat, but it is also a fact that human beings are capable of denying a threat of death that is staring them in the eyes. *When Jews who escaped the early Nazi death marches returned to the ghetto to tell their fellow Jews that the Nazis were machine-gunning men, women, and children and intended to exterminate every one of them, they were angrily hooted at and yelled down by the majority who didn't want to hear the truth.*

Suppose they held a genocide and nobody came? It becomes much harder and perhaps impossible to commit genocide when a victim people is not prepared to be wiped out. In assembling early warning systems data, we seek to identify the extent to which a people makes itself available, even if unknowingly, to play the role of victim if and when such a "request" is made.

THE CANCER OF GENOCIDAL DESTRUCTIVENESS

Early Warning Process 11: Development of Manifest Genocidal Process

We are now at the end of the road. Now the warning system can only record the tragic finale of genocide. However, even at this stage, there still are bitterly significant processes to be determined, even as a genocidal campaign is achieving maximum momentum toward whatever measure of destruction it will achieve. Even now it need not be too late to stop a mounting campaign of genocide if one pays attention to the signals and mobilizes resources to stop the genocidal activity.

In effect, every society, every group within that society, and every individual on all levels of that society are faced with a series of critical decisions whether or not to be unknowing bystanders, knowing bystanders or accomplices, or actual executioners in the unfolding momentum of mass murder. These decisions are necessarily repeated at several stages in the sequence.

As the momentum of oppression mounts, a critical aspect of decision making in every society is what happens to the legal machinery of the society. Is the legal machinery indifferent to the victims? Does it support and legitimize the violences? In the history of many genocides, there have often been early "field experiments" to see how far one can go, and how much one can get away with. What other public and institutional forces besides the judiciary speak up against the victimization? Are there popular protests? Do legislators speak out? Do opposition political parties attack the emerging violence? Do religious leaders stand up against the increasing oppression and violence? What role does the press play?[25]

The terrible end usually approaches step by step. There first may be unofficial executions of groups of the victim people. If these first executions are not stopped, there then follow more-open campaigns of genocidal executions, though these, too, may still be kept "unofficial" so as not to arouse too much concentrated attention. Special squads of killers often are employed at first. Then civilians are encouraged to commit violence against the victims, and regular police and military forces are employed more openly. The process quickens with each wave of executions.

Robert Payne studied genocide in Bangladesh and took that as a basis for examining mass slaughter throughout history. He found that mass murder "obeys predictable laws and assumes predictable stages, despite outward differences." Payne suggests that the universal scheme of a massacre follows a consistent pattern:

1. The future victims are lulled into a sense of security
2. The death blow
3. The victims recover from their paralysis
4. The military mounts another massacre
5. The victims begin to organize
6. The military mounts a third massacre
7. The victim "bites off the enemy's hands and feet" (the tide begins to turn against the killers)
8. The final massacre (the killers continue, relentlessly, up to their last breath)[26]

Should there develop inquiries or investigations by various international sources attempting to track down "rumors" and "unconfirmed reports" of genocide, there are generally efforts at evasion, concealment, and denial. A common phenomenon that attends the gathering momentum of executions and killings is the capacity of the killers, and the host society at large, to deny the experience of killing their victims.[27]

Eventually, there is frankly militant, large-scale genocide. Now we hear openly of the genociders' policy. At this stage, the cancer cannot be stopped, of course, except by destroying the host. Certainly, by now it is too late for the many who have already died while the world ignored, denied, or evaded all the earlier warnings and indications, and it is also too late for the many who will now die during the terminal ravages of the cancer. The last of the many earlier warning opportunities has passed.

TRACKING THE SEQUENCE OF EVENTS

The values and behavior of a society are, of course, subject to considerable change and progression. The long-range goal of an early warning system is to track and predict the sequences of events through which societies characteristically move, often unknowingly, to genocide. In order to understand the characteristic progression toward genocide in different cultures and eras, we studied a great many societies in which genocide had taken place. We found that the sequences through which genocides build were in many ways very similar, despite vast differences in historical and social contexts. On the basis of these similarities, we mapped a "time line" to use in following the progression of a group or society. We discovered that the pattern we observed in studies of genocide was remarkably similar to the pattern described by sociologist Neil Smelser in his study of collective groups.[28]

Smelser defines a series of determinants of collective behavior according to the "logic of a value-added process," which means that each stage in the process adds its value, but only as the earlier stages combine according to a certain pattern can the next stage contribute its particular value. Collective behavior is the combination of all the necessary conditions. Thus, for example: "A racial incident between a Negro and a white may spark a race riot. But unless this incident occurs in the context of a structurally conducive atmosphere, an atmosphere of strain (an atmosphere in which people perceive the incident as symbolic of a troubled state of affairs), the incident will pass without becoming a determinant in a racial outburst."[29] Smelser's stages are:

1. Structural conduciveness: What structures in the societal system promote the collective behavior?
2. Structural strain: What specific strains are operative in the group, within the context of the previously described conducive elements, that will elicit the collective behavior?
3. Growth and spread of generalized belief: The crystallization of value-oriented beliefs that impel and define the legitimacy and necessity of the collective behavior.
4. Precipitating factors
5. Mobilization of participants for action
6. Operation of social control

In our proposed data system, the time line essentially follows Smelser's concept of the collective process, but our time line is elaborated and adapted to the specific phenomenon we are tracking, genocide. We use the following categories:

1. Societal forces supporting human life versus societal forces moving toward destruction of human life
   a. Cultural values and tradition
   b. Structural processes and institutions
   c. Human rights status
2. Key historical, economic, political, legal, and social events and transitions
3. Formation of genocidal fantasy and ideology
4. Precipitating factors or context
5. Mobilization of means to genocide
6. Legitimation and institutionalization of genocide
7. Execution of genocide and experience-denying mechanisms

SOCIETAL FORCES SUPPORTING HUMAN LIFE VERSUS SOCIETAL FORCES MOVING TOWARD DESTRUCTION OF HUMAN LIFE

Supporting human life: The ways in which the psychocultural processes are turned toward the support of human life by peoples and cultures who guard against destructiveness and seek the common welfare of all people

Moving toward destruction of human life: The ways in which psychocultural processes are turned toward inviting and implementing destructiveness

The concept of an early warning system requires that we describe a baseline or starting point for any given people or group some time before there are any forces building to the point of programs of genocidal extermination. Our proposed framework begins with entries of societal case history data, recorded first as objective descriptions of processes and events and then classified, to the best of our judgment, as to whether the values and behavior processes of the society are turned toward supporting human life or the destruction of human life, or both.

Everything that we have been saying about the human condition argues that from the outset, we are all involved in experiences of creating life and destroying life. Indeed, we speculated that so long as the constructive and destructive processes balance each other and are integrated with one another in the inner individual human experience, one achieves the most vivid experiences of aliveness. Although we are far from proposing an extension of this theory to the behavior of collective groups, we do say that all societies in our world do all manner of things on behalf of life and all manner of things against human life. In our picture of each society, we want to get a picture of the flow of the forces on both sides of the ledger. Note that in all cases, the value is assigned to behavior, as much as possible, without regard to the particular cultural and historical "clothing" in which the behavior is "dressed." For example, violence in the name of a group's ideology is treated as assault and destruction of a target people, regardless of what it is called in the ideology of those doing the violence.

The information we seek as to how a given society is organized both in the direction of supporting life and in the direction of potential destructiveness is organized along three major tracks of cultural values and tradition, structural processes and institutions, and human rights status.

That classification partly derives from the work of A. Paul Hare on the basic needs that all groups must meet if they are to survive: Members of a group must share a common identity; members of a group must be able to generate the skills and resources necessary to reach a goal; members of a group must have rules that allow them to coordinate their activities and enough feeling of solidarity to stay together; and the group must be able to exercise control over its membership if it is to be effective in reaching the common goal.[30] But, the classification we use also relates to the "functional autonomy" of behavior, or how certain behaviors continue long after the original reasons for them have ceased to exist.

Cultural Values and Tradition

The prevailing collective orientation and tradition of a society, what has been called in sociology at times "national character," in history the "historical tradition," or in folklore the "folkmyth"; the ideological values of a people, e.g., the traditional value placed on warring and violence or the emphasis traditionally placed on family relationships; also the goals articulated by a society, e.g., an emphasis on scientific progress, an emphasis on rescuing one's people from being victimized, a goal of military domination, a desire for peace, the pursuit of industrial supremacy

A society's cultural values and tradition determine, to a large extent, the structures and processes that it creates, how it responds to the dilemmas that develop from structural and institutional processes, and how it responds to the inevitable tensions and pressures that can easily invite and seemingly justify the destruction of human life. Although a society that places a high value on life to begin with should have fewer threats of violence, it is inevitable that sooner or later, tense and explosive situations will arise in all societies, and the prevailing values of a culture are then of enormous importance in determining how far the buildup toward destructiveness will go. *A military commander gives the order to imprison a group of aliens at a time when war with their homeland threatens; the press protests vehemently against the imprisonment of the alien population. A head of state threatens nuclear warfare against another nation; the legislature calls for impeachment of the executive. Discriminatory legislation is passed calling for the expropriation of land belonging to members of a minority group; the courts issue an order against the expropriation on the grounds that it is unconstitutional.*

New events and theories are colored by the accumulated historical memories of a people, that is, the national consciousness of the society's readiness for violence and genocide, how the society responds with emergency measures at times of great distress, the tradition of freedom or suppression of expression and artistic diversity, the extent to which the people accept their polarization into more and less privileged classes. Also important are the society's prevailing beliefs about the "goodness" or "badness" of basic human nature and whether strong authority and power are required in order to contain bad elements or whether one can trust the free play of the democratic process to contain threats against the fabric of society.

In general, the prevailing atmosphere of a society is a critical index of the value system. There is no mistaking the difference between a societal atmosphere that is permeated with fear and terror and a societal atmosphere that encourages freedom of expression, initiative, and risk.

Structural Processes and Institutions

The means a group chooses in pursuit of its goals and the structures and institutions created by the group, which develop in the course of the momentum of the societal system, e.g., a policy of military conquest and extermination by a political system that assigns unchecked power to a single leader or a system of justice that checks and balances the executive power of the state; a free press, a controlled press, or a demagogic press

The structures and institutions of a society are, first of all, expressions of the value system of the group, but these structures and institutions themselves produce various dilemmas that grow out of the "laws of structure," not just because people "want" what is happening. *The brilliant ideas of a pioneering scientist are celebrated and adopted by students; however, as the years pass, these disciples may create an idolatrous cult around the "master's" ideas that interferes with new learning. A mental hospital permits ward personnel to make decisions about the patients' therapies, such as medication or electric shock "treatment," and the result is that many decisions are based on considerations of keeping a patient quiet and tractable rather than on the patient's real needs.*

There are "politics" or system dynamics in each of the subsystems of economic, political, legal, and social services of a society, and these service systems influence one another. It is important to see whether or not check-and-balance controls are instituted to correct the inequalities that arise in any system so that the rights of the weaker members of the population are guaranteed.

A similar set of considerations obtain as to the relationship of each society to other societies. To what extent does it attempt to impose its interests on peoples in other countries or on minorities within its boundaries whose culture and ideological identities are different?

Human Rights Status

The actual status of human rights in a society, including the society's relationship to minorities and to members of other societies and the actual actions undertaken by the collective group as to human life and dignity

Human rights data are powerful in their own right and also from the point of view of their place in a larger system of social indicators as critical indications of whether a society is likely to move in the direction of more-severe infringements of life and possibly genocide. We look at the human rights status of people in connection with each of the early warning processes. Thus, the valuing of human life as a basic process to which all societies must relate finds expression in a society's attitude toward the death penalty, the nature of the military training, the presence of legal and internal professional review machinery for monitoring life-terminating events, and so on.

The quality of human rights in a society is indicated by such factors as freedom of the press, freedom of education, the right to work, decent conditions of work, the right to marry a consenting person of one's choice, and freedom of association. How does a society define human rights under conditions of stress and crisis? *Can a citizen sue in court against being inducted into the army on grounds of a moral commitment to nonviolence? Do government officials or university lecturers lose their positions if they oppose a policy of military intervention?*

The ultimate test of human rights comes when a societal process moves tragically closer to a policy of genocide toward a target group. The acid test of a society is whether some combination of the courts, legislature, press, or public opinion struggles to stop a policy of extermination, whether by the police, military, secret service, or government leaders.

KEY HISTORICAL, ECONOMIC, POLITICAL, LEGAL, AND SOCIAL EVENTS AND TRANSITIONS

Life is marked by never-ending problems and changes that demand major readjustments: from without, by way of natural forces of climate, ecology, biology, and so on; from within, by way of momentous historical events and definitive transitions in maneuverings for power. These major forces and events, interpreted within the prevailing value system of the group, generate powerful dynamics, which greatly influence the subsequent collective process.

The data of major historical, economic, political, legal, and social events that have a huge impact on a people's collective experience are the data that students traditionally have gathered in their efforts to account for genocidal violence. *In Germany, a major economic depression unleashed great bitterness and stimulated a powerful, compensatory nationalism. These processes fed the emergence of Nazi fascism and the megalomaniac persecution of Jews and other "inferior" peoples, from which the Nazis drew so much of their power.* Traditional historical analyses that relate only to these powerful historical forces fall far short of explaining genocidal violence, because they ignore the critical dynamics of human experiencing that are at play both in the determination of historical events and in the response to historical forces. But it would be no less absurd to account for the unfolding of collective behavior only on the basis of psychological dynamics and without reference to these major events in human beings' lives.[31]

To a considerable extent, the major historical events that so influence us are outcomes of the issues all people and societies must deal with, e.g., how a society organizes the distribution of its power resources and whether a society scapegoats others for its difficulties as opposed to concentrating its resources on efforts to rebuild itself. And all major historical events, in turn, shape how people define their basic values and attitudes. The ways in which individuals, groups, and larger communities experience and perceive events and the impact these events have on the values people then define for their lives interact constantly.

Vahakn Dadrian's analysis of the genocide of the Armenians by the Turks during World War I is a good illustration of the interplay between psychocultural dynamics and sociohistorical processes, which, together, forge a momentum toward genocide. Dadrian traces the history of the stigmatization of the Armenians to the stigma the Moslems attached to subject races and to the scorn the Turks attached to the fields of commerce and industry, which had been ceded to the Armenians. The Armenians grew powerful in those pursuits but never developed accompanying legal and political strengths. Dadrian then places the genocide in the larger sociohistorical context of a world war—a time of disequilibrium of cataclysmic proportions—and in the context of the crumbling Ottoman Empire and its need for antidotes to internal discord to recapture lost Pan-Turkic glory. The stigmatization of the Armenians was a necessary condition of the genocide, but it was not sufficient in itself to set off the deadly process.[32]

Also included in the data of major events and transitions are eruptions of violence in societies—how they are authorized and planned and how the society responds to them by way of containing and controlling the violence or by approving and legitimizing it. We need to see the sequences that unfold as societies turn toward increasing violence. As violence climbs and previous unheard-of brutality occurs with increasing frequency, do the society's basic institutions stand by and tacitly allow what is happening? Do the political and legal institutions openly assist, legitimize, and authorize the violence?

Note, of course, that even highly violent societies do not necessarily go on to commit genocide. The wild and woolly American West with its six-shooting cowboys had its limits—although, in truth, it is an entirely fitting subject of study to examine the relationship between the classic cowboy culture and the genocidal campaigns that did take place against the American Indians. Fiery black people's riots in any number of communities around the world need not go on to become a full-scale genocidal campaign against whites; but in some cases, these riots could very well have a larger genocidal momentum in the future.

FORMATION OF GENOCIDAL FANTASY AND IDEOLOGY

The progressive unfolding of a fantasy or goal of genocide articulated either by the leadership of a group or through the prevailing motifs of the group as a whole and progressing to the point of being codified and ritualized in the basic ideology of the group, but not the expression of extremist personalities or fringe groups

In this category, we identify the first major transitions from societal strains and violence toward the specific direction of possible genocide as a culminating collective expression of the society. We seek to identify first what we call the formation of the genocidal fantasy and then the elaboration of an accepted genocidal ideology. Genocide is too serious and vast a matter to spring up in a vacuum of nondefinition or nonideology. There is generally a guiding ideology, and before that there generally is a fantasy of power or redemption or salvation through ridding society of a given target people. We are interested in identifying in any given society the original emergence of such a fantasy and the emergence of the ideological goal of genocide as they are articulated by a leader or an elite and/or through the motif of the group as a whole. We specifically seek to exclude expressions of genocidal fantasies by extremist personalities or groups within a culture, which, as far as can be seen at the time, do not have a significant influence on the total process of a people.[33]

The emergence of full-scale genocide is made possible by the promulgation of an accepted ideology that justifies the killing as self-defense. "They are out to destroy our people/nation/faith/right to exist/way of life; therefore, in self-defense, we must destroy them first." Typically, the victim people is redefined in this ideology as some manner of lesser or subhuman species and therefore not deserving of the protection or dignity that is naturally due other members of the society.

Precipitating Factors or Context

The dramatic events, whether realistically significant or symbolically charged, that constitute powerful threats and thereby trigger the next latent stages of threat response

The turning point in the collective process often is marked by some dramatic precipitating event(s). Sometimes, these precipitating events have very powerful objective meanings. Famine and drought, for example, or a full-scale war are clear-cut emergencies that trigger all kinds of collective behavior. However, many times, the precipitating events are powerful largely by virtue of their electrifying symbolic meanings for the collective group. Given a society whose basic value system favors superiority over other peoples and in which fantasies and a potential ideology of genocide of another people are operative, the occurrence of a major threat, whether real or symbolic, will trigger the subsequent stages of this society's latent style of response to threat. The precipitating crisis may come in the form of major competition for a society's major industry, it may be in the movement of troops to the border by a neighboring country, or it may be the "trivial" matter of another country's humiliating a nation's ambassador.

One way of testing the objective reality of a precipitating event is to judge whether the same event would be handled differently by peoples and cultures that are prepared to interpret such events as problems that need to be solved more than as threats to survival. It is in this sense that many of us question intuitively the traditional historical explanations of various wars as growing out of this or that affront, insult or challenge, border incident, or dramatic clash between ideological interests and leaders – as if any of these events really could explain and justify the unbearable hells that were unleashed. We have sensed that so much of history is more like a recurring fairy tale, in which the mad forces of war and destruction are ready to erupt and require only some essentially trivial symbol to justify triggering the forces that are lying in wait.

And yet, symbolic precipitating factors and contexts do wield tremendous power as triggers that impel and justify the next stages of a behavior process. It is therefore essential that we learn how these triggers operate and that we prepare alternative strategies to head off the destructive spiral. In collective life, the art of diplomacy concerns avoiding provoking another people, e.g., knowing the dos and don'ts of cultural customs and honoring a people's points of cultural pride. A high point of collective maturity has been reached when one nation does not need to send troops into action when another country threatens border incidents and yet the first nation stands firm and has the appropriate military strength should it be required.

The psychology of brinkmanship or emergency responses to precipitating events is an enormous challenge for statesmen and societies. In the early warning system, we seek to analyze these highly charged precipitating events and the roles they play in the transition from the earlier stages of the sequence toward genocide to the later, more deadly stages.

MOBILIZATION OF MEANS TO GENOCIDE

The mobilization of tools and the organization of the participants for action to effect the fantasy or goal of genocide

Following identification of the fantasy of and ideological plan for genocide, we look for indications within a culture that an operative capacity is being mobilized to implement the fantasy and the ideological goal. A genociding group or society obviously must mobilize a great many tools and resources to carry out its intentions. There need to be managers in the government who administer the genocide, or, in the case of an insurgent or a revolutionary force, in the semigovernmental leadership forces of the group.

LEGITIMATION AND INSTITUTIONALIZATION OF GENOCIDE

The progressively formal codifications of the law and the authorization of the formal institutions of a society to allow and implement destruction of the target group

Whether or not a society moves all the way to genocide is very much a function of the extent to which the people and the institutions agree to the legitimation and institutionalization of the unfolding genocide. Sociologist Irving Louis Horowitz argues that genocide is not a random event but grows out of the structure of the state, which must give its approval. Using genocide as the focal point, he has derived a typology of social systems: genocidal societies, deportation or incarceration societies, torture societies, harassment societies, traditional shame societies, guilt societies, tolerant societies, and permissive societies.[34]

Even when a culture is already at the stage of manifest genocide, there is a great deal of information that we seek not only for the long-range purpose of learning more, but also on the realistic grounds that even early stages of genocide still present choices to people and that some genocidal momentums can be stopped even at a late stage. We want to know, for example, what positions the heads of the major churches in a culture take before, during, and after mass executions that are committed by their religionists. We want to know the position taken by medical administrators and practitioners; e.g., whether medical people make themselves available for cruel experiments that become another chapter in the tapestry of the genocide and what kind of medical treatment is given to the survivors and escapees. What are the reactions of the judiciary–do attorneys and judges fulfill the law's historic role as guardian against killing? Does the fourth estate risk exposing, criticizing, and protesting the horrors of the genocidal events? There are also situations in which local political and other leaders are able to arrest an already ongoing genocidal process–for example, the newly installed Kállay government rejection of German demands to deport Jews. Sociologist Helen Fein, who argues forcefully in her well-documented "accounting" of the Holocaust that genocide is a rational result of choices made by the ruling elites, given the circumstances or potential profits and costs, shows that "where state authorities had resisted discrimination and/or church leaders vocally opposed any attempts to justify anti-Semitism or discrimination against Jews, resistance movements also identified with the Jews. . . . If the threat of deportation would not be deterred by the state, leadership usually arose among Gentiles and Jews to avoid the isolation of the Jews, and finally countered the mobilization of the death machine."[35]

EXECUTION OF GENOCIDE AND EXPERIENCE-DENYING MECHANISMS

The actual extermination of a target victim people and the various ways in which the group or people block out experiencing the human meanings of the now-increasing momentum of violence and destruction

The final, tragic data-entry column refers to the actual leap of mankind into a hell in which all that is precious and decent in the human experience is abandoned and the actual extermination of a target people is pursued. Even at this stage, there are important data to be entered as to the facts, figures, locations, methods, and agents of death. There are, moreover, different types of process structures to genocide that need to be analyzed.[36] We also need to follow the various societal processes we have been examining as they strangely continue to play out some semblance of themselves even when the black night of noncivilization has fallen. *The churches offer communion. The courts remain open. The press functions.* Grotesquely, the civilization seems to continue at a time when the society otherwise has become an agency of the deathhead. But there are also, or could be, signs of remaining life. Just as we study terminal medical conditions and seek every possible way to battle anew for life, so it is in the study of genociding societies. "Sometimes we wonder: What if the conductor of the Berlin Symphony had turned to his audience and denounced the death camps? What if the pope had railed unambiguously against the death rites of the pagan Nazi crucifiers?" Are not the continuing institutions of society potentially the remarkable heart and kidney machines through which we would hope to reassert life in a dying social order that has turned to meting out death?

We also seek to identify what we call experience-denying mechanisms, or the various ways in which people in groups block out experiencing the human meanings of their overt mass exterminations. The mass murderer pyramids onto his already existing definition of the target group as not human a belief that he is doing no more than putting society "in order." For human beings to be able to bear the ultimately inescapable inner experience of what they are doing to living people, they must use powerful psychological defenses to block out the experience. We want to understand the structure of these defenses and how they are picked and supported by the group culture. Even at this terrifying stage of the genocidal momentum, there is still much that might be done to disrupt the unchallenged progression of the typical genocidal sequence.[37]

DEFINING LEVELS OF PROCESS

All of the above steps in the development of genocide take place on several different levels. For example, some events come about as dramatic critical incidents, which at one fell swoop forever change human history. There are other, no less dramatic, changes that come about as the result of a longer-term process of social change.[38]

Critical Incidents and Ongoing Process

Critical incidents: Key events that are seen as shaping the historical process of people, e.g., a major declaration by the constituted leader of a people, a celebrated legal case, economic depression, defeat in war, ecological tragedy

Ongoing process: The less dramatic, steady emergence of processes that are accepted as standard for a people or culture, such as a social tradition of segregation or the legal codification of a segregation policy

In the case of the Holocaust, there were infamous moments when the signal was given to advance violence to new heights: *Krystallnacht*, the night the Nazis burned the synagogues and pulled Jews into the streets, beat them, and in subsequent days removed thousands to concentration camps; the failure of the Conference of Allied Nations at Evian, Switzerland, in 1938 to intervene on behalf of the Jewish victims; the first orders for mass exterminations of Jews during the German push eastward in the early 1940s; the later decisions by the Nazis to proceed to a systematic "final solution"; and so on.[39]

Along with such critical incidents, there are also the day-by-day events, which we call the ongoing process. These are often less dramatic, yet critically significant processes in the pace of a people or a culture toward genocide via policies of segregation, discrimination, humiliation, police brutality, imprisonment, and internment in concentration camps. There must be an ongoing climate in a culture that will permit, invite, and support what become orders to napalm-burn villages, to separate husbands and wives, parents and children, or to execute prisoners. Events like these grow out of the ongoing processes within a people's history and way of life that precede the climactic events. In the case of Nazi Germany, there was the emergence of a fabric of unchallenged social humiliation, discriminatory legislation against the Jews, suspensions of civil liberties and elementary civil rights, police actions such as midnight arrests and removal to an unknown fate, and an increasing brutalization until the brutality escalated to a full-blown program of genocide.

Note that the same sets of events in a society may be recorded in different ways both as critical incidents and as ongoing processes. We attempt in the organization of our early warning system to line these data up alongside each other, while providing for a degree of separation between the two kinds of events so that we can study them independently.

Leadership and Societal Dynamics

Leadership: Policy designs, decisions, announcements, and implementations that are seen as issuing from the leader or leadership of a society—such as the president, prime minister, dictator, or head of the church—or by the legislature or courts—e.g., the U.S. Supreme Court decision to desegregate public facilities or the decision of a military leadership to overthrow a government

Societal dynamics: The behavior flow of a given society that is attributable to the collective social-evolutionary process, e.g., the tradition of a free press, the sanctity of the law, a growing momentum of violence in the streets, and an accepted historical tradition of prejudice against black people

How much the major processes of a society are determined by the acts of its leaders and how much by the larger flows of societal dynamics is a never-ending, fascinating question. It is important, and enormously interesting, to track the buildup of a society toward genocidal violences on the two tracks: the events that are initiated and led by the visible leaders and the events that unfold within the larger, more anonymous process of the collective societal dynamics.[40]

WHAT DO INTELLIGENT PEOPLE DO WHEN THEY KNOW IN ADVANCE?

Among the great advances of modern science is the ability to forecast various possible killers, such as hurricanes and tidal waves, or sources of poison and contamination. People in danger zones often are given advance warning and leave their homes. Yet, in many instances, a considerable number of residents do not leave for safer spots, even when advised to do so by the authorities. One U.S. government study of people who refused to leave their homes in the area of an oncoming tidal wave sought to identify the characteristics of people who refused to accept warning information. A surprising finding was that a fair number of well-educated people were among those who refused to leave.[41] Similarly, in the world of personal health, people frequently ignore early warning symptoms, early professional advice, and all manner of promptings of common sense until it is too late for them to save their life. In the psychoanalytic treatment of individuals, we learn that human beings tend to repeat the same acts over and over again, even though they are deeply self-punishing. In the history of mankind, people also repeat the same mistakes again and again.[42]

Human beings are dangerously unknowing or unable to shift many of their ways, even when they are on their way to death. One of the functions of a Genocide Early Warning System, therefore, is to educate people toward the possibility and desirability of change when they are faced with the knowledge of an impending state of danger. The very existence of an early warning system is a powerful symbol of the importance of knowing and being aware.

As we pointed out earlier, knowledge, in itself, does not bring real change, nor is it impossible that knowledge can also bring about an acceleration of evil. Lewis Coser points out that undercutting human beings' time-honored denial of the evils about them could, paradoxically, increase their denial of people's common humanity, but he also sees the positive potential of a knowledge of evil.

> If the increased visibility brought about by the communication revolution decreases the effectiveness of the denial of knowledge by "good people," and forces reliance upon a second line of defense, the denial of common humanity, then an increasing brutalization of public life is much to be feared. If this comes to pass, we might enter a new brutalizing age in which the "good people," far from trying to protect themselves from the impact of dirty work would condone it with a good conscience. And when the conscience of "good people" rather than being protected by more or less hypocritical maneuvers, atrophies for good, then God help us all.
>
> But then again, an alternative and more hopeful outcome might also be envisaged: the new visibility that certain forms of evil have attained in our days may induce intellectuals, those "antennae of the race," and in their wake educated strata, the young and others who have relatively marginal stakes in the society, to question some of the value premises on which the society is based. . . . In this case the revulsion against manifest horrors may set into operation a process of reexamination of societal values which could, in the long run, lead to a transvaluation of basic values and to a restructuring of the fundamental assumptions upon which the society rests.[43]

In the final analysis, if a Genocide Early Warning System someday serves "only" to save several thousand potential victims by enabling them to flee the clutches of a genocider headed toward their homes, the effort and cost of building such an early warning system will have been justified.

Postscript

SOME CONCLUSIONS AND A REDEFINITION OF "ABNORMALITY"

A young woman in Santa Barbara asked Nhat Hanh what it meant to seek the Buddha and what happened when you found him. Nhat Hanh answered, "I am a Zen master. And, as you know, Zen masters always reply incomprehensibly. So I will say that you only find the Buddha by killing the Buddha whenever you find him."

Then he laughed and said, "But I am a nice Zen master, so I will tell you that the Buddha is truth and the only thing that keeps you from finding truth is your conviction that you have already found it. So whenever you have 'found truth,' you must recognize that it is a lie, 'kill' it, and go on in the search for truth."

– Alfred Hassler

The task is done, but it is also barely begun. I have made an intense effort to write as clearly and as simply as I could on these complex issues and to create a reading experience that will stimulate a significant emotional experience for many readers. The issue of this book is, after all, a deadly real-life cancer that even now is claiming countless human lives, and we need to search passionately as well as thoughtfully for tools to stop the carnage. The issues involved are as big as the unfathomables of life and death themselves.

After eight years of work toward this book, I feel rich with a sense of progress, yet humbled by the cosmic issues of life and death that are our concern as we try to understand the human madness that can put to death millions of people in era after era. I feel happy and excited about the book as it is written. It seems to me that logic and hope find expression throughout this work. At the same time, I feel a deep poignancy that we are still a million light years away from the essence of the profound processes we have been studying.

We are struggling with the fact that we need to understand inter-related, yet separate, planes of human experience on so many different levels, ranging from the generation of basic human energy and aggression to the incredibly complex international system: how we construct our psychological energy; the meanings of good and evil; the paradox of human destructiveness amid loving family relationships; the contagion of evil in group processes; and the staggering mosaics of interrelated historical, legal, political, sociological, and psychological processes in the determination of the real-life events of societies. I think it is largely our not knowing how to link up the processes on one level of human experience to other levels that has kept the social scientists from exploring human destructiveness earlier and in greater depth. As a result, the awesome problem of genocidal destructiveness has been left somewhere out there, to be understood largely in historical and political terms, which we have not dared to relate to our psychological understanding of the everyday human being. It is essential that we learn how to describe the millions of genociders who are really like us, live and die in their homes among their loved ones, are active as members of the community, and appear generally to be quite normal human beings.

Even now, as I conclude this work, it is clear I have not answered the question of how to move from one level of experience to another. Moreover, it would be foolhardy to believe that I have plumbed any one of the levels we have studied with any degree of completeness. Inevitably, there are failings in my philosophical and scientific scholarship, and there are failings in my literary capacity to communicate clearly that which we do understand. It is also abundantly clear that it is impossible to penetrate beyond a certain point in our consideration of any number of processes that relate to the still-and-perhaps-forever mysterious aspects of life and death.

I feel we are closer and yet still so very far from being able to plumb the ultimate horror of how it is that a human being, who, to some reasonable extent, enjoys himself and life and cares for his family and friends, can destroy others without being aware of their humanity. When all is said and done, we still do not really know how man can engage in such terrible genocidal destruction, but we are closer to such an understanding for some of these reasons:

1. We have come to terms with the fact that destructiveness is omnipresent and no longer deny its presence all around us.
2. We have begun to look into the potential for violence in the hearts of all people and to see that destruction is not perpetrated only by mad or sick people who are different from the rest of us.

3. We understand that we are drawn to destroy in large part because we suffer from and fear the terrible dilemmas of life and death.
4. We have seen that even in destroying others, we are often defending ourselves against the terrors of death and may be trying to express our aggressiveness for life.

TWO YEARS LATER: SEARCHING FOR A NEW PRINCIPLE OF PSYCHOPATHOLOGY

While this manuscript was going through the usual process of submission and acceptance for publication and editing and production, I was able to continue struggling with the problem of the evident "normality" of genociders. Following the Holocaust, we wanted to believe that the leader of the German people, his principal followers, and the bulk of the executors were insane, and then it became an important first task to grasp the terrible truth that most of the genociders were not insane by current concepts and standards of mental health.

The reason for that absurdity is that most of the language of psychopathology refers to various incompetencies, weaknesses, and giving up of one's powers, and in genocide — and many lesser abuses of human rights — we are dealing with madmen who are altogether too competent in assuming power over others. Yet it is really inconceivable that we accept mental health concepts that do not define the leaders and followers who execute the mass murders as disturbed and abnormal. It is my strong conviction that we must expand the standard classification system in psychopathology to include abuses and destruction of people.

James Coleman, author of a definitive text on abnormal psychology, has taken the admirable position that "the best criterion for determining the normality of behavior is not whether society accepts it but rather whether it fosters the well-being of the individual and, ultimately, of the group."[1] Coleman takes a clear stand against the many mental health experts who insist that participation in the Nazi extermination programs cannot be considered abnormal in mental health terms: "Unless we value the survival and actualization of the human race, there seems little point in trying to identify abnormal behavior or do anything about it."[2]

Revising the theoretical base of psychopathology will make it possible for us, at last, to define the genociders as disturbed persons who terminate the lives of others to prove their own pseudomastery over vulnerability and death, something we have known intuitively. It does not matter even that the majority of human beings can be disturbed in this way under sufficiently inciting conditions. Men of good will have always known that to destroy life wantonly must be an act of madness — even if an entire group and society of people are mad at the same time — but we have lacked the language or the concepts in our traditional discipline of psychopathology to be able to express this truth and to work with it.

I believe that following the concepts developed in this book about the dialectic of life and death, there is a way of redefining psychopathology to include evil and destruction. Working with the dialectic of strength and weakness, which derives from the ultimate human condition of life and death, we can develop a new way of thinking about psychopathology as either what I shall call "disorders of incompetence, weakness, and vulnerability" *or* "disorders of pseudocompetence, superiority, and invulnerability."

Disorders of incompetence represent a solution to the anxiety of being alive and dying through disavowals of one's power and succumbing to the various forms of emotional and mental distresses and incompetence that we are familiar with in the classical definitions of the most recognizable and unarguable forms of neuroses, personality disorders, and psychoses that make people act sick or uncomfortable and unable to go about their normal everyday lives effectively. Disorders of pseudocompetence represent solutions to the same universal anxiety about life and death through disavowals of incompetence, weakness, and vulnerability. The dread of normal human weakness and needs is answered by an overstriving, an inflated sense of oneself, and claims of power over others and an exploitation and manipulation of others. Even worse, some people go to intolerable lengths to prove their pseudomastery of the dilemmas of existence at the expense of others' human rights and lives and engage in abuses, cruelty, and actual destruction of other people.

Traditional psychopathology has been less than comfortable with those disorders that make people do things to other people that largely make the other person uncomfortable and miserable. We have somehow strained to assign mental health diagnoses to some of these conditions, such as character or personality or behavior disorders or psychopathy. These categories have always been less than clear for mental health professionals in that, for the most part, people with these conditions are not like other "patients" and there is relatively little obvious suffering or "sickness" or discomfort. Yet we know that repeatedly and seriously disturbing other people's lives is very much a disturbance, and it can also be understood as a flight from anxiety about being alive and dying. Admittedly, the remarkable situation is that the "patient" (a would-be Adolf

Hitler, for example) doesn't suffer a breakdown (at least initially) but causes the breakdown of others by transferring the risks and the worst hurts of life to others. (One of the important discoveries of family therapy is that a family can impose on one of its members the weakness or nastiness of the others, who then remain seemingly undisturbed and well functioning.)

There are, of course, disorders that include mixed features of incompetence and pseudocompetence, or a shifting between one and the other — such as an exploitative psychopath who becomes upset under counterpressure from society, or a well-organized paranoiac who calls for persecution of a target group and, under certain sociopolitical circumstances, rises to a position of political power, only to break down into a more disorganized state later on. The extent of the psychopathology is defined by the imbalance between strength and weakness and the consequent damage one allows, seeks, or actually renders either to oneself or to others.

Disorders of pseudocompetence are denials of one's own vulnerability and mortality — and ultimately of one's humanity — and include both everyday and more serious evils that people do to their fellow human beings. This definition can include a family group that drives a child crazy, industrialists who are willing to pollute the water and endanger human lives, militarists and arms manufacturers who are eager to expand their power at the expense of other people, or concentration camp guards, whether they are fully into the excitement of their occupation or "just following orders" and escaping anxiety and responsibility by not being themselves.

Evil and psychopathology, in effect, are two sides of the same coin of denying either power or vulnerability. Both represent a failure to balance and integrate the two natural sides of strength and weakness that are intrinsic to the human condition. The more familiar emotional and mental conditions (being neurotic or mentally ill) largely involve disavowals of power and life, and therefore people unable to perform normal life roles. Evil, characteristically, involves a disavowal and renunciation of vulnerability and death, and thereby people who fail to respect other human beings' needs and weaknesses.

Both types of disorders are seriously influenced by, and often are actually set in motion by, people who give up their real selves in the relationships they maintain with groups — whether a family group, in which they disown their own identity and cling or bury themselves in the identities of others; or a collective group, in which they submerge themselves to the group's authority, charismatic leader, or ideology. Submerging oneself in others, conforming to authority or an ideology, acquiescing to clearly wrong facts (e.g., the classic Asch experiments in which a short line is judged to be longer than a long line under group pressure), acting on otherwise clearly unacceptable values (e.g., the Milgram experiment), blindly participating in cults and orgiastic groups (e.g., Jonestown) are all cardinal expressions of disturbances in the relationship of the individual to the collective (as well as of collective disturbances), and we must enlarge our psychopathological classification system to include them. These disturbances set off and combine with other forms of psychopathology—whether mass collective hysteria; somewhat-laughable, but in their time serious, epidemics of collective madness; pogroms; standing by as a silent bystander when neighbors or colleagues are marched off to unknown fates; or blind obedience to orders to execute masses of victims in concentration camps.

Up to a point, groups provide an enormously helpful sense of security and free great human energies and creativity, and it is still unfortunately quite normal, in the sense of common, to be drawn into feeling powerful through joining in group destructiveness. But when groups are committed to destroying life, participation in them must be considered to be psychopathological. The choice to join with mass killers and their followers is to choose to join in an effort to deny one's own mortality and vulnerability at the deadly expense of others.

As a practicing clinical psychologist, I am hopeful that this new, unifying principle of disorders of exaggerated strength or weakness will provide us with a workable basis for revising the standard classification system of psychopathology to include acts of evil and destruction by quite competent people who are currently classified as "normal." Moreover, I am relieved that there may now be a sound conceptual basis for being able to define as abnormal many everyday forms of claiming power over others, demeaning people, exploiting people, and denying the human rights of others, let alone physical abuses of, cruelty toward, and the irreversible destruction of others.

Normal human beings will stay with the continuous process of finding a balance between their strengths and weaknesses. They will neither surrender to undue weakness or incompetence, nor will they claim pseudopower over life and death by terrorizing others. For the business of life is to both live and die and to be both strong and weak, balanced and integrated with one another in self-respect and in respect of the rights of others.

Genocidal evil is normal (common) in history and normal (readily available) in our human potential; but it is, by every sane standard, distinctly abnormal (undesirable). I think that seeing genocide as the ultimate expression of a disturbed balance between strength and weakness — an extreme form of pseudostrength that is as psychotic as the maddest form of mental weakness and incompetence — may open the door to a solution to the conceptual dilemma in psychology that we have not known how to call this very abnormal (evil) and antilife act what it really is, profoundly abnormal.

APPENDIXES

APPENDIX A   The Flow of Normal Life Experience Processes
That Can Culminate

THE DYNAMICS OF "NORMAL" LIFE EXPERIENCE PROCESSES	EXAGGERATIONS AND DISTORTIONS OF THE NATURAL DYNAMIC BUILDING TOWARD VIOLENCE	INDIVIDUAL LIFE EXPERIENCING		FAMILY LIFE EXPERIENCING		GROUP LIFE EXPERIENCING	
		Generating Basic Life Energy or Aggression	The Individual Process of Means and Goals	The Individual Within The Family	The Family as a Group Process	The Individual Within The Group	The Group as a Group Process
Affirming the Value of Life and Life Strength (01-04)							
01. THE VALUING OF HUMAN LIFE							
We want to live.	But at this stage of evolution we still know too little about how to reconcile the facts of life and death, and too often we are drawn toward the lure of death.						
02. EXPERIENCING ALIVENESS							
We basically seek to experience our own aliveness as well as life all around us.	But when we are driven by fears of our own nonaliveness, we turn desperately to destructiveness as if in the pursuit of life.						
03. GENERATING POWER							
We need aggression energy for building and tearing down, loving and hating, "goodness" and "badness."	But we do not yet know how best to integrate the "positive" and "negative" sides of our humanness, how to gauge and control use of power, or how to commit energy to means and goals that serve life without succumbing to destructiveness.						
04. NATURAL IMPULSES TO VIOLENCE							
We need to accept the naturalness of our violent impulses at every level of experiencing.	But too often we do not differentiate between impulse, fantasy, or desire and the actual doing of overt violence.						
Monitoring and Resolving Threat and Conflict (05-06)							
05. MACHINERY FOR MONITORING AND MANAGING THREAT							
We need to perceive accurately the many real threats of annihilation that face us--from without and within.	But in our terror of annihilation, we tend to become overly violent and are easily drawn into unrecognized sequences of escalation and counterescalation of mounting threat and destructiveness.						
06. FORCE FOR SELF-DEFENSE AND IN THE SOLUTION OF CONFLICTS							
We need to defend ourselves forcefully against real threats of annihilation.	But we often do not know how easily we are drawn to excesses of power and destructiveness while fighting sincerely in the name of self-defense.						

in Individuals, Families, Groups and the Societal System
in Genocidal Destructiveness

Early Warning Processes	THE SOCIETAL SYSTEM			GENOCIDE EARLY WARNING SYSTEM						
	Societal Forces Supporting Human Life	Societal Forces Moving Toward Destruction of Life	Key Historical, Economic, Political, Legal, and Social Events and Transitions	Formation of the Genocidal Fantasy and Ideology	Precipitating Factors or Context	Mobilization of Means to Genocide	XXXX XXXX XXXX XXXX XXXX	Legalization and Institutionalization of Genocide	Execution of Genocide and Experience-Denying Mechanisms
Devaluing Humanness (01-04)							XXXX XXXX XXXX XXXX		
EWP 01. THE DEVALUING OF HUMAN LIFE							XXXX XXXX XXXX XXXX XXXX XXXX XXXX		
EWP 02. THE IRRELEVANCE OF HUMAN EXPERIENCE							XXXX XXXX XXXX XXXX XXXX XXXX		
EWP 03. THE PURSUIT OF POWER OVER OTHERS							XXXX XXXX XXXX XXXX XXXX XXXX XXXX XXXX XXXX		
EWP 04. OVERT VIOLENCE AND DESTRUCTIVENESS							XXXX XXXX XXXX XXXX XXXX		
The Illusion of Self-defense (05-06)							XXXX XXXX XXXX		
WP 05. ABSENCE OF CONTROL MACHINERY FOR MANAGING ESCALATORY SPIRALS							XXXX XXXX XXXX XXXX XXXX XXXX XXXX XXXX		
WP 06. APPLYING EXCESSIVE FORCE IN SELF-DEFENSE AND IN SOLUTION OF CONFLICTS							XXXX XXXX XXXX XXXX XXXX XXXX XXXX XXXX		

THE DYNAMICS OF "NORMAL" LIFE EXPERIENCE PROCESSES	EXAGGERATIONS AND DISTORTIONS OF THE NATURAL DYNAMIC BUILDING TOWARD VIOLENCE	INDIVIDUAL LIFE EXPERIENCING		FAMILY LIFE EXPERIENCING		GROUP LIFE EXPERIENCING	
		Generating Basic Life Energy or Aggression	The Individual Process of Means and Goals	The Individual Within The Family	The Family as a Group Process	The Individual Within The Group	The Group as a Group Process
Defending Against Vulnerability and Disorganization (07-10)							
07. PROJECTIONS OF VULNERABILITY AND THE THREAT OF NONHUMANNESS							
We protect ourselves from the terrors of vulnerability, disorganization, and death through psychological defense mechanisms.	But too often these defenses turn to primitive projections of our own fears of nonliving and death onto another who is relegated to a status of not human and, worse, not deserving of life.						
08. PROJECTION OF DESTRUCTIVE IMPULSES							
We dread and seek to control our destructive impulses.	But too often we project our own destructive impulses onto another who is then seen as threatening our life.						
09. NEED FOR LEADERS AND THE AUTHORITY OF SOCIETY							
We create cooperative societal structures and authorize leaders to head and administer the common effort.	But we characteristically conform blindly to the dictates of authority, individual or institutional, at least long enough for much damage to be done.						
10. GUARDING AGAINST BECOMING VICTIMS							
We seek to guard against falling victim to premature death from whatever source.	But often we make ourselves victims in order to remove ourselves from risking the alternative of trying to feel alive.						
The Cancer of Genocidal Destructiveness (11)							
11. THE CHOICE WHETHER TO BE DESTROYERS, ACCOMPLICES, OR BYSTANDERS WHEN A GROUP'S PROCESS TOWARD VIOLENCE IS GATHERING MOMENTUM							
We wish to see ourselves as not capable of destruction of life.	But at this stage of evolution, we are hugely capable of being drawn to destroying life, often in the very process of seeking to protect and advance life, and we then block and deny awareness of the destruction we wreak.						

Early Warning Processes	THE SOCIETAL SYSTEM		GENOCIDE EARLY WARNING SYSTEM						
	Societal Forces Supporting Human Life	Societal Forces Moving Toward Destruction of Life	Key Historical, Economic, Political, Legal, and Social Events and Transitions	Formation of the Genocidal Fantasy and Ideology	Precipitating Factors or Context	Mobilization of Means to Genocide	XXXX	Legalization and Institutionalization of Genocide	Execution of Genocide and Experience-Denying Mechanisms
The Ideology of Victimization (07–10)							XXXX		
EWP 07. DEHUMANIZATION OF POTENTIAL VICTIM GROUP							XXXX		
EWP 08. PERCEPTION OF POTENTIAL VICTIM GROUP AS DANGEROUS							XXXX		
EWP 09. LEGITIMATION OF VICTIMIZATION BY LEADERSHIP INDIVIDUALS AND INSTITUTIONS							XXXX		
EWP 10. AVAILABILITY OF VICTIM GROUP							XXXX		
XXXXXXXXXXXXXXXXXX	XXXXXXXXXXXXXXXXXXXX	XXXXXXXXXXXXXXXXXXXX	XXXXXXXXXXXXXXXXXXXX	XXXXXXXXXXXXXXXXXXXX	XXXXXXXXXXXXXXXXXXXX	XXXXXXXXXXXXXXXXXXXX	XXXX	XXXXXXXXXXXXXXXXXXXX	XXXXXXXXXXXXXX
The Cancer of Genocidal Destructiveness (11)							XXXX		
EWP 11. DEVELOPMENT OF MANIFEST GENOCIDAL PROCESS							XXXX		

The topics of this flow chart are discussed throughout the book. A discussion of the construction of the chart around basic life experience processes, which are also the basis for the Genocide Early Warning System Indicators, is found in Chapter 13.

Appendix B
THE UNIVERSAL DECLARATION OF HUMAN RIGHTS

Preamble. Whereas recognition of the inherent dignity and of the equal and inalienable rights of all members of the human family is the foundation of freedom, justice and peace in the world,

Whereas disregard and contempt for human rights have resulted in barbarous acts which have outraged the conscience of mankind, and the advent of a world in which human beings shall enjoy freedom of speech and belief and freedom from fear and want has been proclaimed as the highest aspiration of the common people,

Whereas it is essential, if man is not to be compelled to have recourse, as a last resort, to rebellion against tyranny and oppression, that human rights should be protected by the rule of law,

Whereas it is essential to promote the development of friendly relations between nations,

Whereas the peoples of the United Nations have in the Charter reaffirmed their faith in fundamental human rights, in the dignity and worth of the human person and in the equal rights of men and women and have determined to promote social progress and better standards of life in larger freedom,

Whereas Member States have pledged themselves to achieve, in co-operation with the United Nations, the promotion of universal respect for and observance of human rights and fundamental freedoms,

Whereas a common understanding of these rights and freedoms is of the greatest importance for the full realization of this pledge,

Now, therefore, The General Assembly proclaims this Universal Declaration of Human Rights as a common standard of achievement for all peoples and all nations, to the end that every individual and every organ of society, keeping this Declaration constantly in mind, shall strive by teaching and education to promote respect for these rights and freedoms and by progressive measures, national and international, to secure their universal and effective recognition and observance, both among the peoples of Member States themselves and among the peoples of territories under their jurisdiction.

Article 1. All human beings are born free and equal in dignity and rights. They are endowed with reason and conscience and should act towards one another in a spirit of brotherhood.

Article 2. Everyone is entitled to all the rights and freedoms set forth in this Declaration, without distinction of any kind, such as race, colour, sex, language, religion, political or other opinion, national or social origin, property, birth or other status.

Furthermore, no distinction shall be made on the basis of political, jurisdictional or international status of the country or territory to which a person belongs, whether it be independent, trust, non-self-governing or under any other limitation of sovereignty.

Article 3. Everyone has the right to life, liberty and security of person.

Article 4. No one shall be held in slavery or servitude; slavery and the slave trade shall be prohibited in all their forms.

Article 5. No one shall be subjected to torture or to cruel, inhuman or degrading treatment or punishment.

Article 6. Everyone has the right to recognition everywhere as a person before the law.

Article 7. All are equal before the law and are entitled without any discrimination to equal protection of the law. All are entitled to equal protection against any discrimination in violation of this Declaration and against any incitement to such discrimination.

Article 8. Everyone has the right to an effective remedy by the competent national tribunals for acts violating the fundamental rights granted him by the constitution or by law.

Article 9. No one shall be subjected to arbitrary arrest, detention or exile.

Article 10. Everyone is entitled in full equality to a fair and public hearing by an independent and impartial tribunal, in the determination of his rights and obligations and of any criminal charge against him.

Article 11. (1) Everyone charged with a penal offence has the right to be presumed innocent until proved guilty according to law in a public trial at which he has had all the guarantees necessary for his defence. (2) No one shall be held guilty of any penal offence on account of any act or omission which did not constitute a penal offence, under national or international law, at the time when it was committed. Nor shall a heavier penalty be imposed than the one that was applicable at the time the penal offence was committed.

Article 12. No one shall be subjected to arbitrary interference with his privacy, family, home or correspondence, nor to attacks upon his honour and reputation. Everyone has the right to the protection of the law against such interference or attacks.

Article 13.(1) Everyone has the right to freedom of movement and residence within the borders of each state. (2) Everyone has the right to leave any country, including his own, and to return to his country.

Article 14.(1) Everyone has the right to seek and to enjoy in other countries asylum from persecution. (2) This right may not be invoked in the case of prosecutions genuinely arising from non-political crimes or from acts contrary to the purposes and principles of the United Nations.

Article 15.(1) Everyone has the right to a nationality. (2) No one shall be arbitrarily deprived of his nationality nor denied the right to change his nationality.

Article 16.(1) Men and women of full age, without any limitation due to race, nationality or religion, have the right to marry and to found a family. They are entitled to equal rights as to marriage, during marriage and at its dissolution. (2) Marriage shall be entered into only with the free and full consent of the intending spouses. (3) The family is the natural and fundamental group unit of society and is entitled to protection by society and the State.

Article 17.(1) Everyone has the right to own property alone as well as in association with others. (2) No one shall be arbitrarily deprived of his property.

Article 18. Everyone has the right to freedom of thought, conscience and religion; this right includes freedom to change his religion or belief, and freedom, either alone or in community with others and in public or private, to manifest his religion or belief in teaching, practice, worship and observance.

Article 19. Everyone has the right to freedom of opinion and expression; this right includes freedom to hold opinions without interference and to seek, receive and impart information and ideas through any media and regardless of frontiers.

Article 20.(1) Everyone has the right to freedom of peaceful assembly and association. (2) No one may be compelled to belong to an association.

Article 21.(1) Everyone has the right to take part in the government of his country, directly or through freely chosen representatives. (2) Everyone has the right
of equal access to public service in his country. (3) The will of the people shall be
the basis of the authority of government; this will shall be expressed in periodic
and genuine elections which shall be by universal and equal suffrage and shall be
held by secret vote or by equivalent free voting procedures.

Article 22. Everyone, as a member of society, has the right to social security and
is entitled to realization, through national effort and international co-operation
and in accordance with the organization and resources of each State, of the
economic, social and cultural rights indispensable for his dignity and the free
development of his personality.

Article 23.(1) Everyone has the right to work, to free choice of employment, to
just and favourable conditions of work and to protection against unemployment.
(2) Everyone, without any discrimination, has the right to equal pay for equal
work. (3) Everyone who works has the right to just and favourable remunera-
tion ensuring for himself and his family an existence worthy of human dignity,
and supplemented, if necessary, by other means of social protection. (4) Everyone has the right to form and to join trade unions for the protection of his interests.

Article 24. Everyone has the right to rest and leisure, including reasonable limitation of working hours and periodic holidays with pay.

Article 25.(1) Everyone has the right to a standard of living adequate for the
health and well-being of himself and of his family, including food, clothing, hous-
ing and medical care and necessary social services, and the right to security in the
event of unemployment, sickness, disability, widowhood, old age or other lack of
livelihood in circumstances beyond his control. (2) Motherhood and childhood
are entitled to special care and assistance. All children, whether born in or out of
wedlock, shall enjoy the same social protection.

Article 26.(1) Everyone has the right to education. Education shall be free, at least
in the elementary and fundamental stages. Elementary education shall be com-
pulsory. Technical and professional education shall be made generally available
and higher education shall be equally accessible to all on the basis of merit. (2)
Education shall be directed to the full development of the human personality and
to the strengthening of respect for human right and fundamental freedoms. It
shall promote understanding, tolerance and friendship among all nations, racial
or religious groups, and shall further the activities of the United Nations for the
maintenance of peace. (3) Parents have a prior right to choose the kind of education that shall be given to their children.

Article 27.(1) Everyone has the right freely to participate in the cultural life of the community, to enjoy the arts and to share in scientific advancement and its benefits. (2) Everyone has the right to the protection of the moral and material interests resulting from any scientific, literary or artistic production of which he is the author.

Article 28. Everyone is entitled to a social and international order in which the rights and freedoms set forth in this Declaration can be fully realized.

Article 29.(1) Everyone has duties to the community in which alone the free and full development of his personality is possible. (2) In the exercise of his rights and freedoms, everyone shall be subject only to such limitations as are determined by law solely for the purpose of securing due recognition and respect for the rights and freedoms of others and of meeting the just requirements of morality, public order and the general welfare in a democratic society. (3) These rights and freedoms may in no case be exercised contrary to the purposes and principles of the United Nations.

Article 30. Nothing in this Declaration may be interpreted as implying for any State, group or person any right to engage in any activity or to perform any act aimed at the destruction of any of the rights and freedoms set forth herein.

Appendix C

THE UNITED NATIONS CONVENTION ON THE PREVENTION AND PUNISHMENT OF THE CRIME OF GENOCIDE

With amazing regularity genocide has repeated itself throughout history. Despite all advances in our civilization the twentieth century must unfortunately be considered as one of those most guilty of the crime of genocide. Losses in life and culture have been staggering. But deep in his heart man cherishes a fervent yearning for justice and love; among small nations and minorities the craving for security is particularly alive. The . . . Genocide Convention . . . can be traced to the fact that it responds to necessities and desires of a universal nature. The word genocide carries in itself a moral judgment over an evil in which every feeling man and woman concurs.

—Gabriela Mistral, the famous Chilean poet who won the Nobel Prize for Literature, in *The Crime of Genocide: A United Nations Convention Aimed at Preventing Destruction of Groups and at Punishing Those Responsible* (New York: United Nations Office of Public Information, OP/489, 1973).

The Contracting Parties,

Having considered the declaration made by the General Assembly of the United Nations in its resolution 96(I) dated 11 December 1946 that genocide is a crime under international law, contrary to the spirit and aims of the United Nations and condemned by the civilized world;

Recognizing that at all periods of history genocide has inflicted great losses on humanity; and

Being convinced that, in order to liberate mankind from such an odious scourge, international cooperation is required:

Hereby agree as hereinafter provided:

Article I. The Contracting Parties confirm that genocide, whether committed in time of peace or in time of war, is a crime under international law which they undertake to prevent and to punish.

Article II. In the present Convention, genocide means any of the following acts committed with intent to destroy, in whole or in part, a national, ethnical, racial or religious group, as such:

    a. Killing members of the group;
    b. Causing serious bodily or mental harm to members of the group;
    c. Deliberately inflicting on the group conditions of life calculated to bring about its physical destruction in whole or in part;
    d. Imposing measures intended to prevent births within the group;
    e. Forcibly transferring children of the group to another group.

Article III. The following acts shall be punishable:

    a. Genocide;
    b. Conspiracy to commit genocide;
    c. Direct and public incitement to commit genocide;
    d. Attempt to commit genocide;
    e. Complicity in genocide.

Article IV. Persons committing genocide or any of the other acts enumerated in Article III shall be punished, whether they are constitutionally responsible rulers, public officials or private individuals.

Article V. The Contracting Parties undertake to enact, in accordance with their respective Constitutions, the necessary legislation to give effect to the provisions of the present Convention and, in particular, to provide effective penalties for persons guilty of genocide or of any of the other acts enumerated in Article III.

Article VI. Persons charged with genocide or any of the other acts enumerated in Article III shall be tried by a competent tribunal of the State in the territory of which the act was committed, or by such international penal tribunal as may have jurisdiction with respect to those Contracting Parties which shall have accepted its jurisdiction.

Article VII. Genocide and the other acts enumerated in Article III shall not be considered as political crimes for the purpose of extradition.

    The Contracting Parties pledge themselves in such cases to grant extradition in accordance with their laws and treaties in force.

Article VIII. Any Contracting Party may call upon the competent organs of the United Nations as they consider appropriate for the prevention and suppression of acts of genocide or any of the other acts enumerated in Article III.

Article IX. Disputes between the Contracting Parties relating to the interpretation, application or fulfilment of the present Convention, including those relating to the responsiblity of a State for genocide or for any of the other acts enumerated in Article III, shall be submitted to the International Court of Justice at the request of any of the parties to the dispute.

Article X. The present Convention, of which the Chinese, English, French, Russian and Spanish texts are equally authentic, shall bear the date of 9 December 1948.

Article XI. The present Convention shall be open until 31 December 1949 for signature on behalf of any Member of the United Nations and of any non-member State to which an invitation to sign has been addressed by the General Assembly. The present Convention shall be ratified, and the instruments of ratification shall be deposited with the Secretary-General of the United Nations.

After 1 January 1950 the present Convention may be acceded to on behalf of any Member of the United Nations and of any non-member State which has received an invitation as aforesaid.

Instruments of accession shall be deposited with the Secretary-General of the United Nations.

Article XII. Any Contracting Party may at any time, by notification addressed to the Secretary-General, extend the application of the present Convention to all or any of the territories for the conduct of whose foreign relations that Contracting Party is responsible.

Article XIII. On the day when the first twenty instruments of ratification or accession have been deposited, the Secretary-General shall draw up a *proces-verbal* and transmit a copy thereof to each Member of the United Nations and to each of the non-member States contemplated in Article XI.

The present Convention shall come into force on the ninetieth day following the date of deposit of the twentieth instrument of ratification or accession.

Any ratification or accession effected subsequent to the latter date shall become effective on the ninetieth day following the deposit of the instrument of ratification or accession.

Article XIV. The present Convention shall remain in effect for a period of ten years as from the date of its coming into force.

It shall thereafter remain in force for successive periods of five years for such Contracting Parties as have not denounced it at least six months before the expiration of the current period.

Denunciation shall be effected by a written notification addressed to the Secretary-General of the United Nations.

Article XV. If, as a result of denunciations, the number of Parties to the present Convention should become less than sixteen, the Convention shall cease to be in force as from the date on which the last of these denunciations shall become effective.

Article XVI. A request for the revision of the present Convention may be made at any time by any Contracting Party by means of a notification in writing addressed to the Secretary-General.

The General Assembly shall decide upon the steps, if any, to be taken in respect of such request.

Article XVII. The Secretary-General of the United Nations shall notify all members of the United Nations and the non-member States contemplated in Article XI of the following:

a. Signatures, ratifications and accessions received in accordance with Article XI;
b. Notifications received in accordance with Article XII;
c. The date upon which the present Convention comes into force in accordance with Article XIII;
d. Denunciations received in accordance with Article XIV;
e. The abrogation of the Convention comes into force in accordance with Article XV;
f. Notification received in accordance with Article XVI.

Article XVIII. The original of the present Convention shall be deposited in the archives of the United Nations.

A certified copy of the Convention shall be transmitted to each Member of the United Nations and to each of the non-member States contemplated in Article XI.

Article XIX. The present Convention shall be registered by the Secretary-General of the United Nations on the date of its coming into force.

NOTES

NOTES TO CHAPTER 1: INTRODUCTION TO A BOOK ABOUT LIFE AND DEATH

Epigraph from Irwin A. Berg, "Cultural Trends and the Task of Psychology," *American Psychologist* 20 (1965), pp. 203–207.

1. My own conviction about my mother's probable susceptibility to cancer because she was too sweet developed during the course of my psychoanalysis. I have since spoken to others who have come to the same conviction about a parent who succumbed to cancer.

By now, there is significant scientific literature on psychogenic contributions to cancer (among the many causes of cancer). There are many evidences of predisposing personality structure – also that the time of onset often follows a major emotional loss – and there are even data that indicate that the rate of growth of cancers is related to (and predictable by) the personality structure of the patient. In an extensive study of psychosomatic diseases, 1,337 medical students were studied during a sixteen-year period, beginning with their entrance to medical school. "The physicians who developed cancer had personality characteristics and family histories similar to those who became mentally ill or committed suicide. They were low-keyed, quiet, emotional, self-contained and lonely. As children they were not close to their parents" (C. G. McDaniels, "Cancer Can Be Psychosomatic," *Jerusalem Post*, June 10, 1976). Recently there have also been fascinating serious attempts to stem the tide of cancer through integrated psychological and medical treatment (see Chapter 3, n. 12, for references to the work of Texas oncologist O. Carl Simonton, his wife, psychotherapist Stephanie Matthews-Simonton, and James Creighton; also Jeanne Achterberg and G. Frank Lawlis).

2. This, of course, is the larger message in the brilliant book by Ken Kesey, *One Flew Over the Cuckoo's Nest* (New York: New American Library, 1962), and the movie with the same title.

3. Psychiatrist John Spiegel has pioneered significant theoretical concepts of the transactions or interplays among the individual, family, and society. Dr. Spiegel proposes a field of transacting systems composed of six levels: the universe, the soma or biological system, the psyche, the group, the society, and the culture (John Spiegel, *Transactions: The Interplay Between Individual, Family, and Society* [New York: Science House, 1971]).

NOTES TO CHAPTER 2: NORMAL MAN AS GENOCIDER

Epigraph from Lionel Rubinoff, "Auschwitz and the Theology of the Holocaust," mimeographed (Address delivered to a colloquium sponsored by the Division of

Theological Studies of the Lutheran Council in the U.S.A. and the Interreligious Affairs Department of the American Jewish Committee, Lutheran Theological Seminary, Columbus, Ohio, May, 1973).

1. Lewis F. Richardson, *The Statistics of Deadly Quarrels* (London: Stevens, 1960).

2. R. D. Laing, *The Politics of Experience* (New York: Pantheon, 1967), pp. xiv, 49.

3. Throughout this book, I refer to genocide not from the point of view of the strictly legal definition, where there is the implication of a willful attempt to wipe out the identity of another people, but from the point of view of the generic meaning of genocide as mass murder or massacre.

4. Frederic Wertham, "New Dimensions of Human Violence," *American Journal Psychotherapy* 23 (1969), p. 374. In that 1969 publication—so many years after the events—Dr. Wertham makes this telling remark: "The whole matter has been left in a twilight, historically and morally, and not a single psychiatric or pediatric organization in Germany or outside has as yet taken it up" (p. 375).

Dr. Wertham writes of one prominent psychiatrist: "Colleagues of his who knew him well and who condemn him for his 'euthanasia' work nevertheless say of him that he was 'an exceptionally good psychiatrist, especially kind to his patients and concerned about them day and night" (Frederic Wertham, "The Geranium in the Window: The 'Euthanasia' Murders," Chapter 9 in *A Sign for Cain: An Exploration of Human Violence* [New York: Macmillan, 1966], p. 174).

A further description of the execution of the mental patients, and its background in German medical thinking about eugenics, is provided by Stephen L. Chorover, *From Genesis to Genocide* (Cambridge, Mass.: M.I.T. Press, 1979).

5. Douglas M. Kelley, *22 Cells in Nuremberg* (New York: MacFadden, 1961), p. 171 (original publication, 1947).

6. James R. Jaquith, Review of Peter Farb, *Man's Rise to Civilization as Shown by the Indians of North America from Primeval Times to the Coming of the Industrial State* (New York: E. P. Dutton, 1968), in *Transaction* 6:7 (May 1969), pp. 36–37.

7. Stuart C. Miller, "Our Mai Lai of 1900: Americans in the Philippine Insurrection," *Transaction* 7:1 (September 1970), p. 23.

8. Arthur D. Morse, *While Six Million Died: A Chronicle of American Apathy* (New York: Random House, 1968).

9. Judah Pilch, ed., *The Story of the Jewish Catastrophe in Europe* (New York: American Association Jewish Education, 1968). Quotation as cited is from the prepublication mimeographed edition; the same material, although rewritten, appears in the 1968 hardcover edition as Chapter 6, "The World Knew and Was Silent," pp. 205–214.

10. A. M. Rosenthal, *Thirty-eight Witnesses* (New York: McGraw-Hill, 1964). See also Leon Sheleff's remarks about the role of a society as a whole in choices to be bystanders in Chapter 9, text and notes 25 and 26.

11. Stanley Milgram, "Some Conditions of Obedience and Disobedience to Authority," *Human Relations* 18 (1965), pp. 57–76, and Stanley Milgram, *Obedience to Authority* (New York: Harper and Row, 1974).

12. David Rosenhan, "Some Origins of Concern for Others," in P. Mussen, N. Covington, and J. Langer, eds., *Trends of Issue in Developmental Psychology* (New York: Holt, Rinehart and Winston, 1969), pp. 134–153.

13. David Mark Mantell, "The Potential for Violence in Germany," *Journal Social Issues* 27:4 (1971), pp. 101–112.

14. Philip Zimbardo, "On 'Obedience to Authority,'" *American Psychologist* 29 (1974), pp. 566–567. Floyd L. Ruch and Philip G. Zimbardo, in their textbook, *Psychology and Life*

(8th ed. [Glenview, Ill.: Scott, Foresman, 1971], pp. 551–554), report at great length another incredible study that is not as well known. The subjects were students at the University of Hawaii who were assembled to hear a brief speech by a professor asking for their cooperation to assist in the application of scientifc procedures to kill the mentally and emotionally unfit. In the course of his remarks, the professor explained urbanely, "Euthanasia which means mercy killing . . . is considered by most experts as not only being beneficial to the unfit, because it puts them out of the misery of their lives, but more importantly it will be beneficial to the healthy, fit, and more educated segments of the population. It is therefore a 'final solution' to a grave problem." The professor then added, "What is not clear, however, is which method of killing should be applied, which method is least painful and who should do the killing and/or decide when killing should be resorted to. For these reasons, further research is required and our research project is concerned with this problem."

The results of the study were little short of incredible. Ruch and Zimbardo write: "It is likely that all 570 subjects would have said they disapproved Hitler's extermination of 6 million Jews, but when it was labeled differently and disguised as something noble, 517 accepted the basic premise and all but 33 even indicated what aspect of the job *he* or *she* would prefer to take part in. Not one of these college students said he or she would refuse to have a part in the undertaking." The study is credited to H. H. Mansson, "Justifying the Final Solution" (Paper presented at the International Congress of Psychology, London, 1969).

15. I. Shlomo Kulcsar, Shoshanna Kulcsar, and Lipot Szondi, "Adolf Eichmann and the Third Reich" in Ralph Slovenko, ed., *Crime, Law, and Corrections* (Springfield, Ill.: Charles Thomas, 1966), pp. 16–52. I. Shlomo Kulcsar, "The Psychopathology of Adolf Eichmann," in *Excerpta Medica International Congress Series No. 150: Proceedings of the IV World Congress of Psychiatry* (Madrid, September 1966), pp. 1687–1689. I. Shlomo Kulcsar "De Sade and Eichmann," in Israel W. Charny, ed., *Strategies Against Violence: Design for Nonviolent Change* (Boulder, Colo.: Westview, 1978), pp. 19–33.

16. At least those were the results of just about all the traditional mental health examination procedures used with Eichmann. There was, however, one striking exception that must be reported. In the Szondi test, Eichmann was found to select pictures of killers to an incredible extent. This test is based on the subject's selection of pictures of different people from something of a "rogue's gallery." Szondi himself reportedly did a blind analysis of Eichmann's test performance and wrote that only rarely in history does such a killer appear. This writer is untrained in the Szondi test and along with most U.S. psychologists was educated to doubt the validity of the Szondi test because its theoretical underpinning seems contrived and is unsupported by a whole history of experiments done years ago, which showed that people do not extract accurate information from photographs. Given this bias, it is difficult to understand the apparent success of the Szondi test in contrast to the findings of accepted diagnostic procedures such as the Rorschach inkblot technique and the thematic apperception test, which did not show Eichmann as abnormal. In any case, it is still factual to conclude that according to a large variety of traditional measures differentiating normal from abnormal, Eichmann appeared more as a nonperson rather than as a sick person.

17. Thomas N. Merton, "A Devout Meditation in Memory of Adolf Eichmann," reprinted in *Reflections* (Merck, Sharp and Dohme) 2:3 (1967), pp. 21–23.

18. The same conclusion was reached by British psychiatrist Henry Dicks, who went back years after the war to examine in depth Nazi mass killers who were still serving their sentences for war crimes. "Neither fanaticism nor identifiable psychiatric disorders were crucial among them. They are mostly examples of weak-egoed emotionally deprived in-

dividuals. Their *secret* resentment, covered by conformity and unquestioning obedience under originally congenial social and group pressures and sanctions, broke surface, causing them to abrogate their earlier levels of 'civilized' behavior while acting their SS roles" (Henry V. Dicks, *Licensed Mass Murder: A Socio-Psychological Study of Some SS Killers* [London: Heinemann, 1972], jacket description).

What is perhaps most difficult to realize is that the "psychopaths" and "madmen" who are the leaders of many of the huge destructive events in history are also, in some intrinsic sense, human beings just like all the rest of us. The convenience of assigning these terrible men responsibility for the hells of their times should not deter us from the larger realization that at the present state of evolution of humanity, all of us carry a potential for terrible destructiveness.

The documentary *Swastika* depicts Hitler's family life at his Berchtesgaden retreat during the years 1933–1939. The film shows Hitler delicately pouring coffee at a children's birthday party, Hitler letting a baby play with his moustache, Hitler chatting with his secretaries about a movie. In a review of the film in the *Washington Post*, Kenneth Turan wrote: "*Swastika,* though perhaps difficult to take, is the most potent of anti-Nazi films simply because it shows us what people seem to be intent on forgetting, a lesson that cannot be learned too often: Hitler and his friends were not devils or robot clowns, but ordinary, everyday even banal folk. . . . The 'shock' of the film is its depiction of a Hitler who goes strongly against type, a man few people have ever imagined existed" (Reported by Jewish Telegraphic Agency, *Jerusalem Post*, October 13, 1974).

A more recent review of the evidence of the normality of the Nazi killers is Hans Askenasy, *Are We All Nazis?* (Secaucus, N.J.: Lyle Stuart, 1978).

19. G. M. Gilbert, *The Psychology of Dictatorship: Based on an Examination of the Leaders of Nazi Germany* (New York: Ronald, 1950), p. 287.

20. Jack Riemer, in a review of Elie Wiesel's *One Generation After*, writes:

> In one of the early chapters, Wiesel meditates on the mystery of the fact that the men who managed the death camps stayed sane. He wonders how they were able to tend their gardens and water their flowers two steps away from the barbed wire, how they were able to experiment with montrous mutations and still believe in immortality, how they were able to go on vacation, to be overwhelmed by the beauty of a landscape, make children laugh—and then go back to the routine, day in and day out, of being killers.

Had the killers been savages or mere sadists the shock would have been milder, but they were not. They were doctors and lawyers, philosophers and sociologists, even theologians. And by all clinical standards, they were sane.

> If that is true, then we need a new definition of sanity. We need a definition that will reckon with man's capacity to divide his techniques from his purposes, that will take into account man's capacity to separate his morals from his means of making a livelihood. We need a definition of sanity narrow enough to exclude the executioners and the departmentalized managers of murder. A definition of sanity that only measures how well a man does his job and does not concern itself with the nature of that job is insane. . . .
>
> To be sane according to this concept means to feel with and to care about your fellow man, to be a unified personality whose head and heart are integrated. It means that one cannot be a technician who does not get involved in politics, or a manager of a murder machine who does not take a stand on policy questions, or a ra-

tional person who has no feelings. [Jack Riemer, Review of Elie Wiesel, *One Generation After* (New York: Random House, 1970), in *Hadassah*, November 1970]

21. Leo Srole, Thomas S. Langer, Stanley T. Michael, Marvin K. Opler, and Thomas A. C. Rennie, *Mental Health in the Metropolis: The Midtown Manhattan Study* (New York: McGraw-Hill, 1962).

22. In an interesting and important evaluation of the concepts of normality and abnormality in mental health, Offer and Sabskin comment how in the history of medicine, "Koch's and Pasteur's discovery led to the view that individuals either harboured bacteria that gave rise to illness or were free of such bacteria. . . . This is, of course, an oversimplification. . . . The infectious-disease model was generalized far beyond itself" (Daniel Offer and Melvin Sabskin, *Normality: Theoretical and Clinical Concepts of Mental Health* [New York: Basic Books, 1974], p. 6). See also Benjamin B. Wolman, *Call No Man Normal* (New York: International Universities Press, 1973); Israel W. Charny, "Why Are Most (If Not All) People and Families Disturbed?" *Journal Marriage and Family Therapy* 6:1 (1980), pp. 37–47; Israel W. Charny, "The New Psychotherapies and Encounters of the Seventies: Progress or Fads?" *Humanist*, May–June and July–August 1974, reprinted in *Reflections* (Merck, Sharp and Dohme) 10:2 (1975), pp. 1–13, and 10:3 (1975), pp. 1–17, also in I. David Welch, George A. Tate, and Fred Richards, eds., *Humanistic Psychology: A Sourcebook* (New York: Prometheus, 1978), pp. 117–140.

23. Henry V. Dicks, *Marital Tensions: Clinical Studies Towards a Psychological Theory of Interaction* (New York: Basic Books, 1967). George R. Bach and Peter Wyden, *The Intimate Enemy: How to Fight Fair in Love and Marriage* (New York: Morrow, 1969).

24. Jerome Frank comments on a news story that appeared in the *Santa Barbara News-Press*, August 27, 1966:

People may become inured to violence through constant vicarious experience. For example, during the summer of 1966 in Washington the Army staged a weekly open-air show showing "Torchlight Tattoo" which featured demonstrations of strangling, stabbings, and other methods of killing used by soldiers; an announcer offered detailed explanations often in a jovial tone. Over a hundred thousand people saw the show before someone protested, but that is less extraordinary than the especially revealing comment of an Army officer when then asked, "Is demonstrating how to strangle a man with piano wire and the best way to cut a man's throat . . . healthy for the public?" replied, "I think the public is well versed in these subjects. They read it in these detective magazines and see it on TV. Why, my children saw the show and they just shrugged off the Ranger act." [Jerome D. Frank, *Sanity and Survival* (New York: Random House, 1967), pp. 73–74]

25. According to Randall Collins:

One might suppose that the monotheistic or philosophical world religions, with their universal brotherhood and their explicit ethical concerns, would indicate an historical breakaway from explicit cruelty and towards altruism. Some of them, such as Christianity, have even been formulated as primarily religions of "love." But in historical fact, this is not the case. . . . The world religions, far from indicating a break with violence, represent a new form in its organization. . . . The iron-age agrarian in which the universalist churches arose supported some of the cruelest forms of stratification ever seen. The moralities of the world religions, generally speaking, contributed more to the extension of violent cruelty than to its mitigation.

[Randall Collins, "Three Faces of Cruelty: Towards a Comparative Sociology of Violence," *Theory and Society* 1:4 (1974), pp. 415–440]

26. See, for example, Kohlberg's exciting findings of a universal sequence of stages of moral development that culminate in a profound respect for life in Chapter 6, n. 15.

27. Peter Weiss, *The Investigation* (New York: Pocket Books, 1967).

28. Elton B. McNeil, "Violence and Human development," in Marvin E. Wolfgang, ed., *Patterns of Violence, Annals of the American Academy of Political and Social Science* 364 (1966), pp. 149–157. See also Israel W. Charny, "Towards Confrontation of the Naturalness of Evil," *Reconstructionist* 37:5 (July 9, 1971), pp. 7–19.

29. Historian George Kren and psychologist Leon Rappoport have collaborated in a thoughtful examination of the Holocaust as a major crisis in human behavior and values. "If one keeps at the Holocaust long enough, then sooner or later the ultimate personal truth begins to reveal itself: one knows, finally, that one might either do it, or be done to. . . . Auschwitz expands the universe of consciousness no less than landings on the moon" (George Kren and Leon Rappoport, *The Holocaust and the Crisis of Human Behavior* [New York: Holmes & Meier, 1980], p. 126).

30. Simon Wiesenthal, *The Murderers Among Us* (New York: McGraw-Hill, 1967).

31. Psychoanalyst Chaim Shatan has written about psychotherapists:

> Usually, and this is my profession's failing, we too succumb to our training in detachment: we withdraw our feelings, we see and hear and speak as from a great distance, from some computer-like zone of the mind beyond the sway of passion. Another approach to such events is *to personalize* them by an act of both moral and scientific imagination. . . . I believe we professionals can make . . . a contribution only if we transcend traditional scientific and clinical relationships . . . to feel *personally* what the hunt feels like, to immerse ourselves in fear we can almost smell and taste, fear connected with the constant confrontations with death. . . . As psychological habituation to war and evil spreads, the intellectual and professional community has – more than ever – a moral obligation to link its scholarly perspectives with ethical involvement. For, *to know about killing – and to remain silent – is to be an accessory to that killing,* and to face profound moral corruption. To meet the evils of power with professional neutrality is to become a behavior technologist who helps render society holocaust-prone. [Chaim S. Shatan, "The Beginning Not the End of the Age of Genocide: A Psychoanalyst's Encounter with the Slaughter of the Paraguayan Indians," in Richard Arens, ed., *Genocide in Paraguay* (Philadelphia: Temple University Press, 1978), citations from prepublication mimeographed text]

32. The mental health literature is rich with references to men's fears and guilt feelings about their destructive impulses. Throughout this book, I refer to many such observations, such as those by Karen Horney, Melanie Klein, Joseph Rheingold, Harold Searles, D. W. Winnicott, and others.

33. A very moving description of the fears of a schizophrenic patient about the possibility of being too destructive toward others is found in the heartwarming book by Hannah Green, *I Never Promised You a Rose Garden* (New York: New American Library, 1964).

NOTES TO CHAPTER 3: THE CANCER OF EXPERIENCING

Epigraph from Paul Tillich, *To Live As Men: An Anatomy of Peace,* papers by Paul Tillich, Linus Pauling, Abba Evan, Alex Quaison-Sackey, Vijoys Lakshmi Panalit, and Pietro

Nenni, Introduction by Robert M. Hutchens and Message from Pope Paul VI (Santa Barbara, Calif.: Center for the Study of Democratic Institutions, 1965), p. 18.

1. Erich Fromm writes:

> All human passions, both the "good" and the "evil," can be understood only as a person's attempt to make sense of his life. . . . Even though the life-furthering passions are conducive to a greater sense of strength, joy, integration, and vitality than destructiveness and cruelty, the latter are as much an answer to the problem of human existence as the former. Even the most sadistic and destructive man is human, as human as the saint. He can be called a warped and sick man who has failed to achieve a better answer to the challenge of having been born human, and this is true; he can also be called a man who took the wrong way in search of his salvation. . . .
>
> Destructiveness and cruelty . . . express *life turning against itself in the striving to make sense of it.* They are the only true perversion. Understanding them does not mean condoning them. But unless we understand them, we have no way to recognise how they can be reduced, and what factors tend to increase them. [Erich Fromm, *The Anatomy of Human Destructiveness* (New York: Holt, Rinehart and Winston, 1973), p. 9]

2. Richard M. Hunt, associate dean of the Harvard Graduate School of Arts and Sciences, and president of the American Council on Germany, which seeks to promote closer West German–United States relations, writes in a poignant piece in the *New York Times* about his resolution to no longer teach a "'no-fault' view of history." Hunt describes a course in which he and his students studied the many processes that led to the ultimate terrors of the Nazi regime, and then how shocked he was to find that the students had come to "depressingly fatalistic conclusions about major moral dilemmas.

"I read comments and questions such as these: 'In the last analysis what else could the average citizens of these little towns have done but vote for a dynamic leader like Hitler?' . . . 'With the ever present threat of Gestapo terror, who would dare to speak out and resist? Would you? Would I? Probably not!'"

Hunt concludes wryly: "Some day soon I'll be teaching the same course again. But not in the same way. . . . Somehow I have got to convey the meaning of moral decisions and their relations to significant outcomes. Most important, I want to point out that single acts of individuals and strong stands of institutions at an early date do make a difference in the long run" (Richard M. Hunt, "No-Fault Guilt-Free History," *New York Times*, February 8, 1976).

3. An excellent, comprehensive view of man's orientation to death is found in Jacques Choron, *Modern Man and Mortality* (New York: Macmillan, 1964). Choron reviews many ways in which people experience fear of death and the many efforts they make to allay that fear. He concludes his study with these remarks: "For myself, I find some measure of reassurance against the nagging doubt of meaninglessness in the implications of what has been considered by some thinkers as the profoundest, even though unanswerable question: Why is there something rather than nothing? What this question implies is that there is no necessity of there being a world at all. But precisely because it would have been so easy not to have been, the existence of the world and of my own individual self must have a significance" (p. 205).

4. In his analysis of death anxiety, Robert Lifton suggests that the inner idea of death is elaborated from earliest childhood in terms of three aspects of the lifelong interplay between life and death. He calls these three polarities: connection versus separation, integrity

versus disintegration, and movement versus stasis. "At every developmental level all conflicts exacerbate, and are exacerbated by these three aspects of what later becomes death anxiety – that is, disintegration, stasis and separation" (Robert Jay Lifton, "On Death and the Continuity of Life: A 'New' Paradigm," *History of Childhood Quarterly: The Journal of Psychohistory* 1:4 [1974], pp. 689–690).

5. Not only are fears of death statements of fears of being alive, but it has been suggested by several penetrating observers of schizophrenia that in most cases, the psychosis expresses the patient's having surrendered to his fear of dying because he feels there is no hope for him to feel alive. Psychoanalyst Harold Searles has made the point that in this sense, schizophrenia is an equivalent of death on the part of those who are so overwhelmed by their fears of dying that they give up. Searles suggests that as long as one feels dead anyway, there is no longer a reason to fear death; one allows oneself to die, because there is nothing to be gained in life and nothing to be lost in death (Harold Searles, "Schizophrenia and the Inevitability of Death," *Psychiatric Quarterly* 36 [1961], pp. 631–665).

Robert Lifton writes similarly: "The principle of impaired . . . imagery of death and the continuity of life is a unitary theme around which mental illness can be described and in some degree understood. I see this kind of impairment as being involved in the etiology of mental illness but not as causative in the 19th century sense of a single cause bringing about one specific fact. Rather, impaired death imagery is the center of a constellation of forms, each of which is of some importance for the overall process we call mental disturbance" (Lifton, "On Death and the Continuity of Life," pp. 690–691).

Lifton identifies three issues in man's imagery of death as relevant to the emergence of mental illness: The first is death anxiety (see note 4). The second is psychic numbing where the image that man lives by is: "If I feel nothing then death does not exist; therefore I need not feel anxious about death either actually or symbolically; I am invulnerable." The numbing is an attempt not to feel or experience the issue of death. In psychosis, "the schizophrenic experiences a pathetic illusion of omnipotence, a despairing mask of pseudo-immortality because he is blocked in the most fundamental way from authentic connection of continuity. . . . But the productions of the schizophrenic are infused with death: like the Hiroshima survivors at the time the bomb fell, he sees himself as dead, other people around him as dead, the world as dead" (p. 694). The third principle is what Lifton calls "suspicion of counterfeit nurturance" or the idea that life itself must be counterfeit if death is inevitable. Lifton also cites Searles's observation that the schizophrenic defends himself against death and anxiety, and yet in another sense feels himself dead so that he has nothing to lose through death. He also cites Ronald Laing's description of the psychotic patient's "desire to be dead, the desire for non-being" (R. D. Laing, *The Divided Self* [Baltimore, Md.: Penguin, 1965], p. 176).

6. As Arthur Kovacs comments:

In a philosophical sense, our clients seek our services because they know they must die – the life must go out of their previous adaptations – so that they might live. The process terrifies them. They desire to be spared its agonies by some magic we might work in the arcane circle of the office. We will allow them to remain as they are, but without pain. We will see them through the transformation without them having to bloody themselves. The illusions die hard. And for most of the great mass of human lives I review in my mind, something even more pernicious seems to happen. The change is resisted, denied, fought against until it becomes literally life-threatening. Then and only then do my friends, my acquaintances, my clients, myself, seem to find the last desperate courage to die and to be reborn in the next stage of what constitutes a human life. Yet the brush with death is often all too close.

> When I extrapolate from the individual lives of those I know to the broader human condition, I get terrified. Too many people lose heart for the tumultuous processes involved in the successive mastery of the developmental crises in the human life span. Most seem to ossify, some earlier and some later. Our culture seems to consist of a large number of individuals carrying out their "responsibilities" in a mechanistic fashion. They seem joyless, devoid of passion, zest, love, tears, terror or any of the other ingredients which smear the palette of life with vibrant hues and not with sombre tones. . . . In my most despairing moments, the whole human race seems now in this predicament as a collective organism. [Arthur Kovacs, in *Psychotherapy* (Bulletin of the Division of Psychotherapy of the American Psychological Association), July 1975, p. 3]

7. For a sensitive discussion of people who are too helpless, and especially of the death that comes to animals as well as human beings who do not fight to live, see Martin E. P. Seligman, *Helplessness: On Depression, Development, and Death* (San Francisco: W. H. Freeman, 1975).

8. In a review of Alan Watts's *Clouds Hidden—Whereabouts Unknown* (London: Jonathan Cape, 1974), Hilda Basch writes:

> Western man is so worried about becoming that he never gets the chance to be; he tries to categorize, classify, "square," the world, and, in so doing, is under the illusion that he understands it; he wants to transform the transient into something static and permanent.
>
> But all this, claims Alan Watts, can only culminate in frustrated ambition, suffering, a continuous state of unhappiness. . . . The individual or ego divorced from the whole is but an insignificant particle. . . . Death, decay, emptiness, are to life, growth, substance, like two sides of the same coin. Each complements the other. Both are of equal importance. Fear, paranoia, discomfort are the results of alienation from the whole—the illusory dichotomy between self and other. [*Jerusalem Post*, August 19, 1974]

9. Ernest Becker, *The Denial of Death* (New York: Free Press, 1973), pp. 266, 270.

10. Psychoanalyst Ernst Kriss is credited with the beautiful concept of "regression in the service of the ego" as a fundamental basis for creativity. Many recent studies of psychopathology also emphasize that the purpose of much psychopathology is to allow a state of regression through which people can reorganize themselves more effectively. The psychiatric disorder is seen as a period of "creative disorganization," through which people seek to discard unwanted aspects of their personality and reorganize themselves more creatively. Needless to say, the problem with this point of view is that a state of being disorganized and really sick, as in psychosis, in itself takes a toll of people and creates a condition that not everybody has the strength to come back from. But there is still much truth to the basic principle that the creative process calls for creative regression and disorganization.

11. For a psychoanalyst-novelist's gripping fantasy of how a group of people conspire to gain control over their deaths, see Allen Wheelis, "The League of Death," in Wheelis, *The Illusionless Man: Some Fantasies and Meditations on Disillusionment* (New York: Harper and Row, 1971), pp. 57–96.

12. Much of what is known and unknown about cancer today lends itself to provocative analogies to other aspects of life. For example, some research has shown that what happens in cancerous tumors is that the antibodies, which normally should fight off the

cancer, turn and overwhelm the body's natural immunological systems. If we then look at our scheme of the complementarities between the two basic givens of life – life and death – we might suggest that at times, people are overwhelmed by the natural protective process ("antibody") of wanting to seek rest in nonaliveness when, under certain conditions, this "antibody" turns from enabling them to return to life rested and refreshed into a rampant killer that draws them toward actual death. So, too, the natural protective mechanism of fighting against death, which is a built-in complement to the natural process of preparing for one's inevitable death, can turn from its life-protective function to run rampant in an insistence on life at any cost, to a point where the death that was unrealistically denied is actually "invited" to hurry its appearance.

Another notion in contemporary cancer research is that a normal biological cell relies on an information system to recognize the dangers facing it. What happens in cancer is a breakdown in the ability of normal cells to recognize the danger of cancer cells, which are always present in the body. In effect, this notion describes a feedback system of information through which normal cells guard against the spread of death. (In physics, it is observed that any system that strives for equilibrium necessarily provides for a negative feedback system, which renders alerts of excesses and insufficiencies that must be corrected.) It has been suggested that perhaps the larger purpose of the ever-present cancer cells is to spur on the basic immunological process of the body that guards against cancers (personal communication, Alberto Podorgny, Weizmann Institute of Science). It does not seem at all strained to analogize this theory and our need to recognize the ever-present potential for destructiveness in ourselves. There is also a great deal of reason to consider that our very potential for destructiveness normally serves life-saving and life-furthering needs – such as self-defense.

This kind of thinking also provokes conjectures about the psychological forces that may be contributing to physical cancers. See, for example, the intriguing speculations of Pearce and Newton as to the connection between a denial of one's aliveness as a person and the possibility of inhibiting the biological mechanisms that may be required to hold ever-present cancer cells in check. Pearce and Newton also suggest the possibility that the particular psychological relationship a person has to a given organ or organ system of his or her body may play a role in determining that this organ becomes the site of a cancer rather than another part of the body (Jane Pearce and Saul Newton, *The Conditions of Human Growth* [New York: Citadel, 1969], pp. 288–289). In recent years some responsible clinicians have been asserting that cancer not only has psychological causes but may be susceptible to active psychotherapy (see O. Carl Simonton, Stephanie Matthews-Simonton, and James Creighton, *Getting Well Again* [Los Angeles: Tarcher, 1978]. See also Jeanne Achterberg and G. Frank Lawlis, *Imagery of Cancer* [Champaign, Ill.: Institute Personality and Ability Testing, 1973]).

On the other hand, Susan Sontag has written a powerful criticism against treating cancer as psychogenic in any way, and her argument for not blaming cancer patients for their dread illness is important in its own right, but I disagree with her overall thesis (Susan Sontag, *Illness as Metaphor* [New York: Farrar, Straus & Giroux, 1978]).

13. See Seligman, *Helplessness*.

14. See the section entitled "People Flee to Deaths, Little and Big" in Chapter 10.

15. Erich Fromm (*The Heart of Man: Its Genius for Good and Evil* [New York: Harper and Row, 1964]) has written about necrophilic personalities who seem to devote their very living to death. Rather than deferring death to its inevitable place at the end of life, these people call to it and place it at the center of their living experience. As Fromm describes them, these people are devotees of dirt, decay, and all things falling apart and putrid. They have never learned to affirm joyous aliveness. Instead they make death a fetish and vainly

attempt to feel alive by going all out for death. In the process, they are dangerous to life all about them. Fromm sees these people as deeply conditioned to their necrophilia. However, it may well be that they, too, are turning to death as a more certain, therefore less hurting, center for their experiencing after having originally embarked on life with a good many of the same wishes to be alive and feel alive as everyone else. Fromm may well be describing a group of people who demonstrate the extreme humans can be brought to or choose because of their deep fear of risk and/or their culture's emphasis on nonrisking, certainty, and banishing of life's anxiety. If this is true, then these necrophiles are no different from the rest of us in any intrinsic sense, but they have surrendered tragically to an extreme defense against life to the point where they become devotees of death.

16. Pearce and Newton, *Conditions of Human Growth*, p. 168.

17. Becker, *Denial of Death*, p. 85.

18. Kenneth Vaux has written in an important work on biomedical ethics: "The task of faithful men and human men today is to remind us of our mortality. The quest is noble — not for immortality but for wholeness; not for extraterrestrial escape but for ter-restrial responsibility. Man is born to die. . . . Theologically discerned, man's mortality, his conditionedness, is the clue to his destiny. . . . Theologically understood, death signals the meaning of life in its conditionedness and contingency. It is God's ultimate attraction of our energy" (Kenneth Vaux, *Biomedical Ethics* [New York: Harper and Row, 1964], p. 108).

NOTES TO CHAPTER 4: THE SOURCES OF HUMAN AGGRESSION

Epigraph from Abraham H. Maslow, "Some Fundamental Questions That Face the Normative Social Psychologist," *Journal Humanistic Psychology* 8 (1968), p. 147.

1. Obviously, many people, including mental health and political science professionals, use the word *aggression* to refer to hostile intentions and acts. However, I join the many thinkers who see aggression as vitality and energy and rely on other words to describe the applications of "aggression" in either constructive or destructive ways. See, for example, how psychoanalyst Leon Saul differentiates between aggression and hostility:

> What we mean by hostility is the tendency of an organism to do something harmful to another organism or to itself. It is not just aggression: aggression (from the Latin, meaning moving actively) may have a constructive meaning (as in getting a good job done), it need not be hostile, and, conversely, hostility need not be ag-gressive, it may be passively expressed. Nor is hostility anger, necessarily, for anger reflects a transient feeling which can be compatible with love. One can fully, without interruption and alteration, love someone despite periods of anger, as every husband, wife, child, parent and friend knows. . . . For hostility is the essential evil in people. Wrongness in personal and social behavior might well be judged by this touchstone: Is it *for* life, for the development adjustment, happiness and fulfillment of society and its individuals, or is it against it? [Leon J. Saul, *The Hostile Mind: The Sources and Consequences of Rage and Hate* (New York: Random House, 1956)]

A new edition of Saul's book, entitled *The Childhood Emotional Pattern and Human Hostility*, was published by Van Nostrand Reinhold, New York, 1980.

See also experimental psychologist Seymour Feshbach, who makes the point that even a violent act in itself does not tell us the full story of its underlying morality or im-morality.

The moral evaluation of a violent act is a function of the lawful status of the act, the extent of personal versus social motivation and the degree of personal responsibility as reflected in the role of authority, the options available to the individual, the defensive or initiated basis of the violence, the degree of emotional disturbance, the amount of force employed, and the intentionality of the act. To these criteria must be added normative considerations of fair play, the degree and manner of the violence, the age and sex of the victim, and, more generally, the appropriateness of the target. Last to be mentioned, but probably most important, is one's attitude towards the objectives of the violence. [Seymour Feshbach, "Dynamics and Morality of Violence and Aggression: Some Psychological Considerations," *American Psychologist* 26:3 (1971), p. 290]

It is wise always to check how each writer intends to use the word *aggression*. My own suggestion is that this time-honored word of human experience is best turned toward its meaning as a natural force and that we go from there toward further differentiations between good and bad applications of our energies.

2. Irenaus Eibl-Eibesfeldt, head of the Human Ethology Group at the Max Planck Institute for Behavioral Physiology in Germany, basically accepts the premise that a tendency toward aggression is inherent in man but stresses that mechanisms of appeasement and control are equally inherent in human nature, among them especially the mechanism of acquaintance, which makes the known person a friend and the unknown an enemy (Irenaus Eibl-Eibesfeldt, *Love and Hate: The Natural History of Behavior Patterns* [New York: Schocken, 1974]).

3. It is interesting to note how many electrical phenomena have been identified within the human body. Many important advances in medicine are based on the development of machinery for monitoring these electrical phenomena, for example, the electroencephalograph (EEG). There are, apparently, still further frontiers of man's electrical nature to be explored. Thus, some provocative findings are being reported that indicate there is not only an internal electrical environment within each person, but a series of electrical energy fields around organisms that influence the way they grow and function. See *Trend Report*, published by the Institute of Life Insurance in New York, issue 10 (1974) for a brief introduction to the possibilities of an aura surrounding living organisms and various medical researches that are being based on this phenomenon.

4. Helen Singer Kaplan, "Conflict-Intrapsychic Causes of Sexual Dysfunctions," in Kaplan, *The New Sex Therapy: Active Treatment of Sexual Dysfunctions* (New York: Brunner/Mazel, 1974), pp. 137–154, and Israel W. Charny, "How Does Marital Quarreling Affect Sexual Relations?" in Leonard Gross, ed., *Sexual Issues in Marriage: A Contemporary Perspective* (New York: Spectrum, 1975), pp. 121–123.

5. The basic concept of complementary or antagonistic opponent processes is one that appears frequently in many different areas of science. In the course of this and the next chapter, I will refer to several scientific and philosophical observations of the interplay of positive and negative forces in nature and the significance of such a model for interpreting many phenomena. An interesting example is found in the work of Leo Hurvich and Dorothea Jameson, which they presented in their Distinguished Scientific Contribution Award Address to the American Psychological Association in 1973. Hurvich and Jameson applied the principle of complementarities to problems of vision and neurological organization, and they commented about their use of such a model of "opponent processes."

We hope we have not given the impression that we believe the principle of opponent processes to be a newly discovered one in behavior or in physiology. We are, of course, well aware of the history of this general concept in human thought, whether in Hegelian philosophy, the dialectical materialism of Marx and Engels, Pavlovian excitation and inhibition, Sherrington's reflex control of muscle antagonists, matter and anti-matter in contemporary physics, or the fundamental Yin and Yang principle that permeates the Oriental point of view. A general principle, universally applied, usually becomes a useless cliche. But our point here is that the opponent process concept, used as a guiding principle in analyzing specific aspects of particular psychological phenomena, may continue to provide the most useful key to the behavior of the nervous system, as it has already proved to do in the analysis of particular visual phenomena. [Leo M. Hurvich and Dorothea Jameson, "Opponent Processes as a Model of Neural Organization," *American Psychologist* 29 (1974), pp. 100–101]

6. "The essence of the dialectical approach is a liberation of the mind from absolute concepts which in themselves claim to explain phenomena as though the opposite point of view did not exist. According to dialectical thought, a positive concept is always viewed in contrast with its opposite, in the hope that their joint consideration will yield a resolution through a more thorough and productive understanding. The principles of relativity and indeterminacy in physics and the concept of homeostatic regulations of living things are examples of increasingly dialectical orientations in natural sciences" (Ivan Boszormenyi-Nagy and Geraldine M. Spark, *Invisible Loyalties: Reciprocity in Intergenerational Family Therapy* [Hagerstown, Md.: Harper and Row, 1973], p. 18).

7. In his introduction to a journal issue devoted to violence and civil conflict, Lewis Coser writes:

The dialectical tension between order and disorder, between the making and the breaking of internal peace and harmony, are likely to characterize the future of mankind as they have characterized its past. Man's best hope is not the eradication of conflicts, for that is impossible, but rather their channeling and regulation, their domestication if you wish, so that their more destructive impact can be successfully minimized. A great poet once put this in two terse sentences when he wrote: "Without contraries is no progression. Attraction and Repulsion, Reason and Energy, Love and Hate, are necessary to human existence" (William Blake, *The Marriage of Heaven and Hell*). [Lewis A. Coser, "Introduction," in Coser, ed., *Collective Violence and Civil Conflict, Journal Social Issues* 28:1 (1972), p. 3]

8. In an intriguingly titled book, *Call No Man Normal* (New York: International Universities Press, 1973), Benjamin B. Wolman is concerned with how human beings develop what we call energy and how they direct this energy either toward life or toward the destruction of life. "As long as an organism is alive, its energies can be in two directions, either toward the promotion of life or towards its destruction. . . . *All living matter is endowed with biochemical energy derived from the universal energy that, in turn, as explained by Einstein, is a derivative of matter. At a certain evolutionary level this biochemical energy is transformed into mental energy. This mental energy serves survival. The apparatus of discharge, call it drive, instinct, or instinctual force, reflects the most universal urge to stay alive. It is the Lust for Life, the wonderful craving of all living matter to live*" (pp. 41, 77).

9. A discussion of how a steady state differs from a static, unchanging equilibrium is found in an excellent introductory book by Irma Stein, *Systems Theory, Science, and Social Work* (Metuchen, N.J.: Scarecrow, 1974). "The concept of steady state and the principle of equifinality . . . refutes the assumption of vitalists that living organisms follow different

laws than the laws of mechanical or closed systems. . . . Since there are continually altering fluxes of matter-energy and information in open systems, they tend to attain a steady state rather than a static, unchanging equilibrium. . . . This steady state of open system is characterized by the principle of equifinality, which means achieving identical results from different initial conditions" (pp. 12–13).

10. See, for example, Frank Farrel and Jeff Brandsma, *Provocative Therapy* (San Francisco: Shields, 1974).

11. According to an Associated Press report, an estimated 107 men may have died as the direct result of an experimental study of untreated syphilis. In the forty-year study conducted by the U.S. Public Health Service, at least 431 black men from Macon County, Alabama, "were denied treatment for syphilis so that PHS doctors could determine through eventual autopsy what damage the untreated disease had done to their body." Besides the high death rate, reports of the doctors in charge of the experiment "detail a grim series of side effects suffered by participants in the Tuskegee Study" (Associated Press, September 12, 1972).

12. Robert Lifton presented some of his as yet unpublished findings in an address to a conference on the Holocaust at Yad Vashem, Jerusalem, in September 1979.

13. In a discussion of "murder without motive," Rudiger Herren emphasizes that often the barrenness of inner experience is what drives the killer to murder in order to experience at least some emotional connection with people and the life process (Rudiger Herren, "Murder Without Motive," *Psychologische Runschau* 9 [1958], pp. 273–290).

Anatol Rapoport observes: "Cruelty is the property of deriving pleasure from the suffering of others, just as empathy is sharing the suffering of others or of experiencing distress from the suffering of others. The bill of particulars charging man with cruelty is long indeed, and perhaps it is true that man is the only really cruel animal. But this may be precisely because man is also the only animal capable of empathy, since both cruelty and empathy presuppose identification with the object of brutality or compassion. Cruelty and empathy are two sides of the same coin." (Anatol Rapoport, *Conflict in Man-made Environment* [Baltimore, Md.: Penguin, 1974], pp. 121–122).

14. Edrita Fried has described the "ego strengthening aspects of hostility." Fried notes how many deeply disturbed people need hostility as an essential ingredient in the mixture of their innermost emotions, even under conditions of accomplishment or success and offers of warmth, friendship, or sexuality; following an artistic experience, which stirs deep emotions; in group situations where they are exposed to a great deal of stimulation; and other ostensibly happy occasions. The common feature of these people is a form of ego weakness; they are frightened that they will not be able to maintain a sense of their separateness from people and things about them. The purpose of the hostility is to maintain an operative possibility of continuing to function as a separate entity (Edrita Fried, "Ego-Strengthening Aspects of Hostility," *American Journal Orthopsychiatry* 26 [1956], pp. 179–187).

15. In a fascinating study of surviving spouses who had murdered their mates, George Bach found that these marriages had been characterized by an absence of fighting and what he defined as "aggression phobia" (George R. Bach, "Thinging: A Subtheory of Intimate Aggression Derived from Spouse Killing," in "Symposium, Murder Within the Family," mimeographed [Presented at the annual meeting of the American Psychological Association, Washington, D.C., 1967]. The same work is cited in George R. Bach and Peter Wyden, *The Intimate Enemy* [New York: Morrow, 1969]).

The following excerpts are from a front page story by Anatol Wolf Holt in the *Philadelphia Bulletin*, June 5, 1959:

Dear People of Philadelphia:

I write to you this morning, at the rise of dawn, still in the midst of a tormented wake, of the most terrible grief which has ever seared my soul. Yesterday afternoon, on June 4th (as you most certainly read in the papers), I lost the most precious thing that life ever gave me—a 3-½-year-old girl child of surpassing purity and joy, a being profoundly close to the secret well springs of life itself—a closeness from which she derived great unconscious strength which made her irresistibly attractive to human beings with whom she came in contact. She was murdered in the afternoon, in the basement of a house only a few doors away from ours, by a 15-year-old boy. . . .

My letter to you is motivated by an irrepressible wish to contribute my share of understanding to what has taken place in the hope of thus slightly increasing our understanding for one another. The first important facts to which to draw attention are the facts about the boy who did the deed, and his family. So far as one could tell, the family was exemplary. In public appearance they have always been considerate and kind; their house has always seemed very well managed. People and property both, always gave the appearance of great tidiness. The daughter of the house—who is now studying nursing in Washington, D.C.—used to baby-sit for us last year, and always conformed to the highest standards of courtesy and efficiency. The boy himself, as you read in the papers, has also always given an excellent formal account of himself—honor student, gentle in manner, handsome, and all the rest.

How then, you will exclaim in horror, can all this good come to such an ill result? I would plead that it comes from a profound lack of comprehension and admission of the full range of feeling and emotion, which is our common human heritage, and which, for convenience's sake, we are so fond of denying. . . . We are wont to label everything which we prefer to stuff into a closet (even as was done to my child) as "inhuman." So, for example, did we speak of the Nazis with their indescribably horrible concentration camps. It is in this way that we permit ourselves to divide the fullness in each of our breasts into two dissociated parts—one part ascribed to the hero, the model boy, the ideal father, and the other part to the criminal, the deranged, the villain.

I am not—as you might wrongly conclude—suggesting that we are all fundamentally "bad" and should therefore spend our lives feeling guilty for what we are. I say instead that it should be openly recognized that every human being *must*, by his nature, express hostility, rage, fear, destructiveness, as well as love, creativeness in action, pure joy of life, and other generally recognized desirable responses. As in regard to the need for expressing these "positive" as well as "negative" responses, there is an iron-clad law according to which all that goes unexpressed will not thereby be eliminated, but will assert itself in often uncontrolled ways. . . . You will understand that I am not lecturing to you for the pure joy of sounding wise. I am hurt to the depths of my being, and I cry out to you to take better care of your children.

My final word has to do with the operation of the machinery of justice. Had I caught the boy in the act, I would have wished to kill him. Now that there is no undoing of what is done, I only wish to help him. Let no feelings of caveman vengeance influence us. Let us rather *help him* who did so *human* a thing.

A Sick Father

16. Silvano Arieti, "Manic-Depressive Psychosis," in Arieti, ed., *American Handbook Psychiatry*, vol. 1 (New York: Basic Books, 1959), see pp. 431–438.

17. In the traditional theory of psychoanalysis, narcissism is seen as the original and ultimately unwelcome level of baby-level selfishness, and the goal of personal maturity is to renounce such narcissism and attain a level of object love and love of others. Heinz Kohut's theoretical repositioning of narcissism describes the sequence of development as beginning from what is indeed a primitive level of self-love, but then the same self-love is transformed (not renounced) into empathy, creativity, wisdom, humor, and so on. The base remains one of a healthy self-love, not abandonment of self-love as in the original concept (Heinz Kohut, *The Analysis of the Self* [New York: International Universities Press, 1971]).

18. An interesting treatment of nightmares is found in John E. Mack's book, *Nightmares and Human Conflict* (New York: Basic Books, 1970). Mack suggests that when one dreams of an intense threat of danger to oneself, the aggression not only often bespeaks one's own aggression to the party one sees as threatening, but the intense threat that is directed at oneself may very well be an attempt to deflect the destruction from the other party so as to protect oneself from destroying the other. In effect, the nightmare can represent a *sacrifice* of the dreamer.

19. See Rollo May's beautiful treatment in *Power and Innocence: A Search for the Sources of Violence* (New York: Norton, 1972).

20. O. H. Mowrer, *The Crisis in Psychiatry and Religion* (Princeton: Van Nostrand, 1961); Saul, *The Hostile Mind*; William Glasser, *Reality Therapy* (New York: Harper, 1965).

21. Karen Horney, *The Neurotic Personality of Our Time* (New York: Norton, 1937); Karen Horney, *Self Analysis* (New York: Norton, 1942); Lionel Rubinoff, *The Pornography of Power* (New York: Ballantine, 1969).

22. There is also the dynamic of projecting onto the victim blame for being a victim. One very fascinating linkage is proposed by Rubin and Peplau to the effect that we blame victims for their plight because we need to sustain our otherwise insistent innocence that life is just and fair—hence, they must deserve what they're getting. "Everyone may have a version of the just world belief in early childhood (Piaget's 'immanent justice'), but some people outgrow the belief quickly and some apparently never do." The continued belief in a just world has been found to be related to a greater tendency to derogate victims ("they get what they deserve"), thus permitting the believers to sustain the myth that people are dealt with justly. "When such believers observe apparent instances of suffering, they are often prone to conclude that either (a) the suffering is not really taking place (or, at least, is greatly exaggerated) and/or (b) the victim is in fact blameworthy. For example, many Germans living under the Nazi regime either denied the fact of mass murders or else concluded that those who were sent to the death camps were members of an impure race who must have deserved their fates. Surveys conducted in the United States at the time indicated that far from evoking sympathy, the Nazi persecutions apparently evoked a rise in anti-Semitism" (Zick Rubin and Letitia Anne Peplau, "Who Believes in a Just World?" in Melvin J. Lerner, ed., *The Justice Motive in Social Behavior, Journal Social Issues* 31:3 [1975], pp. 66–67).

23. Robert Jay Lifton, *Home from the War—Vietnam Veterans: Neither Victims Nor Executioners* (New York: Simon & Schuster, 1973).

24. See, for example, the earlier reports of Drs. Shlomo and Shoshanna Kulcsar's examination of Adolf Eichmann (Chapter 2, text and n. 15). Henry Dicks studied imprisoned Nazi mass murderers (Chapter 2, n. 18), and he also describes the chronic process of brutalization. Chaim Shatan, who also worked with returning Vietnam veterans, describes how "for many combat veterans, the world of dead things remains their spiritual condition"

and how "psychological habitation to the torture of remote or faceless others occurred among United States civilians as well as among active duty military" (Chaim Shatan, "Genocide and Bereavement," in Richard Arens, ed., *Genocide in Paraguay* [Philadelphia: Temple University Press, 1978], citations from prepublication mimeographed text).

25. United Press International, March 11, 1976:

> Heidelberg, West Germany—Albert Speer, who organized the economy of conquered Europe for the German war effort, admitted yesterday that he knew of the Nazi extermination of Europe's Jews. But, he told an interviewer, he simply pushed the knowledge away out of a "cowardice" he now regrets. The 71-year-old Speer was speaking to promote the second volume of the memoirs he composed during his 20 years in jail for war crimes—a volume that stresses the "warm, human qualities" of many Nazi criminals. . . . As to the murder of European Jewry, "I knew what was happening," Speer said. "I did not know it directly by Hitler telling me or saying in my presence that there was an action to kill the Jews. But I knew how Hitler was and how decided he was when he had something in his mind. So, I knew."
>
> Why did he do nothing to stop the annihilation of the Jews? "It was many things coming together," Speer said. "The main thing was this adaptation one has when one is working so long in such a system with a man like Hitler. One gets really used to cruelties. . . . All of these things I heard and I knew. But to go on existing self-consciously one just pushes those things aside and says, well, it's not me who makes the decisions. Of course, it is cowardice and I am ashamed of it nowadays, that it was so, but it would be wrong not to tell people that such a reaction is possible, also among the generals, who were listening to him, too."

26. Kenneth Vaux, *Biomedical Ethics* (New York: Harper and Row, 1964), p. 97.

27. Sigmund Freud, *An Outline of Psychoanalysis* (New York: Norton, 1938), p. 21. Quotation and citation from an article by Benjamin B. Wolman, "Human Belligerence," *International Journal Group Tensions* 2:1 (1972), pp. 48–66.

28. An intriguing treatment of positive and negative aggression is to be found in the work of psychologist Carl Frankenstein, who also treats the origins of destructive energy as embedded within the very formation of natural aggression. Frankenstein traces the development of aggression to the interrelationship of what he considers the two basic life drives of expansion and staticness. Healthy or positive aggression is the ability to break up or tear down existing wholes and to build or reorganize new levels of organization. The two processes work hand in hand, hence the "uninterrupted continuity attaching to any process of normal development, growth or change." Pathological or negative aggressiveness is brought about by a relative disruption of the normal interrelatedness of expansion and staticness and an exaggeration of either dimension of life unbalanced by the other (Carl Frankenstein, *The Roots of the Ego: A Phenomenology of Dynamics and of Structure* [Baltimore, Md.: William & Wilkins, 1966], p. 126).

Distinguished psychoanalyst Roy R. Grinker, Sr., has similarly suggested that on a societal level, the polarities that yield the greater understanding are those of personal or individual freedom versus social structures that maintain, regulate, and control. What Frankenstein refers to as expansion and staticness, Grinker calls on the societal levels freedom and regulation. "I believe that we are witnessing at all levels of our social network a conflict based on dualistic thinking, the polarities of which are personal or individual freedom as against social structures maintaining the functions of regulation and control. Each has moved speedily and quantitatively to become antagonistic and reactionary to the other. The greater the demand for freedom, the more repressive measures are set into action. The more restrictive controls to dampen freedoms, the more protest and violence as the final common pathway of many causes" (Roy. R. Grinker Sr., "What Is the Cause of Violence?" in Jan Fawcett, ed., *Dynamics of Violence* [Chicago: American Medical Association, 1971], p. 64).

29. In Freud's writing, where Eros and Thanatos are not joined in life-death battle and the two do join forces (as Freud indicates they do in any number of complex human behaviors), the combined, integrated impact is largely seen as pathological. In a major treatment of the concept of human belligerence, Benjamin Wolman reviews Freud's thinking and notes how for Freud, fusions of love and aggression underlie many features of pathology in sexual life, such as sadism and masochism. At the same time, it is our sense of Freud's writings—which in their own right represent a powerful developmental process with changes and elaborations over the course of that great thinker's work—that there is also a quality of integrity and energy potential attributed to the fusion of the positive and the negative. This positive energy is implied in the very emphasis on the pathology of disturbed fusions. Thus, Freud would see the differences between an overly shy or impotent person or a lover or a sexual murderer as differences in the extent to which aggressiveness intermixes with sexuality ("a surplus of sexual aggressiveness will change a lover into a murderer"). The implications of such thinking are that there must be an optimal point where a healthy blending of just enough aggressiveness and just enough sexuality makes for a good all-around lover.

Certainly this is the direction in which most psychoanalytical observation and thinking has gone on from the beginnings of Freud. Without any doubt, we are drawing from Freud's thinking when we work with the concept that the ways in which we mix the contradictory sides of ourselves make an enormous difference ("modifications in the proportions of the fusions between the instincts have the most noticeable results"). Actually, who precisely said what and when in the long run isn't that important, nor is it crucial that we account exactly for the boundary lines between our present metaphor and the previous contributions. Although science and scholarship do call for responsible awareness of how a sequence of ideas builds, trying to say exactly who said what first often is actually an exercise in ritualism and a narcissism of trying to prove that we are doing something new and worthwhile. Whether this or that aspect of the metaphor is truly new or old matters far less than whether the proposed model might help us to move forward in our struggle to think about man's destructiveness more effectively (quotations from Freud are from Wolman, "Human Belligerence"; Freud's position on the fusions of love and aggression in pathology is in Sigmund Freud, *New Introductory Lectures in Psychoanalysis* [New York: Norton, 1933], p. 21).

30. Erich Fromm, *The Anatomy of Human Destructiveness* (New York: Holt, Rinehart and Winston, 1973), p. 235. For Fromm's analyses of different forms of violence, see pp. 24–36.

NOTES TO CHAPTER 5: THE INTEGRATION OF "GOOD" AND "BAD" IN HEALTHY AGGRESSION

Second and third epigraphs from Charles Drekmeier, "Knowledge as Virtue, Knowledge as Power," in Nevitt Sanford and Craig Comstock, eds., *Sanctions for Evil* (San Francisco: Jossey Bass, 1971), pp. 242–243, and Erich Neumann, *Depth Psychology and a New Ethic* (New York: Putnam's, 1969), pp. 45, 147.

1. Ernest Becker, a profound theorist of life and death, also attaches the integration of these basic experiences to the emergence of one's ethical qualities. A book that addresses

the issue of evil directly is Ernest Becker, *Escape from Evil* (New York: Free Press, 1975).

2. In Thomas P. McDonnel, ed., *A Thomas Merton Reader* (New York: Harcourt, Brace & World, 1962), p. 349.

3. Granted, the meanings of terms on one level of behavior are not exactly the same as on the next level. Inner good and bad on the level of basic forces of power are not the same as good and bad overt acts in life. Still, it is often legitimate to use the same terms to represent an evolving continuity from more elemental to more complex levels of essentially the same process. In no event are the metaphors proposed as descriptions of tangible aspects of man's physical reality.

Here is as good a place as any to remark on the critical importance not only of hypotheses in science, but also of fictions or constructs, which are designed to help scientists study processes and solve problems so long as the scientist realizes fully that he or she is working with metaphoric fictions. In *The Philosophy of 'As If'* (London: Routledge & Kegan Paul, 1968; original edition, 1924), H. Vaihinger points out how the acceptance of such fictions as the atom in physics and the zero in mathematics have made possible significant developments. There are, of course, many other references to the role of constructs or fictions in psychology and in the philosophy of all sciences, and we need not belabor them here.

4. Gustav Bychowski, *Evil in Man: The Anatomy of Hate and Violence* (New York: Grune & Stratton, 1968), pp. 75, 76, 79.

5. Not all humanistic psychologists limit themselves to the conception that man is naturally good, but many of them do hold entirely to that viewpoint, and some emphasize freeing man's potential wholeness and goodness so strongly that for all practical purposes, they are taking the position that badness need not be an issue in human beings' lives so long as people are able to fulfill their realness and potential. The one-sidedness of this emphasis, which is easily seen in the programs of meetings of humanistic psychologists as well as in their journals, has led to a ground swell of criticism by thoughtful humanistic psychologists, along with criticisms of other "pagan" qualities of the human potential movement, such as implied or actual promises of "short methods" or "rapid paths" to personal fulfillment and emotional health. Thus, Larry LeShan writes: "Even in Zen, where we are constantly treated to the idea that solving a koan causes us to tremble, burst into profuse perspiration, and be 'enlightened,' the lesson is plain if we simply turn the page. We then see that the Zen student is given another koan, goes back to work, and that there is no further talk of his having arrived somewhere. He had only made some slight progress on the life-long, never-ending road. How strange it is that we have not learned that there is no easy way" (Larry LeShan, "The Achievement Ethic and the Human Potential Movement," *Newsletter of the Association of Humanistic Psychology*, July 1975, p. 13).

So, too, Eleanor Hoover, in an award-winning summary of the humanistic psychology movement for the *Los Angeles Times*, quotes one of its leaders, Sam Keen, as favoring "a more 'Zen, homogenized way of living . . . some neurotics reach the point where they need peak experience all the time'" (Eleanor Hoover, "New Psychology," *Newsletter of the Association of Humanistic Psychology*, August 1975, p. 12).

6. David Rosenhan attempted to differentiate between personalities of those subjects in the Milgram experiment who were obedient and those who were not, but he was unsuccessful (David Rosenhan, Address in a panel on "Psychosocial Design for Nonviolent Change" at the annual meeting of the American Orthopsychiatric Association, Washington, D.C., 1971).

The only information I have found that successfully differentiates those people in the Milgram experiment who are obedient and those who are not comes from the exciting work of Lawrence Kohlberg (see Chapter 6, text and n. 15). Subjects in a Milgram study were scored on the Kohlberg scale of moral development. Seventy-five percent of those who scored on the highest level—where value is placed on human life, equality, and dignity—refused to complete the shock process, whereas only 13 percent of those who scored on lower levels did not agree to go the full punishing route of shocking the subject. Since Kohlberg's scale is, fundamentally, a statement of the natural sequence of development through which all human beings must evolve, to whatever stage of development they reach, these results do not differentiate absolutely between different groups or types of people, but they do give us a way of measuring what level of development people reach. There is a potential for violence in all of us, but some people can develop into nondestructive people given their successful growth or evolution (Lawrence Kohlberg, "Education for Justice: A Modern Statement of the Platonic View," Ernest Burton Lecture on Moral Education, Harvard University, April 23, 1968 [mimeographed]).

7. Erich Fromm, *The Heart of Man: Its Genius for Good and Evil* (New York: Holt, Rinehart and Winston, 1964), p. 123.

8. The Israeli government has taken a clear-cut position against the killing of civilians. See, for example, the story of the trial of Israeli soldiers who did murder Arab civilians who innocently violated a military curfew during wartime. The court ruled: "These acts were not simply manslaughter, but constitute acts of homicide in the full sense of the word. . . . *Every officer and soldier is obligated by the knowledge that his weapons are intended for war against the enemy and not for murder of non-combatant civilians. The eight accused have stained the honor of Israel's armed forces"* (Moshe Kordov, *The Kefar Kassim Trial* [Tel Aviv: Narkis, 1959], p. 255, in Hebrew). The Israelis, like all people, are not exempt from the potential to be murderers, but the record shows they struggle actively against that potential. A powerful literary document that describes the potential seduction of Israeli soldiers to war crimes is Aharon Meged's short story, "The White City," in James A. Michener, ed., *First Fruits: A Harvest of 25 Years of Israeli Writing* (Greenwich, Conn.: Fawcett, 1973), pp. 123–190.

9. Ernest Becker goes further than most in his interpretation of Freud. Becker suggests that the meaning of Freud's solution of the death instinct (the organism's desire to die) through its fusion with the life instinct is that "the desire to die, then, is replaced by the desire to kill, and man defeats his own death instinct by killing others." However, Becker also goes on to acknowledge that Freud's formulations on the death instinct are "tortuous" and that "he seems to have been unable to reach for the really direct existentialist level of explanation" (Ernest Becker, *The Denial of Death* [New York: Free Press, 1973], p. 98). See chapter 9, section on "Death: The Ultimate Vulnerability," for Becker's citation of Rank's more decisive explanation of this dynamic.

10. Albert Einstein and Sigmund Freud, "An Exchange of Letters on the Subject of Why There Is War, 1932," reprinted in *International Journal Group Tensions* 1 (1971), p. 19.

11. This theme is developed in various places throughout the book. See, among others, citations of George R. Bach and Peter Wyden, *The Intimate Enemy* (New York: Morrow, 1969); Israel W. Charny, *Marital Love and Hate* (New York: Macmillan, 1972); and Selma H. Fraiberg, "The Origin of Human Bonds," *Commentary* 44 (December 1957), pp. 47–57.

12. Here are two commonplace examples of news stories that describe the contradiction that is built into extreme denial of aggression:

BIBLE-CARRYING YOUTH HELD AS GIRL'S SLAYER
Hackensack, N.J.—An 18-year-old youth who always carried a Bible in his pocket was charged with murder here yesterday. [Associated Press, May 27, 1957]

'MODEL BOY' ADMITS ROBBERY KILLING

Los Angeles – 16-year-old . . . is the son of a civic leader and school principal in suburban Norwalk. The youth is an Explorer Scout, attends church regularly and works after school in a supermarket for spending money. . . . Sheriff's deputies yesterday told a shocked father the boy is a killer and a member of a teen-age gang of liquor store robbers. "This murder thing is so unbelievable I don't know what to say – and so out of character," said the father. [Associated Press, January 8, 1958]

See also the touching letter of a father in Chapter 4, n. 15, and the references in Chapter 13, n. 20, to the work of Edwin Megargie on the violence of people who are too cut off from the naturalness of their aggressive emotions.

13. Rollo May, *Power and Innocence* (New York: Norton, 1973), p. 232.

14. S. M. Silverman, "Conflict Avoidance and Resolution: Problems and Prospects," *International Journal Group Tensions* 3:3–4 (1973), p. 128. It is an enjoyable intellectual task to put together various attempts to formulate a concept of an integrated reality or process of good and bad in the philosophical and psychological literatures. On the one hand, there are many such attempts, but on the other hand we are clearly only at the beginning of developing such an understanding. We are certainly far from having either a systematic orientation or a language that teaches us how to see good and bad as parts of a single whole, with each as intrinsically valuable as the other.

William Mountcastle, Jr., approaches this issue in the course of examining the relevance of various religious traditions to contemporary ecological problems. He notes that the cosmological model that appears in the famous *I Ching* [Book of changes] only appears to be dualistic; when it is understood in the light of Taoist philosophy, "we see that it is really a monistic metaphysics. The great *Tao*, 'beyond shapes and features,' produces and sustains the phenomenal realm of nature which appears as dialectical processes of birth, growth, disease, death and decay. That the Universe is an eternal cyclic process manifested in the precarious and delicate balance between man and nature is the dominant theme of *Tao hsueh*" (William W. Mountcastle, Jr., "The Ecological Problem from the Perspective of Comparative Religion," abstracted in *International Humanism* 1 [1974], p. 5).

A powerful differentiation between the "old ethic" and the "new ethic" is developed by Jungian psychologist Erich Neumann:

> The old ethic is, basically, dualistic. It envisages a contrasted world of light and darkness, divides existence into two hemispheres of pure and impure, good and evil, God and the devil, and assigns man his proper task in the context of this dualistically driven universe. . . . The individual is now essentially split into a world of values, with which he is required to identify himself, and a world of anti-values which are a part of his nature and can in fact be overwhelmingly strong, and which oppose the world of consciousness and values in the shape of the powers of darkness.
>
> The dualism of the old ethic, which is especially marked in its Iranian, Judaeo-Christian and Gnostic forms, divides both man, the world, and the Godhead into two tiers – an upper and a lower one, an upper and a lower world, a God and a Devil. This dichotomy is effective on the practical level in spite of all philosophical, religious or meta-physical declarations of ultimate monism. The actual situation of Western man has been essentially conditioned by this dichotomy right up to the present day. . . .

The new brand is based on an attempt to become conscious of both the positive and the negative forces in the human organism and to relate these forces consciously to the life of the individual and the community. . . . The main function of the new ethic is to bring about a process of integration, and its first aim is to make the dissociated components, which are hostile to the individual's programme for living, capable of integration. The juxtaposition of opposites which makes up the totality of the world of experience can no longer be resolved by the victory of one side and the repression of the other, but only a synthesis of these opposites. [Erich Neumann, *Depth Psychology and a New Ethic* (New York: Putnam's, 1969), pp. 44–45, 94, 101]

In a remarkable though entirely brief statement that is very much in the vein of the metaphor of aggression described earlier, Neumann writes: "Out of the multitude of conflicting forces, the plurality of the opposites, a structure has to be built which will combine these opposing forces, and in which the manifold diversity of the pairs of the opposites will be held together in the firm embrace of a supra-ordinated unity. The value of the structure which is finally achieved will be proportionate to the strength of the tension between the combined opposites and the number of the polar forces which enter into the new combination" (p. 101).

An exciting development in modern psychology and psychiatry toward the synthesis of opposite characteristics of humans is represented in the work of Italian psychiatrist Roberto Assagioli, who described his approach as "psychosynthesis." Assagioli sees psychological health, like biological health, as a dynamic equilibrium that is ever threatened and ever restored between a series of polarities.

> *Psychological life can be regarded as a continued polarization and tension between different tendencies and functions, and as a continual effort, conscious or not, to establish equilibrium.* Among the most important psychological polarities are: impulse-inhibition, feeling-reason, extraversion-introversion. . . . The dynamism of their fusion brings about the birth of a new organism. . . . In the fields of drives, emotions and feelings, the balancing of opposite qualities requires the intervention of a higher regulating principle of a mental or transpersonal nature. The first task is to prevent the drives and the emotions from overwhelming and submerging the reason and the will. The best way to achieve this is to learn how to disidentify oneself from them at will, in order to be free at any time to maintain the "I," the center of consciousness, on a higher level above them, in order to be able to observe and evaluate them, and to wisely regulate them as needed. [Roberto Assagioli, *The Balancing and Synthesis of the Opposites* (New York: Psychosynthesis Research Foundation, 1972), pp. 5–8]

Thus, Assagioli poses as a model of "equilibrated human force" the integration of poles of weakness and violence into spiritual energy.

15. See Johan Galtung, "Theories of Peace: A Synthetic Approach to Peace Thinking," mimeographed (Oslo: University of Oslo, 1967).

16. See Chapter 2, n. 15.

17. Jay Haley, *Strategies of Psychotherapy* (New York: Grune & Stratton, 1963), pp. 161–162.

18. R. D. Laing, *The Politics of the Family* (New York: Vintage, 1972), p. 124.

19. Obviously, much of the traditional psychotherapy literature on psychosomatic problems involves learning to control energy commitment to various psychophysiological functions. In the matter of sexual energies, for example, the work of Karl Abraham, early in

the history of psychoanalysis, includes a brilliant penetration into the configuration of underlying emotions or mind habits of the premature ejaculator, and in modern days we see a more behavioral-management approach to the same problem in the seminal work of Masters and Johnson. So too with just about any other psychophysiological function (Karl Abraham, "Ejaculatio praecox," in *Selected Papers of Karl Abraham* [New York: Basic Books, 1957], pp. 280-298 [original publication of essay in 1917]; William H. Masters and Virginia E. Johnson, *Human Sexual Inadequacy* [Boston: Little, Brown, 1970]). Recent studies of biofeedback illustrate dramatic new technologies for gaining mastery over autonomic nervous system functions that previously could be reached only through tedious (though otherwise exciting and potentially meaningful in larger ways) psychoanalytic therapies.

20. See, for example, a series of cassettes on biofeedback treatment techniques for alleviation of pain, inducing relaxation and the treatment of hypertension, sleep disorder, circulatory disorder, headaches, and other problems: John V. Basmajian and Johann Stoyva, eds. *Biofeedback Techniques in Clinical Practice*, vols. 1-2, each ten cassettes by different clinicians (Bio-Monitoring Applications, 270 Madison Ave., New York 10016, 1975-1976).

21. See, for example, the beautiful book by Erich Fromm, *The Forgotten Language* (New York: Random House, 1955). See also I. S. Kulcsar, "The Education of the Psychotherapist Through the Medium of Psychodrama," *British Journal Social Psychiatry and Community Health* 6:1 (1972), pp. 20-25.

22. Sidney M. Jourard, *The Transparent Self* (New York: D. Van Nostrand, 1964).

23. Philip P. Hallie, "Sadean and Institutional Cruelty," in Frances F. Korten, Stuart W. Cook, and John I. Lacey, eds., *Psychology and the Problems of Society* (Washington, D.C.: American Psychological Association, 1970), p. 303. See also Philip P. Hallie, *The Paradox of Cruelty* (Middletown, Conn.: Wesleyan University Press, 1969).

24. See Israel W. Charny, "And Abraham Went to Slay Isaac: A Parable of Killer, Victim, and Bystander in the Family of Man," *Journal Ecumenical Studies* 10:2 (1973), pp. 304-318.

25. In a discussion of socialist thinking and efforts to define the proper "antithesis" to prevailing social problems, Vadim Belotserkovsky observes: "The pathological death wish results, in my opinion, from the fear of death, the fear of seeing time run out—moreover, from the life/death duality. . . . Whereas one man may espouse the 'antithesis' in the name of life, in the name of love, another does so in the name of destruction and death. Both may be found equally guilty of carrying the antithesis to apocalyptic extremes" (Vadim Belotserkovsky, "The Destructive Pendulum of Extremes," *Humanist*, July/August 1975, p. 33).

26. The concept that emerging human consciousness includes people's ability to choose their own evolutionary future, rather than being swept along deterministically by evolution, has been developed most powerfully by Sir Julian Huxley. In a day of tribute to Huxley convened by the New York Society for Ethical Culture, Gerald Piel, publisher of the *Scientific American*, spoke of Huxley's teaching of the connection between evolution and ethics. Quoting Sir Julian:

> Biological or organic evolution has at its upper end been merged into and largely succeeded by conscious or social evolution. . . . Insofar as the mechanism of Evolution ceases to be blind and automatic and becomes conscious, ethics can be ejected into the evolutionary process. Before man, that process was merely amoral. After his emergence onto life's stage it became possible to introduce faith, courage, love of truth, goodness—in a word, moral purpose—into Evolution. . . . Evolution, after a thousand million years of blind and automatic operation, has finally

generated purpose as one of the attributes of our own species. . . . Man's ethics and his moral aspiration have now become an integral part of any future. [*International Humanism* 2/3 (1975), pp. 16–17]

27. Lewis A. Coser, "Some Social Functions of Violence," in Marvin E. Wolfgang, ed., *Patterns of Violence, Annals of the American Academy of Political and Social Science* 364 (1966), pp. 8–18.

28. A useful discussion of the problem of violence by revolutionaries will be found in Henry Bienen, *Violence and Social Change* (Chicago: University of Chicago Press, 1968).

29. According to Arthur Kovacs:

There is a growing body of literature and empirical investigation all suggesting that the entire sweep of human existence is organized in terms of periodic developmental crises which must be mastered by the growing human psyche so that the next higher stage of existence might be entered. A period of rest and consolidation then occurs. But after a time, the new identity, the new work activities, the new value system, the new human relationships characteristic of the era become stale. The life begins to go out of them. Like the snake, the human organism retreats into a kind of depressed, preoccupied premonitory molting phase. And after a sufficient period of preparation, once again primordial change, accompanied by great angst, wild mood swings, and some decompensation in previous regularities in behavior ensues. The person thus dying gives birth to the person yet becoming. And so the seasons of the human life then rest and recycle. [Arthur Kovacs, in *Psychotherapy* (*Bulletin of the Division of Psychotherapy of the American Psychological Association*), July 1975, p. 4]

30. Veteran psychopathologist Joseph Zubin of the New York State Psychiatric Institute has written recently that a better interpretation of schizophrenia, even when of the chronic variety, should not center around a disease process, or even the episode itself, but around the basic vulnerability of the patient to become disturbed at various times in his life. "A good deal of controversy has been engendered by attacks on the model that considers mental disorders as diseases. . . . By shifting our view of a person as suffering from a continuing mental disorder to suffering from a temporary episode, and further by regarding him as *vulnerable* rather than as *diseased*, much of this controversy ought to become superfluous" (Joseph Zubin, "Vulnerability – A New View of Schizophrenia," *Clinical Psychologist* [Newsletter of the Division of Clinical Psychology of the American Psychological Association], Fall 1975, p. 16).

31. Rollo May, *The Meaning of Anxiety* (New York: Ronald, 1950); Benjamin B. Wolman, *Call No Man Normal* (New York: International Universities Press, 1973), pp. 68–99.

32. For an excellent summary of data as to which children grow up to be altruists, activists, and nonviolent shapers of the future, see Elise Boulding, "The Child and Nonviolent Social Change," in Israel W. Charny, ed., *Strategies Against Violence* (Boulder, Colo.: Westview, 1978), pp. 68–99.

33. An interesting study of the characteristics of unusually peaceful societies will be found in Matthew Melko, *52 Peaceful Societies* (Oakville, Ont.: Canadian Peace Research Institute Press, 1973). British anthropologist Geoffrey Gorer has written fascinatingly of

a few societies where men seem to find no pleasure in dominating over, hurting or killing the members of other societies, where all they ask is to be at peace and to be left in peace. . . . Among these gentle societies are the Arapesh of New Guinea . . .

the Lepchas of Sikkim in the Himalayas (whom I studied), and, the most impressive of all, the pygmies of the Ituri rainforest in the Congo. . . . What seem to me the most significant common traits in these peaceful societies are that they all manifest enormous gusto for concrete physical pleasures – eating, drinking, sex, laughter – and that they all make very little distinction between the ideal characters of men and women, particularly that they have no ideal of brave, aggressive masculinity. . . . When the tribes are broken, individuals, unsupported by the traditional ethics, might easily revert to rat-pack mentality. . . . Nevertheless, they may offer a paradigm of ways to diminish the joy of killing in the uninhibited human race. [Geoffrey Gorer, "Man Has No 'Killer' Instinct," *New York Times Magazine*, November 27, 1966]

34. For example, there are fascinating comparative data on the rate of suicide in different societies. An especially intriguing subset of data concerns the different rates of suicide in the three Scandinavian countries – Denmark, Norway, and Sweden. The suicide rates in Denmark and Sweden are comparatively high; the suicide rate in Norway is comparatively low. Some social theorists propose as an explanation of these intriguing data that the underlying psychosocial basis for the high suicide rate in Sweden derives from a constant emphasis on performance and the pain that attaches to a failure to perform, together with a culturewide orientation toward child rearing as a chore and emphasis on avoiding expressions of anger. These pressures combine to build a pattern that gives people a sense of being trapped with terrible feelings of rage and shame for which they have no outlet. In Denmark, child rearing is approached much more happily, but there is still a heavy burden of guilt attached to expressions of aggression. In Norway, anger is much more open, and so there is less repression and internationalization of aggression. In fact, in Norway, one is prone to see oneself as the injured party and to nurse one's anger (see H. Hendin, *Suicide and Scandinavia* [New York: Grune & Stratton, 1964], in James D. Page, *Psychopathology: The Science of Understanding Deviance* [Chicago: Aldine-Atherton, 1971], pp. 258–259).

NOTES TO CHAPTER 6: DESTRUCTION IN THE QUEST FOR LIFE

Epigraph from Robert A. Clark, "Psychiatrists and Psychoanalysts on War," *American Journal Psychotherapy* 19 (1965), pp. 554, 556.

1. Israel W. Charny, "The New Psychotherapies and Encounters of the Seventies: Progress or Fads?" *Humanist*, May-June and July-August 1974; Morton P. Lieberman, Irvin D. Yalom, and Matthew B. Miles, *Encounter Groups: First Facts* (New York: Harrow [Harper] 1970); Lawrence N. Solomon and Betty Berzon, eds., *New Perspectives in Encounter Groups* (San Francisco: Jossey Bass, 1972).

2. Albert Bandura, "Behavior Theory and the Models of Man," *American Psychologist* 29 (1974), p. 861.

3. J. Glenn Gray's description of the battle experience and its "enduring appeal" has rapidly become a classic. In an introduction to a reprint of his book, *The Warriors: Reflections on Men in Battle* (New York: Harper and Row, 1967), Hannah Arendt observes, "Among the great merits of the book is that it makes opposition to war forceful and convincing by not denying the realities and by not just warning us but making us understand why 'there is in many today as great a fear of a sterile and unexciting peace as of a great war'" (p. xii). Gray is exciting reading as he describes the passion and lust and love that accompany war. The appeal of a certain love "is always greatest when destruction is close at

hand and threatening to overwhelm us. . . . The delight in destruction is its complete antagonist: therefore, we ought not to be surprised that love as concern is most impressive in time of conflict" (pp. 87–88).

4. Following the Yom Kippur War, an unusual case was reported in Israel of a patient who had been hospitalized "in virtually every psychiatric facility in the area without significant improvement in his condition." When the war broke out, he was on leave from the hospital, and he was mobilized the first day. He served successfully in an artillery unit with only an occasional rest, whereas prior to the war he had ceased to function completely. The patient's "recovery" lasted as long as the war, following which he again collapsed and began a new series of hospitalizations (see Avner Falk and Ruth Mann, "War as Therapy," in Abstracts of the International Conference on Psychological Stress and Adjustment in Time of War and Peace [Tel Aviv University, January 1975], p. 110).

5. In a fascinating review of many systemic theories of conflict ("from the mystical idealism of Hegel to the austere materialism of Marx, from the pacificism of Richardson to the sadistic enthusiasm of Kahn"), contemporary scientist-philosopher, Anatol Rapoport concludes that all of them point to the same conclusion: "The 'psychology' of the system may be entirely independent of the psychology of its human components. If this conclusion is correct, we need not search the human psyche for attributes that explain the murderous tendencies of certain forms of human organizations" (Anatol Rapoport, Conflict in Man-made Environment [Baltimore; Md.: Penguin, 1974], p. 173).

6. Ernest Becker, The Denial of Death (New York: Free Press, 1973), pp. 26–27.

7. Rollo May, The Meaning of Anxiety (New York: Ronald, 1950).

8. The concept of an "empty center" is, of course, related to the ultimate truth of the nothingness or death that we all face, hence the continuing vulnerability of man throughout life. But it is also the ultimate truth of our aliveness that the reality we experience in life is so huge and majestic that none of us can possibly encompass it or do justice to its many-faceted invitations and challenges (see J.F.T. Bugental, The Search for Authenticity: An Existential Analytic Approach to Psychotherapy [New York: Holt, Rinehart and Winston, 1965], pp. 401–402; Rollo May, "Contributions of Existential Psychotherapy," in Rollo May, Ernest Angel and Henri F. Ellenberger, eds., Existence: A New Dimension in Psychiatry and Psychology [New York: Basic Books, 1958], pp. 37–91; Ernest Becker, "Human Character as a Vital Lie," in Becker, Denial of Death, Chapter 4, pp. 47–66).

9. Israel W. Charny, "Injustice and Betrayal as Natural Experiences in Family Life," Psychotherapy: Theory, Research, and Practice 9 (1972), pp. 86–91.

10. Commenting on Hall's The Meaning of Dreams (New York: Dell, 1959), Robinson writes:

> Calvin S. Hall, Jr., of Western Reserve University collected 10,000 dreams. . . .
> To be certain that he obtained a faithful picture of our national dream life, he carefully screened out mental patients and people with severe psychoneurosis. The chief emotion expressed in dreams, according to Dr. Hall, is hostility. Unfriendly or even murderous dream acts outnumbered friendly or loving dream acts by almost three to one. Only 2 percent of the hostile dreams involved actual homicide, but in 63 percent of dreams violent acts were performed or hostile feelings experienced. The friendly dreams were mild by comparison. [Leonard Wallace Robinson, "What We Dream – and Why," New York Times Magazine, February 15, 1959, pp. 52–60]

11. Donald W. Winnicott, Collected Papers: Through Pediatrics to Psychoanalysis (London: Tavistock, 1958), and Donald W. Winnicott, The Maturational Processes and the

Facilitating Environment: Studies in the Theory of Emotional Development (New York: International Universities Press, 1965). An excellent critical review of Winnicott's thinking is presented by David Holbrook, "The Wizard and the Critical Flame: Implications About Moral Growth from the Work of D. W. Winnicott," *Psychiatry and Social Science Review* 4:5 (1970), pp. 2–16. Holbrook suggests that we do not have to make children moral because morality is not rooted in reason, which is the level on which we educate for the most part, but in the original experience stream, especially of the child's ability to fuse loving and hating. The child who is confident that he is a loving and constructive person, even when he hates, will be a moral person.

12. This is also the problem of many reform movements that state that they will not be in any way evil, aggrandizing, or exploitive as their enemy has been. Randall Collins has written about a comparative sociology of violence: "Most of the major humanitarian reform movements of the modern era, above all Marxism, but also to a lesser degree piece-meal reformisms, are especially prone to ascetic cruelties. Their very universalisms and their intense mobilization makes it easy; wherever their gaze is turned outwards towards their enemies, and not inwards towards their own dangers, it becomes all the more likely" (Randall Collins, "Three Faces of Cruelty: Towards a Comparative Sociology of Violence," *Theory and Society* 1:4 [1974], p. 436).

13. Israel W. Charny, "The Psychotherapist as Teacher of an Ethic of Nonviolence," *Voices: The Art and Science of Psychotherapy* 3 (1967), pp. 57–66.

14. Ibid.

15. Lawrence Kohlberg, "Moral Education in the Schools: A Developmental Review," *School Review* 74 (1966), pp. 1–30, and Lawrence Kohlberg, "The Child as a Moral Philosopher," *Psychology Today* 2 (September 1968), pp. 24–30. Kohlberg describes six stages of moral development: primitive orientation to physical and material punishments and rewards (stage one); a hedonistic orientation – you scratch my back and I'll scratch yours (stage two); "good boy" orientation where morality is defined by ties of relationship (stage three); an orientation to the authority of law and duty (stage four); only relatively few people reach the higher levels of development where emphasis is first on the social contract of equality and mutual obligation (stage five); then, finally, a morality of individual principles of conscience where the highest value is placed on human life (stage six).

Erik Erikson also postulates that an ethical core is built into all of us phylogenetically. This ethical core evolves in a step-by-step development through increasingly differentiated stages whose final outcome is an ethic that all human beings owe one another the opportunity to maximize the possibilities of everyone's development (Erik H. Erikson, *Life History and the Historical Moment* [New York: Norton, 1975]).

16. D. W. Winnicott has written brilliantly and touchingly about the inevitability of the mother's hatred of the child. *"The mother hates the baby before the baby hates the mother, and before the baby can know his mother hates him."* Winnicott offers a representative list of many ways in which babies necessarily frustrate their mothers and thereby evoke the mother's hatred:

The baby is danger to her body in pregnancy and at birth.

The baby is an interference with her private life, a challenge to preoccupation.

To a greater or lesser extent a mother feels that her own mother demands a baby, so that her baby is produced to placate her mother.

The baby hurts her nipples even by suckling, which is at first a chewing activity.

He is ruthless, treats her as scum, an unpaid servant, a slave.

She has to love him, excretions and all, at any rate at the beginning, till he has doubts about himself.

He tries to hurt her, periodically bites her, all in love.

He shows disillusionment about her.

His excited love is cupboard love, so that having got what he wants he throws her away like an orange peel.

The baby at first must dominate, he must be protected from coincidences, life must unfold at the baby's rate and all this needs his mother's continuous and detailed study.

For instance, she must not be anxious when holding him, etc.

At first he does not know at all what she does or what she sacrifices for him. Especially he cannot allow for her hate.

He is suspicious, refuses her good food, and makes her doubt herself, but eats well with her aunt.

If she fails him at the start she knows he will pay her out forever.

He excites her but frustrates—she mustn't eat him or trade in sex with him.

[Donald W. Winnicott, "Hate in the Countertransference," *Voices: The Art and Science of Psychotherapy* 1:2 (1965), pp. 107–108; reprinted from *International Journal Psychoanalysis* 30 (1949)]

For a discussion of the inevitability of parental hostility for structural reasons that have existed throughout human history, see Leon S. Sheleff, *Generations Apart: Adult Hostility to Youth* (New York: McGraw-Hill, 1981).

17. Parental hostility takes many forms. Indeed, the point made by many clinicians is that to the extent that parents deny their negative feelings toward the child, the more likely those negative feelings will find expression in far more destructive transmissions. This process is seen as central in many cases of children's psychopathology. See for example, the discussion of autism in Chapter 7, especially n. 2. See also the contribution of William Goldfarb and his colleagues, who describe how many feelings of passivity and bewilderment by parents are, in fact, derived from the inhibition of their rage, because they feel potentially capable of destroying their child (William Goldfarb et al., "The Concept of Maternal Perplexity," in E. James Anthony and Therese Benedek, eds., *Parenthood: Its Psychology and Psychopathology* [Boston: Little, Brown, 1971], pp. 411–420). See also Chapter 11, text and n. 20, for a further discussion of the murderous feelings parents harbor toward their children.

18. Erich Fromm, "Different Forms of Violence," in Fromm, *The Heart of Man* (New York: Holt, Rinehart and Winston, 1964), pp. 24–36.

19. Harry F. Harlow and Margaret K. Harlow, "Social Deprivation in Monkeys," *Scientific American* 203 (1962), pp. 2–10. The Harlows describe how when female monkeys who are raised in total isolation become mothers, they either totally ignore or violently abuse their babies. In some instances, a few of the "motherless mothers" succumbed to their babies' persistent efforts to nuzzle and cuddle; some mothers were also able to be "treated" by exposure to a group of younger, more normally raised monkeys who would persuade the isolates to join them in play activities. There are many rich implications to this series of experiments, but for the moment the most relevant implication is how parental destructiveness can be traced to its roots in the parents' own deprivation when they were growing up (Harry Harlow, "Aggression and Love," Third International Kittay Award Address, New York Academy of Medicine, October 31, 1975, as reported in the *American Psychological Association Monitor*, December 1975).

20. See David Gil, "A Conceptual Model of Child Abuse and Its Implications for Social Policy," in Suzanne K. Steinmetz and Murray A. Straus, eds., *Violence in the Family* (New York: Dodd, Mead, 1974), pp. 205–212.

21. The latest accepted figures in the United States are that close to one out of two marriages end in divorce. Moreover, there is now disturbing information that even the heretofore vaunted remarriage leads to no better and even worse outcomes: "A higher percentage of second marriages break up than of first marriages" (Leslie Aldridge Westoff, "Two-Time Winners: For More and More People, the First Marriage Is Only a Training Period for the Second, with Divorce the Diploma," *New York Times Magazine*, August 10, 1975).

22. Edward Hoedemaker has written an intriguing analysis of the process of distrust in generating spirals of aggression, or attacks on behalf of one's self-defense, when in truth the underlying wish is to make contact with another. Hoedemaker's analysis is particularly instructive because he casts his work in the two frames of the everyday process between people and the process that takes place between peoples as nations. "Pathologic distrust and the resultant retreating, uncooperative behavior represent an unconscious plea for a nondefensive, nonplacatory, yet cooperative response from the other person" (Edward D. Hoedemaker, "Distrust and Aggression: An Interpersonal-international Analogy," *Journal Conflict Resolution* 12 [1968], p. 71).

23. Alfred Hassler, longtime executive secretary of the pacifist organization Fellowship of Reconciliation, recorded on the occasion of his retirement some of his thoughts about pacifism, in which he emphasizes the centrality of the pacifist's compassion, humility, and understanding, no matter what the circumstances. Hassler refers to his predecessor, world-renowned A. J. Muste, who once said, "If I can't love Hitler, I can't love." Says Hassler: "You can't get anywhere with it unless you realize that love means understanding and compassion. Then it opens up. Compassion, not in the sense of lessening your opposition to what Hitler was doing, but compassion for a man who clearly had suffered terribly, who was terribly distorted, who had so little real happiness and joy" ("An interview with Alfred Hassler," *Fellowship*, September 1974, p. 8).

24. See the description of the model by Alan Newcombe in Chapter 11, section on "Positive and Negative in the Foreign Policies of People and Nations."

25. "The sight of someone being hurt is a reinforcement of aggression for angry people. As a reinforcement, this perception can lead to increased aggression, but may also produce a pleasant tension reduction, especially if the injured person represents a source of frustration" (Leonard Berkowitz, "Experimental Investigation of Hostility Catharsis," in Jan Fawcett, ed., *Dynamics of Violence* [Chicago: American Medical Association, 1971], p. 143).

26. R. D. Laing, *The Politics of the Family* (New York: Vintage, 1972), pp. 94–95.

27. Philip G. Zimbardo, "On 'Obedience to Authority,'" *American Psychologist* 29 (1974), pp. 566–567.

28. A simple and clear discussion of how we live in an equilibrium between loving and hating is in Benjamin Spock, *Decent and Indecent: Our Personal and Political Behavior* (New York: McCall, 1969).

29. See Winnicott, "Hate in the Countertransference"; also see Joseph Rheingold in Chapter 7, text and n. 6.

30. The British psychoanalyst Melanie Klein has made what many psychotherapists believe to be the definitive contribution to date to our understanding of how, from early in life, we see in our mothers our own feelings toward them. A discussion of Klein's basic concepts is in Chapter 11 in the section "The Naturalness and Necessity of Putting Together Positive and Negative Feelings."

31. Melanie Klein conceptualizes the projective position as a definite developmental phase in all child development (see Melanie Klein, *Psychoanalysis of Children* [London: Hogart, 1937], and Melanie Klein and Joan Revere, *Love, Hate, and Reparation* [New York: Norton, 1964]).

32. Ezra F. Vogel and Norman W. Bell, "The Emotionally Disturbed Child as the Family Scapegoat," in Bell and Vogel, eds., *A Modern Introduction to the Family* (New York: Free Press, 1968), pp. 412–427 (original publication 1960); Israel W. Charny, "Family Interviews in Redefining a Sick Child's Role in the Family Problem," *Psychological Reports* 10 (1962), pp. 577–578; Richard L. Cohen, Israel W. Charny, and Pernilla Lembke, "Parental Expectations as a Force in Treatment: The Identification of Unconscious Parental Projections onto the Children's Psychiatric Hospital," *Archives General Psychiatry* 4 (1961), pp. 471–478; and Lyman C. Wynne et al., "Pseudo-Mutuality in the Family Relations of Schizophrenics," *Psychiatry* 21 (1958), pp. 205–220.

33. Irvine Schiffer, *Charisma: A Psychoanalytic Look at Mass Society* (Toronto: University of Toronto Press, 1973), pp. 72, 74–75, 79–80.

34. Lawrence Edwin Abt and Stuart L. Weissman, eds., *Acting Out* (New York: Grune & Stratton, 1965).

35. In 1973, for example, the World Health Organization reported, among others, the following murder rates per 100,000 population: Venezuela, 8.4; United States, 6.4; Hungary 1.9; Australia, 1.5; West Germany, 1.4; Japan, 1.4; Canada, 1.4; Italy, 0.9; France, 0.8; Britain, 0.7 (*International Herald Tribune*, July 13, 1973).

36. A book by two criminologists, *The Subculture of Violence*, presents this point of view most effectively. The very title of the book bespeaks an excellent conceptual tool for analyses of the violent events of a given community as to the particular processes that encourage and facilitate violence in that community's culture (Marvin E. Wolfgang and Frances Ferracutti, *The Subculture of Violence: Towards an Integrated Theory in Criminology* [London: Tavistock 1967]).

37. Jerome D. Frank, *Sanity and Survival* (New York: Random House, 1967), p. 109.

38. Pascal, *Pensees*, sec. 14, no. 894.

39. M. Lionel Rubinoff, "Violence and the Retreat from Reason," in Sherman M. Stange, ed., *Reason and Violence: Philosophical Investigations* (Totowa, N.J.: Littlefield, Adams & Co., 1974), pp. 85–86.

40. Robert Jay Lifton, *Death in Life: Survivors of Hiroshima* (New York: Random House, 1967).

41. Lifton describes five modes of immortality: the biological, the theological, that achieved through man's work, that achieved by being survived by nature itself, and a mode of "experiential transcendence." Dr. Lifton describes the last as "one so intense that time and death disappear . . . includes various forms of ecstasy and rapture associated both with the Dionysian principle of excess, and with the mythical sense of oneness with the universe that Freud referred to as the 'oceanic feeling.' . . . The symbolic modes of immortality are not merely problems one ponders when dying. They are constantly perceived inner standards, though often indirect and outside of awareness, by which we evaluate our lives, by which we maintain feelings of connection, significance and movement so necessary to everyday psychological existence" (Robert Jay Lifton, *Boundaries: Psychological Man in Revolution* [New York: Random House, 1969], p. 23).

42. Schiffer, *Charisma*, p. 160.

43. Collins, "Three Faces of Cruelty," p. 422.

44. The concept of emotional contagion as an aspect of group experience goes far beyond what happens within specifically defined subgroups to contagious processes within the larger societal groups in which we live. Social psychologist Leonard Berkowitz has been an important spokesman for this point of view, both in basic laboratory work on the problem of contagion and with respect to implications for societal management, such as in the critical area of weapons control (see Leonard Berkowitz, "Impulse, Aggression and the Gun," *Psychology Today* 2:4 [September 1968], pp. 18–23). According to Berkowitz, even

dramatic instances of mass slayings by mentally ill people may be contagious, with each crime triggering the next one.

> The news reports and photographs can serve as a stimulus or spark that sets off a person who had been made predisposed by other circumstances, Dr. Berkowitz said. . . . As a good example of contagious homicide, Dr. Berkowitz cited the three multiple murders . . . in July 1966: Richard Speck killed eight nurses in Chicago. A couple of weeks later Charles Whitman climbed to the top of a University of Texas tower and killed 14 people. Then in November in Mesa, Arizona, Benjamin Smith killed five people in a beauty shop. He said he got the idea from the Speck rampage. [Donald C. Drake, "Mass Slaying May Be Contagious, Psychologist Believes," *Philadelphia Inquirer*, November 2, 1967]

45. Urie Bronfenbrenner, *Two Worlds of Childhood: U.S. and U.S.S.R.* (New York: Russell Sage Foundation, 1970).

46. Interestingly, some critics of the collective movement in Israel have observed that the same emphasis on allegiance to one's group siphons off a good deal of the richness and complexity of individuality. It is this richness of individuality that characteristically nourishes the development of artists, philosophers, writers, psychologists, and so forth, that is, people who turn their sensitiveness to their own vulnerability toward creative outlets (see Bruno Bettelheim, *The Children of the Dream* [London: Collier-Macmillan, 1969]).

47. A dramatic example of the madness of the collective process shocked the U.S. public in November 1978, when 900 Americans, members of a religious sect, committed mass suicide in their jungle camp in Guyana after members of the group had ambushed and killed members of an investigative commission that was led by a congressman. An observer, attorney Mark Lane, reported "that they went to their deaths 'smiling'; they looked genuinely happy" (Associated Press, November 21, 1978).

48. See David M. Levy, "The Act as a Unit," *Psychiatry* 25 (1962) pp. 295–314, and R. D. Spitz, "The Derailment of Dialogue: Stimulus Overload, Action Cycles, and the Completion Gradient," *Journal American Psychoanalytic Association* 12 (1964), pp. 752–775.

49. The classical formulation of cognitive dissonance is generally credited to Leon Festinger (*A Theory of Cognitive Dissonance* [Evanston, Ill.: Row, Peterson, 1957]). An excellent summary of the concept is in the chapter, "Cognitive Dynamics," in Leroy H. Pelton, *The Psychology of Nonviolence* (New York: Pergamon, 1974), pp. 27–53.

50. James C. Coleman, *Community Conflict* (New York: Free Press, 1957). Criminologist Shlomo Shoham is another thinker who has emphasized the escape from cognitive dissonance, which he calls the congruity principle, as a basis for the tendency to classify people as similar and dissimilar, good and bad, like us and not like us (see Shlomo Shoham, *The Sociology of the Absurd* [Tel Aviv and Jerusalem: Schocken, 1970], in Hebrew). See also Shoham's excellent treatment of the whole process of dehumanization and identification of the other as victims in *The Mark of Cain: The Stigma Theory of Crime and Social Deviation* (Jerusalem: Israel Universities Press; Dobbs Ferry, N.Y.: Oceana Publications, 1970).

51. Wilhelm Stekel, *Sadism and Masochism: The Psychology of Hatred and Cruelty* (New York: Liveright, 1953), pp. 24, 29. In an introduction to the reissue of Stekel's 1929 book, Emil Gutheil comments that Stekel's stipulation that hate and aggression are primal reactions that precede reactions of love has never been challenged or replaced.

52. Helm Stierlin, *Conflict and Reconciliation: A Study in Human Relations and Schizophrenia* (New York: Science House, 1969), p. vii.

53. Coleman, *Community Conflict*, p. 14.

54. Frank, *Sanity and Survival*, p. 288.

55. However, we do believe human beings experience the victims' humanity somewhere inwardly even when they do not allow themselves to experience it knowingly. One source of evidence for the fact that people do experience inwardly the harm they do others is the laboratory studies of "transgression and compliance."

> The basic paradigm in experiments on transgression and compliance involves inducing subjects to engage in some form of transgression and then observing the extent to which they comply with the request made, usually, though not exclusively, by the victim of the transgression. The general finding is that the transgression produces a dramatic increase in compliance rates. The theoretical explanation often advanced for this finding is that the harmdoer, feeling guilty for his transgression, seeks to absolve his guilt through altruistic behavior. When one considers the manipulations involved in these studies, what is most intriguing is that the harmdoer feels any guilt or responsibility for the transgression. In no instance does the subject intend to do something wrong—he is always the victim of circumstances. [Michael Ross, and Don DiTecco, "An Attributional Analysis of Moral Judgments," in Melvin J. Lerner, ed., *The Justice Motive in Social Behavior, Journal Social Issues* 31:3 (1975), p. 96]

56. Joost Meerloo, a Dutch psychiatrist and psychoanalyst, who himself made a hazardous escape from occupied Holland to England in World War II, has written a heart-breaking—and infuriating—sketch of the cruel behavior of many doctors hired by the German government (including from the United States) to examine former concentration camp inmates who were claiming reparations.

> To them "man" is a machine, a little bit bigger than a bread box. . . . One cannot help but wonder what motives for rejection simmer in the minds of the medical bureaucrats hired by the German authorities. First, they deny the suffering of those who are still living in despair. During the interview, they shout at the poor targets, accusing them of being exaggerators and hysterics. After a few minutes of angry harangue, they presume to make the illuminating diagnosis of "simulation of symptoms." They forsake all vestiges of empathy and sympathy, inflicting irreparable psychological damage. The only thing some of these victims have left, pride in their suffering, is brutally denied them. . . . People have asked me how such persecution can possibly be perpetrated. "Are they so corrupt that they only speak in the tongue of those who employ them?" The answer is yes. They are and they do much more often and more vehemently than their bosses want them to. It is part of a strange medical psychological dilemma. . . . They do not believe in psychic and emotional causes, they think that leaves no imprint on man's psyche. [Joost A. M. Meerloo, "Second Time Around: The Echo of Nazi Persecution," *Voices: The Art and Science of Psychotherapy* 5:1 (1959), pp. 46–47]

57. Modern Israeli novelist, Amos Oz, observes: "I believe a Crusader and a Jew coexist in every man." In his novel, *Unto Death*, Oz paints a subtle relationship between Crusaders and Jews. "The same fanaticism compounded by superstition which initially prompts the Crusaders to torture and murder Jews leads them to destroy one another" (Marc Saporta, "The Splendid Madness of Amos Oz," *Le Figaro*, excerpted in *Atlas World Press Review*, December 1975, p. 52).

NOTES TO CHAPTER 7: THE HUMAN BEINGS WHO ARE TO BE THE GENOCIDERS

First and second epigraphs from Rabbi Alan Miller, *Reconstructionist*, June 1967, p. 30, and Herbert A. Otto, ed., *The Family in Search of a Future: Alternative Models for Moderns* (New York: Appleton-Century-Crofts, 1970), pp. 185–186.

1. Kahlil Gibran, in *The Madman* (New York: Knopf, 1962), writes:

In the town where I was born lived a woman and her daughter, who walked in their sleep. One night, while silence unfolded the world, the woman and her daughter, walking, yet asleep, met in their mist-veiled garden. And the mother spoke, and she said: "At last, at last, my enemy! You by whom my youth was destroyed – who have built up your life upon the ruins of mine! Would I could kill you!" And the daughter spoke, and she said: "O hateful woman, selfish and old! Who stand between my freer self and me! Who would have my life an echo of your own faded life! Would you were dead!"

At that moment a cock crew, and both women woke. The mother said gently, "Is that you, darling?" And the daughter answered gently, "Yes, dear."

2. Bruno Bettelheim's beleaguered voice stands out relatively alone among many observers of the dread condition of infantile autism when he states, "The precipitating factor in infantile autism is the parent's wish that his child should not exist." Many observers have pointed out that the condition of autism is probably of greater importance to the development of the science of psychology – that is, to our understanding of the basic nature of man – than it is in its own right as a tragic but still relatively rare condition. It is my opinion, too, that many – though not all – autistic children are victims of emotional destruction. Bettelheim emphasizes that it is not simply parental ambivalence to the autistic child that develops once the child is already autistic and therefore a source of terrible pain to the parent, but "only the extreme of negative feelings in the parents can set the autistic process in motion." The autistic child lives out a "single-minded preoccupation with a specific issue . . . his unremitting fear of destruction" (Bruno Bettelheim, *The Empty Fortress: Infantile Autism and the Birth of the Self* [New York: Free Press, 1967], pp. 125, 127, 459). See also Israel W. Charny, "Recovery of Two Largely Autistic Children Through Renunciation of Maternal Destructiveness in Integrated Individual and Family Therapy," in Lewis R. Wolberg and Marvin L. Aronson, eds., *Group and Family Therapy 1980* (New York: Brunner/Mazel, 1980), pp. 250–281.

3. Erich Fromm, "Different Forms of Violence," in Fromm, *The Heart of Man* (New York: Holt, Rinehart and Winston, 1964), p. 24–36.

4. Over the years, U.S. mental health professionals have recognized increasingly the tragedy of the "too much" in the lives of well-to-do children, who often turn up as adolescents with severe personality disorders precisely because they have not been taught how to handle frustration, hurt, and danger in their formative childhood years.

5. See Chapter 6, n. 16, for quotation from Winnicott's work on the inevitability of mothers' hating their children under the healthiest of circumstances.

6. Joseph C. Rheingold, *The Mother, Anxiety, and Death: The Catastrophic Death Complex* (Boston: Little, Brown, 1967). See also Rheingold's original book, *The Fear of Being a Woman: A Theory of Maternal Destructiveness* (New York: Grune & Stratton, 1964). For this author's review of both books and of Rheingold's essential thesis of the unknowing and unknown hatred of children by their mothers and the impact this hatred has on them, see *Psychotherapy* 6 (1969), pp. 145–147.

7. P. G. Zimbardo, C. Haney, W. C. Banks, and D. Jaffe, "The Mind Is a Formidable Jailer: A Pirandellian Prison," *New York Times Magazine*, April 8, 1973.

8. David L. Rosenhan, "On Being Sane in Insane Places," *Science* 179 (1973), pp. 250–258. See also Chapter 2, n. 12, for Rosenhan's replication of the Milgram study.

9. Thomas S. Szasz, *The Myth of Mental Illness: Foundations of a Theory of Personal Conduct* (New York: Hoeber [Harper], 1961).

10. D. G. Langsky, K. Flamenhaft, and P. Machotka, "Follow-up Evaluation of Family Crisis Therapy," *American Journal Orthopsychiatry* 39 (1969), pp. 753–760.

11. See Chapter 2, text and n. 10.

12. News reports of people who stand by without helping in the face of a disaster are an unending phenomenon of modern life. The crucial thing to realize is that they occur even under circumstances in which the bystanders would not have endangered themselves had they tried to help. For example, the following excerpts from news stories:

DALLAS YOUTHS STALL FIREMEN AS BABY DIES

Firemen attempting to reach a burning home in south Dallas Thursday night were blocked by a group of 60 yelling, heckling youths who refused to move out of the street.

40 HERE IGNORE SCREAMS OF RAPED OFFICE WORKER

At least 40 persons heard the screams of a beaten, raped naked girl in a busy Bronx neighborhood – but not one of them lifted a finger to help her or even to summon police.

An interesting summary article on bystander researches, and how individuals who see another person in trouble lose a sense of themselves as individuals to the extent that they lose themselves in their identity as members of a group or crowd of onlookers, is John M. Darley and Bibb Latane, "When Will People Help in a Crisis?" *Psychology Today* 2 (December 1968), pp. 54–57, 70–71. Many people succumb to an unconscious justification of the victim's plight precisely because they cannot bear feeling that they can't help the victim. "If we can't help a victim, we're likely to decide he richly deserves everything that's happening to him" (Melvin J. Lerner, "All the World Loathes a Loser," *Psychology Today* 5 [June 1971], pp. 51–54, 66).

13. Darley's research is described in a news article in the *American Psychological Association Monitor*, November 1973: "Princeton Researchers Find Charity Ends in Lab."

14. Israel W. Charny, "Why Are So Many (If Not Really All) People and Families Disturbed?" *Journal Marital and Family Therapy* 6:1 (1980), pp. 37–48.

15. Israel W. Charny, "And Abraham Went to Slay Isaac," *Journal Ecumenical Studies* 10:2 (1973), pp. 304–318.

16. Shalom Spiegel, *The Last Trial: On the Legends and Lore of the Command of Abraham to Offer Isaac as a Sacrifice: The Akedah* (Philadelphia: Jewish Publication Society, 1967).

17. Marvin E. Wolfgang, *Patterns in Criminal Homicide* (New York: Wiley, 1958).

18. Stuart Palmer, "Family Members as Murder Victims," in Suzanne K. Steinmetz and Murray A. Straus, eds., *Violence in the Family* (New York: Dodd, Mead, 1974), pp. 91–97.

19. David G. Gil, "A Conceptual Model of Child Abuse and Its Implications for Social Policy," ibid., p. 206. See also David Bakan, *Slaughter of the Innocents: A Study of the Battered Child Phenomenon* (San Francisco: Jossey-Bass, 1971). In Chapter 11 (text and n. 20), I discuss further parental hatred of children and how far some theoretician-observers go in formulating the universality and extent of natural parental hatred.

20. Ronald Laing devotes many of his writings to developing the dilemmas that are at work in otherwise happy looking and even successful family groups because of the constant interplay of destructive feelings within the family. It is inevitable that each family member has to struggle to separate, to rid himself of – indeed to "destroy" – the presence of others within him, and once a person is so engaged in destruction, he is necessarily triggering sequences of destructive feelings in other members of the family who respond to his destructiveness and, in fact, are themselves engaged in their own needs to separate. "If I do not destroy the 'family' the 'family' will destroy me. I cannot destroy the 'family' in myself without destroying 'it' in them. Feeling themselves endangered, will they destroy me?" (R. D. Laing, "The Family and the 'Family,'" in Laing, *The Politics of the Family* [New York: Vintage, 1972]. See also Laing's delightful and penetrating book of poetry on the interlocking relationships of family members, *Knots* [New York: Random House, 1970]).

21. A landmark study that describes the tragic destructiveness wrought by make-believe family relationships, in which all differences are swept under the rug, is that of L. C. Wynne et al., "Pseudo-Mutuality in the Family Relations of Schizophrenics," *Psychiatry* 21 (1958), pp. 205–220.

22. See the twenty-year study of marital process conducted at the Tavistock Clinic in London by Henry Dicks, who also observes that the family group that avoids conflict sets itself up for serious breakdowns on one or another level of the family structure and of its members (Henry V. Dicks, *Marital Tensions* [New York: Basic Books, 1967]). An excellent paper on the critical importance of separateness in family emotional health is Murray Bowen, "The Use of Family Theory in Clinical Practice," *Comprehensive Psychiatry* 7 (1966), pp. 345–374. Jules Feiffer has written a play that portrays with deep irony the notion that family members who are empty of emotional experiences in their relationships can find a common meeting ground in murderous violence toward others. (Jules Feiffer, *Little Murders* [New York: Random House, 1968]).

23. Thomas Merton, "Chants to Be Used in Processions Around a Site with Furnaces," in Thomas P. McDonnell, ed., *A Thomas Merton Reader* (New York: Harcourt, Brace & World, 1962), pp. 404–406.

24. Simon Wiesenthal, *The Murderers Among Us* (New York: McGraw-Hill, 1967), pp. 18–19.

25. Ivan Boszormenyi-Nagy and Geraldine M. Spark, *Invisible Loyalties* (Hagerstown, Md.: Harper and Row, 1973).

26. Ibid., pp. 54–61.

27. Ibid., p. 66.

28. Ibid., pp. 64–73.

29. Ibid., p. 177.

30. Louis Linn, in Heinrich Z. Winnik, Rafael Moses, and Mortimer Ostow, eds., *Psychological Bases of War* (New York: Quadrangle; and Jerusalem: Jerusalem Academic Press, 1973), pp. 187–188.

31. G. Le Bon, *The Crowd*, translated from French (London: F. Unwin, 1903), pp. 28, 29.

32. Ibid., p. 36.

33. Silvano Arieti and Johannes M. Meth, "Rare, Unclassified, Collective, and Exotic Psychotic Syndromes," in Arieti, ed., *American Handbook of Psychiatry* Vol. 1 (New York: Basic Books, 1959), p. 552.

34. See, for example, the Nader Report on Community Mental Health Centers, which recommends that mental health centers be converted to "human service centers" that help individuals with "problems of living." *Behavior Today*, a hard-hitting newsletter published by the editors of *Psychology Today*, commented editorially: "If it did nothing else right – which is not the case – the report would be worth its weight in something better than

gold for fingering THE issue. That is the question of distinguishing between medical issues and human service of life problem issues. . . . Mental health pros . . . have helped forge the attitude that you gotta be sick before you need help and if you need help, then you gotta be sick" (*Behavior Today*, July 31, 1972, p. 6).

35. Silvano Arieti and Johannes Meth (ibid., p. 129) describe a psychological epidemic of St. Vitus's dance between the eleventh and fifteenth centuries, especially in the German and Flemish countries. People affected by the disease would gather in the vicinity of churches, and they would dance and sing for several days and nights until they lost consciousness. Many had convulsive seizures. In the year 1278, two hundred such patients gathered on a bridge on the Rhine, and the bridge collapsed. In the light of our newer perspective of how men in groups go "crazy" in a collective lack of restraint, one can only wonder whether all the dancers really suffered St. Vitus's dance. Among the particularly interesting reports of collective epidemics are those of convents where all the nuns suddenly become possessed by "an illness," abandon their discipline, and give vent to hysterical and bizarre actions. One such report in 1700 tells of all the nuns of a convent starting to meow as if they had been turned into cats (to which our contemporary and Freudian-educated naughtiness mischievously associates a veritable cathouse).

36. J. David Singer, "Man and World Politics: The Psycho-Cultural Interface," *Journal Social Issues* 24:3 (1968), p. 129.

37. Bryant Wedge, "The Individual, the Group, and War," in Winnik, Moses, and Ostow, eds., *Psychological Bases of War*, pp. 65–82.

38. The studies of Solomon Asch are classic for establishing the vulnerability of people to group pressure to an extent that subjects agree to "see" what they do not really see when they are given to believe that everyone else sees things in a certain way. (Solomon E. Asch, "Studies of Independence and Conformity: I. A Minority of One Against a Unanimous Majority," *Psychological Monographs* 70:9, No. 416 [1956]).

See also the important analysis of "groupthink" in international affairs by Irving Janis, who describes the problems of consensus leading to decisions that are apparently acceptable to all, when in reality the decision is not really fully endorsed by most or all present except the proposer, especially if the latter is the chairman. Janis reviews a succession of historical fiascos – including the Bay of Pigs, Pearl Harbor, and Vietnam (Irving L. Janis, *Victim of Groupthink* [New York: Houghton, Mifflin, 1975]).

39. According to Gary Marx, collective riots have a profoundly expressive function that goes beyond any protest at social injustice or any demonstration of a political claim, grievance, or ideological position. There are, in fact, "issueless riots" and in riots that are about real issues, there is also at play the same expressive process that is, in truth, issueless and seizes on the ostensible issue of the day only by way of camouflage and expediency (Gary T. Marx, "Issueless Riots," in James F. Short, Jr., and Marvin E. Wolfgang, eds., *Collective Violence, Annals of the American Academy of Political and Social Science* 391 [1970], pp. 21–33).

40. This is the point that psychoanalyst Irvine Schiffer makes in his study of the relationship between charismatic leaders and the collective process: "The masses are made up of you and me, a collection of individuals each with his own intricate psychic apparatus. It seems only reasonable, if we are to talk about such an apparatus *en masse*, that we start first with an examination of the individual psyche and then determine to what degree and in what way one's psyche becomes modified as one blends into the group structure. . . . Everyone has a psyche with striking similarities to his fellows; herein lies the basis for group psychology. And in any psychology of groups, there is always the potential for mass behavior" (Irvine Schiffer, *Charisma: A Psychoanalytic Look at Mass Society* [Toronto: University of Toronto Press, 1973], p. 57).

41. A fuller understanding of group processes calls for an analysis of several inter-

related yet separate dynamics such as diffusion of responsibility in a group, the power of persuasion, the pleasure of feeling familiar with one's group and, hence, the inclination to go along even with group choices that otherwise would be unacceptable, and identification with the ideology of the group. A useful review of some research along these various lines will be found in Kenneth L. Bion, Robert S. Baron, and Norman Miller, "Why Do Groups Make Riskier Decisions Than Individuals?" in Leonard Berkowitz, ed., *Advances in Experimental Social Psychology*, Vol. 5 (New York: Academic Press, 1970).

42. Arthur Koestler, *The Ghost in the Machine* (New York: Macmillan, 1967), p. 399.

NOTES TO CHAPTER 8: THE TRAGIC ILLUSION
OF SELF-DEFENSE

Epigraph from "Notes and Comments" in the *New Yorker*, October 2, 1971.

1. See the telling satire by Kenneth Keniston, "How Community Mental Health Stamped Out the Riots (1968-78)," *Transaction*, July 1968.

2. How spouses defend themselves in marital stress is a direct and indirect subject of virtually all major treatments of the marital process; among others, George R. Bach and Peter Wyden, *The Intimate Enemy* (New York: Morrow, 1969); Israel W. Charny, "Marital Love and Hate," *Family Process* 8 (1969), pp. 1-24, and Israel W. Charny, "Injustice and Betrayal as Natural Experiences in Family Life," *Psychotherapy: Theory, Research, and Practice* 91 (1972), pp. 86-91 — both papers are included in Charny, *Marital Love and Hate* (New York: Macmillan, 1972); Henry V. Dicks, *Marital Tensions* (New York: Basic Books, 1967); Bernard L. Greene, *A Clinical Approach to Marital Problems* (Springfield, Ill.: Charles C. Thomas, 1970); Nena O'Neill and George O'Neill, *Open Marriage: A New Life Style for Couples* (New York: M. Evans, 1972).

3. The pattern of denying conflicts has been given the name pseudomutuality (see L. C. Wynne et al., "Pseudomutuality in the Family Relations of Schizophrenics," *Psychiatry* 21 (1958), pp 205-220.

4. See Marcia Lasswell and Norman Lobsenz, *No-Fault Marriage* (Garden City, N.Y.: Doubleday, 1976).

5. One of the first daring experiments in simultaneous psychoanalytic therapy of married mates was reported by Bela Mittlemann in "The Concurrent Analysis of Married Couples," *Psychoanalytic Quarterly* 13 (1954), pp. 479-491. However, for many years the tradition persisted that psychotherapists, especially practitioners of psychoanalytic therapy, were not to treat both mates. In fact, the tradition was to refuse even to see the spouse of one's patient when that spouse (almost inevitably) asked to be seen.

6. In his brilliant contribution to integrating the then new family therapy with traditional psychoanalysis, Martin Grotjahn revealed that many analysts would say that they never saw the husband or wife or other members of an analysand's family when, in fact, this was not true — they did see them (Martin Grotjahn, *Psychoanalysis and the Family Neurosis* [New York: Norton, 1960], p. 243). Jay Haley has described how at psychiatric meetings in the fifties, one would hear nothing about family therapy in the actual convention sessions, but sitting around at night, relaxing with a small group of friends, many therapists would "confess" in "furtive conversations" that they had begun to treat families (Jay Haley, "Whither Family Therapy?" *Family Process* 1:1 [1962], p. 69). A variety of marriage counseling approaches are summarized in Ben N. Ard, Jr., and Constance C. Ard, eds., *Handbook of Marriage Counseling* (Palo Alto: Science & Behavior Books, 1969).

7. James H. Craig and Marge Craig, *Synergic Power: Beyond Domination and Permissiveness* (Berkeley, Calif.: Proactive Press, 1974), p. 109.

8. "The first serious Western effort to apply humane criteria to war practice was that

of St. Augustine (354–430). While he deplored the restless ambition that promoted wars for sovereignty, he did believe that there were conditions under which it was just to extend an empire. If empires could not be morally extended, then nations already under the control of wicked rulers could not be righteously aided in revolt. Even where the war is just, however, the good man mourns the misery caused; and eschews needless slaughtering, plundering, burning and torturing" (Donald A. Wells, *The War Myth: The Rationalization of War-Making in Western Thought with an Analysis of the Human Dilemmas That Cause War* [New York: Pegasus, 1967], p. 32). There are many discussions and extensions of the just war concept in subsequent works of philosophy and theology, and various authorities through the ages have posed different criteria for the definition. John Calvin, for example, is identified with the following criteria: "To inflict public vengeance by a king, to preserve the tranquility of a territory, to suppress disturbers of the peace, to rescue victims of oppression, and to punish crime" (ibid., p. 35).

9. Percy E. Corbett, "Laws of War," *Encyclopedia Britannica*, vol. 13 (1968), p. 832.

10. Theodore Weber, *Modern War and the Pursuit of Peace* (New York: Council on Religion and International Affairs, 1968), material selected from pp. 29–31.

11. William H. Blanchard, "Messianic Feeling Can Lead Us Into Trouble," *Los Angeles Time Opinion*, December 15, 1968, quotation abstracted from several sections of the article. See Blanchard's full-length book, *Aggression—American Style* (Los Angeles: Goodyear, 1978). A chapter with the same title appears in Israel W. Charny, ed., *Strategies Against Violence* (Boulder, Colo.: Westview, 1978), pp. 164–183.

Frederick Struckmeyer emphasizes a critical distinction between our natural right to defend ourselves, which we must continue even in limited wars, and the fight to impose our own ideology on others or to correct their sinful ideology: "It is not our place as men to punish the sins of 'mistaken' ideologies of other men. We have a general right, even if not a duty, to defend ourselves as a nation. But we manifestly do not have the right to wage unlimited war, and to seek the destruction of the enemy *because* we think him deserving of death. To fight in self-defense and to fight for this latter reason are two vastly different things. . . . It still seems possible to wage some purely defensive wars, wars which are limited in scope and which do not have the effect of destroying what they originally intended to save" (Frederick R. Struckmeyer, "The Just War and the Right of Self-defense," *Ethics: An International Journal of Social, Political, and Legal Philosophy* 82:1 [1971], pp. 52–53).

12. Y. Harkabi, "The Position of the Palestinians in the Israel-Arab Conflict in Their National Covenant (1968)," mimeographed (Revised text of a lecture given at Tel Aviv University, May 18, 1969).

13. See Ken Kesey, *One Flew Over the Cuckoo's Nest* (New York: New American Library, 1962); Thomas S. Szasz, *The Myth of Mental Illness* (New York: Hoeber [Harper], 1961); Ronald Leifer, *In the Name of Mental Health: The Social Functions of Psychiatry* (New York: Science House, 1969).

14. See A. S. Barram, "Modern Trends in Violence," *Reconstructionist* 61:3 (April 1975), pp. 7–18. The *Congressional Record* of February 24, 1972 (118:2), carries a criticism of the "return" of lobotomy in recent years to new heights of frequency and popularity in certain neurosurgical and psychiatric circles. Several reports of physical abuses of mental patients are found in the September 1974 edition of the *APA Monitor*, the newspaper of the American Psychological Association.

15. Anatol Rapoport, *Conflict in Man-made Environment* (Baltimore, Md.: Penguin, 1974), p. 113.

16. Strategist-futurist Herman Kahn has described an escalation ladder with forty-four rungs, each of which is separated by "thresholds"; passing a threshold changes the quality of a conflict. For example, conflict progresses from verbal declarations to traditional crises in which no nuclear threats are made, to intense crises in which conventional

wars begin, to limited nuclear exchanges, and so on. Note, however, that Kahn's intention is also to describe how the escalation process can be controlled and does not have to run amok (Herman Kahn, *On Escalation: Metaphors and Scenarios* [New York: Praeger, 1965]).

17. See Ralph K. White, *Misperception and the Vietnam War, Journal Social Issues* 22 (1965). See also White's reference to Urie Bronfenbrenner's catching concept of "mirror image" processes between peoples as they escalate toward wars, and Gustav Iccheiser, *Appearances and Realities: Misunderstanding in Human Relations* (New York: Jossey Bass, 1970).

18. Morton Deutsch, *The Resolution of Conflict: Constructive and Destructive Processes* (New Haven, Conn.: Yale University Press, 1973).

19. Alan Newcombe, "'Lovemate': A Personal and International Foreign Policy for Peace," in Charny, ed., *Strategies Against Violence*, pp. 3–18. See also discussion of Newcombe's work in Chapter 11, section on "Positive and Negative in the Foreign Policies of People and Nations."

20. See, for example, Thomas Gordon, *Parent Effectiveness Training: The "No-Lose" Program for Raising Responsible Children* (New York: Wyden, 1970), and A. M. Levi and G. Metonomski, "A Computer System to Aid Decision Making in Large Groups: A Practical Proposal," mimeographed (Haifa: University of Haifa, 1975).

21. Alberto Podorgny of the Weizmann Institute points out that in the history of evolution, overspecialization characteristically leads to the extinction of a species. When a species overspecializes a particular evolutionary feature (however much that feature originally served the purposes of self-defense and survival), it can lose control of its own nature or evolutionary adaptability and can no longer cope constructively with change. Man might be thought of as a creature that has overspecialized its mechanisms for self-defense (personal communication).

22. From "Notes and Comments" in the *New Yorker*, October 2, 1971.

NOTES TO CHAPTER 9: SACRIFICING OTHERS TO THE DEATH WE FEAR OURSELVES

Epigraphs from Harry H. Shapiro, "A Search for Conscience," *Philadelphia Jewish Exponent*, March 29, 1968, and A. Anatoli Kuznetzov, *Babi Yar* (New York: Farrar, Straus & Giroux, 1970), p. 351.

1. R. D. Laing, *The Politics of Experience* (New York: Pantheon, 1967), p. 67.

2. In his book of poetry, *Knots* (New York: Random House, 1970), R. D. Laing sketches how family members lock horns in projecting their impulses and shortcomings onto one another, and then their further reprojections of their projections onto one another, *ad absurdum*.

3. Benjamin Spock, *Baby and Child Care* (New York: Pocket Books, 1945).

4. Konrad Lorenz, *On Aggression* (New York: Harcourt, Brace & World, 1966).

5. "The way in which the old ethic provides for the elimination of . . . feelings of guilt and the discharge of the excluded negative forces is in fact one of the gravest perils confronting mankind. What we have in mind here is that classic psychological expedient – the institution of a scapegoat. This technique for attempting a solution of the problem is to be found wherever human society exists" (Erich Neumann, *Depth Psychology and a New Ethic* [New York: Putnam's, 1969], p. 50).

6. A study by E. Walster showed that the more severe an accident, the more an observer blames the innocent victim of the accident, because attributing the accident to chance would mean that the same misfortune could occur to anyone else, including the observer (E. Walster, "Assignment of Responsibility for an Accident," *Journal Personality &*

Social Psychology 3 [1966], pp. 73–79; reported in Michael Ross and Don DiTecco, "An Attributional Analysis of Moral Judgments," in Melvin J. Lerner, ed., *The Justice Motive in Social Behavior, Journal of Social Isues* 31:3 [1975], pp. 91–110). Assigning responsibility for an accident to the victim has been termed by one researcher, R. G. Shaver, "defensive attribution." Ross and DiTecco write of those who themselves do the harm. "Defensive attributions by harmdoers would presumably take a different form. They may deny personal responsibility for any harmful consequences of their actions by ascribing to only the most sophisticated interpretations of responsibility. By doing so, harmdoers would transfer blame to the environment and deflect it from themselves" (ibid., p. 95).

7. Ernest Becker, *The Denial of Death* (New York: Free Press, 1973). Becker citation is from Otto Rank, *Will Therapy and Truth and Reality* (New York: Knopf, 1946), p. 130.

8. Irvine Schiffer, *Charisma: A Psychoanalytic Look at Mass Society* (Toronto: University of Toronto Press, 1973), p. 83.

9. John Toland, *The Last 100 Days* (New York: Bantam, 1967), p. 252.

10. Becker, *Denial of Death*, p. 138.

11. Philosopher Lionel Rubinoff says in no uncertain terms: "The deliberate infliction of pain and death on others is only too easily facilitated by the linguistic magic enacted through the invocation, 'I was forced to it by the circumstances, I was merely obeying orders.' Such language, I suggest, is nothing less than celebration in black magic" (M. Lionel Rubinoff, "Violence and the Retreat from Reason," in Sherman M. Stanage, ed., *Reason and Violence* [Totowa, N.J.: Littlefield, Adams & Co., 1974], p. 91).

12. A disturbing survey by Herbert Kelman and Lee Lawrence following the conviction of Lt. Calley for mass murders in Vietnam presented people with the question of what they thought they would do if they were soldiers in Vietnam who were ordered by their superior officers to shoot all inhabitants of a village that was suspected of aiding the enemy — including old men, women, and children. Fifty-one percent said they would follow orders; 33 percent said they would refuse to shoot. "In short, the cognitive and ideological grounding for mass violence in an authority situation seems to be present in large segments of the United States population" (Herbert C. Kelman, "Violence Without Moral Restraint: Reflections on the Dehumanization of Victims and Victimizers," *Journal Social Issues* 29 [1973], p. 41). The study itself is reported in detail by H. C. Kelman and L. H. Lawrence, "Assignment of Responsibility in the Case of Lt. Calley: Preliminary Report on a National Survey," in Lewis A. Coser, ed., *Collective Violence and Civil Conflict, Journal Social Issues* 28:1 (1972), pp. 177–212.

13. See Chapter 8, text and n. 11.

14. A. S. Barram, "Modern Trends in Violence," *Reconstructionist* 61:3 (April 1975), pp. 7–18.

15. There is a good deal of evidence that even in democratic societies, police functions naturally carry a high potential for sadism and totalitarianism, so that the argument that a squad of police in the United States today could be expected *not* to carry out an order to execute prisoners is an apt illustration of how a group's decisions are made by members of the group and not only by their leader.

Data from World War II show that in many instances, even in otherwise democratic countries, the police cooperated readily with the Nazis. The story of how Swiss border police turned back Jewish refugees is in the quotation preceding Chapter 12. Hannah Arendt writes about the cooperation of the French police with the Gestapo even at the time of Leon Blum's decidedly anti-German popular-front government:

> Long before the outbreak of the war the police in a number of Western countries, under the pretext of "national security," had on their own initiative established

close connections with the Gestapo and the GPU, so that one might say there existed an independent foreign policy of the police. This police-directed foreign policy functioned quite independently of the official governments. . . . That the Nazis eventually met with so disgracefully little resistance from the police in the countries they occupied, and that they were able to organize terror as much as they did with the assistance of these local police forces, was due at least in part to the powerful position which the police had achieved over the years in their unrestricted and arbitrary domination of stateless and refugees. [Hannah Arendt, *The Origins of Totalitarianism* (Cleveland: Meridian, 1968), pp. 288–289]

16. Irving Janis, *Victims of Groupthink* (New York: Houghton Mifflin, 1975).

17. Information about Franco will be found in the *Encyclopedia Judaica*, vol. 6 (1971), pp. 160–161. See also the quotation preceding Chapter 13. Information about Trujillo will be found in the *Encyclopedia Judaica*, vol. 5 (1971), pp. 244–245.

18. The story of the Hungarian Jews can be found in Raul Hilberg, *The Destruction of the European Jews* (Chicago: Quadrangle, 1961), especially pp. 521–526.

19. S. M. Silverman, "The Victimizer: Recognition and Character," *American Journal Psychotherapy* 29:1 (1975), p. 15.

20. Vahakn Dadrian, "A Typology of Genocide," *International Review Modern Sociology* 5:2 (1975), p. 204.

21. Elie Wiesel, *The Town Beyond the Wall* (New York: Holt, Rinehart and Winston, 1964), p. 151.

22. Robert Jay Lifton, *Death in Life* (New York: Random House, 1967).

23. A similar picture of an absence of emotions in individual situations of loss and grief has been described by Eric Lindemann in his study of reactions to deaths of family members (Eric Lindemann, "Symptomatology and Management of Acute Grief," *American Journal Psychiatry* 101 [1944], pp. 141–148).

24. Lifton, *Death in Life*, pp. 509–510.

25. Leon Sheleff, "The Innocent Bystander: Socio-legal Aspects," in Shlomo Shoham, ed., *Israel Studies in Criminology*, vol. 2 (Jerusalem: Jerusalem Academic Press, 1972–1973), p. 229.

26. Leon Sheleff, "The Criminal Triad: Bystander, Victim, Criminal," *International Journal Criminology & Penology* 2 (1974), p. 170. See the later book-length treatment: Leon Shaskolsky Sheleff, *The Bystander: Behavior, Law, Ethics* (Lexington, Mass.: Lexington Books, 1978).

27. Schiffer, *Charisma*, p. 10.

28. Lionel Rubinoff, "Auschwitz and the Theology of the Holocaust," mimeographed (Address delivered to a colloquium sponsored by the Division of Theological Studies of the Lutheran Council in the U.S.A. and the Interreligious Affairs Department of the American Jewish Committee, Lutheran Theological Seminary, Columbus, Ohio, May, 1973), p. 61.

29. A useful introduction to the concept of choice making, and how it is based on an interplay of rational and emotional factors, is in John C. Glidewell, *Choice Points: Essays on the Emotional Problems of Living with People* (Cambridge, Mass.: M.I.T. Press, 1970). For a deeper, often beautiful study of the responsibility of a choice, see Jungian analyst Frances T. Wickes, *The Inner World of Choice* (New York: Harper and Row, 1963).

30. Psychologist Eugene Gendlin has made noteworthy contributions to our understanding of the experiencing process and how it is the manner of the experiencing that counts more, in many cases, than the outcome itself. In terms of choice making, the issue often is not simply which choice one makes, but how much the process of making the

choice is carried out with integrity and completeness. "The experiential *process, not the value-conclusion alone,* tells us what a value really is in an individual. The same verbal value-conclusion can mean very different concrete process conditions and very different resulting behaviors" (Eugene T. Gendlin, "Values and the Process of Experiencing," in A. H. Mahrer, ed., *The Goals of Psychotherapy* [New York: Appleton-Century-Crofts, 1967], p. 198).

31. Harold Greenwald calls his procedure "direct decision therapy" (Harold Greenwald, *Decision Therapy* [New York: Wyden, 1973]).

32. Barram, "Modern Trends in Violence," p. 17.

33. T. W. Adorno, Else Frenkel-Brunswick, Daniel J. Levinson, and R. Nevitt Sanford, *The Authoritarian Personality,* 2 vols. (New York: Harper and Row, 1950).

34. See text and n. 4 above.

35. Speech by S.S. Reichsfuhrer Heinrich Himmler to a meeting of S.S. generals in Posen on October 4, 1943. Cited by Jean-Francois Steiner in *Treblinka* (New York: Simon & Schuster, 1967), p. 13.

36. Albert Bandura, "Behavior Theory and the Models of Man," *American Psychologist* 29 (1974), pp. 861, 862.

37. J. Spaander, then director general of the National Institute of Public Health in the Netherlands, developed this idea in an address to the 1966 annual meeting of the American Psychological Association. He suggested that we learn how to develop tolerance to the foreign and unknown "by a systematic approach of the individual with effective stimuli in the sensitive period of his life" (mimeographed text). See J. Spaander, "Plans for Developing the Potentialities–Tolerance as One of Man's Potentialities," in Symposium: "What Are Man's Potentialities for Peace?" *International Understanding* 6 (1968), pp. 19–25, and the discussion of education for negative experiences in Chapter 12, section on "Religion and Education on Behalf of Nonviolent Aggression."

38. Louis Coser cites a paper by Everett Hughes entitled "Good People and Dirty Work" (*Social Problems* 10 [1962], pp. 3–11). These are the people who deny awareness of evil deeds about them, such as in Germany and other lands occupied by the Nazis. They have some vague knowledge of what is going on but, nonetheless, manage to hide this knowledge from themselves. They know and yet they don't know. They see themselves and are seen by others as "good people"–they never would do any "dirty work" themselves, yet they are dimly aware of the dirty work done by others and in one way or another condone it as necessary. Dr. Coser writes that these people are "so perturbing just because they seem in some relative respect so much like most of us" (Louis A. Coser, "The Visibility of Evil," *Journal Social Issues* 25:1 [1969], p. 101).

39. See O. H. Mowrer, *The Crisis in Psychiatry and Religion* (Princeton: Van Nostrand, 1961). In truth, all of us must live with a great deal of shame and guilt all our lives, for none of us ever can fulfill what Erik Erikson defines as "the Golden Rule in the light of new insight." Says Erikson, *"Truly worthwhile acts enhance a mutuality between the doer and the other–a mutuality which strengthens the doer even as it strengthens the other"* (Erik H. Erikson, *Insight and Responsibility* [New York: W. W. Norton, 1964], p. 233). Rollo May writes of "normal guilt": "It helps us to do the best we can in presenting our thoughts to each other, and it also gives us a humility as we communicate that makes us more open to each other and more sensitive. . . . Normal guilt can be expressed conceptually by one's being a fellow man, by being open, humble, by loving. . . . Normal guilt must be involved in all aspects of experience, and it can only be lived out" (Rollo May, "The Context of Psychotherapy," in Morris I. Stein, ed., *Contemporary Psychotherapies* [New York: Free Press, 1961], pp. 302–303).

40. Lawrence Kohlberg's consistent scheme of stages of moral development in many different cultures speaks of the universality of man's (potential) experience of the dignity of life (see Chapter 6, n. 15).

One nation that has produced a remarkable literature on the value of life is the State of Israel. Even under conditions of war, the culture-valued experience is to defend one's home and family, and even to mourn the death of one's enemy. A beautiful best-selling collection of children's writings following the 1967 Six Day War included the following excerpts from young Israelis:

AND WE'LL SEND THEM A FLOWER

Yoash:
I suggest that we tell our enemies that it is better
to live in peace, so they won't take our land. We
need it too, not only they—and we'll send them a
flower.

Miki:
We'll tell them not to make war. . . .
You can't buy a daddy.
If he dies it's all over.
Some Egyptian boy won't have a father and he will be
sad all the time.

Guy:
If all the children were nice
If the whole world was nice
They wouldn't want to kill anyone because
the world would be nice.

[*Childhood Under Fire: Stories, Poems, and Drawings by Children During the Six Days War*, ed. Abba Kovner (English ed., Tel Aviv: Sifriat Hapoalim, 1968), pp. 76–77]

See also *The Seventh Day: Soldiers Talk About the Six-Day War* (London: Andre Deutsch, 1970). Writing in his regular column, Cleveland Amory noted: "The Six Day War, Israelis will tell you, was the first in history where there was not a single rape. . . . When the Egyptians did run, the Israelis could have killed thousands upon thousands of them. They not only didn't kill them, but in some cases, they didn't even take them prisoner" (Cleveland Amory, *Saturday Review of Literature*, April 12, 1969).

Elie Wiesel, whose heart and eyes and ears are so incredibly attuned to the roles human beings choose in the grim play of history, noted: "That victory Israel needed in order to survive. But more is required to explain it than the military or human qualities of her fighters, their valor and sacrifice. There was something else, I know not what. I do know this war was not like others. The victors would have preferred doing without it. Saddened, devoid of hate or pride, they returned to their homes, disconcerted, withdrawn, as if questioning themselves on the roots of their secret. Victors like that the world has never known" (Elie Wiesel, "Israel Was Alone," *Hadassah*, May 1969).

41. The critical significance of the choices we make as to both goals and means toward our goals has been underscored in Viktor Frankl's moving book, which is based to a large extent on his experience as a concentration camp inmate (Viktor M. Frankl, *The Doctor and the Soul: From Psychotherapy to Logotherapy* [New York: Bantam, 1967]).

NOTES TO CHAPTER 10: THE HUMAN BEINGS
WHO ARE TO BE THE VICTIMS

Epigraph from *Zohar: The Book of Splendor,* ed. Gershom Scholem (New York: Shocken, 1963), p. 95.

1. Many have written that in the biblical story of Isaac's sacrifice, Isaac too was a conscious participant. As the Jungian psychoanalyst Gustav Dreifus points out, the Isaac story becomes an archetype of self-sacrifice for Judaism and Christianity alike (Gustav A. Dreifus, "Isaac the Self-sacrifical Lamb: A Study of Some Jewish Legends," *Journal Analytical Psychology* 16:1 [1971], pp. 69–78; see also Israel W. Charny, "And Abraham Went to Slay Isaac," *Journal Ecumenical Studies* 10:2 [1973], pp. 304–318).

2. Elie Wiesel, *The Town Beyond the Wall* (New York: Holt, Rinehart and Winston, 1964), p. 151. Philip Hallie (*The Paradox of Cruelty* [Middletown, Conn.: Wesleyan University Press, 1969]) has written of the victim's mingled dread and fascination with his victimizer: When the victim resists being victimized, the spell is broken. This theme, of course, also has had many expressions in great fictional literature.

3. Kurt Vonnegut, Jr., *Slaughterhouse-Five; Or the Children's Crusade: A Duty Dance with Death* (New York: Delacorte, 1969), pp. 99–100.

4. Israel Drapkin and Emilio Viano, eds., *Victimology* (Lexington, Mass.: D. C. Heath, 1974). This volume was published following the First International Symposium on Victimology in Jerusalem in 1973. The origin of the concept of victimology is generally credited to Benjamin Mendelsohn, a Jerusalem attorney.

5. Menachem Amir, *Patterns in Forcible Rape* (Chicago: University of Chicago Press, 1971).

6. The plight of the rape victim can, in fact, be generalized to apply to all victims. It is true that we are wont to heap on victims the blame for what befell them, and this tendency adds salt to an already serious injury. Up to a point, this is an important argument against a victimological analysis of tragedies such as the Holocaust, but it would be equally wrong to go to the extreme of avoiding all analyses of victims' real contributions to their plights.

7. Marvin E. Wolfgang, *Patterns in Criminal Homocide* (New York: Wiley, 1958); see Chapter 7, section on "The Family Life of the Human Beings Who Are to Be the Genociders."

8. These were some of the fascinating findings in Wolfgang's study. In general, "the bedroom has the dubious honor of being the most dangerous room in the house," but proportionately, the women were slain there more than the men. On the other hand, women killed men more frequently in the kitchen (ibid., p. 25).

9. S. M. Silverman, "The Victimizer: Recognition and Character," *American Journal Psychotherapy* 29:31 (1975), pp. 19–25; also S. M. Silverman, "Victim and Victimizer: A Framework for the Problem and Its Solution," *American Zionist,* December 1971, pp. 29–32.

10. An unusually frank acknowledgment of the reality that all of us feel like killing ourselves at times appeared in a major editorial feature in *Life* by columnist Loudon Wainwright some years ago. Wainwright wrote, "Like most of us, I've played a bit with the idea of producing my own death." After describing more of his own suicidal impulses, Wainwright also took note of how many suicides are indirect but all too lethal: "The chronic speeder, the weekend drunk, the excessive smoker who are very often indulging in suicide on the installment plan, and if they are surprised when the purchase is suddenly paid up in full, they shouldn't be. Speaking of that, I imagine that a lot of suicides are horribly surprised to find themselves in mid-air or in that wink of time between the trigger-squeeze and death. Somehow, somehow they didn't mean it to go quite so far." Wainwright concluded, "Maybe the best prevention lies in the unsentimental recognition of one's own self-annihilating

drives" (Loudon Wainwright, "The Suicide That Lives in All of Us," *Life*, October 29, 1965, p. 26).

11. Robert A. Clark, "Psychiatrists and Psychoanalysts on War," *American Journal Psychotherapy* 19 (1965), pp. 540–558. See also the next three references on people's fantasies about their suicide.

12. Karl Menninger, *Man Against Himself* (New York: Harcourt, Brace & World, 1938).

13. Robert R. Litman and Norman D. Tabachnick, "Psychoanalytic Theories of Suicide," in H.L.P. Resnick, ed., *Suicidal Behaviors: Diagnosis and Management* (Boston: Little, Brown, 1968)), pp. 27, 33, 73–91.

14. Edwin S. Schneidman, "Orientations Towards Death: A Vital Aspect of the Study of Lives," Resnick, ed., *Suicidal Behaviors*, pp. 19–68.

15. Chaim S. Shatan, "The Beginning, Not the End, of the Age of Genocide: A Psychoanalyst's Encounter with the Slaughter of the Paraguayan Indians," in Richard Arens, ed., *Genocide in Paraguay* (Philadelphia: Temple University Press, 1978), citation from prepublication mimeographed text. For an important study of the phenomenon of Jewish collaboration with the Nazis, see Isaiah Trunk, *Judenrat: The Jewish Councils in Eastern Europe Under Nazi Occupation* (New York: Macmillan, 1972).

16. Wilhelm Stekel, *Sadism and Masochism: The Psychology of Hatred and Cruelty* (New York: Liveright, 1953), p. 49 (original publication 1929).

17. George R. Bach and Herb Goldberg, *Creative Aggression* (New York: Avon, 1975).

18. Samuel J. Warner, *The Urge to Mass Destruction* (New York: Grune & Stratton, 1957).

19. First and foremost, Wilhelm Reich is still honored for his breathtaking pioneer work on character analysis (Wilhelm Reich, *Character Analysis* [New York: Orgone Press, 1949; original publication in German in 1933]). A fascinating work, one of several in recent years that reappraise the brilliance of Reich even in his later years, is W. Edward Mann, *Orgone, Reich, and Eros: Wilhelm Reich's Theory of Life Energy* (New York: Simon & Schuster, 1973).

20. There are many instances of breakdown reported in the mental health literature that follow not despair and loss but success and forward movement in one's life. For example, one study of fatal one-car accidents found that many of the driver-victims had recently taken or were about to take a significant move up in their life situation (Norman Tabachnick et al., "Comparative Psychiatric Study of Accidental and Suicidal Death," *Archives General Psychiatry* 14 [1966], pp. 60–68).

21. Albert Ellis and Robert A. Harper, *A Guide to Rational Living* (Englewood Cliffs, N.J.: Prentice Hall, 1961).

22. The many possible relationships of controller and controlled to one another are illustrated in a series of terms provided by E. F. Haskell:

Symbiosis/constructive cooperation: advantage to controller, advantage to controlled
Commensalism: advantage to controller, no effect on controlled
Parasitism/imperialism: advantage to controller, no effect on controlled
Allolimy: no effect on controller, disadvantage to controlled
Synnecrosis/destructive conflict: disadvantage to controller, disadvantage to controlled
Ammensalism: disadvantage to controller, no effect on controlled
Predation/guerrilla terrorism: disadvantage to controller, advantage to controlled
Alletrophy: no effect on controller, advantage to controlled
No interaction: no effect on controller, no effect on controlled

(E. F. Haskell, "A classification of semantic errors and its application," unpublished lecture, Gamma Alpha Fraternity, graduate chemical fraternity, New Haven, Yale, 1952; in "Conceptual Gaps and Confused Distinction," *International Associations* 3 [1974], p. 153).

23. Joost Meerloo, a psychiatrist who himself escaped from the Nazis, argues strongly for the universality of suicidal feelings in all people, hence in masses of people, but also suggests that there is a phenomenon of mass suicide. He points out that in biology, there are some reactions of this nature—for example, in the face of great danger, ants will surrender passively—and he notes any number of instances in which groups of human beings have done just the same after defeat. Meerloo suggests that a combination of forces are at play in mass suicide; on the one hand, a sense of catastrophe following the overturn of all of one's values and on the other hand, an effort at renovation or purification and an effort to restore collective self-esteem through the heroism of suicide (Joost Meerloo, *Suicide and Mass Suicide* [New York: E. P. Dutton, 1963]).

24. David A. Rothstein, "The Assassin and the Assassinated—As Non-patient Subjects of Psychiatric Investigation," in Jan Fawcett, ed., *Dynamics of Violence* (Chicago: American Medical Association, 1971), p. 150. John Toland describes graphically how Winston Churchill insisted on being led into the war zones. On one such occasion, Lt. Gen. Simpson was forced to speak to him: "Prime Minister, there are snipers in front of you, they are shelling both sides of the bridge and now they have started shelling the road behind you. I cannot accept the responsibility for your being here and must ask you to come away." Writes Toland: "A look came over Churchill's face that reminded of a small boy being called away from his sand castles on the beach. . . . Churchill had repeatedly been told, 'The way to die is to pass out fighting when your blood is up and you feel nothing.' It seemed now that the Prime Minister was determined to take every possible risk, as if a sudden and soldierly death at the front would be a suitable end and free him from the worries in the post-war world with the Soviet Union" (John Toland, *The Last 100 Days* [New York: Bantam, 1967], p. 312).

25. Vahakn N. Dadrian, "The Common Features of the Armenian and Jewish Cases of Genocide: A Comparative Victimological Perspective," in Israel Drapkin and Emilio Viano, eds., *Victimology: A New Focus*, Vol. 4, *Violence and Its Victims* (Lexington, Mass.: D. C. Heath, 1975), pp. 113, 114.

26. Irvine Schiffer, *Charisma: A Psychoanalytic Look at Mass Society* (Toronto: University of Toronto Press, 1973), p. 38.

27. There are millions of people alive in the world who barely survived one or another era of genocide, and these people can hardly be expected to countenance social science or philosophical "understanding" of what was done to them and their dear ones. In this connection, it is distressing to note that many of the bitter emotional scars (let alone physical scars) that were left by the Holocaust are untreatable by any available means of psychotherapy. H. Graver reports, for example, that of one thousand cases of Holocaust survivors seen in Montreal's Jewish Hospital, fewer than ten people returned for treatment or showed an interest in psychiatric help (H. Graver, "Psychodynamics of the Survivor Syndrome," *Canadian Psychiatric Journal* 14 [1969], pp. 617–622). Israeli psychoanalyst Shamai Davidson observes that the majority of the Holocaust survivors seen in an outpatient psychiatric clinic cannot be helped other than through supportive treatment or symptomatic drug therapy (Shamai Davidson, "The Treatment of Holocaust Survivors," in Davidson, ed., *Spheres of Psychotherapeutic Activity: A Collection of Papers Compiled for the Tenth Anniversary of the Haifa Kupat Holim Health Clinic* [1973], pp. 77–87, Hebrew; pp. 91–92, English abstract).

In a report of his efforts to treat Holocaust survivors twenty-five to thirty years later, psychiatrist Anthony Marcus writes: "I have been quite unable to assist many of these people with the essence of their continuous chronic inner despair. . . . The Holocaust experience and the associated feelings of expendability have haunted those who have survived the concentration camp experience. The quality of having been a survivor has made many of the victims of the concentration camp experience unable to ever live normal lives. It is because they have survived that they are unable to live. Their very survival in a horrendously paradoxical way has been their existential despair" (Anthony Marcus, "Holocaust Survivors: Those Who Never Came Home," in "Abstracts of the International Conference on Psychological Stress and Adjustment in Time of War and Peace," mimeographed [Tel Aviv: Tel Aviv University, 1975], p. 60). Further information on the survivors of the Holocaust can be found in L. Ettinger, *Concentration Camp Survivors in Norway and Israel* (Oslo: Universitatforlaget; London: Allen and Unwin, 1964). See also Henry Krystal, *Massive Psychic Trauma* (New York: International Universities Press, 1968).

28. Yehuda Bauer, *Flight and Rescue — Bricha: The Organized Escape of the Jewish Survivors of Eastern Europe, 1944–1949* (New York: Random House, 1970); Moshe M. Kohn, ed., *Jewish Resistance During the Holocaust* (Jerusalem: Yad Vashem, 1971); Yuri Sobel, *They Fought Back* (New York: Crown, 1968).

29. Hannah Arendt, *Eichmann in Jerusalem* (New York: Viking, 1964); Bruno Bettelheim, *The Informed Heart: Autonomy in a Mass Age* (Glencoe, Ill.: Free Press, 1960).

30. Meerloo, *Suicide and Mass Suicide*, p. 23.

31. S. L. Stebel has written a fascinating, suspenseful novel that illustrates this point metaphorically. The story is of an Israeli who is accused of conspiring with the Nazis. He turns out to have been a Nazi killer who, in his great guilt, unconsciously developed amnesia about his real self and adopted the very identity of his victims (S. L. Stebel, *The Collaborator* [New York: Random House, 1963]).

32. Israel W. Charny, "Teaching the Violence of the Holocaust: A Challenge to Educating Potential Future Oppressors and Victims for Nonviolence," *Jewish Education* 38 (1968), pp. 15–24.

NOTES TO CHAPTER 11: NONVIOLENT AGGRESSION AS AN ANTIDOTE TO DESTRUCTIVE VIOLENCE

Epigraph from Anatol Rapoport, *Conflict in Man-made Environment* (Baltimore, Md.: Penguin, 1974), pp. 221–222.

1. There is now a considerable amount of experimental literature on the conditions under which children learn to be aggressive, but many such studies relate to aggression only or largely in its negative meanings. An example of experimental work which does relate to aggression as potentially both constructive and excessive can be found in the important summary by Leonard Eron and his associates: Leonard D. Eron, Monroe A. Lefkowitz, and Leopold Walter, *Learning of Aggression in Children* (Boston: Little, Brown, 1971).

2. See the earlier discussion of humanistic psychology in Chapter 5, n. 5.

3. The accepted popular conception of emotional and mental problems certainly expects people who show too much aggression to be psychological patients, and perhaps also those who show too little aggression insofar as they are manifestly depressed or withdrawn. But most people do not understand that the pleasant, affable, helpful person who is prepared to compromise and smooth over all situations is also a prima facie patient. The underlying ethic in Western culture continues to be that if you are really a good person, you are not an "aggressive" person. The noted psychiatrist Lawrence Kolb writes: "Some wish for a world in which there is complete suppression or abolition of the ag-

gressive drive. As clinicians we know what the dire consequences would be" (Lawrence C. Kolb, "Violence and Aggression: An Overview," in Jan Fawcett, ed., *Dynamics of Violence* [Chicago: American Medical Association, 1971], p. 12).

Psychologist George Bach, in particular, stands out as a pioneer teacher of what he aptly calls "creative aggression" because, he argues forcefully, a host of personal and interpersonal problems, such as in the marital process, require a healthy flow of aggressive self-expression and self-definition (George Bach and Herb Goldberg, *Creative Aggression* [New York: Avon, 1975]).

4. What is even more bedeviling to laymen (and sometimes also to those mental health professionals who fall into a simplistic pursuit of emotional health and wholesomeness) is to find that many times the people who are far too aggressive in their behavior—the actually violent people and the catalyzers of violence around them — *inwardly* fail to experience normal aggression in their feelings and fantasies. See the references to works by Shlomo Kulcsar and Shoshanna Kulcsar concerning the Nazi mass murder administrator, Eichmann, in Chapter 2, n. 15.

See also a study by psychiatrist Augustus Kinzel of people who have been imprisoned for their violent behavior. There is a striking absence of fantasies of violence in such people. "They did not seem to dream, daydream, or attach much value to thought. Instead, they seemed to express themselves by body action almost exclusively. It is particularly striking that although they spoke relatively freely about their violent pasts, they almost totally denied their own aggressiveness, so that none actually considered himself a violent individual" (Augustus F. Kinzel, "Violent Behavior in Prisons," in Jan Fawcett, ed., *Dynamics of Violence*, p. 161).

5. Theodore Olson and Gordon Christianson, *Thirty-one Hours* (New London, Conn.: Grindstone Press, 1966).

6. Robert A. Clark, "Friends and Aggression," mimeographed (Philadelphia: American Friends Service Committee, no date—about 1965). Clark's observations of Friends' fears of aggression are also consistent with the conclusion of many that people generally fear the eruption of their destructiveness toward others more than they fear being destroyed. See also Joost Meerloo's discussion of the paradox of peace and the "tremendous pressure of hidden hostility and aggression lurking behind some forms of pacifism" (Joost A. M. Meerloo, "The Paradox of Peace," in *Aggression: Theory and Clinical Practice* [New York: Mental Health Consultation Center, 1966], p. 46). In *I Never Promised You a Rose Garden* (New York: New American Library, 1964), Hannah Green describes how a psychiatric hospital attendant who was a pacifist slapped a patient into bleeding submission. The patient, Deborah, Hannah Green's protagonist, reported to the ward doctor the following day. "Why do you want to see him?" the nurse asked. "I have something to tell him." "What is it?" "That a pacifist is one who uses his open hand" (p. 126).

7. Leon Saul, *Psychodynamically Based Psychotherapy* (New York: Science House, 1972), and Leon Saul, *The Childhood Emotional Pattern and Human Hostility* (New York: Van Nostrand Reinhold, 1980).

8. Thomas Gordon, *Parent Effectiveness Training: The No-Lose Program for Raising Responsible Children* (New York: Peter Wyden, 1970).

9. Trigant Burrow, "Neurosis and War: A Problem in Human Behavior," *Journal Psychology* 12 (1941), pp. 235–249, and Trigant Burrow, "Prescription for Peace: The Biological Basis of Man's Ideological Conflicts," in Pitrim A. Sorokin, ed., *Explorations in Altruistic Love and Behavior* (Beacon, N.Y.: Beacon Press, 1950), pp. 93–117.

10. Among contemporary mental health thinkers who sincerely emphasize the significance of assertiveness and self-expression but definitely propose avoiding anger—indeed, they claim that anger is unnecessary—are Thomas Gordon, cited in

note 8, and Albert Ellis: Albert Ellis and Robert A. Harper, *A Guide to Rational Living* (Englewood Cliffs, N.J.: Prentice Hall, 1961). and Albert Ellis, *Reason and Emotion in Psychotherapy* (New York: Lyle Stuart, 1962).

11. R. D. Laing, *The Politics of Experience* (New York: Pantheon, 1967), pp. 48–49.

12. Gibson Winter, *Love and Conflict: New Patterns in Family Life* (New York: Doubleday, 1961), pp. 104, 105.

13. Sheldon Kopp, "The Zaddik," *Psychology Today*, May 1969, p. 29.

14. Anthony Storr, "Possible Substitutes for War," in J. D. Carthy and F. J. Ebling, eds., *The Natural History of Aggression*, Proceedings of a Symposium held at the British Museum, London, 1963 (London: Academic Press, 1964), pp. 139–140.

15. "No child can test out his developing strength . . . if there is no one to oppose. . . . In later life, persons whose parents have failed them in this way often show an alternation between two extremes. They either make no emotional claims on other people, or they make such excessive demands that no one can fulfill them" (Anthony Storr, *Human Aggression* [New York: Athenaeum, 1966], p. 45).

16. George Bach and Peter Wyden, *The Intimate Enemy* (New York: Morrow, 1969), pp. 11, 23.

17. Israel W. Charny, *Marital Love and Hate* (New York: Macmillan, 1972). For an excellent description of a full-scale family therapy that very much works toward renewed warmth and closeness of family members through also working with inner feelings of anger, including forthright communications of anger between family members as well as between therapist and patients, see the existentially oriented family therapy of Carl Whitaker: Carl A. Whitaker and Augustus Y. Napier, *The Family Crucible* (New York: Harper and Row, 1978).

18. A very helpful review of Melanie Klein's thinking will be found in R. B. Money-Kyrle, "British Schools of Psychoanalysis, Number 1: Melanie Klein and Kleinian Psychoanalytic Theory," in Silvano Arieti, ed., *American Handbook of Psychiatry*, vol. 3 (New York: Basic Books, 1966), pp. 225–229.

19. Winnicott's work is discussed in Chapter 6, n. 16, and Chapter 7, in section on "The Individual Who Is to Be the Genocider."

20. A significant, growing number of thinkers have begun to conceptualize much psychopathology and social pathology as a function of unrecognized and undisciplined parental hatred of children, originally a natural process, going amok. Sociologist Leon Sheleff developed a full-scale conceptualization of parental hostility, for which he proffers the name of the Rustum Complex, following an ancient Persian legend of the inadvertent killing of a son, Sohrab, by his father, Rustum (Leon S. Sheleff, "Beyond the Oedipus Complex: A Perspective on the Myth and Reality of Generational Conflict," *Theory and Society* 3 [1976], pp. 1–45. The book-length treatment of this theory is in Leon S. Sheleff, *Generations Apart: Adult Hostility to Youth* [New York: McGraw-Hill, 1981]).

Arnaldo Rascovsky, founder and former president of the Argentine Psychoanalytic Association, is reported in a psychiatric newspaper as saying, harsh as it sounds, that "adults have a basic drive to kill children" (*Roche Frontiers of Psychiatry*, November 1, 1971). See also a discussion of the story of Abraham slaying Isaac as a folk classic of parental availability to destroy one's own child in Israel W. Charny, "And Abraham Went to Slay Isaac," *Journal Ecumenical Studies* 10:2 (1973), pp. 304–318.

Joachim Flescher has written that the basic symbolism of Jesus as God's son may be seen as "a remnant of ritual human sacrifice from our prehistoric ancestors." The basic process he describes is as we have studied: man's effort to spare himself from mortality by sacrificing another in his stead. The point that is especially important here is that men are so desperate for release from mortality that they will focus this magical mechanism of sacrifice even on their own children. Flescher goes on to suggest that in general, the treatment of Jews by Gentiles is a large-scale continuation of the basic misconstruction; the Jews as a nation continue to be the "Jesus-sacrifice" of subsequent Gentile efforts to spare themselves the threat of death. "The treatment of Jews by Gentiles is the most reliable *barometer of mankind's destructive potential*" (Joachim Flescher, *Nazi Holocaust and Mankind's "Final Solution"* [New York: D.T. R.B. Editions, 1971], pp. 23–33).

Another classic, albeit less reverent, piece of literature that speaks to parental destructiveness is Jonathan Swift's memorable, some say mirth-provoking and others say bloodcurdling, satire: Jonathan Swift, "A Modest Proposal for Preventing the Children of Poor People in Ireland from Being a Burden to Their Parents or Country, and for Making Them Beneficial to the Public," in *Prose Writings of Swift*, chosen and arranged by Walter Lewin (London: Walter Scott, 1936), pp. 260–270.

21. Selma H. Fraiberg, *The Magic Years* (New York: Scribner, 1959).

22. Selma H. Fraiberg, "The Origins of Human Bonds," *Commentary* 44 (December 1957), pp. 47–57.

23. Konrad Lorenz, *On Aggression* (New York: Harcourt, Brace & World, 1968).

24. Personal communication; I appreciate very much the permission to use this material.

25. John Bowlby, "Disruption of Affectional Bonds and Its Effects on Behavior," *Canada's Mental Health*, Supplement No. 59 (January-February 1969), p. 3.

26. Albert J. Stolnit, "Some Aspects of Children's Aggressive Behavior During States of Illness and Recovery," in Heinrich Z. Winnik, Rafael Moses, and Mortimer Ostow, eds., *Psychological Bases of War* (New York: Quadrangle; and Jerusalem: Jerusalem Academic Press, 1973), p. 215.

27. The management of such crises of infidelity is the focal example treated in Israel W. Charny, "Injustice and Betrayal as Natural Experiences in Family Life," *Psychotherapy* 9 (1972), pp. 86–91.

28. Jim Forest, "Nhat Hanh on Meditation," *Fellowship*, September 1975, p. 9. The exercises are abbreviated from Nhat Hanh's book, *The Miracle of Being Awake*.

29. Alan G. Newcombe, "'Lovemate': A Personal and International Foreign Policy for Peace," in Israel W. Charny, ed., *Strategies Against Violence* (Boulder, Colo.: Westview, 1978), pp. 3–18.

30. Ibid., pp. 6–7.

31. Ibid., pp. 8–9.

32. Charles E. Osgood, "Suggestion for Winning the Real War with Communism," *Journal Conflict Resolution* 3 (1959), pp. 295–325, and Charles E. Osgood, "Calculated De-escalation as a Strategy," in Dean G. Fruitt and Richard C. Snyder, eds., *Theory and Research on the Causes of War* (Englewood Cliffs, N.J.: Prentice Hall, 1969), pp. 213–216.

33. Newcombe, "'Lovemate,'" pp. 13–14.

34. Bach and Goldberg, *Creative Aggression*.

NOTES TO CHAPTER 12: STRATEGIES FOR NONVIOLENT AGGRESSION IN DESIGNING THE SOCIAL ENVIRONMENT

Epigraph from Kurt Vonnegut, Jr., *Slaughterhouse-Five: On the Children's Crusade—A Duty-Dance with Death* (New York: Delacorte, 1969), pp. 32–33.

1. These four conditions are, in effect, statements of values by which we should seek to direct our behavior. Robert Lifton makes the point very clearly that men, collectively as well as individually, choose and are led to choose behavior such as violence and non-

violence on the basis of their guiding value concepts. "My basic premise is that we understand man through paradigms or models. The choice of the paradigm or model becomes extremely important because it determines what might be called the 'controlling image' or central theme of our psychological theory. Human culture is sufficiently rich that a great variety of paradigms are available to serve as controlling images, including those of 'power,' 'being,' 'instinct and defense,' 'social class,' 'collective unconscious,' 'interpersonal relations,' etc." Lifton cites the work of Kenneth Boulding, *The Image* (Ann Arbor: University of Michigan Press, 1956), in which Boulding stresses that there is present in the organism from the very beginning of life a tendency or direction (which Lifton calls "an *inchoate image*") that emerges as "*an interpretative anticipation of interaction with the environment*" (Robert Jay Lifton, "On Death and the Continuity of Life," *History of Childhood Quarterly: The Journal of Psychohistory* 1:4 [1974], pp. 681–682, 688).

2. Several studies have demonstrated that a commitment to peaceful values adds to personality development and health. A series of studies of students who participated in Children's International Summer Villages (see note 18 below) showed significant gains in personality strength. Psychiatrist Robert Coles observed greater emotional health and maturity in students who took a stand to demonstrate on behalf of peace (Robert Coles, "Psychiatric Observations on Students Demonstrating for Peace," *American Journal Orthopsychiatry* 37 [1967], pp. 107–111). An interesting summary of what is known about how to successfully educate children to nonviolence will be found in Elise Boulding, "The Child and Nonviolent Social Change," in Israel W. Charny, ed., *Strategies Against Violence* (Boulder, Colo.: Westview, 1978), pp. 68–99.

3. At the City University of New York, psychologist Morton Bard developed an outstanding program to study the possibilities of modifying violence in the family through specially trained police units. The police were instructed in how to reduce the contagion of violence in family conflicts rather than to contribute to a further escalation of the conflict. Typically, the arrival of policemen on an angry domestic scene heats up tempers further; in fact, the experience of the New York City Police Department was that policemen were often attacked and injured. In the City University project, the policemen, working with graduate students in psychology, were trained to convey their understanding of the hurt and anger of all parties to the conflict, respect for the people involved, and trust in the peoples' ability to regulate their own behavior without threats of control by the police (Morton Bard, "The Study and Modification of Interfamilial Violence," in Suzanne K. Steinmetz and Murray A. Straus, eds., *Violence in the Family* [New York: Dodd, Mead, 1974], pp. 127–139).

4. *Jerusalem Post*, November 4, 1954.

5. Daniel Glazer, "Victim Survey Research: Theoretical Implications," in Israel Drapkin and Emilio Viano, eds., *Victimology* (Lexington, Mass.: D. C. Heath, 1974), pp. 31–41.

6. A concept of disorder, dissent, difference, and controversy is vital to the structure of a democratic society, but not so civil disobedience, espionage, terrorism, criminality, and so on. See, for example, the monograph of Supreme Court Justice Fortas on a riot-torn United States: Abe Fortas, *Concerning Dissent and Civil Disobedience: We Have an Alternative to Violence* (New York: Signet, 1968). For an interesting analysis of the necessary role of disorder in urban life, see Richard Sennett, *The Uses of Disorder: Personal Identity and City Life* (New York: Knopf, 1970).

7. Ruth Benedict, as cited by Robert A. Smith, "Synergistic Organizations: Humanistic Extensions of Man's Evolution?" *Man's Emergent Evolution*, an issue of *Fields Within Fields Within Fields: The Methodology of the Creative Process* 3:1 (1970), p. 40. The concept of synergy used in the paper refers to union, unity, or partnership. The term was

developed by Benedict and later used by Abraham Maslow, who is also quoted by Smith: "Those societies have high synergy in which the social institutions are set up so as to transcend the polarity between selfishness and unselfishness" (ibid., p. 41).

8. Paul Wehr, "Conflict Education Through Experiential Learning," in John Whiteclay Chambers, ed., "Peace Research and Its Impact on the Curriculum," Conference on Peace Research in History, mimeographed (Faculty of Social Sciences, State University of New York at Plattsburgh, 1972), pp. 115–116. See also Paul Wehr and Michael Washburn, eds., *Peace and World Order Systems* (Beverly Hills, Calif.: Sage, 1976).

9. Johan Galtung, "Theories of Peace: A Synthetic Approach to Peace Thinking," mimeographed (Oslo: University of Oslo, 1967), pp. 216–218. Unpublished manuscript used with the kind permission of the author. A similar point has been made about the very structure of science: The very conflicts within it are ultimately its strength. "Science submits a rational picture of the world, highly differentiated, fraught with conflict, and anything but homogeneous. A power monopoly, on the contrary, exhibits a tendency to operate in what might be described as a magic picture of the world. . . . Empirical data are not welcome unless and insofar as they are in keeping with . . . ideological categories and principles" (Ladislav Tondie, "Conflict Situations in Scientific Communities," *International Social Science Journal* 22:1 [1970], pp. 111–126).

10. Mohandas Ghandi, reprinted from *The Selected Works of Mahatma Ghandi*, ed. Shriman Narayan, vol. 4, in Thomas E. Hackey and Ralph E. Weber, eds., *Voices of Revolution: Rebels and Rhetoric* (Hinsdale, Ill.: Dryden, 1972), p. 312.

11. Excessive violence on television is well documented. George Gerbner, dean of the Annenberg School of Communications at the University of Pennsylvania, has been instrumental in developing much of the data of such "violence counts" from year to year in the United States. An overview of the problem from a larger world perspective can be found in Mary Burnet, *The Mass Media in a Violent World* (Paris: UNESCO, 1971).

12. Claude Lewis, an astute columnist, wrote at the time of the great success of the movie *The Godfather:*

> If you like watching detailed murder, violence, threats, deceit, abuse, blood, terror, anguish, racism, corruption, vice and brutality, you will love "The Godfather."
>
> Movie critics – all far more qualified than I – have generally said it is a great film. They are right if you like mayhem and controlled, organized madness.
>
> If you've never seen (close up) anyone shot in the eye, or strangled by a fine wire, or gunned down in the gutter, or clubbed, kicked or bitten, or walloped with a garbage can, or riddled by a maniac with a submachine gun and then bashed in the face, "The Godfather" is for you. . . .
>
> Hitler happened. But to film his horrible holocausts in dedicated detail on full-color screen would be to glorify his grotesqueness and ultimately serve to bring a kind of bastardized beauty to it all. Because technical achievement almost always tends to mask the true depth of depravity.
>
> What purpose is served – other than to make money – in simulating the most private portions of grievous and vicious deaths on film? Like the Godfather himself, the film knows no subtleties. The atrocities on the screen are often acts beyond murder.
>
> Perhaps what really bothers me most about "The Godfather" is what the film says about us all. The movie makes a genuine appeal to man's basest instincts. And for the most part, it succeeds. [Claude Lewis, "Only a Sick Society Would Applaud *The Godfather*," *Philadelphia Bulletin*, March 26, 1972]

13. Margaret Mead, "Violence and Its Regulation: How Do Children Learn to Govern Their Own Violent Impulses?" *American Journal Orthopsychiatry* 39 (1969), pp. 228–229.

14. U.S. Public Health Service, Surgeon General's Advisory Committee on Television and Social Behavior, *Television and Growing Up: The Impact of Televised Violence* (Washington, D.C.: Government Printing Office, 1972), p. 78.

15. Israel W. Charny, "We Need a Human Language for Reporting the Tragedies of Current Violent Events: Towards a Model for the Content, Tone, and Dramatic Mood of the Broadcaster Reporting the News of Human Violence," *International Journal Group Tensions* 2:3 (1972), pp. 52–62; reprinted in Charny, ed., *Strategies Against Violence*, pp. 200–211. Of course, a variety of codes and guidelines have been drafted in various quarters that propose to define the limits of acceptable portrayals of violence. See, for example, the brief but very sensitive and knowledgeable statement by the British Broadcasting Corporation, *The Portrayal of Violence in Television Programmes: A Note of Guidance* (London, March 1972). See also Melvin S. Heller and Samuel Polsky, "Television Violence: Guidelines for Evaluation," *Archives General Psychiatry* 24 (1971), pp. 279–285.

16. See William A. Nesbitt, ed., *Teaching Global Issues Through Simulation: It Can Be Easy, Intercom* 75 (Summer 1974). A strong statement of the linkage between everyday, local issues of peace and justice and larger global issues of world order is found in Gerald Mische and Patricia Mische, *Toward a Human World Order: Beyond the National Security Straightjacket* (New York: Paulist Press, 1977).

17. A very interesting pedagogical application of conflict theory to teaching young people how to get along with antagonists and themselves is in Anatol Pikas, "We Speak and We Listen: National Conflict Resolution Through Communication," mimeographed (Uppsala: Pedagogistia Institutionen, 1975). This is a prepublication edition in English of a book that has been published in several European languages.

18. See, for example: UNESCO, *Education for International Understanding: Examples and Suggestions for Classroom Use* (Paris, 1959) and UNESCO, *International Understanding of School: An Account of Progress in Unesco's Associated Schools Project* (Paris, 1965). See also the heartwarming program initiated by psychologist Doris Allen that grew into the worldwide Children's International Summer Villages: Doris Twitchell Allen, "Measurement of Effectiveness of a Program for Peace: Children's International Summer Villages," *International Mental Health Research Newsletter* 10:2 (Summer 1968), pp. 13–15, and Doris Twitchell Allen, "Children for a World Community," in Charny, ed., *Strategies Against Violence*, pp. 232–253.

19. An excellent series on education for war and peace was produced in journal pamphlets with the name of *Intercom*, published by the Center for War/Peace Studies, 218 E. 18th Street, New York. Outstanding issues have included: *Conscience and War: The Moral Dilemma* 63 (1969), *Education for War, Peace, Conflict, and Change* 65 (1970), *The Human Person and the War System* 66 (1971), *Teaching About Spaceship Earth: A Role-Playing Experience for the Middle Grades*, 71 (1972).

20. The Consortium on Peace Research, Education, and Development (COPRED), whose secretariat at this writing is at Kent State University, is a central source of current information about such projects.

21. Hostile groups can be placed together under pleasant situations, but that does not necessarily reduce conflict between them (see M. Sherif, *In Common Predicament* [Boston: Houghton Mifflin, 1966]). It is also true that people can be exposed to one another under very positive circumstances and yet turn against one another when war erupts. The critical determinant is the internal perception people have of one another and not just the external circumstances of any contact, however pleasurable it is. There are many stories of foreign nationals who were warmly befriended in some country and then used their knowledge of that country for espionage and warfare purposes against their former host.

22. A large-scale project on the elementary school level that has produced an impressive array of theoretical papers, along with the operational materials of the project

itself, is the Diablo Valley Education Project: Teaching About War, Peace, Conflict, and Change: An Experimental Curriculum Development Project, Initiated and Carried Out in the Schools of Contra Costa County, California. Another example of curriculum development is that of the United Kingdom World Studies Project sponsored by One World Trust, an educational charity foundation founded in 1952 by some members of the nonpartisan Parliamentary Group for World Government in London. The project takes as its goal a curriculum that teaches "loyalty to the human race in all its diversity" (Christoph Wulf and Susan Carpenter, eds., *Peace Education*, special issue of the *International Peace Research Newsletter* 12:3-4 [1974], pp. 17-20).

23. Herman Roehrs, "The International Comprehensive School as a School for Peace," in Wulf and Carpenter, eds., *Peace Education*, pp. 23-24.

24. The information about the Aktion Suhnezeichen is from the *International Peace Research Newsletter* 13:4 (1975), p. 25.

25. Gene Sharp has written a definitive, encyclopedic review of the history of nonviolent action on the part of both peoples and governments: *The Politics of Nonviolent Action* (Boston: Porter Sargent, 1973). Although history shows very little commitment to peace, there are surprisingly many incredible stories of successful nonviolent actions through the ages.

26. Adam Curle, "The Scope and Dilemmas of Peace Studies," Inaugural lecture delivered at the University of Bradford, England, February 4, 1975, as reported in the *International Peace Research Newsletter* 13:4 (1975), pp. 3-5. The same point was implied in another inaugural address by the then director of the U.S. Peace Corps, Jack Vaughn, at a banquet inaugurating the Center for the Study of the Causes of War and Conditions for Peace at Utah State University in 1967:

> Peace, also, has had its lexicon. Peace was good for you. Peace was the re-emergence of "our" way of life—on both sides of the border. Peace was the warmth and healing of sunshine. It was calm and normalcy. It was the resumption of everything good—and the improvement of everything bad. Peace was love, and if not quite love—then at least there was nothing afoot quite bad enough to hate.
>
> Paired off, "war" and "peace" were an expression of total contrast, no blending here . . . no confusion. Life and death. Black and white. Good and bad. War and peace. . . .
>
> Examine mercilessly, and I believe you will discover that history's favorite absolutes—"war" and "peace" are a tragic masquerade.

27. The United Nations Institute for Training and Research (UNITAR) has been active in experiments of models for negotiations. An interesting round table on several projects by different centers will be found in "Observations on International Negotiations," mimeographed (Greenwich, Conn.: Academy Educational Development, 1971).

28. James H. Craig and Marge Craig, *Synergic Power* (Berkeley, Calif.: Proactive Press, 1974). Examples of a very precise methodolgy for no-lose negotiations of serious differences will be found in A. Levi and Benjamin A. Levi, "Jews and Arabs Rehearse Geneva: A Model of Conflict Resolution," *Human Relations* 29 (1976), pp. 1035-1041, and A. M. Levi and G. Metonomski, "A Computer System to Aid Decision Making in Large Groups: A Practical Proposal," mimeographed (Haifa: University of Haifa, 1975).

The no-lose concept of negotiations is a further extension of the concept of shared goals that was demonstrated so brilliantly by the classical work of Sherif in the Robbers' Cave Experiment. Children in a summer camp setting were subjected to a grueling sequence of conditions, which moved them back and forth between alternate bouts of angry competition and prejudice and then reunions in common purpose and friendship after they were presented with a common problem that required their cooperation with one another. The possibilities and necessity of shared goals between combatant peoples in our world are endless if only there is leadership to direct people to respond to the problems. For example, we see repeated everywhere on earth problems of pollution and a poisoning of the seas that are the common boundaries of nations that are otherwise at one stage or another of serious or potential conflict (M. Sherif, O. J. Harvey, B. J. White, W. R. Hood, and Carolyn W. Sherif, *Intergroup Conflict and Cooperation: The Robbers' Cave Experiment* [Norman, Okla.: University Book Exchange, 1961]).

29. Theodore F. Lentz, *Towards the Technology of Peace* (St. Louis: Peace Research Laboratory, 1972).

30. Harold Lasswell has written on the possible contributions of psychotherapists to global peace. He suggests several types of activity, including, naively, counseling political figures and affecting the selection of leaders but also, intriguingly, "surveying and influencing collective tension levels . . . , guiding crash programs at crisis moments, and mobilizing predispositions by world training programs" (Harold D. Lasswell, "The Interconnections of Political Power, Psychotherapy, and World Community," mimeographed [Address to the American Psychoanalytic Association, Los Angeles, May, 1975], p. 12).

31. The one world that is becoming more and more an actuality in our age of air travel brings to mind the conceptualization of the shared goals of all humanity as the irrevocability of the common destiny of passengers on Spaceship Earth. This metaphor was the basis for a series of curricular materials on the elementary school level (Charles Bloomstein, ed., *Teaching About Spaceship Earth, Intercom* 71 [1972]).

32. The author of the concept of an international disaster army is Chanan Rapaport, director of the Szold National Institute for Research in the Behavioral Sciences, Jerusalem, and coauthor of the concluding chapter of this book, "Toward a Genocide Early Warning System."

33. One of the utterly tragic problems of genocidal disasters is what to do with the survivors and escapees. It is not an easy task for other nations to absorb huge numbers of refugees from other lands. At least, that is the "innocent" side of the incredible cruelty that so many nations have shown to refugees; one can hardly escape the feeling that in many cases, the nations that stand by without helping, even when they can, are indirectly sanctioning the extermination of their era's victims. One of the telling epigrams of such cruelty is attributed to British Lord Moynen when discussions were under way about the Nazis' possible release of a million Jews in return for a fleet of trucks. Lord Moynen is reported to have said, "What shall I do with this million of Jews? Where shall I put them?" (Shalom Rosenfeld, *Criminal File 124: The Greenwald-Kastner Trial* [Tel-Aviv: Hes Kerni, 1956], p. 66; in Hebrew – the quotation itself is reported in English). Although the concept of an international disaster army does not address the problem of refugees directly, prior provision for such services to refugees does represent some measure of solution to the problem of what to do for people in disasters. In addition, such international readiness to aid in disasters should contribute to a more hospitable climate for receiving refugees.

34. A. Paul Hare, "Dealing with Collective Violence [with Examples from India and Kent State]," in Charny, ed., *Strategies Against Violence*, pp. 257–279. Hare describes the operation of nonviolent armies in India when religious riots threatened and the work of a nonviolence research team at Kent State University in the wake of the tragic slaying of four students and the threat of still further violence.

35. Gideon Hausner, the state prosecutor for Israel in the Eichmann trial, continues to this day to speak of the failure of the Allies to bomb Auschwitz, even though target-accurate bombing was being carried out by the Allies nearby (Gideon Hausner, "Why

Wasn't Auschwitz Bombed?" Letter to the Editor, *Haaretz* [Tel Aviv], March 13, 1975; in Hebrew).

NOTES TO CHAPTER 13: TOWARD A
GENOCIDE EARLY WARNING SYSTEM

Epigraphs from Milton Mayer, *They Thought They Were Free: The Germans 1933-45* (Chicago: University of Chicago Press, 1966), p. xix, and Anna W. M. Wolf, "Educating for Peace," *Child Study* 25 (1938), pp. 231-234.

1. Marc Pilisuk and Lyn Ober, "Torture and Genocide as Public Health Problems," *American Journal Orthopsychiatry* 46:3 (1976), pp. 388-392.

2. For a time, Amnesty International, which was established in 1961, was viewed in some quarters as somewhat leftist, or at least as an unduly naive, liberal group that failed to distinguish between torture and the legitimate and realistic necessities of military and police functions against revolutionaries, terrorists, and other groups who clothed themselves in "liberation" semantics to disguise their own vicious assaults on human life, while charging the established governments with cruelties. More recently, however, Amnesty is emerging as a responsible organization whose annual report of torture around the world is looked to by citizens rights groups and governments with increasing respect.

At the center of Amnesty's activities is a Prisoner of Conscience Library. Amnesty seeks to maintain information about people who are held as political prisoners (defined as "those physically restrained from expressing an honestly held opinion that does not advocate violence"). Information is collected from friends and relatives of prisoners, a systematic scanning of newspapers, and inquiries, including sending authorized representatives to investigate the situation of a prisoner. The group then works by methods such as approaching embassies and writing letters to newspapers to secure prisoners' releases, at the same time it provides some assistance for prisoners and their families. At this point, at least, Amnesty is concerned primarily with individual cases, and, in fact, it carefully represents itself as an advocate of individual rights rather than as an observer of the larger status of human rights in a given nation, although there is a trend in Amnesty reports toward more overviewing of torture and the legal practices of countries (see Evan Luard, ed., *The International Protection of Human Rights* [London: Thames and Hudson, 1967]; also the *Amnesty International Annual Reports*).

Other agencies, too, concern themselves with monitoring various aspects of civil rights around the world. One important source of information about major world events is Keesing's *Contemporary Archives*. The International Commission of Jurists, based in Geneva, issues very important advice on human rights violations. The International League for the Rights of Man, a nongovernmental organization accredited to the United Nations, follows and reports on offenses against human rights. Freedom House in New York issues meaningful surveys of the status of freedom in different countries. However, to the best of our knowledge, none of these reporting agencies attempts to maintain a systematic information system as to ongoing genocides, or the broader picture of the status of human rights in different countries, and for the most part each agency is committed to its traditional mode for distributing information, not to the development of multimedia means for arousing and alerting an informed world public.

3. In a special issue of the magazine published by the United Nations Association of the United States, which was devoted to the thirtieth anniversary of the United Nations, William Korey, a past chairman of the observer programs of the World Assembly on Human Rights and the conference of UN representatives of the association, writes about human rights in general: "Violations of human rights appear as widespread today, if not

more so, as at any time in the past. The thousands of petitions – 'communications' – reaching the U.N. annually, relating violations of human rights, constitute only the tip of the iceberg. Gross violations of human rights often go unreported. An Amnesty International report last year documented the practice of physical and psychological torture in some 60 countries of the globe. Even terrifying instances of genocide reappeared, beginning in the sixties" (William Korey, "U.N. Human Rights, Illusion and Reality: Violations of Human Rights Appear as Widespread Today, If Not More So, As at Any Time in the Past," *U.N. 30, Interdependent* 2:7 [August 1975], pp. 117).

4. For many years, the United States has stood out as conspicuously absent from the list of signatories to the genocide convention. In a release dated August 7, 1974, the Bureau of Public Affairs of the Department of State noted:

The United States, although participating in the development of the Convention text, and voting for and signing it, has never ratified or acceded to it. President Nixon noted this in a message to the Senate on February 19, 1970 and urged the Senate to consider anew this Convention. He stated that its ratification would reaffirm the stringent United States opposition to the crime of genocide, and he added that the Attorney General and the Secretary of State believe that there are no constitutional obstacles to US ratification.

The Genocide Convention outlaws action that is repugnant to the American people and contrary to the principles on which our country was founded. Our failure to adhere to this Convention is an unnecessary diplomatic embarrassment and leaves us open to criticism despite our condemnation of genocide. Conversely, by ratifying the Convention, we would be publicly reaffirming our faith in the concepts of human dignity and human rights, and we would be helping to strengthen the structure of international law.

5. A noteworthy number of cancer research projects are designed around marking cancer cells in such a way that the body will be able to recognize them as enemies. These studies follow from the conception of cancer as a process wherein the pathological cells have lost contact with the rest of the body because the normal interactive genetic message is not being communicated; hence, the cancerous cells are not triggering natural immunologic reactions that normally fight off the cancer process (personal communication, Alberto Podorgny, Weizmann Institute of Science).

6. Ervin Laszlo, "World System Research and Information Bureau," *International Associations* 16:1 (1974), p. 36.

7. David Weisbrodt, a professor of international law, testified at a U.S. congressional hearing in 1978: "Perhaps the greatest problem facing non-governmental organizations and researchers concerned about international human rights is the need for human rights documentation" (David Weisbrodt, "Testimony Before U.S. House Committee on International Relations," *Human Rights Internet* 3:7–8 [1978], p. 5).

8. Pinchas Lapid has argued that the Turks' massacre of the Armenians was significant not only in its own tragic right, but also as a "dress rehearsal" for the Holocaust that was to follow. Lapid argues that the dress rehearsal took in several levels: not only the actual systematization of mass destruction, but also the attention given to covering up news of the massacre, the actual participation of Germans in the killings executed by the Turks, and the fact that the world was largely silent about the tragedy of the Armenians and did not punish the killers, thereby tacitly encouraging the Holocaust and other genocides in years to come (Pinchas Lapid, "The 'Dress-Rehearsal' for the Holocaust," *Bulletin of Bar-Ilan University*, Summer 1974, pp. 14–20; in Hebrew).

9. Robert Conquest, *The Nation Killers: The Soviet Deportation of Nationalities* (London: Macmillan, 1970).

10. In discussing the concepts of the Universal Declaration of Human Rights, Jorge Dominguez argues that in order to bridge between the different definitions of human rights data that various governments put forth and the real human rights situation one is seeking to evaluate, a data system should be built around concepts of values as well as of facts. He reviews various available frameworks, including the framework provided by the eight basic values of social life identified by Harold Lasswell and Abraham Kaplan: power, respect, rectitude, wealth, well-being, enlightenment, skill, and affection. Dominguez then adds four "modes of enjoyment," which are to cut across those values: security, growth, equality, and liberty. He concludes, "Assessments can be made about human rights conditions by using empirical data. . . . But 'What then' is a question that will continue to face us all" (Jorge I. Dominguez, Nigel S. Rodley, Bryce Wood, and Richard Falk, *Enhancing Global Human Rights* [New York: McGraw-Hill, 1979]. See also Harold Lasswell and Abraham Kaplan, *Power and Society* [New Haven: Yale University Press, 1965] and note 12 below).

William Korey writes about the Universal Declaration of Human Rights: "If the manifesto acts as a powerful beacon that provides light and inspiration for those suffering oppression or struggling for basic rights, it nonetheless lacks the kind of machinery that can bring about compliance with its various provisions. It may constitute international law, but it is devoid of enforcement powers that could give it genuine effectiveness. Implementation machinery, with certain notable exceptions, is missing. . . . HUMAN RIGHTS IS A DANGEROUS PANDORA'S BOX TO MANY OFFICIALS. IF IT WERE OPENED NO GOVERNMENT WOULD BE SAFE FROM ATTACK" (William Korey, "U.N. Human Rights, Illusion and Reality," p. 118).

11. Herbert C. Kelman, "Violence Without Moral Restraint," *Journal Social Issues* 29 (1973), pp. 25, 31.

12. One of the most ambitious proposals for worldwide monitoring of a wide variety of social indicators was put forth by the team of Richard Snyder, Charles Hermann, and Harold Lasswell. Their central focus is that governments can be evaluated for their effects on human dignity. Although the academic world has reacted with many of the usual, if necessary, reservations and criticisms of feasibility, this proposal has generated considerable support overall and, in many quarters, even excitement (Richard C. Snyder, Charles Hermann, and Harold D. Lasswell, "A Global Monitoring System: Appraising the Effects of Government on Human Dignity," *International Studies Quarterly* 20:2 [1976], pp. 221–260).

13. In certain areas of psychiatry, we have had frighteningly real examples of how behavioral science concepts and professionals can be subverted to tasks of destruction. We saw in Chapter 2 how in Nazi Germany, psychiatrists were among the leaders of the first mass extermination programs, which were rationalized as the legitimate treatment of the mentally ill, retarded, and incompetent (Fredric Wertham, "The Geranium in the Window: The Euthanasia Murders," in Wertham, *A Sign for Cain* [New York: Macmillan, 1966]).

14. President Carter's Commission on the Holocaust, under the chairmanship of Elie Wiesel, followed a commendable path toward proposing a Holocaust center that would be both a memorial to peoples who have suffered genocide and an active research center (*Report of the President's Commission on The Holocaust* [Washington, D.C.: Government Printing Office, 1974]). About relating the Holocaust to the plight of the peoples, Wiesel writes: "How to reconcile the specifically Jewish victims with the universality of all victims haunted us throughout the pilgrimage. . . . As if, by speaking of Jews, we were somehow turning our backs on the millions of non-Jews the Nazis slaughtered. Which, of course, is not the case. Quite the contrary: As we evoke the Jewish martyrdom, we also recall the suf-

ferings and deaths of the non-Jewish victims. The universality of the Holocaust must be realized in its uniqueness" (Elie Wiesel, reporting on the trip of President Carter's Commission on the Holocaust to Auschwitz and other death camps in the *New York Times Magazine*).

15. See the same emphasis on values and seeing events as parts of larger patterns in the following comparison between traditional approaches to individual human problems and a world order approach, which appeared in the newsletter of the Institute for World Order in New York, *Macroscope* No. 2 (Winter–Spring 1977), p. 6. (A fuller development is in Burns H. Weston, "Contending with a Planet in Peril and Change: An Optimum Educational Response," *Alternatives: A Journal of World Policy* 5:1 [1975], pp. 59–95.)

Traditional Approaches	*World Order Approach*
1. Analysis presumed value free	1. Analysis is value oriented – aimed at value clarification and realization
2. Ultimate analytical goal is description	2. Ultimate analytical goal is prescription
3. Time dimension is past and present	3. Time dimension is past, present, and especially future
4. Problems seen as separate issues	4. Problems seen as interrelated issues
5. Focuses on nation-states and governmental elites	5. Focuses on range of actors from individuals to supranational institutions
6. Policy goals defined in terms of national interest (designed to maximize national power and wealth)	6. Policy goals defined in terms of global interest (designed to meet human needs)
7. Power seen as basically military and economic	7. Power seen as not only the ability to coerce
8. Large-scale violence considered as an acceptable means to implement policy goals	8. Large-scale violence ordinarily considered unacceptable
9. Human survival assumed	9. Human survival deemed problematical

16. In a series of "commandments" to students of collective behavior, sociologists Marx and Wood comment, "Thou shalt walk an intellectual tight rope that permits collective and conventional behavior to be viewed in light of common theoretical and conceptual frameworks, but that does not claim no differences exist between them" (Gary T. Marx and James L. Wood, "Strands of Theory and Research in Collective Behavior," *Annual Review Sociology* 1 [1975], p. 416).

17. See the discussion of the dynamics of suicide in Chapter 10, section on "Why Do People Ask to be Victimized?"

18. Samuel Warner, *The Urge to Mass Destruction* (New York: Grune & Stratton, 1957).

19. Kurt Wolff calls for a "sociology of evil," that is, a study of the etymology and semantics of evil in various languages, the place of evil in the history of philosophy, the relationships between evil and technology, evil and the law, and so on (Kurt H. Wolff, "For a Sociology of Evil," *Journal Social Issues* 25:1 [1969], pp. 111–125).

20. Edwin I. Megargie, "Matricide, Patricide, and the Dynamics of Aggression," mimeographed (Paper delivered at a symposium, Murder Within the Family, at the annual meeting of the American Psychological Association, Washington, D.C., 1967), and Edwin I. Megargie, "The Role of Inhibition in the Assessment and Understanding of Violence," in Jerome L. Singer, ed., *The Control of Aggression and Violence* (New York: Academic Press, 1971), pp. 125–147.

It is intriguing, and important, that even when there is a bona fide organic basis for an individual's eruption into violence, personal psychological processes and the societal processes that affect the individual's orientation to violence still determine to a great extent whether or not the pressure of the organic process will find its expression in destructive ways. A panel of thirty-two specialists reporting to Texas Governor John Connally about the Whitman case, a man who went berserk on a university campus, called the tumor Whitman suffered "extremely malignant" but they were not convinced that it was responsible for his bloody acts. "The report points out that the murderer had been accustomed since childhood to handle guns. Later, during his military training for sharpshooting, he became an expert in the use of firearms." The same commission suggested that soldiers who have been trained for killing in such a way that their whole thinking process will have been shaped by their training should be reconditioned or reeducated prior to their return to civilian life (*Fellowship* 33:3 [March 1967]; see also Mortimer D. Gross, "Violence Associated with Organic Brain Disease," in Jan Fawcett, ed., *Dynamics of Violence* [Chicago: American Medical Association, 1971], pp. 85–91).

21. A powerful study of witch-hunting by an outstanding student of genocide, Norman Cohn of the Columbus Center at Sussex University, England (a research center that is concerned with the dynamics of persecution and extermination), describes the devastating "collective fantasy" and collective persecution of hapless men and women, especially the latter, who were accused of being witches and then destroyed by the community in its "self-defense" (Norman Cohn, *Europe's Inner Demons: An Enquiry Inspired by the Great Witch-Hunt* [New York: Basic Books, 1975]). Reviewer John Demos wrote in the *New York Times* about the book, "Few previous works have demonstrated so convincingly the power of 'inner' constructs to shape historical events" (John Demos, review of Norman Cohn, *Europe's Inner Demons*, in *New York Times Book Review*, August 10, 1975). See also Norman Cohn, *Warrant for Genocide: The Myth of the Jewish Conspiracy and the Protocols of the Elders of Zion* (New York: Harper, 1969).

Here we might also take note of a book by the brilliant "prophet" Elie Wiesel, who describes, in story form, a twentieth-century blood-libel and pogrom in a small town – using this plot as a metaphor for the Holocaust. The story centers around a missing Christian child. There are rumors in the marketplace that the Jews killed him. An air of pogrom is all about when one Jew, Moshe, steps in to offer himself as the murderer of the child, though he is not, but the moral process has already reached the point that one sacrifice will no longer satisfy the mob. The pogrom must proceed in all its raw passion (Elie Wiesel, *The Oath* [New York: Random House, 1973]).

22. Gene Sharp, *The Politics of Nonviolent Action* (Boston: Porter Sargent, 1973).

23. The pressure for legitimizing violence that previously was not sanctioned becomes greater when a society undergoes major upheavals, such as during wartime or during economic or other disasters, and when the basic ideological definitions in a society change radically. Allen Grimshaw emphasizes two conditions that characterize the emergence of collective violence: (1) when previously stable superior/subordinate relationships between peoples lose their hold and (2) when there is a belief that societal control agencies are either weak or partisan or both (Allen D. Grimshaw, "Interpreting Collective Violence: An Argument for the Importance of Social Structure," in James F. Short, Jr., and Marvin E. Wolfgang, eds., *Collective Violence, Annals of the American Academy of Political and Social Science* 391 [1970], pp. 9–20).

24. William A. Westley, "The Escalation of Violence Through Legitimation," in Marvin E. Wolfgang, ed., *Patterns of Violence, Annals of the American Academy of Political and Social Science* 364 (1966), pp. 120–126.

25. When *The Holocaust* was shown on West German television, the editor in chief of the mass-circulation *Stern* magazine acknowledged: "I knew that defenceless people were being exterminated like vermin in the name of Germany. Yes, I knew about it and I was too cowardly to offer any opposition" (Reuters, *Jerusalem Post*, February 2, 1979).

26. Robert Payne, *Massacre: The Tragedy at Bangla Desh and the Phenomenon of Mass Slaughter Throughout History* (New York: Macmillan, 1973), Chapter 6, "A Schema of Massacre," pp. 76–87. An excellent summary of the stages of the unfolding of the Holocaust will be found in a pamphlet published by Yad Vashem, *The Holocaust* (Jerusalem, 1975).

27. The story of Erich Dorf in the book and television film, *The Holocaust*, is a powerful illustration of such denial of experiencing (Gerald Green, *The Holocaust* [New York: Bantam, 1978]).

28. Neil J. Smelser, *Collective Behavior* (New York: Free Press, 1963). For a critique of Smelser's book and a response by him, see Elliott Currie and Jerome H. Skolnick, "A Critical Note on Conceptions of Collective Behavior," in Short and Wolfgang, eds., *Collective Violence*, pp. 34–45, and Neil J. Smelser, "Two Critics in Search of a Bias: A Response to Currie and Skolnick," ibid., pp. 46–55.

29. Smelser, *Collective Behavior*, p. 262.

30. A. Paul Hare, "Cyprus–Conflict and Its Resolution," pamphlet (Inaugural lecture at the University of Cape Town, South Africa, May 1974), and A. Paul Hare, "Theories of Group Development and Categories for Interaction Analysis," *Small Group Behavior* 4:3 (1973), pp. 259–304. See also A. Paul Hare, *Handbook of Small Group Research* (Glencoe, Ill.: Free Press, 1976), and A. Paul Hare and Herbert H. Blumberg, eds., *Nonviolent Direction Action: American Cases, Social-Psychological Analyses* (Washington: Corpus, 1968).

31. A frightening example of the nonsense of one-sided explanations of human experience is the remark of a well-known family therapist who commented that there should have been relatively little suffering during the Holocaust in Jewish families whose basic family structure was psychologically sound!

32. Vahakn N. Dadrian, "The Structural-Functional Components of Genocide: A Victimological Approach to the Armenian Case," in Israel Drapkin and Emilio Viano, eds., *Victimology* (Lexington, Mass.: D. C. Heath, 1974), pp. 123–136.

33. For example, when a Nazi party in Minneapolis succeeded in a municipal election, the event meant the party was no longer a fringe party but a meaningful indicator, though in the larger perspective, still a low-level indicator (see Jack Porter, "A Nazi Runs for Mayor," *Present Time* 4:4 [1977], pp. 27–31).

34. Irving Louis Horowitz, *Genocide: State Power and Mass Murder* (New Brunswick, N.J.: Transaction, 1976).

35. Helen Fein, *Accounting for Genocide: National Responses and Jewish Victimization During the Holocaust* (New York: Free Press, 1979), p. 325.

36. Dadrian has made an effort to classify different types of genocide as cultural; latent, e.g., via deportation; retributive or localized atrocities, as a meting out of punishment; utilitarian or regional massacres; and optimal or full-scale holocausts (Vahakn N. Dadrian, "A Typology of Genocide," *International Review Modern Sociology* 5:2 [1975], pp. 201–212). Sociologist Jack Nusan Porter argues that genocide presupposes a clear intent to wipe out the target people; all other killing is more like "oppression" or "massacres," not genocide. Porter's argument has the advantage of defining genocide more clearly but the disadvantage of excluding too many situations of mass murder (Jack Nusan Porter, "What Is Genocide?" [Unpublished paper]). See also Lucy S. Davidowicz, *The War Against the Jews 1933–1945* (New York: Bantam, 1976).

37. Fishel Schneorson was a psychologist in Tel Aviv who called out in 1943:

We must alert the peoples of the entire world that the destruction of millions in Europe is not the tragedy of those millions alone, nor of the Jewish People mourning its sons, but this is a worldwide epidemic, in the fullest tragic sense, that threatens death and destruction to the existence of humanity itself. Although everyone knows that the Jewish People are indeed the first victims of the Nazi destruction, they are neither the only ones nor the last. It is enough to recall the slaughter of the Gypsies that the Nazis are conducting in Europe according to their plan for eliminating inferior races, as well as the mass destruction of Soviet prisoners. This is the way of epidemics, the surest victims are the weak, but in the course of time none are spared and more and more victims are added. [Fishel Schneorson, *Psychohistory of the Holocaust and Rebirth: Essays and Researches* (Tel Aviv: Izre'el, 1968), p. 12, in Hebrew]

38. See John C. Flanagan, "The Critical Incident Technique," *Psychological Bulletin* 51 (1954), pp. 327–358.

39. Davidowicz, *War Against the Jews 1933-1945.*

40. "A system flow chart covering many social events . . . would reveal a confluence of multiple causes of violence, where several factors come together at approximately the same time and exceed the threshhold of suppression through mutual reinforcement" (Roy Grinker, Sr., "What Is the Cause of Violence?" in Jan Fawcett, ed., *Dynamics of Violence* [Chicago: American Medical Association, 1971], p. 59).

41. A bibliography of researches of such disasters is in Anita Cochran, "A Selected Annotated Bibliography on Natural Hazards," mimeographed (Institute of Behavioral Science, University of Colorado, September 1972). Increasingly, disaster research centers have been established at various universities, such as Ohio State, which publishes a newsletter about disaster studies, *Unscheduled Events.*

42. Years ago, the brilliant social novelist Sinclair Lewis wrote what has become a byword for the denial of potential destruction to ourselves: *It Can't Happen Here* (New York: Doubleday, 1935).

43. Lewis A. Coser, "The Visibility of Evil," *Journal Social Issues* 25:1 (1969), pp. 108–109.

NOTES TO POSTSCRIPT: A REDEFINITION OF "ABNORMALITY"

Epigraph from "An interview with Alfred Hassler," *Fellowship*, September 1974, p. 6.

1. James C. Coleman, James N. Butcher, and Robert C. Carson, *Abnormal Psychology and Modern Life*, 6th ed. (Glenview, Ill.: Scott, Foresman, 1980), p. 14.

2. Ibid., p. 15.

SELECTED
BIBLIOGRAPHY

Arendt, Hannah. *The Origins of Totalitarianism*. Cleveland: Meridian, 1968.

Arens, Richard, ed. *Genocide in Paraguay*. Philadelphia: Temple University Press, 1978.

Becker, Ernest. *The Denial of Death*. New York: Free Press, 1973.

Choron, Jacques. *Modern Man and Mortality*. New York: Macmillan, 1964.

Chorover, Stephen L. *From Genesis to Genocide*. Cambridge, Mass.: M.I.T. Press, 1979.

Cohn, Norman. *Europe's Inner Demons: An Enquiry Inspired by the Great Witch-Hunt*. New York: Basic Books, 1975.

_____. *Warrant for Genocide: The Myth of the Jewish Conspiracy and the Protocols of the Elders of Zion*. New York: Harper, 1969.

Coser, Lewis A., ed. *Collective Violence and Civil Conflict*. Journal Social Issues 28:1 (1972).

Davidowicz, Lucy S. *The War Against the Jews 1933–1945*. New York: Bantam, 1976.

Dicks, Henry V. *Licensed Mass Murder: A Socio-Psychological Study of Some SS Killers*. London: Heinemann, 1972.

Dominguez, Jorge I.; Rodley, Nigel S.; Wood, Bryce; and Falk, Richard. *Enhancing Global Human Rights*. New York: McGraw-Hill, 1979.

Fawcett, Jan, ed. *Dynamics of Violence*. Chicago: American Medical Association, 1971.

Fein, Helen. *Accounting for Genocide: National Responses and Jewish Victimization During the Holocaust*. New York: Free Press, 1979.

Frank, Jerome D. *Sanity and Survival*. New York: Random House, 1967.

Fromm, Erich. *The Anatomy of Human Destructiveness*. New York: Holt, Rinehart and Winston, 1973.

_____. *The Heart of Man: Its Genius for Good and Evil*. New York: Harper and Row, 1964.

Gilbert, G. M. *The Psychology of Dictatorship: Based on an Examination of the Leaders of Nazi Germany*. New York: Ronald, 1950.

Gray, J. Glenn. *The Warriors: Reflections on Men in Battle*. New York: Harper and Row, 1967.

Hilberg, Raul. *The Destruction of the European Jews*. Chicago: Quadrangle, 1961.

Horowitz, Irving Louis. *Genocide: State Power and Mass Murder*. New Brunswick, N.J.: Transaction, 1976.

Kren, George, and Rappoport, Leon. *The Holocaust and the Crisis of Human Behavior*. New York: Holmes & Meier, 1980.

Kuznetzov, A. Anatoli. *Babi Yar*. New York: Farrar, Straus & Giroux, 1970.

Lifton, Robert Jay. *Death in Life: Survivors of Hiroshima*. New York: Random House, 1967.

Milgram, Stanley. *Obedience to Authority*. New York: Harper and Row, 1974.

Morse, Arthur D. *While Six Million Died: A Chronicle of American Apathy*. New York: Random House, 1968.

Neumann, Erich. *Depth Psychology and a New Ethic*. New York: Putnam's, 1969.

Payne, Robert. *Massacre: The Tragedy at Bangla Desh and the Phenomenon of Mass Slaughter Throughout History*. New York: Macmillan, 1973.

Pilch, Judah, ed. *The Story of the Jewish Catastrophe in Europe*. New York: American Association Jewish Education, 1968.

Rapoport, Anatol. *Conflict in Man-made Environment*. Baltimore, Md.: Penguin, 1974.

Sanford, Nevitt, and Comstock, Craig, eds. *Sanctions for Evil*. San Francisco: Jossey Bass, 1971.

Schiffer, Irvine. *Charisma: A Psychoanalytic Look at Mass Society*. Toronto: University of Toronto Press, 1973.

Sheleff, Leon Shaskolsky. *The Bystander: Behavior, Law, Ethics*. Lexington, Mass.: Lexington Books, 1978.

Short, James F., Jr., and Wolfgang, Marvin E., eds. *Collective Violence. Annals of the American Academy of Political and Social Science* 391 (September 1970).

Steiner, Jean-Francois. *Treblinka*. New York: Simon & Schuster, 1967.

Wertham, Frederic. *A Sign for Cain: An Exploration of Human Violence*. New York: Macmillan, 1966.

Wiesel, Elie. *The Oath*. New York: Random House, 1973.

Wiesel, Elie, chairman. *Report to the President: President's Commission on the Holocaust*. Washington, D.C.: U.S. Government Printing Office, 1979.

Wiesenthal, Simon. *The Murderers Among Us*. New York: McGraw-Hill, 1967.

Yad Vashem. *The Holocaust*. Jerusalem, 1975.

ABOUT THE AUTHORS
AND THE BOOK

Israel W. Charny is executive director of the International Conference on the Holocaust and Genocide. He is an associate professor of psychology at the School of Social Work at Tel Aviv University, where he has taught courses on the Holocaust, genocide, treatment of Holocaust survivors, and the critical implications of the Holocaust for psychological therapy and treatment. He is also senior researcher and codirector of the Genocide Early Warning System Project at the Szold National Institute for Research in the Behavioral Sciences in Jerusalem.

He has been a visiting professor of psychology at Hunter College of the City University of New York and professor of psychology and consultant in counseling at the Reconstructionist Rabbinical College. He was formerly director of Guidance Consultants, a psychological group practice in Paoli, Pennsylvania. He is past chairperson of the American Orthopsychiatric Association's task force on the quality of life and chairperson of the association's study group on mental health aspects of aggression, violence, and war. He was a member of the founding Council of the Consortium on Peace Research, Education, and Development centered at the Institute of Behavioral Science of the University of Colorado and a member of the Council of the American Association for the Advancement of Science.

He is past founder and president of the Israel Association for Marital and Family Therapy and a member of the Council of the Israel Institute for the Study of International Affairs.

Chanan Rapaport is director of the Szold National Institute for Research in the Behavioral Sciences in Jerusalem and codirector of the Genocide Early Warning System Project.

How Can We Commit the Unthinkable? Genocide: The Human Cancer was commissioned by the Institute for World Order in New York and supported by a grant from the Szold National Institute in Jerusalem.

421

INDEX

Actions, 97–98, 110–111, 119–121, 123–124, 181
Affection, 100
Aggression
  acting out, 98, 143–144
  and affectional bonds, 248
  animal, 247–248
  and authority, 144–145
  creative, 255
  and dependency, 99, 100, 192
  and destructiveness, 48–49, 51–53, 54, 58–59, 61, 63–67, 71, 85–89, 258, 336–337, 338, 340. *See also* Dehumanization; Violence
  as energy, 47–48, 49–50, 52, 53, 58, 60–61, 68, 69, 84–85, 87, 104, 241–242, 336
  family, 146–157, 178–179, 243, 339
  healthy, 237–240, 242, 244, 248–249, 255, 257–258
  as instinctual, 48
  and invulnerability, 104–105, 338
  nonviolent, 257, 258–280, 344–347
  and sexuality, 49–50, 51, 80, 186, 220, 249
  types of, 68–69
  See also Bad; Good; Hate; Love; Murder; Self-defense
Airlines, 277–278. *See also* Qantas Airlines
Aktion Suhnezeichen (action, sign of atonement), 271–272
All-Win process, 173
Altruism, 73
American Friends Service Committee, 270

American Indians, 11, 197, 228, 323
Amnesty International, 284
Anger, 98, 106, 178, 237, 241, 245, 247, 249–250, 258. *See also* Dependency, and anger
Annihilation, 99, 100, 101–102, 105, 168, 173, 310–312
Anxiety, 93–94, 105, 110, 123, 161, 181–182
Arab League, 290
Arabs, 173, 176, 178, 260
"Archaic bloodthirst," 100
Arendt, Hannah, 231
Arieti, Silvano, 159
Armenians, 227, 322–323
Asch experiments, 340
Assassination, 226
Atomic bomb, 197
Auschwitz, 205
  as symbol, 129–133
Authority. *See* Eichmann Experiment; Genociders, and authority
Autism, 141

"Babi Yar" (Yevtushenko), 13
Bach, George, 245, 255
Bad, 72, 73, 79–80, 82, 83–84, 243
  defined, 82
  See also Evil
Bakan, David, 67
Bandura, Albert, 91, 208
Bangladesh, 3, 316
Barram, A. S., 198
Battered child syndrome. *See* Child beating
Baylor College of Medicine, 67